ACTIVIST LEADERS OF SAN JOSÉ

ACTIVIST LEADERS OF SAN JOSÉ

En sus propias voces

● ● ●

JOSIE MÉNDEZ-NEGRETE

THE UNIVERSITY OF
ARIZONA PRESS
TUCSON

The University of Arizona Press
www.uapress.arizona.edu

IBSN-13: 978-0-8165-4200-0 (hardcover)
ISBN-13: 978-0-8165-4082-2 (paperback)

Cover design by Carrie House, HouseDesign LLC
Cover photos from top left: Sofia Mendoza, courtesy of Karl Soltero; Mike Garcia, photographer unknown; Jack Brito, courtesy of Karl Soltero; Cecilia and Ron Arroyo, courtesy of Diego Salazar, with thanks to Corinne Gutierrez; Ernestina Garcia, courtesy of Doreen Garcia Nevel; Josie Romero, courtesy of Diana Martinez; Antonio Soto, courtesy of CET; Clare and José Villa, courtesy of José Villa; Esther Medina, courtesy of Cameo Burton. Interior design by Sara Thaxton
Typeset in 10/13.5 Arno Pro (text), Veneer Clean, and Agenda (display)

Publication of this book is made possible in part by a subsidy from the College of Education and Human Development at the University of Texas, San Antonio, and by the proceeds of a permanent endowment created with the assistance of a Challenge Grant from the National Endowment for the Humanities, a federal agency.

Library of Congress Cataloging-in-Publication Data
Names: Méndez-Negrete, Josie, author.
Title: Activist leaders of San José : en sus propias voces / Josie Méndez-Negrete.
Description: Tucson : University of Arizona Press, 2020. | Includes bibliographical references and index.
Identifiers: LCCN 2020010952 | ISBN 9780816542000 (hardcover) | ISBN 9780816540822 (paperback)
Subjects: LCSH: Mexican American political activists—California—San Jose—History—20th century. | Mexican American political activists—California—San Jose—Biography. | Community leadership—California—San Jose—History—20th century. | LCGFT: Oral histories. | Biographies.
Classification: LCC E184.M5 M464 2020 | DDC 979.4/740046872—dc23
LC record available at https://lccn.loc.gov/2020010952

To the Chicanas and Latinos/Chicanos who shared their stories—thank you for the lessons. May we continue walking the paths that you carved in pursuit of social justice and social change.

The photographs in this book were provided by the participants or family members. Some originally appeared in the San José *Mercury News*, *El Excentrico*, *El Observador*, and La Confederación de La Raza Unida Archives under the oversight of Doreen García Nevel.

CONTENTS

Preface   *ix*

Acknowledgments   *xxvii*

1. Families of Origin: Becoming Activist Leaders   3

2. Do You Know the Way? Movement and Migration to San José   32

3. Depression and Baby Boomer Generations Speak   43

4. Marginalization and Exclusion: Family Backgrounds   57

5. Activist Leaders *Legados* in Action   73

6. Social Change Among the Generations: Education and Social Activism   95

7. Latinos/Chicanos of the Depression Generation   145

8. Chicanas of the Depression Generation   166

9. Latinos/Chicanos of the Baby Boomer Generation   206

10. Chicanas of the Baby Boomer Generation   232

11. Chicana Awareness, Consciousness, and Resistance: Systemic and Structural Interactions   271

Conclusion: What Chicana and Latino/Chicano Activist Leaders Teach Us   285

Notes   *291*

References   *299*

Index   *305*

PREFACE

Through the voices of historical actors who have lived inside the complexities of raced, classed, and gendered experiences, I make visible and document the history and contributions of Chicana and Latino/Chicano[1] activist leaders sin San José, California, and Santa Clara County. This social history narrates the lived experiences of two cohorts. I identify the first as the Depression Generation, which includes participants who grew up in the poverty, scarcity, and deprivation of the late 1920s to early 1940s, most of whom migrated from various parts of the Southwest to California, to work in the agricultural fields. To this generation, benefits accrued to those who were conscripted or who volunteered for World War II and the Korean War, yielding them amenities not previously available. The second group is the Baby Boomer Generation, marked by the period of time between 1946 and 1964, who reaped rewards from the civil rights movement and gained entrance into the middle class.

In this study, I focus on the participants' lived experiences, covering the 1930s to the mid-1990s. Eleven Chicanas and twelve Latinos/Chicanos responded to a seventeen-page interview guide, which allowed me to gather memories and recollections of their families of origin, families of procreation, and educational experiences. Moreover, I document their parents' community involvement, along with putting together a historical overview of each participant's respective contributions.

Let me suggest that even when traditional notions of leadership inform the ways in which they access and create change, Chicana/Latino participants do not perceive leadership as positional, whereby an individual is expected to exercise influence over others. Traditionally, leadership, in the normative context, describes a person endowed with qualities, by birth and class, to lead others into action. Also, charisma, influence through position or authority, is most often associated with a grand man style of leadership that comes out of an elite socioeconomic purview in which most are outcasts. While influence and position may play a part in the process because of the relational importance of negotiating power, this, in and of itself, is not the be-all and end-all of their involvement. Even when many of the participants in this study continued to hold positions of power and importance, they maintained connections with the grassroots communities that launched their activism or supported them in carrying out their leadership. And although their constituencies had expanded beyond their initial support base, these activist leaders nurtured interactions with the grassroots. For those who participated in this study, relationships with people in positions of power were not foundational to their formation as activist leaders; their families and communities were their inspiration.

Chicana/Latino activism and leadership has been written about in a variety of ways. Regional accounts such as Mario T. García's study of El Paso, Texas, *Mexican American Leadership,* detailed the activism of the Mexican-American middle-class generation. Rudy Acuña, in his various iterations of *Occupied America,* examined the ways in which Chicanos have been politically involved. Benjamin Márquez (1993) documented the formation of the League of United Latin American Citizens (LULAC) from its inception in 1929 to the 1980s. He traced its evolution during the assimilationist pre– and post–World War II eras, detailing an agenda that initially promoted the shedding of culture and language in an Americanization process that failed to melt Mexicans into the everlasting pot, despite being identified as "White" in the decennials of the 1920s and 1940s, as they continued to remain members of a subordinated class apart.[2] Henry A. J. Ramos (1998), in *The American GI Forum: In Pursuit of the Dream, 1948–1983,* exposed the segregation and discrimination that Mexican people experienced in South Texas, as Raul Yzaguirre had detailed: "Housing and health conditions were dangerously substandard, and local Anglo service establishments, from restaurants and hotels to hospitals and barber shops, were frequently off-limits to Latinos. Much like blacks in the South, Hispanic Americans in Texas and much of the nation were denied equal treatment under the law as a matter of course" (Ramos 7). As the central character and a relentless public figure leading the struggle against exclusion, Dr. Henry P. Garza took on the "local state-supported segregation of Hispanic public-school students. . . . [LULAC] was the first organization to effectively lobby for a program for the special needs of Spanish-speaking Americans" (9). Private Felix Longoria's death in the Philippines during World War II, and the denial of his burial by a Three Rivers, Texas, funeral home, became the catalyst that united and expanded pursuit of Mexican American civil rights.

Carol Hardy-Fanta (1993), in a study of a Latino community in Boston, examined the ways in which men and women view and understand political activism in a participatory democracy, focusing on gender differences and how Latinas and Latinos engage political processes and the ways in which culture and gender intersect in the involvement of ethnic communities. She concluded that Latina consciousness expresses a connected and collective leadership approach that differs greatly from that of Latinos, whose aims are to achieve status, impose hierarchy, and access personal gain. Maylei Blackwell, in ¡Chicana Power!: Contested Histories of Feminism in the Chicano Movement (2011), explored Chicana roles in the 1960s and 1970s in Los Angeles. From a feminist perspective, Blackwell analyzed the struggle over gender and sexuality, drawing conclusions about the ways in which racialized ethnicity, gender, and political identity framed resistance and contestation of representation. She relied on oral histories, revisiting the lived experiences of Hijas de Cuauhtémoc—a feminist organization—to show the ways in which women activists reconfigured their recollections of the time.

Still, in all these accounts, the histories lack the presence or agency of those woman and men of Mexican descent who have contributed to a culture that marginalizes and derides them as Indigenous, migrants, and immigrants to the region. Studies about San Antonio, Los Angeles, and Tucson, to name a few, depict the Mexican American presence in the Southwest, but none focus on documenting and examining the narratives of activist leaders and their contributions to social change.

Chicanas and Latinos/Chicanos who participated in this study showed that they possess an active and reflective mindfulness of being one with their environment, with an imaginary that conceptualizes an active social justice ideology, as they called back recollections of experiences that gave them insight and consciousness to narrate their involvement. In this manner, they relied on their sentient self whereby with mind, body, spirit, and soul they negotiate race and racialized ethnicity, socioeconomic class, gender, and sexuality, as a people who have intimately known poverty and risen above its limitations. Moreover, because they understood how they, as a people, were socially derided as Mexicans, they worked to make things better for Raza, and as such, the interactions they enact are premised on agency and relational notions of change. Informed by ideologies of equality, fairness, and justice, they engaged social change inside their families and communities, without apologizing for their social position as working-class people.

Activist Leaders and Ideologies of Practice. Among models or paradigms relied upon to examine the presence, or absence, of Chicana/Latino leadership, patron strategies or Mexican American assimilationist notions outlined an activism dressed in the limitations of cultural nationalism and post-Chicano reform and accommodation (Acuña 1988; Barrera 1979; Cotera 1976; Gómez Quiñonez 1990; M. T. García 1989; Muñoz 1989, and others). Texts have disregarded or at best obscured contributions by Chicanas/Latinos as agents of change. Thus, rather than examining the ways in which grassroots and community activism and leadership processes emerge in the context of ethnic struggles, they have adopted conventional notions of leadership, using grand men or women theories that ascribe normative attributes to their contributions. To analyze this misconception, I provide an abridged retrospective, beginning with an analysis of the Mexican American generation (García 1989).

According to Mario García, Mexican American leadership accounts for the ways in which Spaniards and Mexicans colonized the Southwest, as settler colonialism by Anglos is intertwined in the development of barrio culture, urbanization and mass movement, bilingualism, and the ways in which religion contributed and stratified cross-cultural identification within the Mexican American community, which serves as rationale for organizing homogenous notions of the group as a political unit. Scholars such as Benjamin Marquez (1993), Rodolfo Acuña (1988), Carlos Muñoz Jr. (1989), and others contend that the U.S. political system failed to make Mexican Americans integral parts of the political process, relegating them to a secondary status as quasi-citizens (Montejano 1987). Thus, thanks to their cross-cultural identity, Mexican Americans have been conditioned by socioeconomic status and ideological views to see themselves as part of an homogenous category whereby they embraced and accepted their position in American history as less than full citizens. On the other hand, Miguel David Tirado (1970) challenged the assumption that Mexican Americans are "politically apathetic and complacent with respect to participation in community organizations" (53). Moreover, he refutes the lack of Mexican American organizational involvement, given their history and the ways in which political and community organizations grew and persevered. Mario García (1989) argues that "despite popular stereotypes that view Mexican Americans as apolitical, marginalized farmworkers, as 'illegal aliens' and as people who selfishly cling to their culture, they have not been isolated from the great struggles and transformations of our age" (1). These and other explanations were also used by Alvarez (1973) and García to discuss the "migrant generation" or the "immigrant era," respectively, during the first two decades of the twentieth century.

Informed by Marvin Rintala's notion of a political generation as "a group of human beings who have undergone the same basic historical experience during their formative years," Garcia (1989) posits that Mexican Americans share a historical experience that distinguished them as such a generation (3). Thus, to locate their origination story, García suggests two historical groups: the ethnic group of the early nineteenth century, and the Mexican American generation of twentieth-century immigrants. Unlike groups that still identify with Mexico as the *madre patria*, he argued that the Mexican American class found itself identifying with the United States as the homeland, no longer aspiring to return to the *madre patria* whence their ancestors came. According to García, for the Mexican American generation,

Achievements were accomplished by breaking down legal and de facto barriers to first-class citizenship. The Mexican-American middle class, especially in the areas of education, political representation, and public facilities and led by groups such as the League for United Latin American Citizens (LULAC), the School Improvement League in San Antonio, the Unity League in Southern California, the Community Service Organization (CSO), the American G. I. Forum, as well as other Mexican American veterans' associations, successfully asserted the rights of Mexican-Americans. (298)

In this way, García creates a trajectory that leads from the immigrant, to the migrant, to the Mexican American generation. While he critiques the absence of a Mexican American middle class in the work of Chicanos, García's narrative does not make visible women and working-class activists who made significant contributions to the leadership formation of Mexican Americans.[3] When García included women, he depicted them as auxiliary to the actions of men. Thus, he wrote about activism and leadership as mutually exclusive. For example, in documenting a LULAC election in 1949, García wrote about "a group of Mexican-American leaders ... headed by a 'long-time LULAC activist' who endorsed ... Telles, who would become Mayor of El Paso and organized south-side voters on behalf of liberal candidates" (117). In his narrative, the men are in charge, with women engaging in the daily work that looks for and brings out the registered voters, even as the women actively work to dismantle poll taxes. Thus, El Paso women activists could be credited with the election of Ernest Ponce as "elected alderman for parks and recreation" (118), as they challenged the political power structure and its policies of exclusion.

On the other hand, García argues that "the Chicano Generation moved to rectify the failure of the past and to break through the ideological handicaps of the Mexican-American Generation" (300). As such, Mexican American activism set the foundation for the formation of Chicano leaders and leadership strategies for social change from a nationalist and idealist perspective (Acuña 1988; Camarillo 1984; Gomez Quiñonez 1990, and others). In this way, a nationalist ideology evolved to inform Chicano activism as well as an organizational leadership approach. For the Chicano generation, reforms were insufficient—they were not interested in becoming hyphenated Americans or in changing the system from within—they wanted change. And, for the first time, "Americans of Mexican descent challenged the very basic ideological foundation of the United States" by questioning the position to which they had been relegated. In García's view, "the Chicano generation was a product of its historical time," as the Mexican American generation had been. Yet, "despite [the Chicano Generation's] rejection of the American experience, it was born out of that experience" (García, 1989, 300).

The Chicano movement, perceived by some as a spontaneous civil rights struggle arising from the student movement, was recognized as just another of the many movements that sprang up in the 1960s. Yet, it was more complex and built on the his-torical foundations of Mexican Americans' ancestral legacies. Albert Camarillo (1984) captured it best when he states that "the Chicano movement meant different things to different people, both within and outside the Mexican American community . . . many disparate groups that sometimes quarreled: middle-class vs. working-class interests, youth vs. older generations, Californians vs. Texans, Marxists vs. non-Marxists, those who wished to work within existing structures vs. those who advocated alternative institutions" (93). Like generations before them, Chicanos advanced their struggles for social justice, although not within a paradigm of equality or within a uniform ide-ology. The group was neither monolithic nor homogenous in practice or thought.

While rejecting accommodationist and assimilationist notions of past politi-cal, social, and cultural activism, the movement's diversity and complexity propelled Chicano activists and their allies toward a struggle for justice, and fairness, without foregrounding equality. Mario T. García (1989) suggested that Chicano leadership "expressed itself as a political generation in relation to the central experiences of this period: immigration and the Mexican Revolution of 1910," from a male-centrist perspective, while women were represented as corollary activists among men (15). Even though Chicanos pursued a political agenda that pushed politics to the left, they demanded the maintenance of culture, language, and self-determination in a conquered land that belonged to their ancestors (Muñoz 1989). García offered that the Chicano generation "built on the successes and failures of the Mexican-American generation . . . [moving] to rectify the failures of the past and to break through the ideological handicaps of the Mexican-American generation. . . . [It] was part of a wide youth alienation and rebellion that sought alternative models of social change in post-industrialized America" (1989, 300). Others, such as Segade (1978), in *Aztlán: Essays on the Chicano Homeland*, credits *la huelga* (strike) with catalyzing the Chicano move-ment, even though other events that influenced it might have concurrently taken place, thus merging urban and rural Chicano concerns. While Carlos Muñoz (1989) placed the birth of the Chicano movement within the politics of identity, and inside theo-ries of social movements, Acuña (1988) minimized its impact, treating prior efforts as evolving and continuous aspects of history. For Muñoz, the movement was a search for identity, with its own ideology and objectives for social change by way of youth rebellion, crediting high school and college youth for much of its ideology, but not including Chicanas and those from working-class origins.

The *movimiento*'s birth is anchored in manifestos and revolutionary plans such as *El Plan Espiritual de Aztlán* and *El Plan de Santa Barbara*, which aimed "to transcend all religious, political, class and economic factions or boundaries . . . the common denom-inator that all members of La Raza [could] agree upon" (*El Plan de Aztlán*, 197, quoted in Barrera 1979, 39), to place Chicanos at the center of the movement. Likewise, *El Plan de Santa Barbara* also emphasized a nationalist ideology that promulgated patriarchy and masculinity, bringing in women as accessories of *la lucha* (the struggle)—Adelitas and Soldaderas of a new revolution. Similarly, Barrera (1979) argues that "nationalism is a political orientation that emphasizes the common identity and common interests of a group of people who see themselves as sharing a similar historical experience and cultural orientation," without accounting for the absence or marginalization of Chicanas (39). He further contends that Chicanos of the 1960s stressed the need for unity and the development of an ideology around which all could rally, yet issues of sexism were excluded from their worldview or agenda for social change. Chicanas were perceived merely as supporters of *la causa*, rather than as equal partners in the struggle for social justice.

Amid a multiplicity of plans from *La Alianza Federal del Pueblo*, *El Partido de la Raza Unida*, and Movimiento Estudiantil Chicano de Aztlán or MEChA, the Chicano movement put forward that "social, economic, cultural, and political independence is the only road to total liberation from oppression, exploitation, and racism" (Barrera 1979, 22). Social, economic, and political aspects of the struggle were factored into the movement, so long as they were in accord with its proposed ideology. For example, Chicanos reclaiming their "indigenous roots" placed a "strong emphasis on the preservation and promotion of Chicano cultural heritage" (22) with roots in a patriarchal Aztlán, until feminists such as Cotera (1976) and Anzaldúa (1987) dug up women from the heap of a male-centric narrative. Liberation, an embedded argument that promoted the abolishment of racist practices within the existing social, educational, economic, and political system, was central. It was presented under a philosophy of *carnalismo*, the strength of *la familia*, the importance of people working together under the men of the movement, and the recognition of the right of "all peoples to preserve their self-identity and to formulate their own destiny," so long as it is organized within traditional norms of *la cultura* (Barrera 1979, 24–25). From an anti-assimilationist agenda, activists were measured by their commitment to "self-determination of our community [as] the only acceptable mandate for social and political action; [because] it is the essence of Chicano commitment," but liberation for Chicanas never was a parallel concern (Barrera 1979, 25).

In this revolution, Chicanas were secondary to men or merely supporters of male activist leaders. This ideology of nationalism suggests that because assimilation focused on shedding language and culture, "the struggle to understand the Mexican-American experience increasingly focused on questions of alienation, ethnicity, identity, class, gender, and chauvinism," without problematizing the state of women among the many structures of inequality with which Chicanos contended, Chicanos were the creators of *la lucha* (Gómez Quiñonez 1990, 103). As such, *el movimiento* came with a set of beliefs and political practices that made a case for "dignity, self-worth, pride, uniqueness, and a feeling of cultural rebirth [which] made it attractive to many Mexicans [because it] cut across class, regional, and generational lines" (104).

For the first time, *mexicanos* did not feel compelled to apologize for their history and could unearth what had been buried in the Spanish or Mexican American identities they had accepted for too long. Gómez Quiñonez (1990) clarified that during that tumultuous time "there arose a variegated burst of activity loosely identified as the 'Chicano Movement.' Initiating forces were the Farm Workers Union, the Alianza, the Crusade for Justice, student organizations and eventually, La Raza Unida. Workers or persons of working-class origin were key to these forces, and women often provided the organizational backbone" (103). Once again, the rich and expansive web of Mexican people reclaimed their dignity and self-respect because no concerted efforts had been undertaken since the middle-class struggles for reform by LULAC. Gómez Quiñonez (1990) argues that Chicano activism

> emerged as a challenge to the assumptions, politics, and principles of the established political and social order. *Chicanismo* . . . encompassed issues of education, civil rights, health, poverty, labor, access to professions, institutionalized racism, political participation, the arts, urban ecology, land rights, and many others. Optimum visionary goals pertinent to these issues were not realized, yet incremental gains of the Chicano community may be dated from the effects of this movement. (189)

It was this all-encompassing movement that paved the way for the formation of activist leaders who would attempt to improve the living conditions of la Raza. Aspirations were not grounded on class mobility or assimilation, rather self-determination informed its agenda but it was not an all-inclusive strategy for change.

Chicana feminist discourse opened up a space to engage a critical examination of *mujeres* in the *movimiento*. Martha P. Cotera (1976), in her collection of essays, profiled Mexican American women, particularly historicizing their location as gendered and classed individuals. "Some Chicano males already in leadership and authority positions, challenged women's participation in activities outside the home. Their claims were that 'everyone knew,' and history, culture, and tradition established Mexican-American women could/should only be homemakers and mothers" (6). Traditionalist and sexist notions of what it means to be "woman" within limited cultural views of women's involvement had failed to recognize Chicanas as change agents. Anna Nieto-Gómez, building on Cotera, points out the contradictions of being traditional or liberal in their conception of Chicana feminism, as Chicanas were subject to "charges of being 'Agringadas,' 'Anglocized,' 'feminists' and 'anti-traditionalists'" (Cotera 1971, 18), cleaving divisions among women activists—neither agreed with the male agenda.

The presence and labor of Chicanas continued to be part of the struggle for social and cultural rights. Because they were seen as traditional reproducers of culture who participated in organizations as secondary supporters, Chicana involvement was clearly marked as inferior and their contributions dismissed. For example, "analyses of communities generally show that women, through mutualistic societies, low-key efforts such as LULAC, G.I. Forum, and church organizations, continued to push for progress and improvement in the community. Often, at the minimum, they helped maintain strong cultural identities through the planning and execution of elaborate May 5th and September 16th parades, *bailes, actos civicos,* and *jamaicas*" (98–99).

The contributions *mujeres* made to their community were seen from a traditional point of view. Cotera (1971) explained: "These older women provided the backbone for the civic and political organizations organized or reactivated in the 1960s and 1970s, [and] had its cadre of these seasoned, stalwart women, whose commitment has been proved" (98–99). Still, because culture and domestic everyday activities were defined as the realm of women, their activism and leadership in or outside this system was unacknowledged or devalued. As already stated, García (1989), in his examination of Mexican American leadership, failed to place women at the center, since he was looking "for actual accounts of leadership based on role and position assigned to women" within traditional notions of a patriarchal analysis (2). Not isolating Mexican American women's leadership for its own value, he concluded that leadership "was mostly dominated by men" (2).

In a patriarchal culture, accommodation, rather than inclusion, was the order of most Mexican American organizations. For example, "while LULAC members accommodated to more aspiring Mexican-American women and even encouraged them to be like their Anglo female counterparts, they did not share authority equitably with the women" (García 1989, 39). Tokenism and paternalism serve to explain the place of women in Mexican American leadership venues. García acknowledges that, "within the type of second-class position, the women made important community contributions, although in activities still closely related to 'women's work'" (39), neutralizing and minimizing their involvement. He argues, "Women engaged purely social affairs . . . [did] work in the barrios . . . orphanages and health clinics, sponsoring youth activities, and collecting and donating toys and clothes to underprivileged children. Along with the men, they registered voters, raised money for college scholarships, and taught English and citizenship to Mexican nationals. All this did not make LULAC women feminists but . . . more Americanized Mexican-American woman" (39–40).

Contrarily, Cotera argues that Chicanas were not willing to replace one oppression for another owing to cultural and socioeconomic explanations. They challenged the racism of the dominant culture as it affected Chicanas and their male partners, while also challenging their mistreatment at the hands of Chicanos. As feminists,

Chicanas began with the premise that their involvement did not emerge with the birth of the movement. As documented by Acuña (1988), Camarillo (1984), McWilliams (1990), Muñoz (1989), and others, Chicanas were a presence in the struggle for social change—for example, Emma Tenayuca, Josefina Fierro de Bright, Luisa Moreno, and Jovita Gonzalez—although their contributions were analyzed from a grand woman perspective.

Their centrality in the movement would not be acknowledged until the early 1970s when feminism took hold. Nieto Gómez (1974) writes that as their consciousness emerged, women began to speak out "against the sexual racist oppression with which 'Chicana women must contend'" (34). Furthermore, she highlights the Chicano movement's indifference, for Chicanos conceived of the "Chicana only as a member of the Chicano people in general who are economically oppressed as a culturally different people," dismissing the structural differences of classist, racist, and sexist points of departure (34). In her perspective,

> The movement has been indifferent to the specific issue of 51 percent of the Chicano people as women. At the same time, the Anglo headed popular women's movement has only viewed Chicanas as potential members of the ranks of women because all women are oppressed by the sexist attitudes against them. It has then ignored the issues the Chicana must contend with as a member of a minority culturally different, lower income group. In so doing, it has ignored how the Chicanas social and economic status as a woman is also severely determine by her race as well as her sex. (34–35)

Within these contradictions, ideological camps emerged whereby male-identified women were classified as pro-family *loyalistas*, while *feministas* were depicted as "anti-family, anti-cultural, anti-man and therefore anti-Chicano movement" (Nieto-Gómez 1974, 38). According to Nieto Gómez, "loyalists do not recognize sexism as a legitimate issue in the Chicano movement" (38). *Feministas* did not see their struggle for equality as anti-man or anti-Anglo, rejecting white feminist accusations of desiring to separate from men. In these feminists' views, Chicana notions of oppression stemmed from racism, classism, and sexism (A. García 1989). Given their social location, Chicanas saw themselves as having no option but to confront economic, racist, and sexist oppression.

Moreover, *feminista* perspectives were further complicated by the intense homophobia that branded Chicanas as not meeting the nationalist expectations imposed on them as good wives and mothers, marked them as "lesbians, and lesbians as feminists," and labeled them *vendidas* or "sellouts" (M. T. García 1989, 226). According to Pesquera and Segura (1990), Chicana feminists parted with the Chicano movement by challenging patriarchy because gender was subsumed into the overall Chicano struggle. On the other hand, Chicana feminists rejected white feminist ideology because it failed to integrate race-, ethnic-, and class-based experiences.

Emma Pérez (1993), challenging discourses about Chicanas in history, argues that "consciousness—whether of race, class, gender, or sexuality—is born from one's intimate awareness of one's oppression" (58). Chicano theorizing presupposes a universal experience, without problematizing the intersectionalities of race, class, gender, and sexuality into ways of being, acting, and behaving. Thus, to amplify an understanding of women's contributions, Cherríe Moraga (2000), alluding to ways in which the lived experiences of those who actively challenge power create a humanist environment as they gain knowledge about themselves and their communities in the process of creating change, theorized in the flesh, meaning that women's lived experiences facilitate engagement with the world, as they account for skin color, environment of upbringing, and sexual identification, thus creating political interactions and relationships that emerge from need (Moraga and Anzaldúa 1983). Gloria E. Anzaldúa (Anzaldúa and Keating 2002), departing from a *mindbodyspirit* holistic philosophy, opens spaces to create and generate knowledge from multiple sites of entry. Mestiza consciousness or coming to knowledge about the self in the context of relational interactions at individual, collective, and tribal levels are thus intertwined with *conocimiento* of self and others, molding a subjective consciousness that facilitates understanding of the self in the context of structural constraints, while stoking the desire to engage in the creation of change, for if we change ourselves, we change the world.

Rather than fragment or universalize Chicana experiences, Pérez (1999) argues that "*feministas* see sexism as an integrated part of Chicana's struggle in conjunction with her fight against racism" and in the context of socioeconomic class (38). Chicanas, perceived as twice or three times removed from equality by men in the *movimiento*, are thus remanded into women's places and spaces in *la familia* and within *carnalismo*, and thus relegated to the reproductive division of labor whereby patriarchy dictates their relationships with men and each other as well as their involvement in the struggles for social justice and cultural rights. For Maxine Baca Zinn, it is in that context that structural notions of familism privileges *compadrazgo* and extended family ties in support of male power to theorize as solidarity or familism, keeping women in their place or whatever social position they are expected to occupy, although enjoined in an unequal partnership whereby they fight for change and social and cultural justice (Baca Zinn 1982/83).

Rodolfo Rosales (2000), in his study of Chicanos in San Antonio, Texas, argues that "because of the intersections of race, class, and gender, the Chicana experience has not been based solely on the advancement of Chicanas" (176). According to him, Chicana involvement for social justice emerges "out of struggle that involved the entire community, [as] the Chicana experience has been shaped by issues and priorities of a community-based strategy which has brought about participatory-oriented political process . . . by Chicana community activists" (176). Vicki L. Ruiz (1998), in *Out of the Shadows: Mexican Women in Twentieth-Century America*, an oral history in the context of "claiming personal and public spaces," brings into this discussion the work of labor and civic activists and feminists or "Mexican women who made history": "Spanish-speaking women as family members, as workers, and as civic-minded individuals have strived to improve the quality of life at work, home, and neighborhood" (73). She argues that "as farm hands, cannery workers, miners' wives, *mutualista* members, club women, civil rights advocates, and politicians, Mexican women have taken direct action for themselves and others." Clearly, even when their ideas diverged, Mexican-descent women "joined together in common cause, particularly in areas as voter registration" (73).

Chicana theorists argue that during strife and struggle Chicanas did not stand on the sidelines. They are and have been historically invested in improving conditions in their community, with the aim of creating a better life for their children, desiring to spare them from the historical trauma of surviving in a racialized, classed, and gendered society that has relegated them to subordinated spaces and places of subjugation as Mexicans. Finally, with her retrospective study of a Los Angeles organization, Maylei Blackwell (2011), documents the ways in which activists challenged each other and male leaders of the Chicano movement, recording the "ways young women faced a form of sexual initiation into the movement whereby men, under the guise of mentorship and political education, would initiate sexual relationships with incoming freshmen women" (70). In telling their memories, these *mujeres* "reclaimed a counter narrative of revolutionary women and the image of the Soldadera through the lens of Chicana resistance" (113).

Countless books exist that study the everyday lives of Mexican-descent people in Southern California, while few texts have examined the specific case of San José and the struggle for social justice and equal rights there. Along with theses or dissertations, some texts have presented research on daily life in San José.[4] For example, in *Get Out If You Can*, published in 1953, Fred Ross records his organizing efforts among San José's residents on "the other side of the tracks," pointing out that, as in many other California cities named after Spanish saints, "the forebears of some of [the residents] were here when the Pilgrims landed. Many came from Mexico in the early 1900's," however, "the majority are the children and grandchildren of the early immigrants, born and raised in California," even though the "1950 Bureau of the Census lists them simply as 'Whites of Spanish Surname'" (1). He describes the "stooped forms" of Mexicans working in the fields. They "hold common labor jobs in most of the factories . . . [and] their bruised and bleeding faces [are] pictured in the files of various Police Commissions under the heading 'Alleged police brutality: Case closed for lack of evidence'" (1). Ross writes about the ways he motivated Eastside residents of Sal Si

Puedes to become involved in the electoral process, so that they could access amenities that they were denied because they lacked the power to vote. Ross recalled that the residents dismissed the electoral process, but most addressed their need to improve the lives of their children.

Ross wrote about the founding of the Community Services Organization (CSO) and the house visits they conducted, recalling that with the support of the Spanish radio station and the Central Labor Council of the American Federation of Labor, they created a partnership that convinced residents to register to vote, increasing the number of deputy registrars from the one that had been allotted to sign up 20,000 unregistered residents (15). Ross documented that in almost three months, with "3,000 man-hours," they registered "4,000 folks out here in Sal si Puedes" (18). But their efforts did not focus solely on registration; to ensure that voters were not discriminated against on election day, poll watchers were assigned to the voting sites. Ross was instrumental in training César E. Chávez, who soon became an organizer for CSO.

In his autobiography of Chávez, Jacques Levy (1975) wrote about the family's move to San José and what the neighborhood was like at the time.

> The barrio wasn't large, just two unpaved dead-end streets running into Jackson and bordered on three sides by fields and pasture. . . . Sal Si Puedes was a rough barrio . . . the saying goes that if trouble developed, a neighbor would say, "If you think you can handle it, sal si puedes." The second version [of how the barrio got its name] developed because the streets were unpaved. When the rainy season started, people who thought ahead parked their cars on Jackson Street. They would say to the ones stuck in the mud, "Sal si puedes, get out if you can." (50–51)

It was there that Chávez met Father Donald McDonnell, with whom he "became great friends" (89). When Chávez finally met the "best organizer," whom he had been trying to avoid, Fred Ross came to see him at home. Chávez recalled: "It must have been in June 1952 when I came home from work one day, and [my wife] Helen told me this gringo wanted to see me" (97). Suspicious of any whites that came to the neighborhood, such as police or researchers who often asked irrelevant questions—the Eastside of San José was a living research laboratory for social scientists who often came to extract the knowledge of the community—Chávez continued to avoid Ross until Helen told Chávez she would not lie for him. Chávez then agreed to meet with Ross, although with a plan to discourage him. "I invited some of the roughest guys I knew and bought some beer," having arranged that he would give them a signal and the group would throw Ross out of the house (98). But instead of getting rid of Ross, Chávez found himself absorbed in his presentation. "Fred spoke quietly, not rabble-rousing, but saying the truth. He knew our problems . . . a creek behind Sal Si Puedes which carried the waste from a packing house ... the kids would play in it, and they'd get sores.... Fred did such a good job of explaining how poor people could build power that I could even taste it" (Levy 1975, 98–99).

Other residents of the community would participate in the creation of knowledge, as San José State College enabled Chicano students to document the city's history, advancing alternative and insider approaches for engaging in research and recording community histories, rather than reproducing hypotheses informed by a culture of poverty and problem-ridden theses advanced by research outsiders from surrounding universities. For example, in his 1991 thesis, Arturo Villarreal examines the everyday lives of residents, focusing on the Black Berets, an activist organization formed in 1965 from the Jackson Kings, a social group established 1959 and led by Anselmo "Chemo" Candelaria,[5] who grew up in Sal Si Puedes. More recently, Nanette Regua and Arturo Villareal (2009) collaborated on a pictorial book about San José, titled *Mexicans in San José*, in which they examine the everyday experiences of Mexicans as working people who labored in agriculture and the canneries.

Stephen J. Pitti, in *The Devil in Silicon Valley: Northern California, Race, and Mexican Americans* (2003), studies the economic organization of the region. The book is a narrative written inside a race argument that situates Mexicans and Mexican Americans as miners, in agriculture and cannery work, as well as janitors and service workers. Pitti takes the reader on a journey of Spanish and Mexican times, with an immigrant narrative of a group that has been exploited and derided. The practices that segregated Mexicans on the Eastside of San José surface thorough documentation of the structural inequalities of race and class. The agency of the historical actors who lived in those times support the thesis he advances. Even though some of their voices are interwoven to support Petti's arguments, women's stories remain buried in the ashes of culture.

In *Ethnic Community Builders: Mexican Americans in Search of Justice and Power* (2007), an anthology of oral histories, Francisco Jiménez, Alma M. García, and Richard A. Garcia depict the "1960s through 2000, a period of social change, social tensions, and community mobilization" (1). In this book, four Chicanas and one Chicano from the Depression Generation speak about the ways in which they worked to create social change. Foregrounding their stories are summaries of the setting, the shift from agriculture to a technologically advanced economy, and an overview of the historical context that framed social protests and community activism (5). Claiming that the struggle for change did not begin with the movement, the authors clarify that "these community builders inherited a legacy of movements to achieve equality for Mexican Americans in the United States from earlier historical periods" (5). They also point out that a history of organizing for "citizenship rights, fighting racism, registering voters, winning political elections, reforming the educational system, and addressing other community issues" (6) has always been part of the daily existence of people of Mexican descent, as they fought to retain and celebrate the cultural enrichment they had been taught to recognize by their families and community, in opposition or resistance to Americanization. The authors document previous oral histories, tracing the practice of interviewing to Manuel Gamio in 1931 California. Like them, I rely on this tradition to document the lives of Chicana and Latino/Chicano leader activists as I write a social history in the voices of those who experienced life in San José.

LIVED EXPERIENCES AND HISTORIES OF ACTIVISM

Lived experiences of activist leaders in San José provide an understanding of the ways in which they negotiated relational leadership as they struggled to bring about social justice and social change. Embedded in Chicanas' daily interactions are the gendered relations in the internal dynamics of the nation, along with class and race interactions, and an understanding of marginalization. On the other hand, Latinos/Chicanos more readily engage race and class differences as the principle contradictions in their involvement, given that their masculinity is seldom a point of contention.

The participants all grew up in a patriarchal family, with some fathers fully in charge and some wives totally dependent on them as stay-at-home mothers. For example, Mike Garcia stated that growing up in such a family led to his gendered and masculinist views in regards to family formation, and while others recalled their upbringing in a working-class background with males in charge, most recalled spouses and children contributing to family wages. Some grew up in urban communities, while others were raised with relatives as part of their household. Without exception, the activist leaders in this study were raised in two-parent families, with more than half experiencing extended family relationships, like Felix Alvarez, who grew up in a rural agricultural community with paternal and maternal relatives living nearby. In those instances, elders tended to the children to assist parents who worked.

Among these activist leaders, some Chicanas and Latinos left school and went to work so that their family could make ends meet. When they worked and went to school, they contributed their income to the family budget. Other than poverty and the traditional experiences of growing up inside economic constraints, the recollections they shared provide an understanding about what compelled them to work on improving conditions for their people. For them, life was not easy or without sacrifices. The jobs they held were the worst paid and the most dangerous, a practice that continues to keep Mexican-descent people in a marginal status. For example, José Carrasco links his background to field work, particularly with sugar beets. He lived in dire poverty growing up, a poverty that marked him but also gave him the compassion to advocate for justice and to fight for social change. Still, none questioned their economic circumstances. They did their part to lift their family and community without fear of participating in the labor market and without shame, understanding that their lives were constrained by the social arrangements of race, class, and gender.

Despite the adversities they experienced, families in this study were repositories of tradition and models for social change. Parents—mothers as well as fathers—instructed their children inside a worldview that promoted an ethic of community service and support. Some were active in unions and in politics, while others tended to their neighbors and participated in the religious activities of their communities. Their legacy of activism did not focus on self-promotion or self-gain, but on improving their community and creating a just and equitable life for others. Their philosophy of involvement began with the premise that creating change for the group resulted in an improved life for the individual, since when the lives of others improved, so would their own lives. Still, their legacy of work would begin at the bottom.

LEGACIES OF WORK AND STRUGGLE: CANNERIES AND THE FIELDS

Among Mexican and Mexican-descent workers, the drive to organize the canning and packing industry began in the period of the Depression Generation. Because labor discriminated against Mexican participation in unions, and because agriculture was excluded from the National Labor Relations Board regulations since work was paid by piece-rate, those who worked in the fields and the canning industries were excluded from worker protections and collective bargaining. As agriculture became mechanized it was reclassified and subject to the 1935 National Labor Relations Act. The American Federation of Labor (AFL) signed a contract to negotiate with the California Processors and Growers, setting working conditions, and thus extending unemployment benefits to seasonal workers. The United Cannery, Agricultural, Packing and Allied Workers of America (UCAPAWA), affiliated with the Congress of Industrial Organizations (CIO), began organizing canning plants, accusing AFL of being a company union. Despite an aggressive grassroots effort, the UCAPAWA failed to unseat AFL locals. In 1945, the International Brotherhood of Teamsters (IBT)—those who transported their product to market—threatened to boycott canneries who continued to recognize AFL representation. Because of fear that their products would remain in the warehouses, the corporations caved in and negotiated with the Teamsters. This change did not improve conditions for seasonal workers, who continued to be ignored by the Teamsters (Zavella 1987).

According to Dave Bacon (2015), by 1930 "the Santa Clara Valley was the fruit processing capital of the world, owing to the labor of thousands of immigrant workers.... Thirty-eight canneries—some run by huge corporation like Libby's, Hunt's and

Calpak—employed up to 30,000 people." The anticommunist witch hunts compelled radical Chicano labor and community leaders to organize in San José. For example, after being blacklisted by the Coast Guard on the Los Angeles docks, Bert Corona came to organize workers in San José. He and Lucio Bernabe, a cannery organizer, encouraged strikes among Braceros, organized food caravans when Braceros stopped work, and tried to prevent their deportation.

Ernesto Galarza, a resident of San José, organized Mexican and Filipino farmworkers into the National Farm Labor Union in the late 1940s, which struck growers in the Central Valley. That union's successor, the Agricultural Workers Organizing Committee, began the great grape strike in 1965 under the leadership of Larry Itliong, and later merged with the National Farm Worker Association to form the United Farm Workers (UFW). Bernabe later helped found the Cannery Workers Committee (CWC) in the 1970s and '80s. The CWC challenged discrimination under the Teamsters contracts, since Mexican workers, mostly women, had only temporary jobs working on the line during the season, while white workers, mostly men, held permanent jobs in the warehouses and maintenance departments (Bacon 2015). Some mothers who participated in this study found jobs in the canneries to augment their family wages. For example, the Salazar family was able to save money to purchase the home in which Cecilia Arroyo and her siblings would be raised.

From 1948 to the 1970s, Mexican Americans were the largest ethnic group of cannery workers.[6] Those Mexican women who were promoted to office work or supervisory jobs during this period were fluent English speakers and were born in the United States. After World War II, cannery managers promoted primarily Italian and Portuguese women as floor ladies, who had the power to dismiss workers and were in charge of enforcing rules, instructing workers, and pushing for faster and more accurate work—ethnicity and language were issues (https://www.sourisseauacademy.org/niLADS/July2017LADS.pdf).

In 1969 concerned cannery workers formed the Mexican-American Workers Educational Committee, later known as the Comité de Trabajadores de Canería, or Cannery Workers Committee. The CWC fought against race and sex discrimination practiced by the Del Monte Corporation and the Teamsters. In their organizing endeavors, the comité published union materials in Spanish and taught workers how to vote in union elections. Their effort was unsuccessful but resulted in the opening of the Cannery Workers Service Center in 1978 (http://onlineexhibits.historysanjose.org/cannery life/through-the-years/1967-1999/unions.html).

It was these working women of Santa Clara County that collaborated with Patricia Zavella (1987) in the study that produced the book *Women's Work and Chicano Families: Cannery Workers in Santa Clara Valley*. The book is an examination of women's dual labor responsibilities in the domestic sphere and in the factory as they became employed as seasonal cannery workers. Zavella found that the women were segregated by race and gender as they carried out their duties. Also, they earned less than the men in their families, further reinforcing the traditional division of labor in which husbands continued to be seen as the main breadwinners while, despite outside employment, wives were perceived as responsible for domestic work. Still, cannery workers gained status and influence in the decision making of the family because of their contributions to their standard of living, but did not gain their husbands' support with housework; they continued to carry the load of the household work along with their outside employment.

With the globalization of work, and driven by profits, canneries began to relocate to Mexico. In less than ten years, all or most moved to the *bajío* region of Mexico, which includes the states of Aguascalientes, Jalisco, Guanajuato, and Queretaro. Efforts to stop the relocation of these multinational corporations came to naught, and those who relied on the canneries for supplemental family income found themselves unemployed or working in the vestiges of the agricultural economy that were still available in Santa Clara County. Some found work in the service industry as janitors, and still others provided family day care or became employed in other service jobs. Some would move on to find employment in the electronic industry—an area of employment for ethnic and minority women that has yet to be studied.

The chapters that follow document activist leaders' upbringing and relationships with their families of origin as they recall their cultural, social, and political lives in San José, California. Inside a legacy of hard work and self-sufficiency, they sought to create a better world for their people, reaping rewards for themselves only when it benefited all. Finally, I discuss their families of origin and the ways in which they became activist leaders who fought for Raza rights.

ACKNOWLEDGMENTS

This book is the realization of a dream to record the lives of Chicana and Latino/
Chicano activist leaders who fought and continue to struggle for justice and social
change in San José, California. They inspired many to make things better for others,
and in fighting for Raza rights they mentored many and imparted lessons of activism.
Chicanas and Latinos/Chicanos of the Depression Generation have left a mark in our
hearts and minds. With the passing of José Villa, whose life work focused on educational rights at all levels and who struggled against police violence and fought for
bilingual education, it is more urgent to tell these activist leader stories. Because Antonio R. Soto taught many of us to embrace our intellectual and spiritual lives, I write
about him. To record the memories of Esther Medina, Sofia Mendoza, and Ernestina
García—strong women who fought for educational access and equality for Mexican
Americans—we must continue organizing for Raza women's rights. To Jack Brito, an
education and community activist leader whose mission focused on corrections and
who left a legacy of making the sociocultural environment a better place for all, we
owe a great debt.

While activist leaders of the Baby Boomer Generation continue to model ways
to improve our lives, Cecilia Arroyo, Josie Romero, and Mike Garcia are no longer
with us, and they have left a gap in county planning, county mental health, and democratic politics, as well as in the unionization of service employees and undocumented
workers. Those who remain continue to work on improving Raza lives: Victor Garza,
José Carrasco, George Castro, Lou Covarrubias, Bea Vasquez Robinson, and Blanca
Alvarado work to create better living conditions for all. Wherever retired or residing
out of the area, these activist leaders continue to focus on creating change in their

respective communities. Delia Alvarez, Rose Amador, Elisa Marina Alvarado, Kathy Chavez Napoli, Felix Alvarez, Pete Carrillo, and Tony Estremera, in their own ways and motivated by a desire for service, still struggle for social justice.

In San Antonio, Texas, my home away from home, inspired by activist leaders who came before me, I have had immense support in the work I undertake with the goal of improving the lives of those with whom I come in contact. At the center of this invest-ment have been graduate students such as Drs. Norma E. Cárdenas, Sandra D. Garza, and Donald Allison, as well as colleagues—Drs. Marie Miranda, Marco Cervantes, and Lilliana P. Saldaña—who continue to support and inspire me. I owe a debt of gratitude to Dr. DelliCarpini, dean of the College of Education (COEHD) for her support. I also thank Patricia and Carolina Carrillo for their support in the early days of this work; and Gabby Sanchez, who walked alongside me in the process of publication for this book; thank you for being the beacon of light in which I can do work that matters. To Doreen Garcia Navel, Carol Carrasco, Clare Villa, Michal Mendoza, Cameo Burton, Felisa Méndez Carrazana, and all who answered my calls and provided photographs of their loved ones, I extend my appreciation—I am forever grateful for your words of encouragement. George R. Negrete, my most passionate and critical voice, I am the person I have become because you have been part of my life. Finally, for each and every one of you who participated in this project, I have done my best to share your stories.

ACTIVIST LEADERS OF SAN JOSÉ

1

. . .

FAMILIES OF ORIGIN

Becoming Activist Leaders

When Chicana and Latino/Chicano activist leaders in this study spoke about their lives in San José and Santa Clara County, they credited their relatives, particularly mothers and fathers, and other leaders in the community for inspiring them to become involved. Some shared insight about their daily experiences confronting injustices in the household or community, while others reported fighting for peoples' rights when they saw or experienced unjust or unfair situations. From an early age, these activist leaders consciously embraced justice, equality, and fairness—not in a rhetorical sense, but in interaction with the ethical conundrums of quotidian life. Thus, I argue that commitment to their people and community drove Chicanas and Latinos to work on creating a better world, inside an ethic of service, work, and responsibility. This study considers the experiences of Chicanas and Latinos/Chicanos in order to illustrate the ways in which they understood structures of inequality and domination in the context of ideologies learned at home and in the communities where they grew up.

Their voices and words serve as the text for analysis. Their observation and listening skills—such as noticing how adults spoke about each other as men and women, black or white, or rich and poor—generate a map for self-understanding in the context of interactions with peers, parents, and others with whom they engaged inside the structural makeup of their respective communities. For it was their lived experiences that gave them a foundation for understanding and negotiating social change as they struggled for their peoples' rights.

For Chicanas, race, while a salient and continuous intersectional space in their everyday lives, did not surface as an urgent problem. Although race and class encumbered their daily experiences, it was their recollections of gender difference, oppression, and subordination that molded their interactions in the family. In contrast, Latinos/Chicanos, who occupied a more privileged gender status, readily discussed class and race as sources of discomfort in their leadership interactions.

WHO ARE THEY?

Blanca Alvarado, councilwoman and vice-mayor of San José, and the first Chicana elected to Santa Clara County Board of Supervisors, remembered growing up in Cokedale, Colorado, a small mining town in the central southern part of the state, near the New Mexico border. She recalled that "it was a small mining town . . . now designated as a historical landmark. It's a special place . . . I still have wonderfully fond and loving memories of being raised there." Brought up in a community inhabited primarily by Spanish-speaking[1] families, Alvarado felt the security of inclusiveness. As an invested member of her community, she did not experience exclusion. This communitarianism served her well; she understood herself as belonging.

Esther Medina, a contemporary of Alvarado's, spoke about rural life in the agricultural fields of California during the Great Depression. She lived in a camp[2] with her brothers and sisters until the family migrated to Santa Clara County when she was four. Medina remembered her father as a labor activist with concern for fellow humans. She offered, "He was very involved . . . the family has a philosophy from him. He really emphasized looking out for other Latinos. I still hear his voice saying, 'Bring them in, son hermanos de Raza. Hoy será por ellos y mañana será por nosotros [they're blood brothers. Today it will be for them, tomorrow may be for us].'" Medina has no memories of her mother complaining, rather "we just made room for them." In this way, Medina expressed the philosophy that guided her family, pointing out that she was the only activist leader among them.

President of Service Employee International Union, Local 1877, Mike Garcia spoke about the internal dynamics of family, which primarily reflected traditional patriarchal notions often assigned to Mexican Americans (Madsen 1973; Lewis 1979). Garcia elaborated: "I guess it was very macho; the male dominated the familia. As far as positions, they're working-class—all my uncles were working-class. Our families were held together by traditional values of the family—strong working male symbols with subordinated women." Garcia's family values were embedded within the patriarchy and a structure of domesticity.[3] Responsibility for producing children and caring for the family and maintaining the home was the role assigned to women. "My mom stayed at home—that's the way he wanted it—he had complete control of the family. He was the dominant person." Thus Garcia described his father's power, which shaped his notions of gender and colored his expectations for a family relationship.

FIGURE 1 Blanca Alvarado, second from left, Alianza Hispano Americana, Cokedale, Colorado. Courtesy of Blanca Alvarado.

Also focusing on the internal dynamics of the family, but in a rural environment, Felix Alvarez, a cultural worker and community activist and a contemporary of Garcia's, remembered growing up in a large, close-knit family under the influence of his grandparents. For him, it was "not a Brady-bunch type of family; we grew up in a two-bedroom house—one bedroom was for my mom and dad and for the smaller siblings that grew up literally in their bed. The other bedroom was for my grandparents—the rest of us grew up pretty much in the living room or anywhere else there was floor space." For Alvarez, sharing such close quarters with all the members of the family was not deprivation or poverty. He explained, "We didn't feel deprived. It was not until I went off to college that I had a room to myself—dormitory room. For the first time, I had my own bed and sheets; I never grew up with that, but my family was very supportive." Insightfully, he indicated that family life and educational preparation were always a priority. At the same time, within a normative frame of reference, Alvarez viewed females as nurturers and caregivers of the household. His grandmother, replacing the absent mother who was participating in the public world of work, is idealized for her domestic contributions because she made *tortillas a mano*.

Born in Fort Morgan, Colorado, José Carrasco,[4] an educational leader and master organizer, was raised in Santa Clara County. He spoke about growing up in an agriculture-based economy, that is, before the cannery, and later manufacturing, became available as a source of employment for his parents. The poverty experienced by Carrasco and his family still causes him emotional discomfort. He spoke of the circumstances—a father who was ill for an extended period and a large family—that compelled him to act on his hunger, which subjected him to ridicule; it was a heart-wrenching recollection:[5] "I think I'd probably have to start by talking about the time that I was a kid in elementary school and I got caught by a couple of guys going through garbage cans, kind of getting, you know, sandwiches and food that people would throw away. The next Monday they came into my classroom—I was maybe in second or third grade at the time—they announced it to the class." This memory was framed within a personal understanding of the humiliation and isolation he felt when he came face-to-face with poverty and the class-based intolerance directed against him by middle-class students with whom the teacher colluded by remaining silent. Carrasco continued: "The reason I raise that is because I remember coping with what was happening at that moment. I couldn't say, 'I'll show you, you sons of bitches.' I was totally incapable of defending or dealing with it."

The struggle of growing up under those conditions is not easily forgotten, as shown by the emotional energy and *coraje* Carrasco discharges to fuel the courage that have driven him to create social change. Poverty launched him forward, and it still shapes his activist leader vision; the desire for social justice and social change is embedded in his recollections of marginalization, which inspires him to organize Raza and poor communities of color.

UPBRINGING AND TYPES OF FAMILIES

Some participants recalled growing up happy and without problems in a large family.[6] Some spoke about poverty, and the difficulty and burdens that a large family places on its members. Still, embedded in these *recuerdos* are valued memories. Despite the hardships, few respondents expressed regret at having grown up in their families. Their upbringing informed their views on social change. Whether in the family or the community, everyday experiences influenced these activist leaders' struggle for social justice.

A longtime supporter of the United Farm Workers, and a community and mental health activist, Josie Romero remembered growing up in a family where money was never a big issue.[7] She recalled the closeness and support she experienced in her large extended family. "Grandpa and grandma were always watching to make sure that mom and dad did the right thing—if mom and dad weren't doing the right thing, grandpa would get on them, especially grandpa on mother's side." In her upbringing, responsibility for children did not end with the nuclear family, since relatives and community members often took charge. Grandmothers and grandfathers were closely tied to the family and often lived with them and were usually the most present around the home.

Romero had access to her extended family, but a small number of the respondents grew up without the presence of their extended kin. For example, Elisa Marina Alvarado, a cultural activist and mental health social worker, recalled, "I'm the oldest of six children. So, there was the dealing with a big family and a lot of activity in the house. Everybody had a sense of my dad working really hard to try to provide a certain quality of life—a sense of security." Alvarado remembered the struggles experienced by her parents, who wanted to have a stay-at-home mother to establish a strong foundation for their children. Alvarado mother's strove to provide a milieu that would culturally and intellectually stimulate their traditional family. She recalled how others in her middle-class neighborhood perceived her family. Alvarado had privileges not available to some of her contemporaries; she had access to resources others did not have. For example, she spoke of traveling: "We went to Mexico once a year; to visit *familia*, and we would stop and visit my grandmother. . . . I always felt I was more related to being Mexican than Chicana, until I moved out at eighteen, and into the Chicano movement." Middle-class status did not prevent Alvarado from developing a cultural identity that would later shape her involvement in the Chicano movement. Her parents provided her a historical engagement with her ancestral Mexican culture and exposed her to alternative educational venues, creating divergent ways for understanding her position and that of others whose life trajectory was unlike hers.

In addition to poverty and the traditional experiences of growing up in economic constraints, most of these activist leaders recollected experiencing a poverty that compelled them to work to improve conditions for their people. Recognizing that life was not easy or without sacrifices, both Chicanas and Latinos/Chicanos participated in the daily life of the family to meet their needs, in whatever way was necessary.

FAMILY HARDSHIPS AND A LEGACY OF EMPLOYMENT

Ernestina García, homemaker and community activist, recalled that her family relied on agricultural work for economic survival, describing the difficulty of making do within a large family. She spoke about entering the world of school and about interactions with the rancher's family and their children, confronting boundaries in public life as both spaces created a great deal of conflict, pain, and confusion. Her school experience, in particular, was filled with sadness and tears. She spoke about juggling the responsibilities of working as a family for the ranchers who hired them, noting that all her family members participated. She will never forget the ranchers' names, including one called "Big Nosed One," or *narizón*. García spoke about her parents' toiling in their daily life:[8]

> Mi 'amá trabajaba very hard—*muy duro porque trabajaba en la casa*—she washed clothes, not only ours, but also sometimes *lavándole ropa a la dueña del rancho. Mi hermana*, the oldest, *trabajaba limpiándole la casa a la Señora*—My sister cleaned the rancher's house. *Yo no entendía, at an early age, no podía entender porque es que los hijos de ellos, del ranchero, podíamos jugar con ellos mientras que estábamos allí en la casa*—but in school we were separated. At such an early age, I could not comprehend why their children, we could play with them while they were there at home, but when it came to school, we could not.

For García, this physical separation was irrational—race and poverty converged in her socialization—and segregation by race or ethnicity was no less difficult than poverty. Such a separation left an indelible impression, informing the ways in which she navigated and contested the treatment she experienced as a result of how she was socially positioned in relationship to whites, and the rancher's family in particular. Early in life, García learned to see herself and her environment on the basis of class and race, although she was cognizant that gender issues were no less burdensome for her and the women in her family.

Similar to most of those from the Depression Generation, Victor Garza, a political and community activist, also spoke about growing up poor in a rural community and normalizing it: "When you don't know anything outside the immediate surroundings, you feel that you have the world in your hands, even though you may be the poorest of the poor. . . . My mom—she was the strongest of the two—always led us to believe that we were not poor, even though we were sometimes barefooted and we'd have raggedy clothes, for she . . . always felt that we were not really poor . . . we were just as good as anyone else." Garza credited his mother's creativity and resourcefulness for their security. He saw her efforts, not as a protection, but as a fostering of self-esteem so they would not feel less valued than the people around them.

Josie Romero spoke about her family's philosophy of self-sufficiency. She attributed the family's notion of economic independence to her parents: "Being as poor as we were, I can tell you honestly that we never applied for welfare, or anything like that. I'm sure we would have qualified because we had so many of us. But, my father always told us that he had brought us to this country and he alone was going to support us." For these activist leaders, there was no shame in being poor or in doing whatever was available for the family. However, no one desired to make their progeny dependent on the state, they'd rather work than ask for assistance.

Growing up in the Salinas Valley, Delia Alvarez, was raised with an ethic of self-sufficiency that encouraged the family to take whatever work was available. In that context, with the knowledge that she was not rich, she recalled interacting with people in the workplace and the community. Still, with a father who was a blue-collar worker, Alvarez said, "We lived from paycheck to paycheck, and he was a hotheaded young Chicano changing jobs a lot; when Dad started drinking, the teen years were rough. The earlier years we were with a lot of family and took excursions to the beach. From an economic standpoint, we were poor. However, I had stability because mother stayed home to raise us." As was the case for Alvarez, familial difficulties emerged as issues. For some it was drinking and for others, excessive work schedules and other family conflicts. However, the family's everyday survival depended on factors besides work, and education was promoted as the route to success and social change.

Unlike Alvarez, Bea Vasquez Robinson, an organizer and political activist, experienced much trauma growing up in a poor family. "It was not a happy childhood . . . there was a lot of poverty." Given the family's dynamics, Vasquez Robinson found herself negotiating interactions in the household and, like Alvarez, worked to achieve excellence in school. For her, academic achievement was an escape from her everyday struggles at home. But while school was a place where Vasquez Robinson felt competent and successful, her life was filled with sadness: "My father was an alcoholic. Mother was very timid when she was with him and afraid of being sent back to Mexico because she had been here illegally for a long time. We were a very large family, we followed the crops, and we lived in tents."

Most migrated to the United States for work, but not all worked in the fields. For example, growing up with a stay-at-home mother in her early years, Cecilia Arroyo was raised around Cupertino, "close to where De Anza College is now located." She lived in a community "that was all Chicano except for a few Oakies." Her "paternal grandmother lived on one side and maternal grandmother around the corner," and there were fictive kin such as her godmother "down the block and so it was a family neighborhood." It would be about ten years later, when her brother was born, that the family moved to Santa Clara.

Her father, who was securely employed outside of agriculture, did not smoke or drink but could be volatile. Arroyo saw herself as having grown up in "a very typical Chicano household," where she had to mediate as the peacemaker when her parents' "interactions escalated." Nevertheless, "the only thing that was different is that women in my family are very strong. My mother is a very strong role model and my maternal grandmother is still strong to this day. As for me, setting the peace for other people, that was my job." For Arroyo, her community was her family. She explained: "My parents were not very religious so we didn't have the religious community to relate to and they didn't do a lot of civic things. They didn't do anything because they still don't even vote. So, we didn't have that community and all we had was our extended family; we are very close-knit." Arroyo's mother entered the labor force, securing employment as a seasonal cannery worker. It was through her efforts that the family purchased a home, thus sheltering their children from poverty.

Low socioeconomic status and an urban upbringing were two distinguishing characteristics of those who were raised in San José during the Depression and Baby Boomer eras. One exception is Antonio Roberto Soto, community leader and activist and a professor emeritus at San José State, who came from a ranching family in Arizona. "By ranching I mean *en el desierto*—in the desert. In 1888, my grandfather Ramón Soto, under the Homestead Act, established a ranch in the middle of the desert." Given his class position, Soto recalled no options available there for Mexicanos. More unusual was his entrance into the priesthood: "At the age of thirteen and a half, my aunts and mother sent me to a Franciscan Seminary in Santa Barbara where I studied Latin, Greek—six years; a year of novitiate or boot camp where they isolate you from everything; three years of philosophy; and, four years of theology. So, thirteen years mostly away from family, although I would visit summers." The preparation Soto received would ready him for a life of education and activism. He began his involvement in the mid-1950s, working with Braceros in Southern California.

Like Antonio Soto, Jorge Gonzalez, president of Raza Si! and a community and political activist, came from a nonagricultural background. Gonzalez grew up in Mexico City with the freedom to be independent, surrounded by intellectuals and left-leaning refugees from different parts of Latin America. He saw his experience growing up as comprising two stages: one in Mexico, where he was exposed to many different perspectives and interests, and the other as a young immigrant to the United States. Gonzalez elaborated, "In Mexico City, our family took two or three apartments—aunts, uncles, grandparents—it was neat because my aunts and uncles had different interests. So, they influenced me. For example, I had an aunt into things Spanish and she was a Flamenco dancer. An uncle who was a bullfighter was more into things that were Mexican. Many friends, people from the province, who would bring their guitars and sing."

That multiplicity of activists and their different interests motivated Gonzalez, fanning his curiosity and desire to learn from the many perspectives he heard. To complement his Latin American exposure, Gonzalez's mother contributed an internationalist perspective that was U.S. influenced. Gonzalez said, "She listened to U.S. music mirroring Mexico City as a cosmopolitan city. Our family was lower middle class. In this country we would be considered poor, we lived paycheck to paycheck,

FIGURE 2 Antonio Soto, OIC/CET founder. Photo from the CET Fifth Anniversary Program. Courtesy of CET.

but we were not poor in the kind of poverty that exists in Mexico." Though Gonzalez was surrounded by intellectual discussions and political ideologies, he did not experience the privilege of wealth in Mexico. While he enjoyed growing up in a supportive family environment, things changed when his mother married an American citizen who brought them to the United States. Still, intellectual curiosity, the encouragement to question and to read, and issues of social justice and equality, as well as kindness, were values that guided Gonzalez.

Chicanas I interviewed would differ, not only in their upbringing but also in the ways they interacted and related to others. They acknowledged the influence of family members. For example, Delia Alvarez's parents participated in mutualistic or service organizations. She said, "What got my father more involved was a gang fight—I believe it was Chualar or Gonzalez—when Mexicans were depicted as gangsters. So, my dad was part of a CSO committee; they used to go to San José for the big conventions." Derisive images and the mistreatment of Mexican Americans thus became a catalyst for involving many parents in activities that would improve their group.

For some, union activism became a site of involvement at the local level, albeit limited to their respective unions. George Castro, a community and educational activist, cites his mother's membership in the International Ladies Garment Workers Union (ILGWU); his father too joined later. Jorge Gonzalez's parents are another example: "My stepfather became active when the UFW boycott started—that was around 1965 or '66. My mother was equally active, and when they moved to Ventura they were extremely active against the Vietnam War, still supporting the farmworkers, but against the Vietnam War. They had a committee called The Action Committee, and they even ran candidates for city council, that was the height of the '60s." Even though his mother was involved, the depth of activism was much broader for male parents. Fathers were active through their unions, with one respondent's father being in the "boss" position.

Community activism and political involvement emerged as another area of investment for some fathers. Blanca Alvarado's father was very active in the Mine Workers Union. She recalled, "He was the treasurer. My parents would get involved with the elections. So, my early political formation began with my dad and mother—from my dad, I learned about the power and good that individuals are capable of, and from them I grew up knowing that role models play a part." Alvarado saw her father as the activist parent. However, she pointed out that her mother also was involved in electoral politics.

Sofia Mendoza, too, a community activist and organizer, spoke about her union activist father. Rose Amador's father combined community and political activism. She remembered that "in Pennsylvania—with very few Hispanics or Mexicans or any in the whole state—but, he managed to start up a Latino group; he was always involved—in the GI Forum and with Image." Her mother, on the other hand, focused her involvement on community service and activism. Both parents were active in electoral politics, supporting and working with Democratic and Raza candidates.

Josie Romero came from a long line of activists. In our interview, she focused on her mother's contributions: "My mother was always very involved in *el barrio*, helping little old ladies that were alone, made sure that they ate, washed their clothes, and sent us with anything special we would make like tamales, or caldo. She remembered the lady that was sick or a lady that was alone—we sort of like adopted them, and when they got well move on to others." Similarly, Kathy Chavez Napoli, from Sal Si Puedes, the community of entry for San José's Mexican immigrants, recalled her mother's involvement: "Mother was always being asked to translate because she's native born here." She explained, "Most acquaintances where I grew up on Summer Street in San José were limited English speaking, so she was always being asked to do translations and to help ease the way in different situations."

Some mothers who were not active during their children's upbringing became active in later life, often in religious activity. This was the case for Vasquez Robinson's mother: "She became very involved and very active in the church, a leader in her *Carmelita* group, attended many meetings, and visited the poor. Valued in her religious circles for saying the rosary, she was always called upon to say the rosary when people died; she was known for the beauty of her prayers." For Vasquez Robinson, that her mother, Francisca, fulfilled this type of need in the community was a great service. She was a well-respected community figure, playing a prominent part in stage-of-life ceremonies having to do with religious rituals and celebrations.

In describing his mother's community activism, Pete Carrillo, a political and community activist, saw her involvement as traditional. Carrillo's mother did not limit herself to Democratic politics—the expected venue for Hispanic participation. She also worked for the election and reelection of Barry Goldwater. From his mother, Carrillo learned about pragmatic politics and self-interest, the art of compromise or a quid pro quo exchange of political power—strategies Carrillo's mother demonstrated.

Ernestina García and José Villa spoke about relying on agricultural and migrant work for economic survival. Both experienced the difficulty of making do in a large family, while recalling blissful childhoods. García remembered feeling happy within the confines of her family, yet talked about confronting boundaries to negotiate public life. She remembered being happy in the private space of the home, even when "we were many—seventeen of us. I didn't meet the two oldest, but altogether to give you an idea of the size of the family that I came from, there's twelve of us living; the home environment was a happy one." Contrary to her own family experience, García perceived her mother's life as hard, because segregation was no less difficult than the poverty they experienced.

García shared many painful memories of how she and her Mexican classmates were discriminated against and humiliated at school. Early in life she recognized that her environment was based on distinctions of class and race, although gender would also come into play. Rather than learning to fear those who had sociocultural power, García learned to understand the freedom of their entitlement as she contested their power in the struggle for social change. For her, rather than experience it as a limitation, movement and migration would be a venue that offered options for change.

José Villa, of the same generation as García, also recalled that his nuclear and extended family immigrated "during the *Revolución*—it was 1916." He elaborated, "My father, his family—his father and mother, widowed sister with two children, a younger brother, my mother and my two oldest brothers, *vinieron de Mexico*." His father had lived here before, and he came with notion of settling in the States. "We set roots in Clovis. He built a little adobe house in the barrio, as he had come to the area *a ver donde había trabajo*; he knew there was *ferrocarril*—railroad work." That was how "he spotted the place to set up a base to work." Through their relocation, Villa's father aimed to create a home for his family that was free of the violence they had experienced in Mexico. Others were driven by a strong work ethic and a philosophy of self-sufficiency, a theme that emerged in the participants' family values—regardless of gender. Since they were actively part of the labor process, seeing Raza as not having a choice but to work, many of the participants in this study saw their legacy of work as foundational to becoming involved with social justice and in pursuit of social change.

FAMILIAL INFLUENCES ON LEADERSHIP FORMATION:
LEGACIES OF ACTIVISM

Participants stated that family influenced their development as activist leaders. Romero credited her motivation to her parents and grandparents. Her political activism, however, she attributed to her paternal grandfather, who was the mayor of a municipality in Mexico. Antonio Soto's grandfather, a founding member of the Alianza Hispano Americana in Tucson,[9] was instrumental in contributing to his formation as an activist, although family members on both sides inspired him to fight for social justice and strive for social change.

George Castro, a political, community, and educational activist, cited his parents' union activism as inspiring. Jorge Gonzalez's parents provided a broad picture of parental activism, but the breadth of involvement was much greater for fathers. Community activism and political involvement emerged as another area of focus for male parents. While Blanca Alvarado saw her father as the activist parent, her mother participated in electoral politics. While one father was religiously active, four fathers among those in the Depression Generation were not involved in religious activities. For Rose Amador, her mother focused her involvement on community service and activism, while both parents were involved in electoral politics, supporting and working for the Democratic Party and the election of Raza candidates. Romero, who came from a long line of activists, identified her mother's community activism as inspiring her to act on behalf of the community. Kathy Chavez Napoli also named her mother as the one who made a difference in the needs of her community.

Most mothers of both generations found a way to become invested in their children's upbringing, but Felix Alvarez was one of only two males in the study inspired by their mothers' activism. He recalled, "She was involved in trying to get Raza to vote back in the '60s and in many other community issues at the neighborhood level. I would characterize my mother as an activists' activist. She was a natural leader." He recalled that people were often attracted to her and her desire to "always stop and help people." Both Romero and Alvarez found their mothers' contribution to the welfare of the community and their support of individuals inspirational. To provide a place to sleep and to serve a meal to those in need was not perceived as something foreign in their household—such actions were congruent with a philosophy of service.

On the other hand, Pete Carrillo, in describing his mother's activism, saw his mother's involvement as traditional. He said, "My mother was active in her own family because she was the one that went to school." She did all the paperwork for her parents—she was literate in both Spanish and English—and it was from her that Carrillo "got his political bent. She knew everybody in the neighborhood, I mean literally knew everybody in the neighborhood." With some hesitation, Carrillo said that his mother worked for the election and reelection of Barry Goldwater, later campaigning for Senator Paul Fannin, both staunch Republicans. He explained, "It wasn't until later that I figured out—although she didn't have the strategy mapped out in her mind— that down the street from our house was Goldwater Farms owned by the Goldwater family—she and her neighbors wanted . . . the city to transform it into a park. And, indeed, that is exactly what happened." Thus, it was from his mother that Carrillo learned about pragmatic politics and the art of compromise.

Those who did not consider their parents to be political or active in the community remembered other qualities that influenced their own vision for social change. Villa, reflecting on his father, said he was not involved "in a union kind of thing" because "at the time they practically dragged you out and shot you if you even thought about it." His father's involvement rested in organizing his large family and in instilling in them skills and qualities necessary for becoming productive individuals. In his view, "Father was surviving with us and the family and arranging to take us *a las escardas,* to make sure the *troquita si se quebraba se componía*—that the truck was fixed, if it broke. He was so busy taking care of us that he didn't have time or energy for anything really." For Villa, organizing and arranging activities required to get a work crew established, for example, entailed leadership. His father got things done, assuming responsibility for the welfare of not just his family but also of relatives who relied on his father for employment. In the everyday duties of life, that was his way of exercising leadership and contributing to social change.

NEGOTIATING RACE AND CLASS: GENDERED SYSTEMS OF UNDERSTANDING

While race and class were power intersections for Chicanas and Latinos in this study, gender was more often a focal point of relational interaction for Chicanas. Gender conflicts were not at the center for males of both generations, but Chicanas found themselves engaging raced, classed, and gendered constraints within and outside the family and community. Still, race and class were more readily visible and impactful in the lives of Latinos, even when engaging gender as a position of privilege and entitlement. What follows are narratives of race and class in the participants' words.

In his memories of growing up in Tucson, Antonio Soto recalled that there was much racism in his community. "But, it wasn't so evident, because the two races didn't mix too much." Still, at fourteen years of age, he says, "I wasn't aware of it. Of course, for the next four or five summers I spent the whole summer there, and became aware." For him, class was a source of conflict, and the contradiction eventually became clearer, especially when it came to his private education. Soto explained:

> I remember coming home weekends, back to my family home wearing my green and gold University of San Francisco (USF) jacket, and, the kids would look at me real odd and would say, "What's the matter? Either you're going to the university or you don't live here in this area." I'd ask, "Tell me why?" They said, "Anybody who goes to the university doesn't stay here; we don't know of any kids in here who have ever gone to the university." I said, "Oh my God! That tells me a lot of this neighborhood." I thought I knew it well, because I was very involved in the Church.

Sheltered from poverty and protected by his involvement in the church, Soto had not realized that life was more complicated for others.

Felix Alvarez recalled his family's class position as a wedge in his South Texas community. However, differences were found in the professional classes, such as among "the doctors, business, medical . . . you'd see stuff in the paper, where you'd see the socialization of that, where you'd have your upper-class kind of Mexicanos or Tejanos and then you'd have the barrio. But, I mean, socialite kind of stuff, you know, the *familia* so and so, *y la hija* of so and so, you know, that kind of stuff, which is kind of Mexicano, that you had some of that." Like Soto, who did not experience mixing between Raza and Anglos, Alvarez did not recall interactions among classes. "There were no interrace relations—issues of concern had more to do with sexism and misogyny—it was an in-your-face racism, rather than the 'subtler' racism of California." He remembered, "Getting in a lot of fights as racism was very blatant, even when I always considered California to be more racist but subtler."

George Castro spoke about his upbringing in Los Angeles. For him, outright racism became a moot point, as he resided among people who looked like him and shared similar living conditions in a community that also incorporated blacks. Castro said, "There were no whites—we were all minority. And everybody looked, we all looked as if we were part of the underdogs. The Japanese looked like the whites, and the white is something we saw on TV. We played against them in high school, but they didn't go to our school . . . we were East LA, we were the bottom. Amongst us, I would say, race relationships were very good, as we integrated the black and the Mexicano." In his community, difference was a point of inclusion; it was when those with privilege—such as whites—were in their midst that race would become contentious. In this context, Castro simultaneously experienced injuries of race and class, although most present was the psychological injury of the color hierarchy, as he believes that it was their darker complexion that motivated him and his sister to become involved in the struggle for Raza rights. He said, "The two of us are much more committed to *la causa* and Mexican people . . . and it's simply because we're darker . . . there was no mistaking my sister and I—we're clearly Mexican—my sister and I are just completely involved."

As far as socioeconomic class is concerned, Castro said that "class was associated with where you lived and whether you resided in public housing or not." He elaborated, "Mexicanos, we were richer than the other ones, and the biggest social class that I remember is whether you lived in the projects or not. And, you could live in the dumpiest shack next to a project, but there was a real distinction [between] the people who lived in the housing project versus the nonhousing project."

Castro identified relative poverty to demonstrate the distinction of living in your own house. The stigma of class and poverty attached to those who lived in the projects because "the housing projects were rougher; it was the heart of the biggest gangs." He described the only class distinction he could recall: "We had some rickety houses. We never lived in a housing project; we were never that low, always were a little higher. Dad and Mom, they both had work, we were not going to live in a housing project." Class differences would be another way to separate the group, while gender would become the wedge that separated Chicanas.

GENDER, CLASS, AND RACE: NAVIGATING STRUCTURAL INEQUALITIES

Chicana activist leaders brought up gender subordination or inequality, which was often construed as their place as women. For example, Bea Vasquez Robinson spoke about treatment women received at the hands of fathers, husbands, brothers, and society at large. In their relationships with males, Chicanas often were relegated to second- or third-class citizenship. Vasquez Robinson stated that "things were as things have always been; there were no laws that made it illegal to discriminate based on sex, so if you were brown and a woman it was very, very difficult. You had to endure remarks—not only were you discriminated against in terms of employment and in terms of buying power, all these redlining practices, but also socially."

In her view, the negative treatment of women was pervasive: "Even kids, boys knew that it was okay to belittle the mother because she was a woman." Misogyny was alive and well in the Mexican American culture.

> Yet, we stuck very close to other Latinos. We had to because of the marginal existence that we had. We had to and so we did. So, I never felt I fit in because of all these things and so, to me, there were different worlds, but the white world was alien and cold and you could never enter, never, never. There were a lot of rebuffs when I did try, both from children and adults. So, it just reemphasized repeatedly that there was a separation and you had to stay within those boundaries.

As Vasquez Robinson matured, she learned to navigate both white and brown worlds. Because of fundamental influences in school and in her community, she had an opportunity to overcome some of the barriers she confronted in her early years, learning to make decisions based on an individual's value instead of racial background.

Like Vasquez Robinson, Esther Medina experienced discrimination and humiliation at a very early age as a person of color, including overt race discrimination in school. In addition to physical separation and the enactment of distinctly racialized rituals, in second grade the teacher placed Mexican and Mexican American children in what she considered a "Mexican" place. As Medina saw it, this teacher's "sick little game" would never place her on a par with or ahead of the children of bankers, doctors, and lawyers; by that community, she was considered an outsider. This treatment was not limited to her teachers and the children in her classroom. The Mexican American children were also ridiculed, publicly taunted, and humiliated outside the classroom, for example by the actions of a public health nurse assigned to her school: "The nurse would . . . line us up in the hall—all brown kids—we had to take our shoes and socks off to be inspected—to see if we had lice. With those sticks—tongue depressors—she'd look between your toes to see if we were clean enough—this is the kind of humiliation that we would have to put up with; it took hours."

Medina equated the humiliation, hurt, and anger with the feeling she experienced when she saw old movie reels about the Holocaust. She credited her parents for helping her overcome such horrors, saying that without their help she would have been unable to overcome the traumatic experiences of her school days; they gave her positive reinforcement and reassured her that she was a good, loved, and valued child. She was repeatedly told, "'You're worth a lot. You come from this culture,' and they'd talk to us about the culture and how ignorant people were. They'd tell us not to hate them because they were ignorant people. That we had to remember what we were worth, and they would counter all this negative stuff that was going on at school." The mental, emotional, and physical abuse Medina experienced as child inside educational institutions prepared her to understand the human condition and to differentiate groups of people by their intentions—adults and children alike.

Josie Romero also spoke about experiencing blatant racism. She too was protected by her parents, although they were unable to prevent the racial biases she encountered as a member of a marginalized people. For instance, she recalled a time in 1954, "when I was just eleven or twelve years old, and we were coming from Texas to Washington, you know, we had to cross the state of Utah, and Utah is lily white." Romero remembered that the family stopped to have breakfast in a small town in Utah. On the father's instructions, she and her brother went ahead of the adults while the adults went to wash their hands: "'Get us a table. I'll be there in a minute.' As we walked in and sat down, the waitress came and said, 'We don't serve Mexicans,' and, of course, . . . that didn't make a lot of sense." Not having experienced this type of treatment before, Romero did not understand what the waitress meant by her comments. To make sure that she was accurately hearing what she was being told, she asked the waitress to repeat herself. "We don't serve Mexicans," was her response. When her father arrived, the waitress gave him the menu and told him to sit, which led Romero to unpack the privilege of color:

> My dad is blond and blue-eyed because he's German. But speaks no English, so I turned around and said, *"Dicen que aquí no sirven a Mexicanos. Que tenemos que salir."* [They say they don't serve Mexicans here. We have to leave.] My dad's face turned red . . . and *el dijo,* *"Dile que vaya a chingar a su madre . . ."* [he said, "Tell them to go f---- her mother"]. I couldn't say that in English then. I didn't know how to translate that, so he dropped the menu and we left.

This incident taught Romero never to accept unequal treatment. However, her father's coping strategy was to avoid restaurants, to protect his family from racism.

"From that day forward, my dad was very selective where we stopped; he didn't want to put us through this. To protect us, he just started stopping at the grocery store. He would buy us the food, and we would eat it in the car." That would not be her only experience with overt racism. Romero continued to experience unequal treatment at the hands of those who were outside the group. The racial experiences she had to live through, as she and her family worked the migrant stream from Texas, would have been more unbearable had it not been for her parents' protection. It was these and other experiences that laid the foundation for Romero to complete an education and pursue a service profession where she would struggle for and protect the rights and dignity of those marginalized by structural barriers such as race, class, and gender.

As a member of the Baby Boomer Generation and one of the two participants born in San José, Kathy Chavez Napoli brought up race and class experiences growing up in Sal Si Puedes when she spoke about her transition from Mayfair Elementary to Mildred Goss Elementary. "It was very much a white school in a nice neighborhood with brand-new tract homes and a brand-new school," which middle-class children attended. She recalled "one negative time, when this one girl kept picking on me; she called me 'a beaner,' and we got sent to the principal's office and I got in trouble and she didn't." Despite these type of conflicts, Chavez Napoli experienced no academic difficulties:

FIGURE 3 Kathy Chavez Napoli at Mildred Goss Elementary. Courtesy of Kathy Chavez Napoli

FIGURE 4 Rose Amador. Courtesy of Rose Amador LeBeau.

"Most of the time I did well in school and I liked the teacher and I remember at least three or four times when I used to be called one of the teacher's pets, because I loved school." Still, it was in high school that she would deal with class differences between "poor and middle class, and that's where I really learned that I was real poor."

For Rose Amador, who grew up in Pennsylvania, race relations were confined to black and white. Amador's father reproduced such binary practices at home when speaking about blacks. She said, "Dad used to tell us, 'You don't play with them, you don't talk to them, only in class.' And all the kids acted that way, it must have been all those parents saying that to kids. When I think about it, when I got older and realized how racist it really was."

In one way or another, race and class were structures of inequality these activist leaders encountered inside a complex understanding of difference at home and in the community. The concepts of justice, equality, and fairness were imbued with nuanced qualities they strove to understand as they struggled for their peoples' rights and social justice.

INSPIRATION POINTS: ENGAGING SOCIAL CHANGE

Romero began advocating for workers' right in the agricultural field where she also served as a translator. While Blanca Alvarado, Esther Medina, and Bea Vasquez Robinson worked in agriculture, Delia Alvarez, Sofia Mendoza, Elisa Marina Alvarado, Cecilia Arroyo, and Kathy Chavez Napoli grew up in an urban environment. Alvarado, Medina, and Vasquez Robinson, when they settled in Santa Clara County, countered racism by doing well in their academics. Still, for those who grew up around the time of the Great Depression, education was not an option for Mexican women. Of the five Chicanas from that generation, only Sofia Mendoza attended San José State College, later dropping out to organize.

Of those who grew up during the Baby Boomer Generation, three out of five born in the early years of that era pursued higher education, with two obtaining degrees after having established themselves as professionals. The most obvious racial aggression experienced by women in this generation was described by both generations. Some recalled that teachers and counselors failed to encourage them to higher education. There were never any questions or any doubts about white students—even girls—but for Mexican Americans, a higher education escaped their grasp.

These activist leaders' gender, class, race, and educational identities are built on the legacy of their family histories. How they were shaped can be attributed to their family socialization, although they acknowledge and recognize the influences other people had on their formation. Their mothers, fathers, grandparents, and teachers often are credited with influencing their leadership and activist practices. In addition, many identified Dr. Ernesto Galarza and César E. Chávez—activist leaders in their community—as role models and mentors.

SIGNIFICANT OTHERS: THE IMPORTANCE OF MENTORS

In their accounts, participants shared recollections about individuals outside the family who contributed to their activism and leadership. While many emphasize Galarza and Chávez as points of inspiration, Pete Carrillo identified José Carrasco and Humberto Garza, who brought him into their circle. Carrillo recalled, "Humberto Garza and José Carrasco—they allowed me to be part of their group of people. They were very tough. I think the reason I could withstand their barrage of probing questions was why I was able to stay with them, not initially, but as it progressed—I was able to argue as effectively as their students. This enabled them to have respect for me, because I have tremendous respect for them, and still do." The relationship that evolved developed naturally, rather than being planned by design. Carrillo recognized that circumstances made possible a relationship that helped form his leadership skills.

While José Carrasco and Humberto Garza served as mentors for Carrillo, Carrasco himself acknowledged Dr. Alice Scoffield's influence. He elaborated on her mentorship.

> Scoffield was the one that got me into teaching, because I got into teaching by accident. I wasn't looking for it. She literally dragged me into the damn thing and the next thing I knew, I was out there. And, so, I met with her, and I didn't have my credentials yet, and I was an intern—since she was the director [of a teacher's education program] she got me into it, and then she got me into the classroom, and so she had an idea and that once you started teaching you finished up—you didn't worry about the credential.

She would not be the only person to support him. When speaking about "so-called mentoring" relationships, Carrasco explained these interactions as "somebody liked me enough to care about me." He reflected on his relationships with Jack Brito and Ernesto Galarza:

I don't think Jack was trying to teach me a whole bunch of stuff. Jack is a survivor; that's what makes him so honest—he is surviving. Jack, I think, wanted me close because he felt comfortable with me around because I also was strong, and, so, in a way, we comforted each other. But, it wasn't as if Jack was trying to teach me, I learned tremendous things. And, what's so powerful about mentorship is that you're not trying to teach anybody anything; you're just learning yourself. It's in that informal kind of reaction, action, kind of learning that you sort of share with someone else.

Carrasco highlighted the importance of self-learning and motivation in his relationship, emphasizing honesty as a key aspect. For him, a foundation of trust fostered the productive interactions that went beyond the instructional aspects of leadership. Still, as an activist leader, Carrasco did not see himself as the product of a system or as an individual; rather, he saw himself as constituted by a compilation of the circumstances and influences that shaped his actions.

Still, of all the persons who influenced Carrasco in his leadership formation, the one individual who began with mentoring in mind was Dr. Ernesto Galarza, whom many in the community perceived as a mentor, recognizing him as a master organizer who made many contributions. For example, he contributed to the development of bilingual education programs in the local college and school districts.

For Sofia Mendoza, it was her involvement in grassroots activism that brought her into a relationship with Galarza. She recalled their first meeting when she was a young mother living in the Eastside of San José and Galarza visited her at her home: "Dr. Galarza came to my house and he wanted to talk to me. And, God, I think about it; it was almost like yesterday. I feel so honored. I wish I could've recorded what this man had to say to me. He was wearing a raincoat, and he took his raincoat off, played with my kids for a while, then he sat down, and said, 'I want to talk to you. I've been reading your name in the newspaper.'" Mendoza thinks that Galarza visited her because of her involvement in the community, and others may have suggested it. She paraphrased the concerns that brought him to her house.

"I just want to talk to you about what it means to be a leader. To see if you even understand what it means and what it is." He said, "If you're going to get into this just for short terms, don't hurt the people. They don't need to be hurt anymore." He says, "If you're going to be here and you're just going to disappear just don't do it. But, if you're going to be in it for the long haul, then go ahead and do it." He says, "But I don't know if you know what being a leader is." He's telling me all this stuff. It was so wonderful to hear.

Like Mendoza, José Villa respected Galarza as a leader and said that he had exercised a great influence on him as an activist for social change. Villa elaborated,

Ernesto Galarza did influence me very profoundly in that he said, "Stay close to the community. Don't be seduced by high wages, high salaries or big jobs. Stay close to the community where you can help it." So, my motivation has been to stay close to the Mexican community. I've been part of that community. And if there's anything that distinguishes me from leadership—broad leadership—is that I stayed close to my people. I refused to give up my identity, or my relationships with my people.

Galarza encouraged Villa and supported his work with Mexican Americans, instructing him to hold on to his ethnic pride and to maintain alliances with his culture by not rejecting his identity. Galarza offered Villa criticism to help him productively examine his actions and involvement. However, Galarza was not always direct with his criticism and often started with an analogy of somebody else's shortcomings. For example, Villa remembered how he would say, "'So, and so is a very bright guy, but he doesn't know how to dominate an idea, master it so that you make it more than an idea, bring it into action.' And, I think he was saying that to me rather than, he had a funny way of talking, he was saying, '*el que mucho abarca, poco aprieta*' [he who attempts much, achieves little] sort of thing. So, part of the mistakes I made was taking on too much and not focusing on one issue or on one thing." In this way, Galarza cautioned Villa from spreading himself too thin.

In contrast to Villa's long-lasting relationship with Galarza, differences in approach lead to a parting of the ways for Galarza and Carrasco when Carrasco took the institutional path. Carrasco explained, "I had to challenge [his willingness to] let a very good friend of mine be wasted just to achieve his ends. That to me was the end of a very critical point. We could have continued working [together] in some way, but that probably had more to do with our parting of the ways than other things that came up." On the other hand, Villa recalled Galarza's constructive criticism: "The biggest compliment I ever got from him was that I was a general among generals in manipulating a bureaucracy—the Chicano community needed someone who understands institutions and systems, and how to massage them. To me that was a game; a game I'll miss playing—a game to be played, like on a chessboard and I like to play chess, and, as in chess, sometimes you must sacrifice pawns or knights to checkmate the opposition." This example illustrates the pragmatism and instrumentality of leadership as sites where Galarza and Villa merged their ideas. On the other hand, Galarza's approach became a point of contention and disagreement in Carrasco's visionary perspective.

Victor Garza, Esther Medina, Antonio Soto, and Josie Romero saw Galarza as a leader and activist who made important contributions to their community. Even though these activist leaders did not share the direct relationship that Brito, Carrasco, Mendoza, and Villa experienced, they, too, felt influenced by him in their work. Brito credited Galarza's tenacity and diligence in the struggle for farmworkers' rights as the foundation for organizing the UFW. Brito stated that "Galarza was one of those few people who worked so hard and so diligently," emphasizing that "without him there would have been no César Chávez; Galarza was one of the originators of the farmworkers movement way back in the '20s." Among the Depression Generation, Galarza was recognized as a leader and respected for his accomplishments. As George Castro put it: "The only person that had made it—that anybody would listen to—was Ernesto Galarza. And, teachers, even teachers were unusual, a lawyer was really unusual, and they weren't very involved. They weren't giving back to the community. I didn't see that. It was kind of like getting away from their culture."

Among these activist leaders, Galarza is recognized for his contributions to education and his pioneering spirit with farmworkers. He is valued for his part in pursuing the educational rights and advancement of Mexican Americans. He is also respected for returning to his community and remaining rooted in the culture he never rejected, even though he was a successful scholar activist. Finally, Felix Alvarez reflected on Galarza's involvement in Raza communities, while questioning the direction taken by his mentees. "Galarza was a leader . . . I've read several of his writings—they are profound; he's so Mexican, he's one who bridges Mexicanos and Chicanos. It's too bad that a lot of his students didn't continue." In Alvarez's account, Galarza was a bridge between Mexicanos and Chicanos. However, Carrasco would assess him as more interested in immigrant Mexicans rather than Pochos or Chicanos like himself. Still, Felix Alvarez pondered why individuals who were touched by Galarza in all his complexities of activism and leadership have failed to carry forward his tradition. No such questions or criticisms emerged about César E. Chávez.

CÉSAR E. CHÁVEZ: A LEADER AMONG US

Prior to his prominence as a founder and leader of the United Farm Workers of America, César E. Chávez was a resident of, and activist leader in, San José. In his work and organizing endeavors, Chávez interacted with many of the Depression Generation participants in this study.[10] In the field and collecting life histories at the time of his death, I heard many activists speak about the ways in which Chávez influenced their lives as leaders, organizers, and human beings. Sofia Mendoza saw him as one of her mentors. Among the many interactions she had with him, Mendoza recalled Chávez telling her: "With us organizers it's just different. It's like all our feelings come into play when we do our work." Because of her prior experience with farm labor struggles—her father was an organizer during the Lemon Grove Strike,[11] which took place in the 1930s in Fillmore—Mendoza's affiliation with the UFW was a lifelong relationship.

When recalling their interactions with Chávez, these activist leaders spoke about the community organizer who understood the meaning of mobilizing from the bottom, and the migrant urban Chicano who selflessly returned to the fields to organize farmworkers. From Sofia Mendoza, another story emerged. "He was a common everyday person who loved people, regardless of color. Fearless. Never stopped struggling. He always gave and never took. Wore in the fields what he wore everyday—his plaid shirt and work clothes—a hard worker." Chávez understood working individuals; he accepted workers regardless of their social, political, or ethnic attributes—he was one to pursue the greater good rather than personal gain.

Blanca Alvarado saw Chávez as a compassionately committed human being. She voiced her regret for not remaining as strong a supporter of his later struggles with the boycott of pesticides: "I didn't do more for him and for his cause; he was a wonderful model of humanity, dignity, and respect. A gentle giant, he believed strongly in his cause, and, because he believed so strongly in his cause, the rest of us embraced his cause and felt passionately about it, like he did."

Alvarado presented a complex image of a quiet yet intensely committed organizer and leader, while Ernestina García valued his commitment to others as a source of strength for the movement.[12] For both activist leaders, Chávez was the reflection of selflessness whose concern for self always came after concern for others. As García saw it, César Chávez *"siempre miraba por el prójimo; él no miraba ¿qué hay en esto para mi? No se hizo rico, y si había injusticia allí te decía 'esto esta mal y* correct it'" [always looked out for his neighbor; he did not look into what's in it for me. He did not become rich, and if there were injustices, he would tell you then and there, "This is wrong, correct it"].

Chávez's sense of justice was so great that he always tried to call out injustices he witnessed. However, he would only bring these issues to the attention of others, expecting them to correct whatever weaknesses they recognized. Ernestina García observed that Chávez *"no andaba buscando crédito* . . . he would not instigate or *quebrar la unidad que tenían, él se sentaba y oía*; he would support. He would support whatever was going on, and that's what I call a leader." As she saw it, for Chávez, confrontation was an aboveboard and open process, and jealousy was not in his vocabulary; he worked to unify.

Themes of selflessness, unity, and commitment arose again when Felix Alvarez spoke about Chávez's devotion to his people: "Committed to the whole group rather than to himself, he fought for farmworkers, for a union, for a religiosity, even. He was multifaceted; he wasn't just one thing, even though people identified him with farm labor." Chávez was more than a leader of farmworkers; he influenced goals and policies in other arenas. While working with the union, Chávez "touched many other points, and he went from a leader to a great leader who went beyond his immediate group, reached a status of international focus."

Internationally recognized as a man of peace, Chávez was a humanist concerned with the welfare of those who work for their sustenance. For these leaders and activists, Chávez was an accurate representation of the farmworkers he struggled to defend.

Like Galarza and others participating in this study, Chávez never failed to own and maintain his ethnicity. Felix Alvarez said, "His identity as a Chicano, being Mexicano, being Indio. . . . He didn't have to tell you that he was brown; he was brown. He didn't tell you he thought in Indian ways, because he acted in an Indian way."

Clearly, Alvarez did not perceive Chávez as a monotypic leader who professed to have the traditional influence and authority accorded to a union president. In Alvarez's reflections, Chávez did not autocratically dictate the direction of his movement, but guided it using humility, commitment to change, and investment in the workers whom he considered the most dispossessed. For these activist leaders, Chávez directly and indirectly influenced many by his life, his vision, and his actions.

WHAT DOES CÉSAR CHÁVEZ REPRESENT FOR ACTIVIST LEADERS?

For many, Chávez was a figure of mythic proportions. He embodied hope because—in the idealism of the 1960s and early '70s—he had a sense of power that inspired many with his call to resist all that was unjust and unfair. Participants remembered Chávez as a humble person who actively refused to pursue material goods for himself. Mendoza most admired him for his will to struggle for his beliefs: "I just think of César as a warrior; he did things because he had to. He never lived in fancy homes. He never had fancy things. He was with the people. He was extremely intelligent." Moreover, Chávez acted out his values and beliefs even when not in public view. Mendoza recalled being with him during one of his many fasts: "I remember going to see him. He was in a little building even without a bed, just a mattress on the floor. He would tell us, 'Don't give up.'" According to Mendoza, Chávez had no more and maybe even less than the workers he so avidly supported.

For Ernestina García, Chávez evidenced genuine qualities of "a leader and he's still our leader, and he'll be the only leader that I would recognize in my life." She too lauded his humanity and revered him for what he represented, always in the context of family. She connected to his humble beginnings as a farmworker and expressed an appreciation for his efforts to improve conditions for all who worked in agriculture, sharing in the common experience of working in the fields and the hardships that came with it. García said, "*Antes que hubiera union de César Chávez se sufría mucho, y él fue el que took the stand y se quedó en el fil and stuck with it, pa' que se hicieran unos cambios.*" [Before there was a César Chávez union, we suffered much, and it was he who took a stand and remained in the fields, but he stuck with it so there would be some changes.]

For the participants in this study, Chávez's call to leadership was not limited to the farm fields. In the urban setting, where Chicanos began to fend off race and class oppression, Chávez also inspired students and other activists to pursue justice and equality. He showed them the way, and many of their contemporaries took stands against injustice, regardless of their station in life. Bea Vasquez Robinson saw Chávez as a "crusader who embodied humility and didn't kowtow to anybody." Citing his example, Josie Romero contested the notion that only educated and professional people can engage in social change and advocacy, adding, "César Chávez has shown us that you don't need to be professionally educated to be a leader, and you don't have to have millions of dollars to create change." With her words, she challenged the grand men theories of leadership by those with position and wealth.

Chávez and his followers reshaped notions of leadership and who could be leaders in our communities. He inspired many to fight for the rights of those who work to harvest our food. He supported women in leadership by recognizing them and bringing them into the fold of the UFW, including those who were economically better off, and recruiting leaders of national stature like Bobby Kennedy. Chávez also incorporated racial and cultural minorities into the movement for farmworkers' rights. In her reflections about Chávez's ability to attract people from many walks of life, García spoke about being influenced by the way he formed coalitions with people who had never been able to work in unity for the same objective. Filipinos, Jews, and liberal whites joined in his call for justice in the fields. She noted that before coalitional politics were in fashion, Chávez amassed a multiethnic, multiclassed, and multigendered coalition to work toward a common mission. For her, the simple man, the humble man, the pacifist, and the farmworker could inspire action on the part of many who prior to this call had remained content with the status quo.

For those invested in social change, there were countless lessons left behind by César Chávez: for one, the notion that leaders and activists in the Chicana/o/Latino community must continue to work for the betterment of the people, for a better quality of life; second, that work must be done because it is the right thing to do. Like Chávez, those who work for social justice and social change must do so without expectations of fame or a place in history. Whether they get the credit or the recognition is not the point, as there is much work to be done: the one lesson all learned from Chávez was to get the work done regardless of the cost. As Felix Alvarez insightfully noted, "Had this gentle giant been a part of the upper crust, the revolution inspired by Chávez would have called for the writing of many volumes to document the brilliant strategist and tactician that he was." While none of the activist leaders in this study achieved César Chávez's stature, they share the knowledge he inspired and have the passion to continue the struggle for Chicana and Latino/Chicano rights.

Testimonials provided by leaders who worked with Chávez or for *la lucha* recall a man who embodied goodness and possessed a generous heart. Without exception, all perceived Chávez as the spark of the *movimiento* and as a leader without equal. From their perspective, Chávez was not simply a farmworker who rose to the rank of union president; he was a brilliant strategist, with the moral character and gift to move a nation and a government to recognize the rights of farmworkers. In their eyes, while he is acclaimed as a humanist of peace in the international world, the nation of his birth has yet to fully acknowledge the value of the man who died while waging war against corporate greed and the inhumanity of multinational corporations, corporations that strip Mexican workers of their dignity, then categorize them as unworthy of a living wage.[13]

Without exception, organizers, activists, and leaders who knew and worked with or supported Chávez saw him as a leader. For Kathy Chavez Napoli, "He was a true leader who led people into more benefits or more action." Blanca Alvarado offered that "some people were born to be great musicians, some people are born to be great teachers, some people are born like César Chávez to lead a movement—I don't know what it is about the personality. I don't know if it [is] something genetic, I don't know if it is something that is intuitive . . . we are called for different things." Vasquez Robinson added that "on the national level he was one of our leaders," expressing concern about the void he left in Chicano leadership. For all who participated in this study, César Chávez was a man of vision who possessed the drive and the ability to motivate others to become partners in the quest for social change. In one way or another, Chávez motivated many to take on the struggle for farmworkers' rights. He inspired their activism and directly or indirectly influenced their involvement in defense or promotion of Raza rights. Sofia Mendoza, who took part in many door-to-door campaigns in Santa Clara County, shared one direct lesson she learned from Chávez: "To dress like the people, you gotta talk with the people. Don't even drive a car. Don't take lunch. Let the people feed you . . . be where the people are and start organizing where they're at." It was in this way that Chávez inspired Garza's vision and motivation to create change. The implicit leadership lessons they gained are, first, that to organize people one must understand how they experience the social world you are attempting to change;[14] second, that the one way to do that is to be in their social surroundings, to be one of them; and third, that to work on an agenda, you have to begin with peoples' understanding of social reality.

Among those of the Baby Boomer Generation, Jorge Gonzalez said, "César Chávez has become an inspiration. I really didn't work with him. I worked with his organization." Gonzalez spoke to the experiences of those who were involved in the secondary boycotts and participated in the marches that supported his cadre of organizers to bring about change in the farm fields. From these experiences, many activist leaders learned different tactics and strategies for organizing in and outside the farmworkers' movement.

All and all, these activist leaders hoped that the death of Chávez, a humble man, a great leader, and a peace activist, would result in his being recognized for having made great contributions for agricultural workers. In earlier years, the American Friends Service Committee nominated him for the Nobel Peace Prize in 1971, 1974, and 1975, although he did not receive it. Some felt that young people, activists, and leaders were beginning to actively involve themselves in social change. As they examined their own feelings, their interactions with him, and the ways he influenced their work, all agreed that Chávez was a man of principle and a man of honor. An inspiring leader who did not lose his humanity in the process of reaching a position of prominence, Chávez maintained connections with neighbors, leaders, organizers, and activists who chose to continue organizing in their own communities, because he knew they were staunch supporters of the struggle for farmworkers' rights. What most admired about Chávez was his ability to disregard and disentangle racial, gender, and class barriers as he built a coalition like none before or since, even in the face of criticism of his positions on immigration and undocumented workers who were compromising unionization efforts in the fields.

From Chávez, all these activists learned that leaders emerge in relationships, because they experienced his ability to maintain and cultivate them, never forgetting who he was and where he came from. As Elisa Marina Alvarado stated, "With César Chávez's death, we have a responsibility to pick up his *bandera* [banner] and keep it marching." For these activists, if there is one lesson to garner from Chávez, it is the reawakening of moral responsibility to create social change.

CONCLUSION

From the oral histories of those who are part of the Depression and Baby Boomer Generations, genealogies of empowerment emerge to show the ways in which families, communities, and previous leaders have influenced them to improve social, political, cultural, and economic conditions for Raza in San José and Santa Clara County. In carrying out their activism, these Chicanas and Latinos/Chicanos have had their values tested, and what has surfaced in these relational spaces are activist leaders who have been socialized, mentored, and instructed to value and demonstrate concern for working-class Raza. Perspectives gained in their interaction with families and communities informed their involvement in the struggle, regardless of race, class, gender, or sexuality.

All the participants grew up in patriarchal families, with some fathers fully in charge and some wives totally dependent upon them as stay-at-home mothers. Without exception, these activist leaders were raised in two-parent families, with more than half sharing a household with an extended family. Those like Felix Alvarez who grew up in a rural agricultural community, with paternal and maternal relatives residing nearby, received support from relatives who tended to the children in their parents' absence. Among these activist leaders, some Chicanas and Latinos left school to work, to assist the family to make ends meet, and when they worked and went to school they turned their income over to the family. For them, life was not easy or without sacrifices. The jobs they held were the worst paid and the most dangerous, a practice that continues today. Because they understood that their lives were constrained by the social arrangements of class and race, these activist leaders did their part to lift up their family and community without fear of participating and without shame. Despite the economic hardships, none of the participants in this study ever considered public assistance as an option, or resorted to becoming dependents on the state for survival. All of them mentioned this to emphasize self-reliance. They would never have considered economic entitlement programs, such as welfare. Mothers and fathers promoted independence and self-sufficiency, despite abject poverty.

Romero and Soto are but two examples, one from each generation, of the influence families had on an activist's leadership formation. Six mothers and eight fathers were activists and leaders; they were key contributors to their children's leadership development. Moreover, six couples were identified as sharing equal responsibility for shaping the participants' commitment to social change. These couples participated in mutualistic and service organizations, with both fathers and mothers participating in labor union politics. Among these parents and relatives, issues of concern included the preservation of culture, the struggle against negative representation of Mexicans and Mexican Americans, unionization and community activism, and electoral politics. The derision and mistreatment of Mexican Americans were catalysts for involving many of these parents in activities that would improve their group.

Most activist leaders in this study spoke about the influence that their mothers wielded over their involvement in the community and in their respective area of activism. While some fathers—Mendoza's, Gonzalez's, and Medina's—were primary inspirations, mothers present a more nuanced and complex influence of activism and leadership in Raza communities. Activist leaders in this study have shared their lived experiences to establish foundations for understanding and negotiating relational leadership, as they engaged the struggle for social justice and social change. Without exception, each one began with the recognition that structures of inequality embedded in the internal dynamics of the family, such as gendered relations along with class and race, inform their notions of social justice and social change. While Latinos/Chicanos more readily faced race and class differences as principal contradictions in their involvement, Chicanas had no option but to engage sexism as a structure of inequality in their activism, which moved them to create options not previously available to them because of gender.

From families where activism carried strong messages and lessons of involvement, Galarza and Chávez were fellow travelers in the struggle for equal rights. Mothers, fathers, and significant others within and outside their private and public communities, along with gender, race, and class experiences, were foundational for understanding the ways in which relationships informed activist leader interactions. Knowledge of self, knowledge of family history and their respective communities, and awareness of their social, cultural, and political environment, along with historical, contextual, and situational influences, launched these activist leaders to become involved. Race, class, and gender experiences, which were primarily negative, with some positive pushback from their families of origin, encouraged activist leaders to develop an awareness of racial injustices, whether they were raised in Mexico or in segregated Chicano barrios throughout the Southwest.

Clearly, both women and men in the group had struggled with poverty and racism. Yet, women, while socialized within traditional notions of femininity, carved out their support and mustered the encouragement to become involved without being deterred by their gender. While their families of origin and significant others have influenced their formation, an ability to negotiate and engage leadership interactions within class, race, and gender notions, it was their passion for social justice and social change that carved their path.

2

• • • •

DO YOU KNOW THE WAY?

Movement and Migration to San José

A ctivist leaders in this study came from all walks of life. Half migrated with their families to Santa Clara County as children or as young adults, and half were born in various parts of California; only Rose Amador and Kathy Chavez Napoli were born in San José. Among those who participated in this study, one came from Mexico, one returned to California from Pennsylvania as a teen, another migrated from New York, and one was originally from Puerto Rico. Others came from Texas, Arizona, New Mexico, and Colorado. Regardless of their origin, these activist leaders made overall contributions to the cultural, political, and social justice rights of people of Mexican origin and the community at large. Among the twenty-three oral histories shared in this book, seven Chicanas were born to Mexican-born parents, and four were born in the United States. All the Chicana activist leaders are U.S. citizens, with eight from California, one from Texas, and one each from Arizona and Colorado. Seven Latinos/Chicanos were born to Mexican parents, and six to U.S. citizens. Four out of the twelve are from California, two each from the states of Texas and Arizona, and one each from Colorado, New Mexico, Puerto Rico, and Mexico.

Regardless of gender, these activist leaders linked their migration to California to economic need. Although not all came to seek agricultural employment, five out of eleven Chicanas traced their work history to the fields, and eleven Latinos/Chicanos also linked their employment to agriculture in Santa Clara County. The exception was Antonio Soto, of the Depression Generation, who located his origins in Arizona and linked his ancestral history to Spanish colonial times of the 1700s. Soto emphasized his ranching and cattle background, which he considered unique for a Chicano of his generation. He said, "My family goes back to when Arizona was still Mexico and even Spain. So, in a sense, we didn't come from Mexico—the United States came to us.

In fact, my grandmother on my mother's side was born in 1856 before the Mexican troops departed, so she was born while Tucson was still Mexico." He added, "My family ranched, and did a bit of farming because it doesn't rain in Arizona." A major part of Soto's later work would be to minister and provide religious and English-language education to Braceros who came to harvest the fields of California.

Among the Baby Boomer Generation, Romero traced her background to the Southwest before the Treaty of Guadalupe Hidalgo in 1848, with family still on both sides of the Texas border. Among the twelve participants from the Depression Generation, eight linked their family migration to the Mexican Revolution, having crossed the border before implementation of the National Origins Act in 1924. As Kelly Hernández writes in "'Persecuted Like Criminals': The Politics of Labor Emigration and Mexican Migration Controls in the 1920s and 1930" (2009), "The Mexican Revolution had been built upon promises of economic equity and social justice, but unrelenting poverty and hunger continued to define everyday life in postwar Mexico" (220), supporting the notion that poverty and the losses of war influenced decisions to move north.

MOVEMENTS AND MIGRATIONS: ORIGIN STORIES

With migration to California in common, Soto and Romero both spoke about their deep roots in the Southwest. Soto was thirteen years old when he moved to Santa Barbara in the early 1940s; he came to prepare for the priesthood. Romero, on the other hand, migrated as a young married woman to start a new life. Among those reared in an urban professional environment, Jorge Gonzalez was the only activist leader born in Mexico; from the age of nine, he was raised in the United States by his mother and stepfather. Lou Covarrubias, with an Ohlone and Argentinian grandmother and paternal grandparents from Mexico, did not migrate from another state, but had agricultural work in common with those of the Depression Generation. Among those who were born in California, six are from the northern part of the state, and six from the southern. Eleven migrated from other places, including Puerto Rico via New York, with the majority relocating from five southwestern states, and one from Mexico. A discussion and examination of their movement, family, and community involvement follows, as well as an abridged review of the support organizations available to them.

CULTURAL AND SOCIAL LIFE AND ANCESTRAL TRADITIONS

Chicanas and Latinos/Chicanos in San José have a historical presence in the daily life of the community and continue to be integral and active parts of its sociocultural activities and events. According to Gómez-Quiñonez (1990), the Chicano movement was

Migration and Movement Map

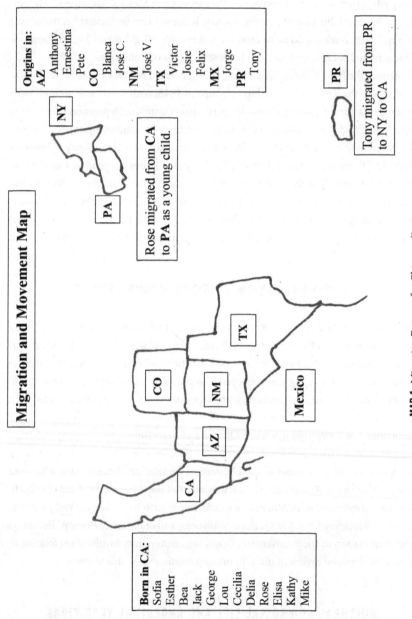

Origins in:

AZ
Anthony
Ernestina
Pete

CO
Blanca
José C.

NM
José V.

TX
Victor
Josie
Felix

MX
Jorge

PR
Tony

NY

PA

Rose migrated from CA to **PA** as a young child.

PR

Tony migrated from PR to NY to CA

Born in CA:
Sofia
Esther
Bea
Jack
George
Lou
Cecilia
Delia
Rose
Elisa
Kathy
Mike

CO

AZ

NM

TX

CA

Mexico

MAP 1 Migration Patterns for Chicanas/Latinos

responsible for creating a "proliferation of community service organizations [with] origins in the demands of barrio residents who joined with a small corps of Chicano and Anglo middle-class professionals to devise solutions to problems" (94). These organizational structures reproduced and promoted individual leadership, such as the Mexican American Movement (MAM), through which Ernesto Galarza became an activist leader as a student and a labor organizer. According to Carlos Muñoz, "MAM sprang from a group of California college students with professional aspirations. It emphasized the development of a leadership group of Chicano professionals, and its membership consisted of school teachers, social workers, lawyers, doctors, and management" (Muñoz 1989, 30 and 36, cited in Barrera 1979). While later influenced by students, cultural and social activism emerged as a communitarian investment from the nineteenth century into the 1920s. According to Barrera, as fraternal insurance societies, these groups focused "on maintaining the physical and cultural integrity of the Mexican communities" (1); Alianza Hispano-Americana, the first mutualista, founded in Tucson in 1884, became the most successful (5).

Within an organizational framework, the Mexican government established Comisiones Honorificas to promote mexicanismo. However, Mexican American leaders saw the involvement of these organizations as an impediment to their leadership because the emphasis was on cultural practices, such as commemorating Mexican national holidays and celebrating Mexican culture, even when they "took action against discrimination, obtained legal advice when possible, and acted as a social agency for Mexican indigents" (Molina-Pick 1983, 9). Barrera (1979) argued that what developed from the 1920s to the 1950s was "an egalitarian ideal, which aimed at securing for Chicanos the statuses and privileges of the dominant, Anglo group" (1). He claimed there was a "shift to equality, motivated by the Mexican Revolution and First World War," premised on internal changes taking place within Raza communities, and the creation of "Chicano organizations with a radically different definition of appropriate ethnic goals" (10). Chicanas were concentrated in the ancillary bodies, with the exception of Josefina Fierro de Bright, Luisa Moreno, and Emma Tenayuca, whose leadership was not fully acknowledged.

Chicanas of both the Depression and Baby Boomer Generations were invested in the everyday social lives of the community. They worked as a group in their agricultural families, did domestic work, or held paid employment positions in service and manufacturing. With the exception of one female who married to leave a difficult home environment, all lived with their family until they formed their own. Both men and women of the Baby Boomer Generation were involved in their community, with mutual aid organizations, in struggles for civic involvement, and with worker rights; parents and their children worked with organizations that promoted Raza rights. See table 1 for a description of organizations that had a presence in San José.

TABLE 1. Organizations in Which Ancestors May Have Participated

Organization	Membership and Activities	Aims
League of United Latin American Citizens, 1929, emerged from an Order of the Sons of America split	Naturalized or native-born citizens of Mexican ancestry who spoke English. It would change with the times, dropping its assimilationist vision to promote Raza educational and political rights.	Promote equality of opportunity with a focus on economic and political action rather than attention to community
Community Services Organization, 1948	Electoral politics and improved community conditions and political action	Improve barrios and raise the political power and voice of Mexican American communities
American GI Forum, 1948	Services to veterans, leadership development, school desegregation, undocumented laborers, and political representation	End discrimination, qualify for GI Bill and other governmental benefits
Mexican American Political Association, 1959	Focus on voter registration, political education, lobbying, endorsing and recommending candidates, and antidiscrimination activities on issues such as police mistreatment and school problems	Promote civic and political involvement
Mexican American Youth Organization, 1950s	Focus on Raza political empowerment	Fight for justice at the political and community level
United Farm Workers of America, 1963	Organized agricultural workers into the union	Improve wages and working conditions for farmworkers
La Raza Unida Party, 1970s	Engaged and civic citizens relying on conventional designs for formation, organization, and leadership	Organize for political power

COMMUNITY GRASSROOTS ORGANIZATIONS

Among the community organizations emerging during the Chicano movement nation-ally were the Crusade for Justice and the Brown Berets in Southern California, and the Black Berets for Justice in Northern California. The Berets included both genders, and "emphasized the right to self-defense against aggression"; according to Gómez-Quiñonez (1990), they best "articulated an explicit call for self-determination" (120). Still, women were expected to adhere to mother and sister roles, as dictated by the bounds of nationalist ideology: "Women participated in the efforts and organizations of the movement across the country, sharing the various tendencies and, on occa-sion, the leadership" (Gómez-Quiñonez 1990, 120). In Gómez-Quiñonez and other accounts, Chicanas are depicted as marginal participants in the political arena, and the authors rely on a framework of conventional male models to understand women's involvement. Other venues for social change were introduced by progressive and leftist organizations.

ALTERNATIVE ORGANIZATIONS FOR CHANGE

One of the alternative and leftist organizations that emerged at the time of the Chicano movement was the August Twenty-ninth Movement (ATM), which originated out of the central Labor Committee of California's La Raza Unida Party "as activists sought to create a multinational (not just Chicano) party which could take the vanguard role in educating and organizing US workers to carry on revolutionary struggle" (Barrera 1979, 31). Both of these organizations relied on Marxist traditions for their ideological foundation. Class assumed primacy as the organizing principle for defining the goals of Chicano groups. As Barrera (1979) writes, "The debate shifted toward a Marxist analysis, emphasizing inequalities between workers, and men and women, as framed by a third world analysis within international relations" (32–33).

> Organizations such as Centro de Acción Autónoma (CASA) and August Twenty-Ninth Movement (ATM) emerged as left organizations. In the 1970s, CASA was primarily responsible for focusing attention on the immigration issue and for redefining the domi-nant Chicano attitude toward undocumented workers from Mexico. In addition to such activities as strike support the organization involved itself in the direct provision of social services to the undocumented. (28)

Built upon notions traditionally embedded in Chicano organizations, Centro de Acción Autónoma (CASA) and ATM "redefined the communitarian ideal." "CASA, while never resolving the issue to its own or others' satisfaction argued that a focus on Chicanos apart from Mexicanos was too narrow." On the other hand, "ATM made the international working class the focus of its allegiance, and considered organizing on an ethnic, or 'national' base to be primarily a tactical manouvre" (Barrera 1979, 33).

These two organizations created community strategies emphasizing their approach, relying on newspaper articles, public forums, and demonstrations as sources of education and agitation for achieving their objectives. Many other community organizations were formed to mobilize youth and educational rights. In the 1980s cultural and community activism continued to be arenas of leadership that were targeted for change during the Chicano movement, and educational involvement became a site for Chicano leadership interactions.

LEGACIES OF ACTIVISM

Common points of entry into activism for the Depression Generation were mutualistas, Comisión Honorífica Mexicana organizations, and social and regional clubs connected to ancestral lands such as the San Felipe Club, organized by people who had previously resided in Del Rio, Texas. For the Baby Boomer Generation, their activism and leadership were informed by and modeled on the involvement of their parents to better their communities, showing that apathy had been but a myth promoted to disempower a group that had a history of involvement in the struggle for social justice and political rights. What follows is an overview and discussion of the ways in which family legacies informed these activist leader's involvement for social justice and social change.

UNIONS AND MUTUALISTAS

Among the Depression Generation, George Castro's parents were active in unions. He stated that "my folks were extremely liberal, left-wing kind of politics. Mom was always a part of the International Ladies Garment Workers Union," while dad "made wood frame in the mills" until he advanced to the level of "foreman, becoming more involved with the unions because he got a little upset with the bosses." On the other hand, Sofia Mendoza, whose paternal family had money, "didn't suffer during the Depression but gave away a lot, as my father tried to help in any way he could." Times were so difficult for Raza that her father became "active with all the organizing efforts," including various unions. "There was a lot of activity, a lot of stuff going on in the '30s, and he was involved in all of that."

Likewise, Esther Medina's "father was very involved with workers' rights issues, with the union." Her mother endorsed his involvement, and Medina never heard her complain about providing shelter to others; she supported her husband, Goyo, in assisting those who found themselves away from their families. During the war, he brought "Latino soldiers' home, because he'd say, maybe somebody would be taking in his sons also; my brothers served in World War II. So, he would invite soldiers that looked kind of lonely, and would bring them home." The Medinas had always been invested in helping those in need. Esther explained, "My family is very aware of giving in their own way, but as far as involvement in social change, I am the only one that's involved directly, but my father was a big activist." In addition, the Medinas would participate in Mexican organizations to promote and celebrate the culture.

Antonio Soto carried a history of involvement that linked him to Arizona's first mutualista, which was co-founded in the late nineteenth century by his grandfather Ramón Soto. José Carrasco's parents also participated in mutualistas. "My dad belonged to [a], that's sort of political, mutualista," Carrasco said, and both his parents "were active here in Santa Clara." While it was not clear to him how they became involved, Carrasco suggested that "it was after my brother and I first got into trouble. Because we were both, at least myself, I was in and out of jail since maybe eleven years old or maybe ten, somewhere around there. But they were already involved in activities so I don't think it had to do with us specifically, in that sense." Like other parents of that generation, the Carrascos were involved in the cultural organizations and mutualistas in San José and in Santa Clara County, in "the

FIGURE 5 Victor and Maxine Carrasco. Courtesy of José Carrasco and Antoñio Carrasco.

same group that José J. Alvarado was with," as "he and my father were very close," and he was "sort of the leader of a lot of the Chicanos in Santa Clara," who originated from the same region. It was through the Comisión Honorífica Mexicana that Carrasco's parents first crossed paths with José J. Alvarado, a noted political leader and husband of Blanca Alvarado, a participant in this study.

It was the memory of her parents' involvement with Community Services Organization that influenced Delia Alvarez's activism. The CSO helped the community, with funeral insurance and immigration services. Her parents became active when she "was a junior in high school." Her father became a member of a CSO committee and would attend their conventions. He became involved because of "a gang fight in Chualar or Gonzalez . . . [also because] Mexicans were negatively depicted in the newspaper."

Generationally, agriculture linked many who migrated to work in California from other parts of Mexico and the Southwest, and as a people they were exposed to extreme poverty and work exploitation. Regardless of place of employment and community of residence, these activist leaders would become involved in righting the wrongs they experienced in multiple sites of interaction as workers and as Mexican people.

CHURCH, COMMUNITY SERVICE, AND POLITICS

Ernestina García's father was "active during the *Revolución,* and after that *en un tiempo cuando trabajo en las minas, y después* [for a while when they were working in the mines, and afterward] they were active in church." Bea Vasquez Robinson's mother, a small business owner who ran La Rosa Restaurant, was not involved "as long as she was working." However, when she retired, "she was often called upon when people died. . . . Everyone would always want Francisca Vasquez to say the rosary." Similarly, José Villa discussed the interconnection of community and religious activism: when he spoke about the connection between the church and community, he spoke of participating in "building experiences that were very instructional and very involving in church activities, because it seems that there was always something to build." He credited a master builder who worked for the church for supervising everything, "from mixing the muds, to making the adobes, raising monies to buy the materials for some of the buildings," for organizing "jamaicas and festivals, and celebrations, bingo," and for lessons learned. For Villa, "these were socializing and work activities."

Jack Brito offered that his family activism focused primarily on church involvement. His parents "were deeply involved with the Catholic Church in Los Angeles at La Soledad on Brooklyn Avenue, a street they renamed after César E. Chávez." They also belonged to "El Santo Nombre Society" and "were both together in a very active social group called El Grupo de Santa María." However, not all their efforts focused on religious activism. Brito's parents were also involved in "all functions that went into celebrating the Fifth of May and the Sixteenth of September." He said, "My mom was very active, but my dad provided the leadership. And, then they had the women's auxiliary—she did backup work with catechism, Holy Communion, and confirmations, using her skills as a seamstress when needed—*pos todas eran costureras*—she was a very, very, active person."

Victor Garza's parents were "mainly involved during election times: they put candidate signs on their yards, [held] fund-raisers—my dad was a strong supporter of César Chávez." However, his mother was involved in the schooling of the children. He recalled the time "one of my sisters was elected as the homecoming queen, but the school didn't print her picture because she was a Chicana. Mom was incensed and immediately got the family together to fight with the school district and forced them to take her picture; she was homecoming queen, but her pictures were set aside because she was Mexican."

Although her own schooling was only to the third grade, his mother made every effort to help her children in school, and helped with "my courses when I was in the eighth grade." Education was important, and even though families relied on their children's labor and wages, parents supported the educational advancement of their children, although less readily for their daughters. Many of the participants recall that both their parents were strong leaders, and also that their fathers were more readily involved in politics.

In addition to community service, parents of the Baby Boomer Generation were politically involved. Jorge Gonzalez stated that his "dad was a political refugee in Mexico during the '40s, when he participated in the overthrow of a dictator named Jorge Ubico."[1] His father was part of the student movement of the time. "Then, in the U.S. both my stepfather and my mom organized one of the first boycott committees for the United Farm Workers in San Diego; they actually got me into the Chicano movement."

Many of these activist leaders were inspired by their parents' political activity. Tony Estremera said his parents were "pretty involved with us. I mean it really took a lot. My father worked graveyard for about six or seven years, I remember when I was a kid, and so it was very time-consuming and it was pretty hard for them" "My father was very political,

FIGURE 6 Jorge Gonzalez, co-founder of Youth Getting Together and Raza Si! Courtesy of Raza Sí!

ideologically political. He understood, he was real demanding of government, and, you know, he understood where things were; he had a pretty good understanding." Also, Elisa Marina Alvarado's father was active and supportive of *el movimiento*. For example, "he organized a walkout during the Cambodian bombings, and he fought for the just treatment and respect for Chicano students, for curricula, and for Latino teachers," but "he was always struggling; I remember him being extremely frustrated." Her mother's involvement was more traditional. For example, during "the Kennedy election, she was really excited about the campaign," and she "had a pretty liberal perspective and was against the Vietnam War." Rose Amador attributed her passion for social justice to her father. She said, "In Pennsylvania and there were few Hispanics or Mexicans, yet he managed to start a Latino group." In Chicago, "he always belonged to the Legion, American Legion and the Masons." When the family moved, "I was about twelve years old, and that was a different experience coming to California." Her father became active in San José "with the GI Forum, with all kinds of ethnic and veteran's organizations."

CONCLUSION

Both Depression and Baby Boomer Generations were influenced by parents who were active. From investment in their communities of origin, to membership in cultural, civic, and social organizations, these parents imparted an awareness of the need to care for others and an ideology of service that promoted the well-being of the community, focusing on the most marginalized. Parents of the Depression and Baby Boomer Generations led the way for their children to invest themselves in creating change, premised on the notion that their lived experiences provided them an understanding of agency to change and improve the world for others.

In addition to relying on the knowledge of their parents and ancestors, these activist leaders learned to identify and confront unequal and differential treatment in the spaces they themselves occupied. For that reason, Chicanas and Latinos/Chicanos gained an understanding of the ways in which inequality and disparities are reproduced; learning to take a stand, they struggled against race, class, and gender oppression. By their example, parents supported their children, helping them understand that if they improved conditions for their people, they themselves would ultimately gain from their efforts.

3

• • •

DEPRESSION AND BABY BOOMER
GENERATIONS SPEAK

Of the participants in this study, the Chicana activist leaders of the Depression Generation were Blanca Alvarado, Ernestina García, Sofia Mendoza,[1] Esther Medina, and Bea Vasquez Robinson. The Latinos/Chicanos from this generation were Jack Brito, José Carrasco, George Castro, Lou Covarrubias, Victor Garza, Antonio Soto, and José Villa. In the Baby Boomer Generation, the six participating Chicanas were Cecilia Arroyo, Delia Alvarez, Rose Amador, Elisa Marina Alvarado, Kathy Chavez Napoli, and Josie Romero, while the Latinos/Chicanos were Felix Alvarez, Pete Carrillo, Tony Estremera, Mike Garcia, and Jorge Gonzalez.

Participants for this study were gathered through presurvey interviews conducted with twenty reputed leaders in the community, who also provided a definition of the meaning of leadership, described a leader and his or her attributes, and provided the names of five Chicanas and five Latinos/Chicanos who met their criteria for leadership. One hundred and twenty-seven names were collected, of which twenty-five rose to the top—thirteen men and twelve women. One person refused to participate, and one dropped out later, leaving twenty-three participants. Their stories follow, beginning with Chicanas of the Depression Generation.

CHICANAS OF THE DEPRESSION GENERATION

Blanca Alvarado's father was born in Ranchos de Taos and her mother in Las Vegas, New Mexico. Alvarado (née Sanchez) linked her legacy of hard work to her mother, who "at twelve or thirteen was already doing man's work." She would "go high in the mountains of New Mexico and Colorado with her dad. They would cut down trees, and with a horse and buggy bring them down and split them into ties they used for the railroads." Alvarado's mother had a difficult life: "She was forced to marry a man when she was twelve or thirteen—a very young age—and from the stories that she has told me, it was a very brutal marriage. He literally kept her enslaved and locked behind closed doors and brutalized her. At some point, like less than a year after they were married, he abandoned her." After this terrible experience, her mother entered into a common-law marriage with Blanca's father—a relationship that endured the rest of their lives.

The migration of Blanca Alvarado's family, the Sanchezes, was precipitated by the closing of the mines, forcing the family to move to California with the intent of settling in Los Angeles. However, not finding Los Angeles to their liking, they moved north and "set up residence in Santa Clara County, where the family was contracted to do agricultural work for a local rancher in San José," the city that would become Alvarado's hometown.

Ernestina García, whose parents were born in Mexico, remembers that "*'apá* and *amá* taught us a strong identification with the culture and instilled in us the responsibility of fulfilling civic duties and democratic participation." A transnational migrant, her father came to the United States first before bringing his family.

> *Apá se venía y se iba pa' atrás. Después que se acabó la Revolución se casó con mi 'amá—* very young age, *mi 'amá*—and then *trajo a su mamá, y su hermana, y a mí 'amá, y a mis hermanas—las que nacieron allá.* [Father came and went. After the Revolution ended, he married my mother . . . he brought his mother, a sister, and my mother and sisters who were born over there.] He was not an activist. *Trabajaba para el ranchero para poder mantenernos a todos, y procuraba trabajar con contrato que acababan* after a certain time. [He worked for the ranchers to be able to support all of us, and he worked with contracts that ended after a certain time.] *Le daban la casa, pero tenían que trabajar—se lo descontaban, no le daban nada.* [They provided a house, but they had to work—took it out of their wages, they gave him nothing.]

García spoke about the hardships of working in the fields, attributing the family's migration to the turmoil and poverty of the Mexican Revolution, which pushed her paternal relatives, including her grandmother, an aunt, and their children, to flee. After immigrating to the United States, García's father was so busy supporting the family that he had no time for any involvement in labor struggles; his concern was with making enough money to make ends meet for the family.

Unlike García's family, Sofia Mendoza's father was an activist. He "came from a family of twenty-eight children—eleven from the second marriage—he worked as a union organizer in the mines and agricultural fields" and was involved in historical labor struggles. In the early years of the twentieth century, her father "organized a strike of citrus fruit pickers in the biggest ranch in California, and they evicted everybody." Soon after that, the family moved to Santa Clara County and set up residence in Campbell, where her dad bought an acre of land. Mendoza reminisced, "There were no other kids around; it was just our own family. As the eldest, I'd keep the kids together, to mind, to do this or that; I was like a sergeant with my brothers and sisters (laughter). That's where it started with me—I took my responsibility seriously." Taking responsibility for family and investing in their well-being is something activist leaders of this generation had in common. Her parents were born in Mexico, and Medina said her "father could not read or write. He came to this country because he was tired of the killing in Mexico, having fought in the Revolution. And, even after the Revolution, he witnessed a female being hanged."

Even though illiterate, Esther Medina's father, Goyo, was an organizer who promoted the celebration and maintenance of Mexican history and culture. Medina took much pride in acknowledging that her father was active in the community. For example, she said that "in Santa Paula, my father had an organization for Fiestas Patrias. They pooled their money and brought a teacher from Mexico—la Señora Ortea—I don't remember her first name, but I remember her face." Along with this strong commitment to the preservation of Mexican culture, Medina learned from both parents a philosophy of service to the community. When they arrived in San José, they settled in Willow Glenn, a place that was like "Saratoga is now—it was like the in place to live— there was a distinct order there, where poor kids had to go to school with the rich kids." She remembered walking to school and the poverty that surrounded them, a poverty she has never forgotten: "There was this *campo de la mora*—a berry field—and it had, I don't know how many families, it was right across the road from where I lived, these poor families sharecropped the berries. So, we went to school with these kids that had money." With empathy toward those who were the most downtrodden, those of the Depression Generation displayed an awareness of the need for families to help each other. This practice continued for a lifetime.

Bea Vasquez Robinson, whose father came from central Northern Mexico, recalled that her parents "met in El Paso, that they traveled across the country in a little old Ford truck . . . we would pitch up tents and work the crops." In her view, her family life "was just poor. When you think of Okies, when you think of the Depression, it was that kind of poverty." For Vasquez Robinson, "growing up in the family was just hideous. I wouldn't wish it on anybody." She did not have "kind thoughts about childhood or growing up." As for others of her generation, poverty and racism were part of her upbringing in Gilroy, a place she recalled as "racist, and separatist, and in terms of Latinos, you were second-class all the way." She recalled that "even if you are little and you don't know that you are second-class, you feel it, you feel the treatment given to you, and you don't know the label but you sure know you're not liked or wanted. You're on the fringes, on the sidelines because of your skin color; because you are not wanted there." In a life affected by physical and psychological injuries, Vasquez Robinson spoke about experiencing "discrimination and that made me thick-skinned, but not so thick-skinned that I would have put up with it." In the midst of poverty, "work was probably the most dominating force. We were expected to work and to be productive, and, consequently, I have very strong work ethics. Everyone in my family."

LATINOS/CHICANOS OF THE DEPRESSION GENERATION

Jack Brito grew up in an urban area, but his "daddy was born in El Paso, Texas, and mother grew up there." He explained, "My mother is from Santa Cruz de Rosales, Chihuahua; she was part of the clan that saw the Revolution taking place. She was six years old, when my grandfather said, 'No.' He had one, two, three, four, five daughters and one son. And in 1903 he just decided, 'No, I'm not going to take any chances,' and moved to El Paso, after that Arizona, wound up in Pasadena, and eventually settled in Los Angeles."

When Brito was in the tenth grade, the family moved to Santa Clara. In that new high school, which he perceived as "a waste of time, and still learning about Columbus," Brito was not allowed to enroll in algebra, "so I stopped going to school—when truant officers still chased you, they caught me, and made me quit." Soon after, "I went to work for Pick Sweet, and after that, I walked up and down First Street in the '40s and cleaned windows and swept out places. Nobody gave you work, but I never quit trying." It was during his rounds that "at the post office, I saw the sign, 'Uncle Sam Wants You!'" Since he had nothing to lose, Brito went to "the sergeant and before I knew it I'd already signed up for the services. Wound up in Korea, and I got out in August of 1947." Upon his discharge, rather than use the GI Bill to enroll in San José College, Brito went to work pruning trees.

Another 1930s generation Chicano with roots in Chihuahua and El Paso, José Carrasco said his family had a farm-worker background and that they lived in an agricultural community when the family was initially formed. Carrasco reminisced: "Our family came out of the sugar beets, and we settled in Santa Clara. Both my mother and father had to work two jobs; they would work daytimes in the fields and then at nights find a job as a custodian or whatever they could find. We were raised in part by my older sister, who herself was working full-time by the time she was in the sixth grade." His growing-up years in Santa Clara were difficult, as living conditions were dire for

FIGURE 7 Jack Brito, far right, Korean Conflict. Courtesy of Karl Soltero.

the entire family. He explained: "I lived in a little chicken shack, and the old landlady herself was kind of eccentric, but her son's family was just very decent with us, especially since they certainly had options at the time." He recognized their economic differences. "They owned their own home, they had their own homes."

A high school graduate, Carrasco's schooling was in Santa Clara—Fremont Elementary, Wilson Intermediate, and Santa Clara High School. In addition to social class, language was an impediment for Carrasco. "I stayed back because in kindergarten I was speaking Spanish, and then in the fifth grade, I was fighting all the time. In fact, . . . we all went to school there. We went to Intermediate in the sixth grade and stayed there through the eighth grade, then went to Santa Clara High School for ninth, tenth, eleventh, and twelfth." Carrasco' parents were "active in the mutualistas."

Unlike Carrasco, who grew up in the area, George Castro migrated to San José at the age of twenty-four in 1968, when he accepted a position at IBM. Like others of his generation, his family immigrated from Mexico during time of the Mexican Revolution. Castro was born in United States, and his father did farmwork and worked on the railroad. For Castro, poverty was relative. "We were not poorer than other Mexicanos, but we were better off." It would not be until they moved near whites that their poverty became obvious.

For the Castro family, urban migration was not in search of employment. Relocation and movement "was Dad's strategy for keeping us out of gangs; you couldn't stay in a gang if you kept moving out of the neighborhoods." Both his parents worked; his mother was "real hardworking, very strict." Still, the hardship of urban migration was a reality for them. He recalled that "by the age of nine we were taking care of the babies. In my family, we were, all three brothers were close together, the oldest, and then there was a big gap between a girl and another boy, seven or eight years—we learned to take care of each other. Most of this was in East Los Angeles and in the suburbs, Norwalk, El Monte, and other parts of Southern California." Practicing self-reliance, the Castros coped with constant relocation. As best they could, they dealt with the circumstances of their relocations, with the ultimate goal being staying out of gangs.

Growing up in Irvington or Mission San José, Lou Covarrubias claimed Indigenous ancestry, since his "grandmother was 100 percent Ohlone Indian, and she married a gentleman from Argentina, and my grandfather was from here, from California." He explained, "*era mexicano de California*—they were Mexican born here." On the paternal side, his "grandfather and my grandmother were from Chapala, Jalisco, which is right near Guadalajara." He and his brother were raised by their grandparents after their mother died. "I was three, my brother and I were taken in by my grandparents," and because "neither of them could speak English, I didn't speak English myself until I started grammar school." Covarrubias was brought up in a family with a "grandfather that was nonmaterialistic. He did not want to buy a home here because *siempre se quería ir pa' México*," he longed to return to the homeland—an immigrant dream of his day, which came with the notion of making money and returning to live out the rest of your days in Mexico.

Covarrubias remembers that "we moved around a little bit as we lost some homes, we lived in some shacks actually, as kids." Theirs was a difficult childhood. Covarrubias recalled feeling embarrassed to tell his friends where he lived, "but being raised by his grandparents, the home itself was good." His grandfather was strict, and his grandmother was "very religious—she said the rosary every night and made us pray along with her. . . . We always had plenty to eat, and she always took care us, our clothes, and patched us." When his grandfather was hired by Lesley Salt Company, their constant movement ceased. That was when the family stopped "following the crops" and gained "a degree of stability." It was also then that his grandfather gave up his dream of returning to Mexico, remaining in the United Sates until the end of his days.

Victor Garza had an immediate connection to Mexico through his father, who came from Piedras Negras, Coahuila. Garza himself was raised in Eagle Pass, where his mother was born. That was the home base from which the family followed the migrant stream, migrating from Texas to the Midwest.

Garza worked in the fields until the age of "twenty-six when I finally realized that wasn't for me, and I moved from Texas to Sanger, near Fresno, and we worked there in the fields for a while." Garza moved to Los Angeles as soon as he could after getting out of the service. "I was a welder and I used to repair submarines and work in ships.

So, after working as a welder for about nine years, I moved to San José because my family was growing up in Sanger and moving to San José, and they were all going to college." Still, with much pride in his agricultural background, Garza added that in the 1940s the family sharecropped in Michigan. For him and his siblings, "it didn't matter whether you were six years old or fifteen, everybody worked together in the family-type setting—those were extremely happy years"—it was the work they knew. Still, the concept of vacation was beyond his experience. "It was when summer came about and you weren't in school no more, and then you were going to go work again in the fields and have fun—that was vacation."

Unlike Garza, Antonio Soto came from an educated family with involved and active parents, and movement for the Soto family was localized to a small area of Arizona. He said he came from "very traditional, well-established families that had been there for a hundred years." Soto proudly proclaimed, "The family had the tradition of education, they weren't moving around and they weren't migrants, which is what I'm trying to say, they were kind of a different kind of a Spanish family. So, they were established there, they stayed there, and their lives followed a very good pattern of going to school." From an upper income family, living in a community where they had status, there was no need for the Sotos to migrate or do agricultural work. Their movement was an urban professional migration.

As was the case with others of José Villa's generation, the Revolution and income insecurity launched the family's migration. During their entry into the United States on their way to New Mexico his "grandfather died in Sterling, Texas." The family settled in Clovis, New Mexico, where the they found employment in agriculture, migrating to work in the fields. Villa recalled, "My father couldn't earn enough for us just holding a railroad job. So we'd go work in *los campos de algodón, las escardas* [weeding the crops] and pulling broomcorn, and all that—so we did work." The Villa family became a resource for their community. He recalled, "We used to have a *troquita* [a small truck] that one of my brothers bought to go out to *las escardas,* and he contracted labor, or gave rides to people, out and around the Texas panhandle—Littlefield, and Middle-ship, Texas."

Class and race were structures of inequality that shaped these activist leaders' daily interactions. Chicanas and Latinos/Chicanos of the Depression Generation relied on lessons learned in their interactions, developing a philosophy of life that inspired them to carve a path for social and cultural change. Chicanas dealt with inequalities of gender differences in their families and in their communities, while Latinos/Chicanos engaged with racism and class differences as people of Mexican heritage. Even coming back from Europe after having served in the U.S. military, many men returned to the same jobs, without the option of accessing better employment readily available to others.

Among the many hardship stories of survival, no narratives of repatriation emerged from the Depression Generation. The Depression Generation comprises Chicanas and Latinos/Chicanos who survived the hardships of difficult economic and racialized times. While they recognized and understood their socioeconomic status, they associated poverty with the conditions of the time, particularly as it pertained to Mexicans. However, their dire circumstances, rather than leading them into reproducing poverty, inspired them to improve conditions for their people and themselves. In so doing, they carved a path for the next generation to follow.

CHICANAS OF THE BABY BOOMER GENERATION

Dalia Alvarez's "mother was born in Colton, California. Father is from Jerome, Arizona. Grandparents came from Guanajuato and Jalisco." She identified her mother's side of the family as Indian, and "my father's as the *español* side, they come from Teocaltiche, that's the *españoles*; mestizos but more of the Spanish, my dad's very light, and my mom's dark." Her relatives from Jalisco moved to Arizona to work in the mines, when "mexicanos could travel back and forth to work."

Alvarez was born in the agricultural community of Salinas, California. Like Soto of the Depression Generation, her family owned property and were not employed in agriculture. She was raised in an "Oakie" community, rather than a Mexican barrio. She explained, "We lived in the Eastside. We were poor but I didn't know the difference—I knew we were poor. My dad was a blue-collar worker, so, we lived from paycheck to paycheck." Still, Alvarez had fond memories of "the earlier years . . . while I was about twelve or ten; we were poor, and Dad was a kid in many ways, but I had stability because Mother stayed home to raise us." For her, "the bad part began when my dad starting drinking. So, that got rough. The teen years were rough." From her "grandmother's side, I knew the importance of owning your own land—we lived in town, and most of the Mexicanos lived in labor camps." These lessons would serve Alvarez well when she became a property owner in her own right.

Born in Cupertino, California, Cecilia Arroyo had a father who came from Mexico and a mother from Arizona. Her father was the primary provider "until Mother became employed as a seasonal worker in the cannery." The family lived "in Monte Vista, an unincorporated area of Santa Clara County," until her mother decided to secure employment. Arroyo said, "Mother put her foot down and told my dad that she had to work to buy a house. Dad was just totally appalled and said, 'No, no, you can't work.' She says, 'I have to.' My dad said, 'Oh, I don't know if we can do this.' She went to work the night shift at the cannery at Libby's, and that started her work every summer." Arroyo grew up near the area that would become De Anza College, where "except for a few Oakies, our neighborhood was all Chicano." Both maternal and paternal relatives lived in the neighborhood. Ten years later, when her brother was born, the family moved to Santa Clara.

Josie Romero's family came from Texas. Although they were poor, she was brought up "in a healthy, supportive environment." She recalled, "I remember having very little to eat; we were very poor, but you always felt you belonged, you always felt that somebody was always there." The presence of her extended family, where "grandpa and grandma were always watching to make sure Mom and Dad did the right thing, and they would scold them if they didn't," added to her security. On her paternal side, it was a different story. "The German extended family were cold and distant, even though they were all raised in Mexico. On my mother's side, they were Indian and Mexicanos, and they were much more united, and involved."

With a home base in South Texas, the family followed the Pacific Northwest migrant trail, "from Texas to Washington State, and from Washington to Oregon, then to Montana, then to Arizona, and back to Texas," for twenty years. "So, I learned to adjust and make the best of it." Despite the

FIGURE 8 Josie Romero speaking at Cultural Competence Summit. Courtesy of Diana Martinez.

constant interruptions to her schooling, Romero dealt capably with her situation: "[I was] in school for two or three weeks; I loved it, it was easy for me, *no me daba vergüenza*—I was not ashamed—to ask questions or of being the new kid on the school. I was there for a purpose. I did what needed to be done, and at about fourteen or fifteen it became difficult to keep up, and I quit to go to work." Romero did not lose her passion for learning; she would return to obtain her GED and eventually obtained an MSW and became a licensed mental health practitioner.

Rose Amador's "father was born in Mexico and raised in Chicago, and [her] mother was born in Michigan." She herself saw the light of day in San José, but she did not remain there long. "So, after I was born they went back to Chicago," then they moved to Pennsylvania, "where I pretty much grew up the first twelve years of my life." In Pennsylvania, Amador lived in a community that had minimal diversity. "I didn't experience much discrimination," growing up in a "close-knit community with the same kids from the time you started kindergarten all the way through sixth grade. It was a comfortable, secure, and good experience."

The eldest in the family, Elisa Marina Alvarado (née Coleman) was born in San Francisco. Her father came from Mexico and is "of Irish and Purépecha ancestry, and mother is Irish and English on one side, and Cuban on the other." As a professor of Spanish, her father was the sole support of the family, and her mother was a home-maker. Because they were a one-income family, frugality was encouraged: "We had a sense of what it was like to contribute, we had to help out. Also, my mom sewed our clothes." The children "did not get lavish gifts and allowances." They got one set of clothes per school year, and "if we needed anything else we would earn the money through babysitting, and we never went out to eat and stuff, we struggled." With a stay-at-home mother and a single wage–earning father, the Coleman family experienced limitations, but they were comfortable.

Kathy Chavez Napoli, a native of San José, traced her ancestry to California. During her childhood, "father was concerned with providing for the family, while mother was active in and around her barrio as a translator and interpreter." She had seven siblings—three older and two younger brothers, and two younger sisters. She recalled that "there were always people around, and my parents, my mother comes from a very large family: aunts, uncles, cousins, and friends." Though poor, Chavez Napoli never felt deprived: "In some families . . . they didn't have meat every day, we always had meat every day. If father ate meat, we ate meat; if he got an ice cream, we got an ice cream." When "my dad used to go to the Burger Bar, he'd buy two or three bags of hamburgers," and unlike in some families where "the head of the family was fed first and got the best, and if there wasn't enough, they got nothing—that's not the way we were raised." In her family, they all ate what was available, regardless of status. She added, "I didn't know we were poor, and surely didn't know that we lived in Sal Si Puedes until my best friend was taking some classes at City College and said, 'Kathy, I just found out about our street, it used to be called Sal Si Puedes, and everybody is writing about it in Chicano studies.' And, I go, 'Our street?' I never knew."

Poverty and movement linked the experiences of these activist leaders. While a few owned their home, most have memories of limited space and having to make do with what they had. Some experienced economic limitations, but most did not recognize they were poor until they were exposed to those who had more. Sites of conflict were not founded on economic needs; the social conflicts with which they would contend centered more on gender inequality within the intersections of the raced and classed experiences they navigated in their respective communities.

LATINOS/CHICANOS OF THE BABY BOOMER GENERATION

Felix Alvarez and his parents came from South Texas. In sharing the story of his father, Alvarez unveiled a narrative of repatriation as he spoke about his father's return to the United States. "At the age of ten or eleven, because they had been victimized by the *repatriaciones*—when the United States kicked out a lot of supposedly undocumented illegal aliens, they also kicked out Raza who had been born here; they carted them off to Mexico. So, when they [his father and uncle] realized they were American citizens, they came back on their own." Felix Alvarez was from a working-class background, and farmwork was the family's source of livelihood, both as migrant workers and later as residents of California. The family was a large one, including "five brothers and two sisters, parents, and one set of grandparents. It was a close-knit family, because we always lived together." Alvarez elaborated, "I grew up in a two-bedroom house, one bedroom was for mom and dad and the smaller siblings that grew up literally in their bed, also, and then the other bedroom was for my grandparents. And, the rest of us in the living room or anywhere else there was floor space or whatever, but we were happy."

Language was important for them, "because we grew up in South Texas about eight miles from the border, and there's something different or special, when you grow up on the border." There were no rules about language and how they spoke, although "at home it was mostly Spanish; my grandparents spoke Spanish." Alvarez grew up in a bilingual environment inside a transnational life between the cities of McAllen and Reynosa, where his grandparents lived on the other side of the Rio Grande. He was comfortable going back and forth. "As a teenager, I'd be out there working in the fields picking tomatoes and stuff, on the Texas side, I'd joke I would jump in the river and swim to the other side."

In addition to an appreciation of culture and language, Felix Alvarez developed a deep consciousness of place and culture. From his family, he learned about the contradictions they confronted as Texas Mexicans. "I grew up knowing that Texas had been part of Mexico, that much of the land had been stolen by Anglos from the South. We always had this historical perspective about who we were as a people and always promoted pride in who we are." His ethnic pride went beyond embracing his Tejano roots; it was also about being Mexican. Although in the early days Chicano was not used as an identifier, "we were proud of being Mexican, and being Tejanos, and when we say Tejano, you really mean Mexicano; it was not a Mexican American thing." Rather than becoming Americanized, the Alvarez family embraced a cultural heritage that provided linguistic and cultural resources.

With no immediate ties to Mexico, Pete Carrillo proudly noted that both his parents were born in Arizona—his father in Ray and his mother in Gilbert. His father was a blue-collar worker, and his mother an activist involved in politics—both Republican and Democrat, as needed. For Carrillo, life in the family was fast paced. Carrillo recalled, "There was always something happening in the house—a large family of seven brothers and sisters, and my mother and father in the house. It was exciting from the standpoint that being the youngest in the family I had a tremendous amount of attention paid to me and that was good while I was growing up, and it also created problems as I became an adult. We had a good stable family—different aspects of good and bad."

At work, his father was a foreman or supervisor, "a steady blue-collar worker for thirty-seven years." According to Carrillo, his father "had an opinion about politics but didn't get involved"; it was from his mother that Carrillo got his "political bent." She taught him about politics and self-reliance. His father, on the other hand, told him "you would not feel good about yourself if you didn't have a job, so my father's idea of self-sufficiency was through retention of a job." His father's words have guided his thinking about work. "It doesn't matter what kind of job you have. If you go in there with the attitude that it's a job for now and you are going to learn how to keep that job, you are going to learn the skills necessary to be able to keep that job, so that you can move forward." Carrillo appreciated that his father "taught me the value of work." He valued his mother's political mentoring as well, pointing out that "when I turned eighteen I was very excited to cast my first vote; I have voted in every single election since."

South Phoenix was a source of education for Carrillo. "When I go back there now and I see my friends, they are drugged-out or dead, in prison or out of prison—it has given me a different perspective." Because of negative influences and associations, and invited by his uncle, Ernie Abeytia, a local Chicano leader, at the age of twenty-two Carrillo relocated to San José. He thought of this move as a temporary one because he was employed at North Phoenix High School as a community worker. "I had just completed my second year on a ten-month contract." The move was not an easy one. He said, "Right before I came from Phoenix, I had a need for community and civic involvement, doing things for the community, and, at the same time, to hang around with friends. I had a good job but there were drugs and alcohol—something was going to break; I was headed to prison because that's where a lot of my friends were." When he found employment at the Center for Employment Training, where he would stay for a long time and become involved in the community, Carrillo relocated permanently to San José. This vocational program would become not only a source of employment but also a site of job preparation. Carrillo would be among a handful of young adults who created a new life in his adopted city.

Tony Estremera, a self-described Chicorican and Chicano movement activist, was born in Puerto Rico. His mother was a homemaker, and his father a farmworker. The Estremera family migration began when his father relocated to Florida to work in the fields; later the rest of the family joined him in "upstate New York, where he worked until he saved enough money to send for us." Estremera was five years old when the family first landed in a place with "a lot of hustle and bustle, exciting. I still remember to this day how I felt when we landed in the airport in New York City." The clothes he wore and the harshness of the English language, which they did not speak, are seared in

Estremera's memory. He explained, "We had little tee shirts. I remember the first time I saw snow and things like that, it was really a real significant change, and English was really heavy; it was a foreign tongue."

In Brooklyn, when he was old enough, Estremera joined Job Corps, ending up in Pleasanton, California. From there, he moved to Sal Si Puedes, "because I met a few guys from Eastside." But, it would be Phil Marquez, a postal service employee, who urged Estremera to explore college. "He'd come out and sort of talk to me, 'Hey, how're you doing? How come you're not in school?' So, I told him, 'Well, I was thinking of going to school.'" In this way, Marquez became a source of encouragement and talked Estremera into returning to school and recruited him into the movement. "'Look, why don't you come to this gathering, like, next week there's a community meeting, and if you come, I'll introduce you.'" At the age of sixteen, Estremera made a home in San José, becoming active in United People Arriba, the Community Alert Patrol, the Mexican American Student Confederation, and the Movimiento Estudiantil Chicano de Aztlán. "Then, there was law school, I was involved in Centro Legal and in La Raza Student Association." It was his education and access to the community that inspired Estremera to develop as a professional, and San José gave him access to education.

Mike Garcia and his parents were born in East Los Angeles; his grandparents were from Mexico. His father grew up "in Depression-era East Los Angeles—no father, at least a father that was around—they had a real rough life." His father, who retired from the Los Angeles Fire Department, never forgot that he was working-class. Garcia attributed his work ethic to his father, who "never got involved politically, but always ingrained in me hard work and not questioning authority." It was that ethic that compelled his children "to work at an early age; he really pushed work. He never gave us any money; he made us work for it." In Garcia's view, his father was "a source of strength for the family," but he saw himself as unlike his father. "I revolted against a lot of what he stood for. He wasn't political; he was more subordinate than I liked or would accept. But that was his era. I came from a different era, a different reality in the '60s and the '70s, and the Chicano movement." The family relocated to San Fernando at a time when there were very few Mexicans living in the suburbs. Among the first to relocate there, and coming from an inner-city Mexican barrio, Garcia did not understand the social relationships. He explained, "My first six years was all Mexican—in Mexicano East LA there was like a war going on; I didn't understand it, it affected my self-image and [I was] subjected to name-calling. However, by the time I went to high school it was 50 percent Mexican—now, there are no whites."

Jorge Gonzalez, from the same generation as Garcia, was born in Mexico City. He immigrated to the United States with his mother, becoming an urban migrant in Ventura County. Gonzalez later moved to San Diego, where his stepdad obtained his master's degree and introduced him to the *movimiento*.

CONCLUSION

The participants provided various reasons for their migration and movement. Some from the Depression Generation migrated from urban and rural areas to San José and Santa Clara County to counter the effects of poverty, while others were pushed to relocate because of the Mexican Revolution or as a result of economic need. Their lived experiences and social circumstances framed their notions of equality, justice, and fairness, along with the ideologies of the home and their sense of community that were imparted by their parents and invested members of the community. It was within the intersectionalities of the structural inequalities of their lived experiences that Chicanas and Latinos/Chicanos conceived of the relational spaces in which they could fight for social justice and create social change. Internalizing the inequalities and oppressions they had to contend with, these activist leaders expressed the agency and power to confront race, class, gender, and sexuality in a variety of venues where inequalities played out.

Among those who participated in this study, most had adopted a strong work ethic and self-sufficiency as core values, perceiving themselves as not having a choice but to work. Alternatives like welfare would never have been contemplated. In the context of the greater good for the family and their community, their parents promoted independence through work and self-sufficiency as the route to success and social change. In their quest to create a better world for their people and for themselves, both generations internalized injuries and traumas of poverty, race, class, and gender, which became the frame of reference from which to engage their agenda as activist leaders. The Baby Boomer Generation, however, migrated primarily to flee crime, poverty, and the squalor of their communities, and thus gain access to the middle class.

4

· · ·

MARGINALIZATION AND EXCLUSION
Family Backgrounds

The activist leaders in this study begin from a premise of belonging, despite raced, classed, and gendered marginalization and exclusion. In speaking about their origins, six identified themselves as being born in the United States of Mexican descent, either first or second generation. One was a Chicano from the Depression Generation who underscored his lineage to Spanish and Mexican colonial times, linking his status to cattle and entrepreneurial capitalism, while others connected their migration to the Mexican Revolution or spoke about having been pulled by railroad and agricultural employment. Chicanas from the Depression Generation interacted in public and private spaces as a continuum rather than as separate sites of engagement. Although no one among both Depression and Baby Boomer Generations identified as a feminist, Chicanas expressed affinity with third space feminist ideas.

In this chapter, by sketching out these activists' education, origins, and areas of involvement, I explore the ways in which family and community relationships have shaped their identities, and how they experienced being derided and excluded from the sociocultural geography of the daily life.

DEPRESSION GENERATION: CHICANA EDUCATIONAL TRAJECTORIES

Chicanas of the Depression Generation surpassed their parents, becoming a generation of firsts: four completed high school and one graduated from the eighth grade. Among their parents, mothers had no formal education, and only two fathers completed the second and third grades. Although not given the option to pursue a higher education, most worked to create openings for those who came after them. For example, Sofia Mendoza and Ernestina García promoted and fought for educational rights. In addition, all became invested in the education of their children, participating in teacher-parent meetings, raising funds, and creating cultural events that promoted cultural backgrounds—a duty that was often assigned to mothers, although fathers also became involved when asked.

Table 2 provides a demographic overview of the educational legacy of Chicanas in the Depression Generation. Blanca Alvarado completed middle school in Cokedale, Colorado; after coming to San José as an adolescent, she graduated from San José High, as did Sofia Mendoza, Esther Medina, and Bea Vasquez Robinson. Ernestina García attended elementary school in Arizona and finished the eighth grade in an East Bay middle school. Mendoza graduated from Campbell High and attended some college.

PERSONAL AND SOCIAL IDENTITIES

From an early age, Chicanas understood structural exclusion. Always watchful and engaged in their surroundings, they relied on multiple ways of self-understanding in their relationships with peers, parents, and other adults. As they looked back on their upbringing, poverty and socioeconomic class, race, and labor conditions foregrounded their worldviews. While Alvarado expressed fond and loving memories of her birthplace, she also remembered a company town that limited and restricted her. For her and most of those in the Depression Generation, the agricultural fields beckoned, and they "migrated all over, then settled in Santa Clara County." Esther Medina's family moved to San José because of employment opportunities and her oldest brother's marriage.

Despite economic scarcities, Ernestina García recalled a happy childhood. García was deeply moved as she recalled her home "as a very happy house full of crowdedness—we were seventeen." But her memories of school overflowed with grief. "I went to a segregated school, and I haven't been able to—I don't think I ever will—erase the memories of those times, and how we were treated as mexicanos. For some reason as I get older I seem to feel more . . . *me da mucha tristeza*—it saddens me much."[1] García expressed that class and race traumas and personal injuries become sharper and more emotional with age. When speaking about the public world of an agricultural community, García said she was born between Glendale and Tollison, repeating her words, then switched to Spanglish—her language of comfort: "*Yo nací, entre medio de* Glendale and Tollison, close to Phoenix, *ahí vivíamos, y trabajaba mi 'apá pa'l ranchero, y nosotros* [we lived there, and my father worked there for the rancher, to support us], and as we grew up, of course, we helped *trabajar el algodón*—work the cotton or whatever."

TABLE 2 Origins and Education: Chicana Leaders of the Depression Generation (1929–36)

Name	Place & Year of Birth	Parents' Place of Birth		Education & Involvement			Area of Activism
		Mother	Father	Self	Mother	Father	
Blanca Alvarado	Cokedale, CO 1931	New Mexico	New Mexico	High school	None	Second or third grade	Community and political
Ernestina García (7/9/05)	Tolleson/ Glendale, AZ 1929	Sonora	Culiacan, Sinaloa	Eighth grade	None	None	Education, community, and political
Esther Medina (10/17/12)	Rancho Cespes, Fillmore, CA, 193	Zacatecas	Zacatecas	High school*	None	None	Social and community
Sofia Mendoza (3/14/15)	Fillmore, CA 1934	Arizona	Mexico	High school^	None	None	Education, community, and political
Bea Vasquez Robinson	Ventura, CA, 1934	Durango	Zacatecas	High school*	None	Third grade	Community and political

Note: Date of death in parentheses.

*Has honorary degree. Esther Medina received an honorary PhD from Santa Clara University, and Bea Vasquez Robinson an honorary AA from San José City College.

^Attended some college.

FIGURE 9 Ernestina García, on the right, with relatives. Courtesy of
Doreen Garcia Nevel.

As she talked, García allowed her emotions to surface. She linked her pain to the
unjust treatment and attitudes still experienced by Chicanas/os—miseducation and
separation. *"En medio de la yarda tenían una* faucet—there was one faucet in the middle
of the yard, *y allí tomábamos agua, y por el* cyclone fence *tú mirabas que habían—eran
tres o cuatro—*las fountains *de los Americanos corrían muy bien, y nosotros en línea* [there
we drank water, and through the cyclone fence you noticed that there were three or
four fountains for the Americans that ran well, and we were in line]. *Esas cosas se le
grababan a uno* [Those things stay in one's mind]." School reproduced the unfairness
of their living conditions: she talked about the lack of amenities and the segregation at
school. García contrasted the experiences of the rancher's children to her own experience and that of her peers, reflecting that on the ranch they could all be children, unlike

their experience at school, where they were kept separate and apart. She continued, *"Yo no entendía por qué en la escuela tenían un* [I did not understand why in the school they had a] *cyclone fence, y al otro lado tenían columpios, y el* [and on the other side a swing and the] slide; *nosotros no teníamos nada* [we had no swings, we had nothing]. *Nomás allí en la yard la mexicanada cantando, aguaté, matarile-rile-rile. aguaté, matarile-rile-ron* [Just there in the yard, all the Mexicans singing call-and-response children's songs, I want tea water, Matarile, rile, rile. I want an tea water, Matarile, rile, ron], we only had our songs." The cyclone fence and the lack of amenities represented the many barriers García confronted as a Chicana who was forced to live in a different world of class and race, even though her pain and trauma were mediated by culture. On the one hand, social boundaries symbolized by swings, slides, and fountains became symbols of the inequality of race, which she struggled to overcome. Her consolation came from Mexican cultural knowledge, games of the imagination, and the education she received at home from her parents. Despite it all, their lives were enriched.

Bea Vasquez Robinson grew up in poverty. Because of the internal dynamics at home, Vasquez Robinson found herself dealing with gendered contradictions. To make life more bearable, she focused on excelling in school, as academic success became a way to escape the everyday struggles of the home: "We were a large family, we followed the crops, and we lived in tents. We had no toys—it was a very hard luck story." She had nine brothers and sisters. As evidence of their stark poverty, Vasquez Robinson spoke about the loss of a young brother. "My father didn't believe he was sick and wouldn't let my mom take him to get treated. We didn't have a regular doctor or medical insurance, so she took him to Santa Clara County Hospital; his appendix burst, and he died."

Rather than attribute her brother's loss to the politics of race, Vasquez Robinson assigned it to poverty. However, race and class were salient and continuous intersectional spaces in the everyday lives of Chicanas.

GENDERED INTERSECTIONS OF RACE AND CLASS

From early childhood, race and class were ever-present contradictions that often became relational processes to negotiate. As Vasquez Robinson recalled how she was treated by the males in the family, she noted that girls and women were relegated to places of subordination. As she saw it, "Girls were second- or maybe third-class citizens—things were as things have always been and there were no laws that made it illegal to discriminate based on sex. So it was okay to discriminate. The good-old-boy network was in place. If you were brown and a woman it was very difficult in terms of employment and buying power. To joke about women was nothing. Everybody laughed, including many women." Negative treatment of women was rampant.

"Even kids—boys—believed that it was okay to belittle their mother because she was a woman." In Vasquez Robinson's view, misogyny was endemic, but "we stuck very close to Latinos; we had to because of our marginal existence." Of course, it was not only gender that separated Chicanas, it also was race and class. "I never really fit in so, to me, there were different worlds. There was 'our world' and then there was the 'white world.'" And, in her growing up experience, "there was never 'Asian' or 'Native American Indian' worlds. Mostly, it was just the 'white' and 'brown worlds,' and the brown world was home—it was safe."

Home protected Vasquez Robinson from racism and classism. Despite a difficult home life, there she felt "a sense of security," while the "white world was an alien and cold world you could never enter." When she tried to enter it, Vasquez Robinson experienced countless "rebuffs from children and adults, so it just reemphasized separation, and boundaries." Through the years, she learned to negotiate both worlds, overcoming barriers, which allowed her to make decisions based on individual value instead of through the lenses of race and class.

At an early age, Esther Medina, like Vasquez Robinson, experienced race and class discrimination. In elementary school, the teacher and health nurse were primary sources of "some of the stuff I'll never forget." Medina spoke about the humiliation that took place "during second grade, this one teacher, she would divide the whole class and stand us against the walls to do inspection, like in the army. We lost every day, and if you didn't look right, you didn't go out to recess and stayed inside with your head on your desk." By enacting racialized rituals, the teacher relegated students to a Mexican place where "every day, the kids would come in, and they would laugh, and call out, 'You dirty Mexicans.'" In her view, the teachers' practices reinforced disciplinary technologies of race and class, socializing Chicanas/os to think they would never win or advance ahead of the children of bankers, doctors, and lawyers—a constant reminder that they were outsiders. This type of treatment was not limited to teachers; Mexican children were publicly ridiculed, taunted, and humiliated by the actions of a public health nurse who "would line up all the brown kids in the hall to be inspected for cleanliness and lice—it took hours and it happened often." Medina felt the psychological trauma she experienced was tantamount to what she saw in films about the Holocaust.

Her home life would prepare Medina to confront an unequal world. She credited her parents with teaching her to cope, since without their support she would have been unable to handle it; they provided her alternate frames of reference with which to see herself, reassuring her of their love, pointing out she was a "good, loved, and valued child." Rather than foment hate, her parents taught their children forgiveness, attributing the teachers' actions to ignorance.

These experiences taught Medina to become an advocate for her group. Although what she experienced was traumatic, the mental, emotional, and physical abuse she experienced expanded her understanding of the human condition, teaching her to differentiate groups of people by their intentions—adults and children alike. Foundational in the fight for women's rights, these women created women's programs, non-traditional vocational training, and a bilingual-bicultural domestic violence center in their community, creating options for women where none had existed. Both Medina and Vasquez Robinson built resources and organizations that addressed the needs and improved the status of women.

Esther Medina and Sofia Mendoza shared a common place of birth, along with their fathers' efforts as union organizers. At three years of age, Mendoza recalled "seeing people along the highway with piles of furniture . . . then, when other unions became involved, they put up a lot of tents to house them." Recalling her parents' activism, Mendoza lauded her mother for "helping the striking families"; she often said she wanted "one of my kids to be just like me." Sofia Mendoza would take on the challenge, and while she credited her father for her involvement, she patterned herself after her mother, focusing on "how I affect other people." As "the oldest girl of five children," Mendoza took on much responsibility because she "had a handle on things," as she "bossed everybody, and kept order" to ensure her siblings got things done.

Unlike most of her generation, a middle-class environment sheltered Mendoza from poverty and racism. In high school, she struggled against exclusion through linguicism, a form of language racism. She recalled, "We didn't have a Spanish club. So, I'd come home griping and complaining," to which her father would respond, "You know what you got to do, make sure they have one." Guided by her father, in her first organizing effort she went about talking to the Spanish classes, one by one. When she had gained enough support, "I was appointed to do it; we got the Spanish club." Through that process, she learned that if you're going to take on an issue, it has to be a winning issue.

Racist treatment in school activities was a source of exclusion—Chicanas were not accepted in traditional social groups or sororities established on their campuses. In response, Alvarado, Medina, Mendoza, and Vasquez Robinson established socio-cultural clubs to organize clothing and food drives, as an alternative to their exclusion because of race and class. With work and family at the center, García became active as a young adult, encouraged and supported by her husband, Tony. Guided by their lived experience and knowledge gained in their families and communities, the Depression Generation of Chicanas fought for cultural and social rights.

DEPRESSION GENERATION: LATINOS/CHICANOS IN THE STRUGGLE FOR RIGHTS

Among Latinos/Chicanos of the Depression Generation, Antonio Soto, a Catholic priest who left the church at the age of fifty, was an activist leader and professor of Mexican American studies at San José State. George Castro, a chemist employed by IBM,

FIGURE 10 George Castro. Courtesy of the Society for the Advancement of Chicanos and Native Americans in Science.

became a political activist who was involved with MAPA and the GI Forum, later participating in various educational advocacy programs such the Society for the Advancement of Chicanos and Native Americans in Sciences (SACNAS). He continues to promotes science education in the middle schools of East San José.

José Carrasco, an educator and national organizer, was involved in the nation's first walkout for education in the mid- to late 1960s at Roosevelt Junior High, where he was teaching. Carrasco retired as a professor from San José State University. José Villa, drawn to the city by an employment opportunity, came San José State University as a co-founding faculty member in the first Mexican American Graduate Studies (MAGS) program in the nation created to recruit Raza students. Because of community demands and activism, Villa relocated with his growing family. Victor Garza became involved in the community through his educational journey, aligning with the GI Forum, the Chicano Employment Committee, and other advocacy groups to promote access to employment and political participation. Lou Covarrubias, the first Chicano chief of police, is credited with founding community policing, as well as with diversifying the department by preparing men and women of color for promotion and advancement. Covarrubias also worked with the GI Forum and its Fiestas Patrias, mentored students at Evergreen Valley College, and worked with organizations serving Mexican Americans.

As detailed in table 3, with the exception of Soto, the participants traced their lineage to Mexico. Four of their mothers were born in the southwestern United States, and two originated in northern Mexico. On the paternal side, two were born in the United States and four in Mexico. One mother was from Tucson, others from El Paso and Eagle Pass, Texas, and still others from various parts of California. One father each was from Tucson and El Paso, with eight—three mothers and five fathers—tracing their birthplaces to Mexico.

Latinos/Chicanos of the Depression Generation have more formal education than their parents, with Antonio Soto's parents being the only ones of their generation to have completed high school. Those who joined the service benefited from the GI Bill or the Servicemen's Readjustment Act of 1944, which provided educational and

TABLE 3 Origins and Education: Chicano Leaders of the Depression Generation (1928–37)

Name	Place & Year of Birth	Parents' Place of Birth		Education & Involvement			
		Mother	Father	Self	Mother	Father	Area of Activism
Antonio R. Soto (1993)	Tucson, AZ 1928	Tucson, AZ	Tucson, AZ	PhD	High school	High school	Social Activism and education
George Castro	Los Angeles, CA 1930s	El Paso, TX	Nochistlan, Jalisco	PhD	Eighth grade	Ninth grade	Science and education
Jack Brito (9/20/2017)	San Diego, CA 1929	Chihuahua	El Paso, Texas	Tenth	Fifth grade	Third grade	Political and social
José Carrasco	Fort Mason, CO 1939	Torreon	Chihuahua	PhD	None	Third grade	Organizing and education
José Villa (6/27/2018)	Clovis, NM 1928	Mexico	Mexico	MSW	None	None	Social and education
Victor Garza	Eagle Pass, TX 1930s	Eagle Pass, TX	Piedras Negras	MA	Third or fourth grade	None	Political and social
Lou Covarrubias	Irvington, CA 1930s	California	Mexico	MA	Sixth grade	None	Public service

Note: Date of death in parentheses.

housing access for those who served in the war, making military service an entry point to the middle class. Only two out of seven participants did not serve in the military. Six received higher education degrees, with one attending some college.

BABY BOOMER GENERATION: ADVANCEMENT AND UPWARD MOBILITY

Parents of the Baby Boomer Generation attended school, with four completing elementary and one graduating from high school, and two fathers finished elementary and three attended middle school. Four of Boomer Generation Chicanas received master's degrees, and two completed bachelor's degrees.

While experiences of trauma and hurt often inspired their involvement, these activist leaders took on public and private issues—including the Vietnam War and its high conscription rate and death rate of Chicanos who served in that war—that affected their community in various ways. Motivated to create an equal, just, and fair environment that treated their people as full human beings, they took on issues that adversely affected the lives of their people, such as housing issues, vocational education, health and mental health, cultural activism, and other type of educational and social concerns.

CHICANA ACTIVIST LEADERS AND THE CHICANO RENAISSANCE

Rose Amador worked in educational and social service venues. She began her career in vocational education at Service Employment Redevelopment (SER) Jobs for Progress, later becoming director of the Center for Training and Careers, a program that would become ConXión. Invested in the professionalization of marginalized women and the training of men who lacked a formal education, Amador created a service community for Chicanas/Latinos and other ethnic groups in need of preparation for employment. Delia Alvarez got her start in public service by working for the county of Santa Clara and fulfilling myriad positions in the Welfare Department, the Executive Office, and the Public Health Department. She also became involved in freeing her brother—the second-longest-held prisoner of war in Vietnam. All the while, Alvarez advanced up the ranks in corporate public service but maintained her connections to the community with Oaxinas de Paz and the Chicana Coalition. Cecilia Arroyo, like Alvarez, had a long career with the county of Santa Clara. From the County Planning Department, Arroyo went to the Association of Bay Area Governments, later joining the Chicana Coalition. "I started doing things that nobody else was doing, thus my contribution to Chicana Coalition was to become a political link, because that is my strength." After completing her BA, Arroyo put herself through graduate school, working as a secretary. "I had business training, got a job at City College, and worked in the counseling department. Then, I got a job at the old Economic Opportunities Commission as the executive secretary to the director."

Josie Romero was hired by Santa Clara Country as a paraprofessional "to bridge the mental health services gap in the community, because it was lily-white and there were no bilingual professionals." As a Santa Clara County employee, Romero organized workers into a union. She collected "signatures and we got in, and then I organized the community workers to get approval for a monthly meeting and in the guise of training we also did a lot of advocacy." She was also a founding member of Chicano Mental Health and Trabajadores de la Raza. Romero was heavily invested in politics and supported the Democratic Party and its candidates.

Although employed full-time, Romero continued her education: it took "ten years to get my GED, AA, BA, and my MSW, and I never doubted I would do it." As an MSW, Romero moved up the ranks of administration and became licensed as a social worker and certified as a disaster social worker, utilizing her expertise in times of national emergencies. Romero served as South County Mental Health director, then she was promoted to assistant director of Community Mental Health San José, becoming the regional director in 1984, and entering private practice as a psychotherapist. Also, she was the founder of the Hispanic Institute of Family Development and sat on its board until 1986. Mental health work would be an entry point to employment for several activist leaders in this study.

Elisa Marina Alvarado was a community and student activist who was politically involved before immersing herself in cultural work. With "about twenty-two years as a licensed MSW," she worked in mental health as a "case manager, community worker— and really enjoyed it." However, she found her strength in art and culture, because "I'm an artist, and in my mental health work I try to approach the work as an artist, constantly striving not to define reality, and seeing what else we can see." In that sense, Alvarado has embodied the "role of artist, *curandera*, healer, or a co-journey person" with those whom she has organized and collaborated with, informed by progressive ideologies of the left.

Kathy Chavez Napoli, from Sal Si Puedes, traces her family lineage to Northern California and to her father's Indigenous background. Chavez Napoli was the first to graduate from college on "both sides of my family among at least two hundred cousins, some who are twenty and thirty years older." Her parents had limited education. A leader in the Auto Recyclers Association, with the support of her children she created a multi-million-dollar business that she and her husband administer. See table 4 for more information about this generation of Chicana activists.

Among Chicana participants of the Baby Boomer Generation, all the mothers and daughters were born in the United States, while five out of six fathers were born in

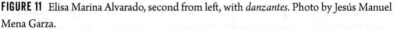

FIGURE 11 Elisa Marina Alvarado, second from left, with *danzantes*. Photo by Jesús Manuel Mena Garza.

Mexico. As first- or second-generation Mexican origin on their paternal side, these Chicanas expressed a strong Mexican cultural connection and were fluent in Spanish. Elisa Marina Alvarado's father, who was a professor of Spanish at the community college, had an MA, while his wife had some college. Amador's mother completed high school, one mother finished the fifth grade, and four went to middle school. Among fathers, two attended elementary and four went to middle school.

Educationally, Chavez Napoli and Romero reflect the legacy of the working poor. Still, throughout the generations, Chicana activist leaders navigated an environment that mirrored a culture and status that continues to be derided and devalued. Except for two parents who completed high school, one in Mexico and one in Guatemala, only one mother graduated from high school. One mother and two fathers had no formal education, and most participants identified both parents as having "some schooling" as their educational attainment. Apart from Elisa Marina Alvarado's parents, most are second generation and beyond.

TABLE 4. Origins and Education: Chicana Leaders of the Baby Boomer Generation (1942–49)

| Name | Place & Year of Birth | Parents' Place of Birth | | Education & Involvement | | | Area of Activism |
		Mother	Father	Self	Mother	Father	
Delia Alvarez	Salinas, CA 1942	Colton, CA	Guanajuato, Mexico	MA	Sixth grade	Eighth grade	Service and public administration
Rose Amador	San José, CA 1949	Michigan	Chihuahua, Mexico	BA	High school	Seventh grade	Vocational education
Cecilia Arroyo (4/4/2009)	Cupertino, CA 1945	Phoenix, AZ	Mexico	MA	Sixth grade	Sixth grade	Health and public administration
Josie Romero (11/4/2004)	Eagle Pass, TX 1944	Eagle Pass, TX	Coahuila, Mexico	MA, MSW	Fifth grade	Eighth grade	Mental health and social services
Elisa Marina Alvarado	San Francisco, CA 1945	Hollywood, CA	Guadalajara, Mexico	MSW	Some college	MA	Cultural activism
Kathy Chavez Napoli	San José, CA 1949	California	California	BA	Eighth grade	Third grade	Public policy and advocacy

Note: Dates of death in parentheses.

LATINO/CHICANO ACTIVISM AND LEADERSHIP

Felix Alvarez began his cultural work with Teatro Campesino, and he founded multiple venues for imparting ancestral knowledge such as Teatro de Los Pobres and the Center for Community and Cultural Activism (CCCA). He served on the board of the Alum Rock School District. Jorge Gonzalez, a progressive political activist, was co-founder of Raza Sí!, a pro-immigrant workers' rights advocacy group, and he was involved with educational issues. Mike Garcia began his activism by working on youth rights, and after obtaining an MSW, he became an organizer for Service Employees International Union (SEIU), where he worked to organize the Justice for Janitors campaign, which focused on undocumented workers. He eventually became president of the union. Pete Carrillo, a political and cultural activist, was involved with the Chicano Employment Committee, and he became the first executive director of the Mexican Heritage Corporation. Under his leadership, the corporation organized the first Mariachi Festival. Tony Estremera, a community activist focusing on educational rights and anti-police violence work, was active with various organizations. Estremera vied for public office and was elected to the San José–Evergreen Community College Board.

Among participants from the Baby Boomer Generation, one activist leader was born in Mexico, another in Puerto Rico, and three traced their birth to Texas, California, and Arizona, respectively. With slightly more educated parents than the previous generation, four participants obtained professional degrees, and one completed an undergraduate degree: Alvarez had some college, Garcia and Gonzalez obtained MSWs, Carrillo completed his BA, and Estremera received his JD and is a licensed attorney. A summary of their origins and educational histories are presented in table 5.

FIGURE 12 Tony Estremera. Courtesy of the San José–Evergreen Community College Board.

CONCLUSION

The five Chicana activist leaders from the Depression Generation all achieved higher levels of education than their parents. Two mothers and three fathers traced their origins to Mexico, and three mothers and two fathers claimed U.S. birth. Among the mothers, none had an education, while two

TABLE 5. Origins and Education: Chicano Leaders of the Baby Boomer Generation (1950–51)

Name	Place & Year of Birth	Parents Place of Birth		Education & Involvement			Area of Activism
		Mother	Father	Self	Mother	Father	
Felix Alvarez	McAllen, TX 1950s	Mission, TX	Hidalgo, TX	Some college	Some schooling	None	Social and cultural
Jorge Gonzalez	Mexico City, 1950s	Mexico City	Guatemala	MSW	High school, Mexico	High school, Guatemala	Political and social
Mike Garcia (3/26/2017)	Los Angeles, CA 1951	Los Angeles, CA	Los Angeles, CA	MSW	High school	Some high school	Union organizing
Pedro "Pete" Carrillo	Phoenix, AZ, 1950	Gilbert, AZ	Ray, AZ	BA	Some schooling	Some schooling	Political and social
Tony Estremera	Puerto Rico 1950s	Puerto Rico	Puerto Rico	JD	None	None	Organizing

Note: Date of death in parentheses.

out of five fathers attended second to third grade. Among the participants, four graduated from high school, one attended some college, and one completed the eighth grade. Latinos/Chicanos of this generation, who total seven, reported that two mothers and three fathers were born in the United States, and that two mothers and three fathers lacked a formal education. Unlike the previous generation, four mothers went from third through eighth grade, with one graduating from high school. Fathers went from third to ninth grade, with one graduating from high school. Among the Chicano activist leaders, three obtained a PhD, two an MA, one an MS, and one attended some college, after having dropped out in the tenth grade.

Baby Boomer Chicanas, along with their parents, had more years of schooling. Mothers were all born in the United States, while only one of the fathers is from California. Mothers of this generation had some formal education, with one completing high school and some college, and others attending sixth to eighth grade. Among fathers, one had an MA, and five went from third to eighth grade. The participants completed four MAs and two BAs. Among the five Latinos/Chicanos in this generation, four mothers and three fathers were U.S.-born, one mother and a father had no formal education, while two mothers completed high school and two had some schooling. Among the fathers, two had no education, while one had some schooling, and two some high school. Latinos/Chicanos of this generation completed a JD, two MSWs, one BA, and one attended some college. With the exception of one activist leader who was born in Mexico, four out of the five participants were U.S.-born.

Each generation, despite the barriers and limitations imposed on them by race, class, and gender, advanced educationally and socioeconomically, while still promoting the rights of their people in their everyday lives. A detailed discussion on the legacies they built follows in the next chapters.

5

• • •

ACTIVIST LEADER *LEGADOS* IN ACTION

These oral histories illustrate the ways in which activist leaders in San José, California, have worked in multiple venues for social change. Despite shifting emphases resulting from conflicts and contradictions that emerged in their daily lives, some remained involved in the cultural and social life of the community for the rest of their lives. Others started in education and moved on to participate in political and policy issues of the city, while still others have been involved in social and community service. A discussion of their contributions follows, with the understanding that their involvement interweaves with multiple areas of focus. The next section unpacks the ways in which multiple inequalities informed their investment in social action and social justice and their commitment to change.

CULTURAL, SOCIAL, AND POLITICAL LIFE

In her daily life, Blanca Alvarado upheld a strong sense of fairness within her family and in the community. Thinking back to her childhood, she recalled two instances of inequality and exclusion. She remembered the Plancarte family, who "came directly from Mexico, and were considered outsiders, and different." She recalled standing up for one of their children, her schoolmate. "I remember Betty Plancarte and feeling tremendous pity for the way in which she was treated, and a couple of times got into confrontations with other people because she was treated badly. But, I also remember feeling resentment towards my own family for the way they looked down on the Plancartes." Inequality and internalized racism were at the core of her sense of justice, fairness, and equality, which shaped Alvarado's consciousness and agency to act. She said, "I have always, for whatever reason, stood up as a champion for someone." For example, she added, "When I was going around with José, I remember an incident in the living room of my parent's home, and my sister making sarcastic comments about blacks," such as, "I wouldn't be caught dead dancing with a black person." Alvarado retorted: "I don't have any problem with that. I dance with a black man all the time." She was referring to her boyfriend José, who was darker than anyone in her family—color had never been an issue for her. Racism was not the only structural inequality she would confront. "I defended myself and other women, not only at CET but also with the Mexican American Political Association, because it was another male-dominated organization."

As far as socioeconomic class is concerned, Alvarado brought up those times in high school when she organized her few Chicano peers: "We gravitated toward each other." With "Mrs. Crist at Catholic Social Services" as their mentor, they organized Club Tapatio—a social group with a cultural vision. Alvarado and the other club members "wanted to do some good, so we managed to organize food and clothing drives for the poor. So, there again is a very small aspect of being organized within a group for a purpose. Without the Club Tapatio de San José High School, it would have been a dismal, boring place."

It was at San José High School that Blanca met José J. Alvarado, her future husband. "He was already a well-established businessman in San José" with a "radio program on KLOK and a little record shop in his broadcasting studio right on Post Street, at First and Market." In addition, José Alvarado promoted a great deal of interest in the political life of the community. For example, "he put together a youth drop-in center right there in his office and a juke box, and we had ping-pong tables with checkered tablecloths, and the Coke machine. It was a place we hung out at." Because "he was creating his own revolution in San José, by being outspoken on some very major issues, police brutality being one of them," Alvarado admired him. Because of his sociocultural position, José gave her access to social amenities. For her, "it was an exciting time in many ways because here I was a very young woman, and he was a very mature, well-established man. He had tremendous popularity, and, in addition to having a radio program and doing his own activism on social issues, he was a dance promoter."

Blanca thrived as part of that social world and enjoyed accompanying José to all his events. In retrospect, she regretted the way she treated her mother. "I was *muy desobediente*—disobedient—and I would just take off with him. I remember going to Salinas, Sacramento, Stockton, and Tracy; he was promoting stars that he brought in from Mexico." Through him, she met and interacted with many famous people or "*luminarios cómo* Jorge Negrete, Pedro Infante, Lalo Guerrero, and Maria Victoria," among other artists of the golden age of Mexican cinema. Alvarado, a Chicana of many firsts, became the "first female, bilingual broadcaster on KLOK."

Later, she would be one of the many faces featured in San José's premier bilingual magazine, *El Excentrico: Magazin Social, Fotográfico Latino-Americano*, which printed seven hundred copies per week. The magazine was published from April 1949 to April 1981, and documented the daily experiences of the community, advertising and promoting small and professional businesses owned by Mexicans and Mexican Americans. The first issue featured Lorraine Caudillo dressed as a China Poblana.[1] The magazine also highlighted social endeavors of the community by including photographs by the likes of Richard Diaz, who was called "*el fotográfo de las estrellas*," and Rudy Belluomini. *El Excentrico*'s inaugural issue promised that, in an effort to "introduce and present its Latino element, *El Excentrico* dedicates and consecrates to its Latino-Americana *colonia* accounts of vibrant messages of cordiality for each one of its Spanish-language members. With each day of publication, *El Excentrico* hopes to improve, to become a worthy reflection of our *colonia* or neighborhood" (April 1949 issue, my translation).

Esther Medina was a columnist for *El Excentrico* from September 5, 1955, to January 1961. She published notices of engagements and marriages and recorded the sociocultural activities of the many clubs that supported the cultural life of people of Mexican descent in San José. She would also document the presence of Mexican artists and singers who came to perform in San José—often hosting receptions for them at her home. In December 1955, Medina herself would grace the cover of the magazine.

As early as high school, Medina addressed her peers' social needs, becoming instrumental in the establishment of the Latin American Club in 1952 or '53. It was her awareness of ethnic and class exclusion that motivated her, since she had noticed that "unless you were really dressed and came from kind of a wealthy family, you didn't belong to any of the clubs." The way she saw it, Mexicans people made contributions, and "people need to know about us—we need to become part of the system." These were the organizing principles that helped the club become the high school's "club of the year."

As high school students of this generation, an experience the participants shared was that higher education was not promoted for Chicanas. For example, Medina was made to believe that success was achieved through marriage, which for women was considered "successful, and counselors never mentioned getting ready for college—no one ever talked to me about college." As a result, she felt the only option available was that of becoming a beautician, with the idea of owning her own shop. Her goal was not easily achieved, though. Needing to amass the financial means to attend beauty college, Medina worked "in a nut-shelling place, and I saved all my checks to pay for beauty school. When I got enough money—it must have been maybe '57—I got to beauty school." After accumulating six years of experience with a large clientele, and with money saved from the business, she opened a shop, hiring "relatives that were hair

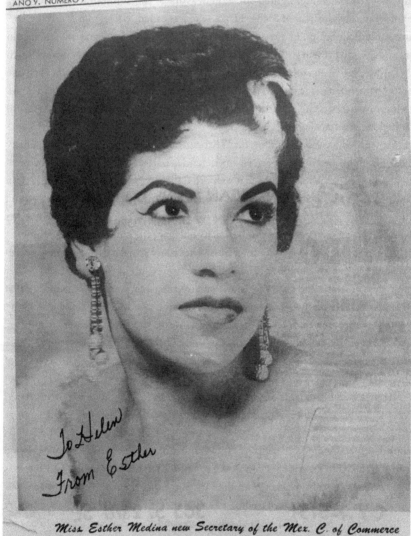

FIGURE 13 Esther Medina, secretary of the Mexican Chamber of Commerce. Photograph from *El Excentrico*. Courtesy of Cameo Burton.

stylists." She became a respected and successful businesswoman, but still her "hope was to enroll in school."

Medina opened other businesses, and her resourcefulness and tenacity served her well. Having learned the culture of business, she guided herself through the process: "To set up a business, you needed a permit, a business permit. You needed a lawyer. You needed a lease for the place. You had to negotiate the lease. You had to buy the equipment. Get a bookkeeper, and the bookkeeper taught me how to keep the books, and then I would just take them quarterly and she told me what books to buy and how to do it. And, I did it." Medina engaged in other endeavors and with a small business loan founded a second business. She explained, "I didn't know what a proposal was at the time, but they wanted a proposal, so I asked, 'What is that?' Then they said, 'Well, right away they tell you why you think you can do it. What kind of experience you have.'" Her husband assisted with the children so she could write the proposal. "I sat at my desk at home and I wrote it in pencil—different sections." In addition to writing the proposal, she had to prepare a budget, and "[I] figured it all out; I don't know how I did it, I just did. And, then we opened the liquor store, because my husband wanted a

FIGURE 14 Esther Medina, with daughter Cameo and son Derek. Courtesy of Cameo Burton.

liquor store." But "just at the time that we were financially able for me to go to school," her husband broke his side of the bargain. The marriage ended in divorce, and she became responsible for bringing up of their children, which prevented her from fulfilling her dream of going to college.

Medina built other businesses, including a hair salon, a supper club, and a liquor store. Her experience as a businesswoman became foundational in her public service as an administrator for the Women's Program at Economic and Social Opportunity and the Mexican American Services Agency, from which she retired after having created a multi-million-dollar operation that provided services for her community and housing to low-income seniors.

Activist leaders from the Baby Boomer Generation devised ways to become involved in the cultural life of the community, thus creating alternative venues for change. The social and cultural life of San José would thrive in the mid-century and experience a renaissance during the Chicano movement.

BABY BOOMERS FELIX ALVAREZ AND ELISA MARINA ALVARADO: CULTURAL ACTIVISTS

As cultural activists, Felix Alvarez and Elisa Marina Alvarado engaged multiple sites in their activism; both were founding members of *teatro*, theater groups that worked to educate and politicize the community on a variety of issues. After leaving Teatro Campesino, Felix Alvarez started Teatro de los Pobres, which he perceived as "a community collective because we weren't like a corporation or a business—we were like another *familia*." He and Lillie Alvarez, who was related to Luis and Lupe Valdez, established the group. As he looked back, Alvarez's experience with theater was foundational to his activism. His involvement was "something that I've done along the path, not as an individual but as a people. It had to do with perceiving that whatever we evolved to; it is anchored on the idea that we're a people."

Involved in social services, education, and mental health, Alvarez also tried to foster collective well-being. From 1979 to about 1985, in collaboration with members of the community, Felix Alvarez was part of "*Misa* [Mass] Chicana over at Sacred Heart Church." To the best of his recollection, "it was about fifty of us, mostly Chicanos who started it, premised on the notion 'you can't have personal salvation unless you have community salvation.'" This effort emerged from "Anglos or Italians and Mexicans not feeling comfortable *porque los Mexicanos tampoco estaban de acuerdo*—because Mexicans also were not in agreement." Their intent was "not compartmentalizing the Movimiento's needs by being only into one area of involvement, just into education, or into mental health." Alvarez explained, "Misa Chicana reinforced who we are as a

FIGURE 15   Felix Alvarez, on the far right, reuniting with members of Teatro de los Pobres. Courtesy of Felix Alvarez.

people and as *familias*. We focus on those values that are there, even though they're traditional. I'm making the distinction between what we view as traditional values versus how we perceive a traditional family to be, and those that emerge." With that, Alvarez demonstrated an evolving activist philosophy. Teatro had become his entry point into activism, which began as "a cyclical thing informed by Maya and Aztec philosophy of the four directions—the idea that we live inside an understanding of the cosmos and how everything flows in motion." It was in San José that Alvarez focused on the evolution of "self—physical, emotional, intellectual, and spiritual planes," which necessarily called for "a balance of the four directions." For him, activism translated into action with others, even those against the cause, citing the willow tree story shared by César Chávez: "In the strongest winds, most trees will crack and break because they're too rigid and they're too set and they don't want to accept change. And that the willow tree is very flexible and in the strongest wind it will bend and fold but it will still come back to its original thing." What Alvarez gathered from that story was that scabs or *esquiroles* are part of your endeavors—that we do not have the luxury of losing those who could become allies, adding that "most people I've met who have been my strongest

FIGURE 16 Felix Alvarez holding a banner of *la Virgen de Guadalupe*.
Courtesy of Felix Alvarez.

opposition or who come up and think you are stupid end up becoming the strongest
supporters, and they end up being the strongest allies in the long run."

Alvarez spoke about the ways he engaged relational approaches through the Center
for Community and Cultural Activism, an organization he formed. Based on the philosophy of the four directions, there are four processes that focus on "awareness that
has to do with thinking in terms of social action." And there are "the more militant or
radical or the social worker types who want to educate." For Felix Alvarez, it all begins
when "the audience is invited to take part or engage." While this is not the process a
traditional director undertakes, Alvarez's interests rely on witnessing those who interact and relate to the process of creating social change. (See table 6.)

TABLE 6. Felix Alvarez's Cyclical Processes of Activism

Phase 1	Phase 2	Phase 3	Phase 4
Has the desire to learn English and joy of getting a job, and contemplates inclusion into society—the audience	Signs up to vote, becomes involved in the democratic process, and celebrates being American—has interest in learning and educating others	Militancy increases, yearns to go into the streets, demonstrate; feels the need to become more militant—creates and provides alternative views	Community is part of the process, partners to change policies and structures—change, education, and services. For example, working within and outside the system to make change from a conscious perspective

With this philosophy, he found himself trying to connect with others—to create social change where feasible. Alvarez spoke about his political involvement as "always connected, as the bottom root of it." He refrained from becoming traditional in his endeavors. He said, "Those were the first things I began to run into. I remember telling people in the teatro and people who support what I do. I didn't want to become like many others who go into an elected office, which changes them, transforms them to become a part of that system rather than remain that part of the community." His entrance into politics began with personal connections, sending "a letter to people I know to ask for financial support, then just talking to people, making my own signs." In a grassroots campaign funded with $1,100 in donations, Alvarez won a seat on the Alum Rock School District Board. Even though his tenure would not be without difficulties.

As he saw it, teatro and activism are interwoven, and it is not a process that remains static: "I saw it as a growing thing, developing, and somebody would come up and say, 'Teatro Chicano is this.' Why does it stay there in 1967, we're in 1993?'" As an instructor at Santa Clara University, Alvarez was doing teatro in which his ideas spring from activism. "I teach a lot of what we've been talking about. I try some of these *pensamientos* with non-Raza audience as to how they respond and helps me in one aspect—I'm not a minister, I'm not here to convert anybody—the things we do are not meant to be how it is or what you should do. It's always, this is how we feel about this, this is how we perceive it, this is how we see it, and what do you think?"

In his cultural activism, Alvarez has focused on education. "I've been involved in student walkouts for getting Chicanos into colleges and universities and marched with *estudiantes*; I've been an *estudiante*." Also, he has worked with UFW—marches, pickets, being part of the Teatro Campesino. And for "Central America, I've organized vigils, processions for Bishop Romero." He has also done solidarity work with people from

"South America, Latin America, Chile." Other struggles have included labor issues, police brutality, health services, immunization projects, and violence—in all of which he takes much pride. However, as regards the cultural work, "I usually don't even mention that, but I've been writing plays about issues and concerns involving the community such as migration—La Migra."

Alvarez's "activism departs from two perspectives: as caretaker of certain cultural traditions, and expressions of a ritual ceremony that is part of our community." For example, he says, "it's twenty-three or twenty-four years that I've been doing the Virgen de Guadalupe play, and the Día de los Muertos," because these practices speak to the continuation of culture, and "I see myself as a part of all those who've come before me who have done that." The way he understands it, "there is no structure or organization to that, because we are the ones who are going to continue" to do work that cultural workers have done and will carry on cultural expression.

FIGURE 17 Felix Alvarez, with Teatro Campesino, in front of an Aztec calendar. Courtesy of Felix Alvarez

Elisa Marina Alvarado, like Alvarez, has been involved in multiple areas, from education, to workers' rights, mental health services, and political and cultural work. Rather than just confronting structural contradictions of race and ethnicity along with class, as had been the case with most male activist leaders, Alvarado brought in the additional tensions of gender and sexism. Even when political work motivated her to engage her creative side, she was inspired by building a support group where they could joke and have fun in the creation of teatro.

After graduation from high school, Alvarado received a scholarship to study at Cornell. Yet, feeling insecure about moving and being around "mostly white people there, I just freaked out at the idea of being so far away and not knowing any Chicanos. I was pretty involved and I just didn't feel ready to do that; I didn't understand that it was an opportunity." So she refused their offer. Later, she applied at the University of California, Santa Cruz, and was accepted. However, "financial aid told me that I couldn't get [support] because my father made too much money, and even though I hadn't lived at home in over three years, they still wouldn't give me financial aid, so I just got myself into San José State, and I took classes, and I got involved." It was at San José State that

FIGURE 18   Teatro de la Gente, the original troupe. Courtesy of Jesús Manuel Mena Garza.

she "met Spider [one of the teatro members], dropped out of school, and instead of studying anthropology, did cultural work." She joined Teatro de la Gente full time, returning to school only when she went back to complete an MSW.

Alvarado's parents did not oppose her choices, since "they knew I was a pretty headstrong, independent person, and they never really worried about me that much." Before pursuing a graduate degree at San José State, Alvarado worked as a tutor. During that time, she became politically involved with the creation of "a Third World Coalition, and at the College of San Mateo, I was very active with BASTA [a Bay Area student organization that challenged the incarceration and violent treatment of men of color by law enforcement personnel—*basta* means 'enough'] as we focused on the Los Site defendants, political prisoners, and MEChA [Movimiento Estudiantil Chicano de Aztlán]—I was in MEChA." It was while participating in all these efforts that her notions of community, which she imagined as concentric circles, shifted to include non-blood-related people who became family. "These relationships were reciprocal, about responsibility and mutual support, and educational for passing along knowledge and making social change." Thus, this self-created family—the Chicano community, arts community, and the left—became the core of her involvement in the labor movement and Central American nonintervention work; these endeavors fed her progressive politics.

Like most Chicanas who participated in this study, Alvarado does not perceive herself as a leader in the traditional sense. Rather, she says she is "a builder, with a good feeling for organizational matters, about how to structure things, how to pull together a committee working and pulling together a goal and monitoring it." For her, "it is a role that I play—I like to build a unit, and then we do it." She felt the community perceived her "as a teatro person, organizer, and actress"; and for "the mental health community I am an adult specialist and an advocate; and among Chicanas, an Indigenous woman and a member of groups or network of women, in terms of our journey." Thus, Alvarado's notion of an activist leader calls for that individual to have awareness as "a teacher, a person who develops in others critical consciousness, self-awareness, the ability to look at options, and to move from an awareness to action whether it's with an individual or a group; it is more facilitating rather than directing a process where people look at a problem, or a situation, or their need, or their desires to move beyond complaining, or wanting, or dreaming, toward manifesting it." In line with this, Alvarado reiterated her involvement "in political things like *Los Siete*; Community Alert Patrol—an organization that monitored police action in a series of police shootings, Henry Dillard, a black man, and then Danny Treviño." After that, she "got involved with rent relief, the farmworkers movement, *Los Tres*," among other efforts.

With Teatro de la Gente, Alvarado became the North American coordinator of the Frente Trabajadores de la Cultura, with branches in Mexico and Latin America. "I also was involved in the Story Road apartments tenant strike" and worked with the "Angela Davis Defense Committee, and American Indian Movement—did fund-raisers for Wounded Knee out of La Confederación [de la Raza Unida], and American political prisoners on campus. I got involved in the walkout because of economic cutbacks in the Economics Department—controversial stuff. And, you know, immigrant rights, and then certainly all along teatro and educational rights, and the Bakke decision."

In retrospect, Elisa Marina Alvarado's activism did not always yield happy and productive times. With Teatro de la Gente, "the women were especially unhappy. There was a lot of manipulation and a lot of people were really being excluded from decision making, feeling exploited yet working their butts off from sunup to sundown." She recalled that their days were long and included much commitment, "rehearsing, raising money, cleaning the theater, getting ready for a tour, and then making the leaflets, and then realizing, 'wait a minute here, there's a better way to have more discussions about—the division of labor.'" In that context, child care became a point of contention and an excuse for placing Alvarado on probation, whereby she was prohibited from talking to anyone outside the group. Explaining how this unfolded, she added: "We tried talking to the director, but he just wouldn't listen to us, so we went to the board and the board turned around and told him that we were going behind his back. So he and I worked that together but the women got scared and intimidated—it was like a cult too."

Because she challenged the director's all-encompassing power, Alvarado was isolated to the point that "even when we went on tour to the Southwest I could only talk when it was a logistical thing, 'this is where we put the luggage.'" In Colorado, things came to a head when somebody told the director, "'Elisa is talking to somebody' and he came and stood over me and I said like, 'Fuck you!' And I just kept on talking, with 'What?

FIGURE 19 Adrian Vargas and Elisa Marina Alvarado performing *norteño danza* for Teatro de la Gente. Photo by Jesús Manuel Mena Garza.

Are you going to put me out on the street?'" This and other sexist experiences inspired Alvarado to create a venue from a women-centered perspective. Despite the difficulties she encountered as an activist leader in Chicano teatro, as a co-founder of Teatro Visión she created a place that reflected the thoughts and actions of a community that actively engaged in the creation of social justice and social change through performance. As a mental health worker, Alvarado also promoted the health and welfare of her community, while embracing its Indigenous roots. Like others of their generation, the participants in this study would continue their involvement as they advanced their education.

GARZA, GARCÍA, AND BRITO: BRIDGING GENERATIONS

Although socialized with those of the Depression Generation, Victor Garza bridged his time as an activist leader with the Baby Boomer Generation. He cut his teeth in Chicano studies classes that taught him the knowledge he lacked about his culture; he minored in the discipline and took courses to better understand the politics of his community. As a result of their education, his siblings too were and continue to be involved. For example, "Humberto was active, along with another brother who had two years of college and has always been a leader; city councilman, a vice mayor, and a school board member." This was something they had in common, as Garza himself was elected to the Berryessa School Board. Garza is so invested in the politics of his community that he only missed "one general election when my dad died, but I've always been active and believe in political participation," adding that he learned that from his mom, "because that's the way she was." When he ran for office in 1975, Garza was "the first Chicano ever elected to the Berryessa Board of Trustees, in a very white community." It was a contested election, and "my literature was torn up and thrown in my face, yet I managed to win two to one." His electoral efforts continued when he ran for city council, losing by seventy-five votes, but he "won in other ways because you develop strength and many people respected me for that."

Garza recalled the first political meeting he attended. This was his "first meeting with Dr. Carrasco and José Villarreal—there were about ten white people and four Mexicans. The two of them would make and second motions, and everybody would vote against it," then "Villarreal would make a motion and Carrasco would second it, and everybody would vote against it, and so on throughout the evening." Confused because "I didn't understand it" and having gone with "the hunch they were going to fight, I stood at the door, listened, and got angry." Then, "the Mexicans went on the side of the white people, and when the meeting ended, Carrasco came over immediately, shook my hand, and hugged me, saying, 'Well, Victor, how did you like it?'" Then, "this white guy came and hugged José and shook his hand, stating, 'Well, José, it's been a while, I haven't seen you, where have you been?' Then, an old white guy came over, hugged him, and shook his hand." Garza pulled José aside, asking, "Weren't we going fight these guys? I was ready to take them all on," to which Carrasco responded, "Victor, there's one thing inside and there's another thing outside." At that time, "I couldn't understand that, but it's been very vividly in my mind—that was my first political meeting and it opened my eyes."

Garza dealt with immigration issues, focusing on the American GI Forum efforts when they took a position against Governor Pete Wilson's immigration initiative—Proposition 187. In strong opposition to the notion that "sons or daughters born of illegal immigrants in this country should be deported as anyone born here is an American citizen," "we sent a very heavy letter to the governor on the behalf of the GI Forum, and a dear friend of mine employed by the governor responded, blasting me" and the organization. Garza assumed that his friend had "taken the position that the governor is doing everything right, or possible, to be able to deal with immigrants," but Garza didn't know "whether I had lost a friend or whether this person is in essence only trying to convey that we should do more research before we write a letter, or open our mouths."

Not a stranger to conflict, in his work with the community Garza learned that it was not only about political power, as he quickly realized that his involvement caused political tensions. For example, in the case of SER (Service Employment Redevelopment) Jobs for Progress, Garza recalled being told to "not touch the problem . . . even with about 300 or 400 people, there were two or three who were speaking to close the program because of the negative publicity." Interested in bringing the issue to a conclusion, "to give the money to another program that would provide the same services as this organization," but more than anything "to stop negative things about Chicanos," Garza took a position to "close the program, providing information to back up that position; the Board of Supervisors felt the information reliable, and funds were given to CTC and CET." That stopped the controversy. Rose Amador was among those who supported Garza. "She was right there with me, and when you get involved on issues that are controversial—that make your stomach tie up in knots and lose sleep—yet, you develop a closeness, a relationship, a bond that no one can break and we continued to work together."

One of the co-founders of La Raza Roundtable, Victor Garza was involved with many issues concerning Raza, such as "the selection of a new police chief when Chief McNamara had to move on, trying to address [the] issue we were looking at, not for

FIGURE 20 Victor Garza, at La Raza Roundtable. Courtesy of Rose Amador LeBeau.

him to retire and leave; he was a good chief, but he made one grave mistake on the issue that we were taking him on."

In his view, McNamara was abusing his power in the treatment of Raza subordinates. "Influential Chicanos were on his side, but I was able to organize and get different organizations in the community to support me." This protected Garza: I "wanted to minimize their attack, because as long as it was the GI Forum, and I was the chair . . . the force behind it," their power was neutralized. Among those groups which he organized were "La Raza Lawyers Association, Latino Issues Forum, Chicano Employment Committee, and MACSA—it was six or seven organizations." The positive outcome was that McNamara decided that it was time for him to leave. He left, and "we were fortunate in getting one of our own hired—Lou Covarrubias."

As Garza recalled, the controversy had to do with Ike Hernandez, who was the deputy chief of police, and under his command the department apprehended the ski-masked rapist, who happened to be a Chicano—George Anthony Sanchez.[2] This man had raped many women. Apparently, "Deputy Chief Hernandez made some statements about some figures [numbers of alleged victims], and the chief didn't like it and demoted him." According to Garza, "The community felt that it wasn't right for the chief to demote Hernandez. The important thing was that the ski-mask rapist was captured and the figures could always be corrected. Instead, McNamara chose to attack Hernandez and demote him. We felt that wasn't right. Hernandez was the highest-ranking Hispanic in the police department and we would not sit idly." Those who supported the chief of police began to attack Garza. For that reason, "I got these other people organized, all these organizations, and we dealt with the issue, and I think that it was a great success." All's well that ends well, said Garza: "Ike Hernandez retired, leaving very happy. Chief McNamara left, and he's very happy at Stanford. We got a Chicano chief of police, and we're very happy with him."

As far as educational involvement and mentoring are concerned, Garza was most proud of his activism "with the American GI Forum, Mexican Heritage Corporation, and the ENLACE Program at Evergreen Valley College." He served as the elected president of the California GI Forum, "then, I ran for office at the national level, and got elected." Locally, he vied for the SER board, and won the vice-chair position by five votes; he would become elected to SER national board, serving a five-year term.

Among Chicanas who bridged activist leader endeavors from the Depression to the Baby Boomer Generation, Ernestina García, like Garza, would take on Governor Pete Wilson's immigration campaign. For García and her husband, it was clearly on attack on Mexicans. Still, in her view "even to this day we don't know how to use our numbers to influence those things we believe." García said she was asked in a television interview about Proposition 187. "'Well, what can we do?' I said, 'there's only one thing that we can do, and that is lobby our local Sacramento legislators, get people to make phone calls, and write letters.'" It was clear that "we must have people mobilize against the so-called immigration reform by Governor Pete Wilson," and "those with the strongest voices, or who could articulate the positions in the most effective way, need to reach out." García elaborated: "We ought to have college students, mothers and fathers, people from all walks of life in our community calling their legislators because a phone call can make a difference. Yet, there aren't enough people who are willing to say, 'Hey, I'm upset about what is being proposed and I'm going to let my representatives know about it.'" García learned about Wilson's agenda because her husband, who had long been a registered Republican in order to access the "enemy's agenda" (she herself was the household Democrat, a practice they maintained throughout their marriage), found out about the impending attacks against Raza. Their approach was a useful organizing strategy that served them well in their efforts to focus on policies and politics targeting poor and ethnic minorities.

A second-generation Chicano, Jack Brito, dealt with racism against Mexicans through work. Growing up, his only employment options were in agriculture or packing sheds. Brito dropped out of school when he was fourteen, and rather than continue soliciting work in the downtown streets of San José, he joined the military in 1946. The service inspired him to become involved in improving the lot of his people, working with the farmworker movement as an active Teamster who sought to teach members their rights and offering presentations on health insurance.

Still, for him, education was the central concern in his activism. Brito said, "I did a bit of dabbling with my own kids in the school and the neighbors' kids. When they got in difficulty I would intercede because their parents couldn't or were ashamed, so I'd go set them straight." In the process, "I made some good friends, and they responded quickly, but it was difficult because I thought I was the only one that gave a damn." He said that "the parents were *humildes* and then *avergonzados porque no hablaban muy bien el inglés,* they were humble and ashamed because they didn't speak English." It was in the struggle for education that Brito joined forces with Sofia Mendoza. He met her when she came to his house to visit one of his daughters, Carmen.

Even though he was proud of his activist endeavors, one regret Brito had was that his children grew up in the turbulent time of the 1960s. For him, "it was an unfortunate time for youth." He said, "My kids all are very bright, every one of them reads and writes well. Unfortunately, they got caught in those ugly '60s and '70s, with the Vietnam War, Black Panthers, and drugs, and free love. Most survived it quite well, [but] a couple of them still have some difficulties from those years past." His son Jack was particularly affected. He "went through sixteen years of unstable development at the hands of the state—went into prison at sixteen, and got out at thirty-two," on August 6, 1981. Those personal difficulties and the trauma of his son's incarceration motivated Brito to work for the rights of Chicanos who ended up inside the corrections system.

One of the most influential Chicanos in the community because of his legacy of activism, Brito was a key player in fighting anti-police brutality and a leader in the anti-police protests against the Danny Treviño killing. He had a powerful voice in the community and displayed a deep understanding of the inner workings of the system. He credited his connections, politics, and his work in corrections for the release of his son from prison. He explained, "I could get him out seven years sooner because of key connections. I was a big-shot highway commissioner with the State of California. And, my very dear friend Mario Obledo was director of Health and Welfare and in charge of prisons; he was instrumental in helping me make the right moves. It was Governor Brown, whom I deeply admire, that got Jack out in August of '81."

The arrest of Brito's son was a blow to all the members of the family, but it most adversely affected his mother. But Jack's incarceration lead Brito "to do an awful lot more things that I might have otherwise done, although I was already pointed in that direction." With the philosophy of "*cuidando al projimo, cuidando al más debil,* or taking care of the neighbor, caring for the most fragile, I formed the unification that's so hard for us to come by, to organize." What "Jack went through and put us through made me stronger, not weaker." While he would have liked Jack to have "found another way to gain strength, still I admired him—he committed one heinous and uncondonable infraction, but he did the time." Yet, it was difficult "seeing him from year to year, chronologically getting older, and then coming out at thirty-two thinking that Levi's were still a buck ninety-nine—he had lost all reality." It took "every bit of ten years to get Jack back on square one."

Brito took great pride in the fact that his son finished school during his incarceration. "He did so well, he became one of their instructors." When Jack was released, Brito guided him in the process of finding employment. He took him by the hand, telling him, "You get the paper. Look for the want ads for something that might interest you. Then, just go make an application, and if you do well, you get an interview to get the job." With Brito's support, his son found a job at the Le Baron Hotel as an assistant accountant, a job for which about fifty people had applied. Jack only "lasted ten months; it wasn't what he wanted. Now, as my assistant, he works in my office, and he's the one I leave in charge."

FIGURE 21 Jack Brito. Courtesy of Karl Soltero, from the memorial program.

The work Brito did in the community, with education and the youth authorities as well as police community relations, prepared him to work with convicts; in particular, he helped create options for addicts and those released from prison. Through his involvement Brito learned that "when you know who you are and understand power, change is possible." He clarified, "Just by the nature of the beast, I can call on five supervisors by first name, and about eight of the eleven members of the City Council" to bring about change. For example, Brito mentioned his relationship with Lou Covarrubias, with whom "I go back about forty years. Joe McNamara is one of my dearest friends, along with three or four sheriffs, and the last three or four district attorneys." Brito said he is on a "first-name basis with the power to garner and know who they're dealing with because relating at those levels makes a tremendous, tremendous difference." Still, the incarceration of poor people of color has increased exponentially, which distressed Brito greatly. For example, in 1975, when he began to work in residential facilities for addicts and those coming out of prison, "We had a $365 million budget at the corrections level, and there were 26,000 people in prison. Eighteen years later, there are 137,000 people in prison and the budget is over $2 billion." Most upsetting for him was that there is "money for building more prisons, but we can't do anything in schools." Brito's most ardent wish was to create options of opportunity. "To provide our youngsters alternatives. Show them that they can become captains of their own boats; they can become masters of their ships; they can be the person behind the wooden wheel with the pegs on it that gives direction to their life—we ought to do that."

On this and other issues, Jack Brito contributed a passionate and strong voice. He also mentored many who would take their concerns to the community, especially to address police violence. His one regret was the lack of mentoring. The way Brito saw it, "We're not providing our youngsters with the benefit of a challenging institution where they can gain a core education, so they can look forward to someday becoming self-sustaining, self-sufficient. That's why so many kids grow up *sin oficio*, involved in drugs, involved in gang activities, and some of our smartest youngsters are out at two or three o'clock in the morning tagging some building somewhere." Brito offered that "these youngsters should be up there demanding their rights, as has been the case with the Police Review Board." Chief Lou Covarrubias was against the Police Review Board, having told Brito that "if they come up with a police review board, I'll quit." Obviously, Covarrubias feared losing control of the department, but Brito did not hesitate to remind him that "a committee selected you. We had a committee to select the auditor, and I don't know what that lady's gonna do because she's got no resources, but if you have enough trust in that committee, why don't you make them the Police Review Board?"

In his activism, Brito could disagree with others but still work with them. When Victor Garza led the GI Forum and allowed a cigarette company to underwrite the

Sixteenth of September (Mexican Independence Day) parade, which "totally co-opted what it was all about," Brito took a contrary position. He did not support "a group of people that put on that red, white, and blue hat" to show their patriotism. In his view, what they ought to be doing is making sure "that any time anybody else declared a war, nobody would come. That whole picture that I love that says, 'War is not good for children, people and other living things.'" For him, the GI Forum's patriotism was misguided. "You can't glorify war or celebrate that we kicked the hell out of somebody at the expense of social services money that people need to survive." In that, Brito and Garza found agreement.

CONCLUSION

With a strong sense of justice and a thirst for equality, Chicana and Latino/Chicano activist leaders, as their parents before them, became involved in the schooling and education of their children, taking oversight over the ways in which Raza children were treated and educated. Even though they advanced beyond the educational levels completed by their parents, overcoming the expectations of the time, Chicanas of the Depression Generation were not identified as having the potential to pursue higher education.

Writing about Raza of the Depression Generation in Texas, David Montejano (1987) noted that "in some districts, local policy restricted Mexican children to an elementary education" (192). This was also the case in California. David G. García (2018) found that parent-teacher associations and school districts colluded to segregate Mexicans, whom they perceived as intellectually inferior. White parents and district personnel and administrators supported the notion that it was an "advantage of both races to be separated up to about the eighth grade" (31). Most of those who were part of this generation recalled that the school trained students of Mexican descent to perceive themselves as less competent and not worthy of an education. In Jack Brito's case, the high school refused to let him take algebra, a move that led him to drop out in the tenth grade.

Despite the difficulties they experienced in their everyday lives, these activist leaders understood that segregation and poverty were not their legacy; they did not believe that Mexicans were deficient or inferior. Still, many carried the trauma and pain of the racist and classist treatment they experienced, taking comfort in the knowledge that they challenged mistreatment. While some complied with inane assignments and rote instructions that they perceived as useless, they ultimately left school. Even though they were not treated equally, some activist leaders focused on school success as a strategy for self-valuation, and their families established *escuelitas* sponsored by the community, creating educational options in Spanish. Thus, home and Saturday schools allowed students to learn about their culture, and they gained knowledge of their history and heritage language—a process that, although burdensome for some, empowered them to take pride in themselves and their people.

These spaces of hurt, even for those sheltered by socioeconomic status, served as foundational for creating a more just and equal place for those whose worth as a people were violated. A strategy of survival, from as early as middle school and high school, evolved when Chicanas figured out ways to create sociocultural and organizational venues for inclusion by organizing groups that promoted their culture, such as food drives to aid the needy. Because they had internalized class, race, and gender oppression, these activist leaders created a place and a space to make things better and to improve the lives of their people. Unlike Chicanos/Latinos from this generation, Chicanas who were raised during the Great Depression experienced oppression within the internal dynamics of class and gender intersections in the family. Thus, from early childhood, Chicanas gained a sense of awareness on the ways in which socioeconomic and gendered structures of inequality excluded and marginalized them. Even when they lacked access to education, through their relational interactions they learned oppositional strategies to deal with difference in their everyday surroundings. Chicanas, as gendered individuals—in contrast to Latinos, whom they perceived as entitled and privileged because of gender—would also engage racism. Latinos/Chicanos fought for their peoples' rights by taking up labor struggles and educational rights, activities which Chicanas would later join.

In their own body and through their lived experiences, Chicanas of the 1930s generation in San José understood the ways in which poverty and class, race, and gender shaped their involvement and the ways in which social boundaries limited and constrained their aspirations.

Those of the Baby Boomer Generation (1946–1964) would fight for social justice as they continued to advance in their respective areas of influence and as access to education became more readily available through the Equal Opportunity Education Act of 1965. The act prohibited discrimination against faculty, staff, and students, targeted the racial segregation of students, and required educational institutions to remove obstacles to equal participation. For the Baby Boomer Generation, the Equal Opportunity Act would become

FIGURE 22 José Carrasco at a march. Photo by Jesús Manual Mena Garza.

the equalizer of higher education for Latinos/Chicanos who did not serve in the military, and for Chicanas, who would later gain greater access to education.

Regardless of generation, Chicanas in this study were aware of the gender inequalities they experienced in their family and communities. Some complied with the expectations imposed on them, while others challenged the rules, stepping outside the boundaries of race, class, and gender. Chicanas and Latinos/Chicanos more clearly understood race and class exclusion as they got older and as they interacted with non-Mexicans and those of higher income. Still, when teachers derided and devalued children of Mexican descent, parents created safe and alternative venues where their children learned about Raza.

For most of the women of both generations, involvement in school issues gave access to activism, although not all achieved the same level of prominence. Sofia Mendoza would contribute much to the early education of children in East San José and to the investment of their parents in the education of their children.[3] Others would also work to improve access to higher education and to retain students in colleges and universities. For example, Blanca Alvarado was a strong supporter of Most Holy Trinity Catholic School, for which she raised funds and worked to provide access for those who could not afford to pay. She became active "because it was a new school, it was a new church, and one of the issues that the Chicano parishioners raised almost immediately was the lack of a mass in Spanish." It was through this venue that Alvarado participated in forming "Los Amigos, which in many ways became my extended family through my community involvement." Although the hierarchy did not look too kindly on their endeavors, and "shortly thereafter the Church decided to remove one of the priests that had been very instrumental in our formation," still, as a community they did not sit idly; they took on the Catholic Church to form their organization, as parochial schools became the place where children received a better education.

Chicanas and Latinos/Chicanos of the Baby Boomer Generation would benefit from policy changes and social change brought about by activist leaders from the previous generation. Education and employment in previously restricted spaces—both public and private enterprises—became available: government, media, and secretarial positions and vocational training served as points of entry into politics for Chicanas and Latinos/Chicanos. With these changes, several ran for public office and sought to run for school boards, with Blanca Alvarado becoming the first Chicana being elected to represent District 5, as a result of a successful challenge to the at-large system of voting—a struggle that had been waged and won by activist leaders of both generations. Chicanas and Latinos/Chicanos of the Depression Generation advanced education as a right, not as a privilege, thus opening the gates for Chicanas and Latinos of future generations to pursue an education and to seek employment options not previously available.

6

• • •

SOCIAL CHANGE AMONG THE GENERATIONS
Education and Social Activism

In any endeavor, be mindful about the ways in which you act and treat others. Treat them as you wish to treated. Begin with an understanding that gains are better achieved when you treat others in ways that honor the common good.

—Ethics of activism adopted by San José activist leaders

Chicana/Latino activists set out to create a better world than they had experienced, relying on the lessons they learned at home, premised on the notion that education equips Raza to show their worth to others. Aware that their work for social justice was not for personal gain but to improve the lot of Raza, Sofia Mendoza and Ernestina García, members of the Depression Generation, entered the struggle for social justice from many angles, but education became central to their involvement. In the early 1960s, Mendoza worked with "sixty children and forty-five different families" at the Community Improvement Center (CIC), "teaching mothers how to teach their children . . . teaching them to be better parents." In this endeavor, Mendoza identified their principal objective as

> convincing parents and children—everybody—that intelligence is something that you're born with; it isn't anything somebody gives you. It's something that you already have, and you have to learn how to use it. We were teaching them how to use their intelligence. And, we were teaching the parents that one day shouldn't go by without telling their children how much they loved them, so they could feel secure in knowing that they have this intelligence to learn.

With United People Arriba, Mendoza took on "leadership and assisted organizations with issues like parades because in the '60s there were no cultural activities for Mexican people." In the late 1960s "the Confederación [de la Raza Unida] became very involved in making sure that this city provided cultural events for our people—even though some people said, 'Oh, those are just parades.' But, I think they're very important." Led by high school and college students, the community called for recognition of Mexican holidays, with the Fifth of May taking epic prominence in the community. "The Sixteenth of September should be a bigger celebration," however, because the holiday takes place almost as school begins, "Cinco de Mayo got more prominence." It was during those organizing efforts that the city of San José tried to reactivate the Fiesta de las Rosas Parade, "something that was oppressive to us." This fiesta celebrated the Spanish conquest of Mexico and derided Mexicans with stereotypic images, such as having children and adults dressed in white cotton pants, and peasant shirts with sarapes, cleaning the waste left behind by the horses. Still, there would be many other struggles to take on, particularly in the schools.

As early as the mid-1950s Mendoza began organizing students and parents around issues of racism and mistreatment, supporting students to organize a walkout, which she perceived as one of the most significant undertakings in which she participated. In the early 1960s Mendoza became involved with "Roosevelt Junior High School . . . because, to me, there is nothing more important to our lives and our people than education—I put education above everything else." She added, "At Roosevelt—children were being discriminated"; she relied on "meaningful parent participation . . . so the children could become educated, by empowering the children to bring changes into the school without getting themselves into a lot of trouble." Using a collective approach, "United People Arriba forced thirty-six teachers, principal, and vice principal out of Roosevelt Junior High School because they were very racist." This was only possible with the information collected by Mendoza, who canvassed the community about the treatment children received at school. That was how she learned that "kids were called derogatory racial remarks such as 'taco benders' by teachers." During her organizing work, she met Joaquin "Jack" Brito, the father of Carmen Brito, who attended Roosevelt, and José Carrasco, a teacher who lost his job for standing with the students.

FIGURE 23 Jack Brito and José Carrasco in East San José. Courtesy of José Carrasco.

Jack Brito recalled meeting Mendoza, saying that even though he was involved in his children's schooling, he had not yet met her. "One day, she came to visit. My daughter had some difficulty at Roosevelt Junior

High School, and they had formed a group, with an adviser that happened to be Sofie; she came knocking on the door—that was sometime in the mid-'60s." He was reading the paper, "so I got up and I said, 'Hi,' and, she said, 'Hi, my name is Sofie Mendoza. Does Carmen live here?' I said, 'Yeah, she lives here. Come on in.'" Brito welcomed her into the house, so *se sentaron*, and they were talking and I'm reading the paper *pero todo oyendo*, and with every word she uttered I thought, 'My God, there's another one here.'" After that, Brito and Mendoza joined forces and formed the Community Progress League, with Mendoza as president and Brito as vice president.

When José Carrasco met Mendoza and Brito, he was an organizer for the Council of Churches in San José. That was a time of much excitement and support for the United Farm Workers, a movement, Carrasco point out, where Protestants were initially the ones who "jumped into the *huelga* [strike] because Catholics were told to stay out" by the hierarchy. Carrasco recalled that "when the walkout took place [at school], I took the microphone and told the kids to go home. Later that day I was fired." Soon after, Carrasco and Brito "chatted about what to do and concluded that unless something happens to get the kids to return, to make them understand those problems, staying out would not help." Carrasco met with the principal and gave him an analysis about the "good staff and bad staff, as well as talked to parents." Afterward, Carrasco "went to school and stood in front," urging students to return. He recalled Liz Cordova and Mrs. Crocket, a black teacher, as the strongest supporters and allies of the students.

Thus, in the early struggles for social justice, activist leaders were invested in the education of children. Brito recalled that in the early 1960s it was "almost a one-man fight when no one else gives a damn." With a passion for righting the wrongs they were witnessing, Mendoza and Brito, with the Community Progress League, worked to improve Roosevelt. Among their major accomplishments was "getting rid of the tracking system that had all the Chicanitos in the Z Group, and made improvements all around in faculty and administration, adding a new cafeteria." Sadly, "the results of our efforts didn't fare too well nowadays because Roosevelt is gone, but the cafeteria is still there."

In Milpitas, California, Ernestina García and her husband, Tony, became involved in the education of their children when they moved to town in 1967 and enrolled their children in public school. Because there was no parochial option, her children "*tuvieron que ir a la pública, y de allí es donde empezamos a meternos*—went to public school and it was there that we became involved." Their objective was to remain invested and involved parents, with Ernestina having been delegated the job of dealing with the institution. Her daughter Doreen told her mother about how the students were treated, and her mother made it a point to visit the school. García recalled, "*Andaba en los problemas, y venía, y nos decía, 'Aquí hay mucha gente mala en esta escuela'*—She was getting in trouble, in the middle of things, and was affected by these problems, and she would come and tell us." Doreen began to contemplate dropping out "*porque decía que los trataban mal los maestros—los más chicos*" [because she said that the teachers treated them badly—the younger ones] were not yet in school, Ernestina's oldest daughter and son would raise concerns about the ways they were treated. For example, Ernestina recalled when Doreen told her, "*En la escuela tienen unos muchachitos mexicanos que andan dando vuelta levantando papeles con un palo, y cuando llega el muchacho* [At school, they had some young Mexican kids going around, picking papers with a stick, and when the boy got there] José and his brothers, *y otros llegan a la escuela, la maestra les dice* [the teacher told them]: 'Go and pick up papers.' *Él no entendía, y le dije 'dice que levanten papeles'* [He did not understand, so I told him, 'She says to go pick up papers']." Placed in the position of translating for the other children, she brought these concerns to her mother. The day came when Doreen asked to be transferred out of a photography class which she didn't want to take because it failed to advance her goal of becoming a nurse. García recalled her daughter's words: "*Yo quiero que me cambien de la escuela porque me pusieron en* photography *y a mí no me gusta. Yo quiero algo de aprender porque cuando yo crezca quiero ser* nurse. *Pero yo quiero aprender algo y yo no pienso que voy aprender nada en eso de traer la cámara.* [I want you to transfer me from the school because they enrolled me in photography, and I don't like it. I want to learn something that will help me to become the nurse that I want to be.]" Doreen would continue to tell her mother when the teachers discriminated against Mexicans. "*Venía y nos contaba que había mucho racismo porque los maestros discriminaban a los mexicanos*" [Back from school she would tell us that there was a lot of racism because the teachers discriminated against Mexicans]. Soon, Doreen informed her parents that "*los negros quieren formar* [the blacks want to start] a Black Student Union. And, Tony Soto, Danny Soto, and their sister, and Los Vázquez—*que son of Eleonor Vásquez y de Bea Robinson y de José Vásquez—andamos a ver si tenemos a* Chicano Student Union." The Garcías told her they would discuss the formation of a student group as a family. So, they sat with her, and Tony García urged his wife to take on the educational system, suggesting that "*tú vas a tener que ir allá. Yo tengo que trabajar . . . y tú te metes, y cuando haiga juntas . . . los voy apoyar,* but you're going to have to quit to deal with it."

With her husband's support, Ernestina García stopped working to dedicate herself to advocating for the education of their children. She reviewed books: "*Ay que feo nos ponían, 'taba un* poem *y una canción de mexicanos*—it actually said 'greasers.' *Decía yo,* 'They can't be doing this. *¿Cómo nos 'stan poniendo?*'" At the request of her children, she visited the schools. There, García approached students and gathered information on their families.

"*¿Qué andan haciendo?* What are you doing?" *Me dijo, "es part of the school*—it's part of the school" and, so, I said, "*¿Y dónde vives?* Where do you live?" *Ya me había dicho que*

FIGURE 24 Tony and Ernestina García at a MACSA dinner. Courtesy of Doreen Garcia Nevel.

eran Aranda—he had already told me that he was an Aranda. So, I got his address and *el nombre de la mamá y el papá.* So, I went to their house and I found—*el papá no estaba—la señora, y le dije, "Miré . . . ¿Sabe qué ha dicho mi muchacha?" Dice, "Pos, sí. Es los que los ponen hacer, pero pos ¿qué vamos hacer?"* [I went to their house and found out that the father was not there. So, I spoke to the woman and told her, "Look, do you know what my girl told me?" She said, "Well, yes. That's what they put them do to, so what are we going to do?"]

García visited the school counselor to see about her daughter's schedule. *"So, fui. Me senté. Callada, y oí lo que estaban discutiendo."* She accompanied her daughter and sat with her daughter and the counselor. Silently, she sat and listened to their conversation. When Doreen said, "My mother doesn't like it either," the counselor, ignoring

García, instructed Doreen to "tell your mother that this would be good for your future education. Tell your mother that photography is good for you because when you get out of school, you could get a good job working in the cocktail lounge, taking pictures in these clubs and make good money. You could be one of the photographers who could get a job like that." Unable to hold back, García said, "Repeat that again?" The counselor ignored her, but García continued, "You think we are low-down people that we're going to let our daughter go to bars and night clubs? Is that what you think of us Mexican people?" It was not García's intent to put down the work, so she added, "People who go into those places to take pictures, they do it out of necessity, because they have a job to do, and they get paid. They're not low-down people, but that is not the kind of a job I want for my daughter." The counselor retorted, "No, no, that's not so. I have a friend of a friend who has told me that Poncita works there and makes a lot of money." Out of patience by now, and intent on making her point, García asserted, "My daughter is as good as the rest of the people and even better, and for that reason, you're going to put her into an academic track because that is what she deserves, and you're going to change things." Unhappy with the counselor's response, García complained about the ways in which the school treated the students. "Kids out there are picking up paper," warning the counselor "to do something about that, too."

With teary eyes, García called on her own schooling traumas to expose the legacy of institutional racism. She expressed her anger, *"De lo que nos hicieron a nosotros cuando yo estaba chica en las escuelas*—what they used to do when we were children in school." The counselor got scared and called the principal, who rushed to her and asked, "What seems to be the trouble?" Undermining Ernestina's concerns, the counselor said, "Well, Mrs. García over here, I can't make heads or tails [of what she says or] make her understand, and she's trying to tell me what my job is supposed to be." In support of the counselor, the principal said, "Mrs. García, you have to understand that this is a school. This is for the education of your daughter and for the good of the school, and for the good of your family."

Unhappy with his response, García asked the principal to transfer the counselor, to which he replied. "We're going to look into it." I said, "No, you're going to do it now." Before long and to her relief, "the school moved the counselor—*pos la cambiaron,*" they transferred her. García put the principal on notice about "what they did with Mexicans—*donde metían al mexicano a coser y a cocinar, a la cafetería a lavar platos, y ayudarle a la maestra a cortar lechuga*—making them sew and cook, wash dishes, and help the teacher cut the lettuce." Other concerns she listed included "putting boys into sports, and *al mexicano no lo ponían aprender cosas que les va ayudar más adelante, sino que en lo más mínimo que aprendan.*" García reiterated her concern that Mexican children were not instructed in topics that would help them later in life, but instead they were taught subjects that would not be very useful.

In this way, the García family fought for the rights of students in their community. Their efforts would continue with the formation of a Chicano Student Union, *"los estudiantes formaron su Chicano Student Union,"* and the parents organized *"el Comité Pro-Estudiantil,"* the Pro-Student Committee, because *"había problemas y no conocía a nadie,* there was no group there" to advocate for Chicano students and their families, and there were problems and the parents knew no one there. Soon after, García and her husband asked the Mexican American Political Association (MAPA) for political support on the educational issues they were confronting. They found themselves participating in the Fiesta de las Rosas demonstration and became involved with La Confederación de la Raza Unida, continuing to tackle educational inequalities in surroundings areas.

García recalled their first MAPA meeting: "MAPA was on East Santa Clara Street, *estaba donde la oficina de Lino López*—where Lino López's office was located—the old beginning of MACSA." For the Garcías, it felt good to be there, *"porque había puras caras mexicanas*—because there were only Mexican faces." Their concerns were listened to, and they were sent to Dr. Cabrera, to whom "I explained *lo que estaba pasando, entonces mi esposo y* what was happening, then I told my husband and . . . we joined MAPA." Through those meetings, the couple would expand their involvement to other issues. It was then that Ernestina García met Raquel Silva, Sofie Mendoza, Rudy Madrid, Jack Brito, and Jack Ibarra. After every meeting, García returned home and shared the information with her husband, *"Y, mi esposo y yo pensábamos*—my husband and I thought: 'Ay, que radicals.' . . . *Que revoltosos, como les gusta el barullo, como son averiguados. Porque unos gritos que se oían en las juntas;* we were not used to that—*en la iglesia,* at the church, the meetings were very quiet." García and her husband believed those involved to be rabble-rousers who liked to make trouble and create discord. In the meetings, husband and wife thought their shouts were too loud.

As they had planned, García continued as a full-time activist and organizer, with her husband joining when possible. Initially intimidated, *"andaba rezando 'Diosito, ayúdanos.'* I was praying, 'God, help us.'" During the Fiesta de las Rosas, she expressed concern that the city was wasting funds on parades when *"la pobreza que estaba feo— calles sin cemento y debían de usar el dinero para mejorar el pueblo, instead of celebrando los conquistadores . . .* poverty was ugly, unpaved streets for which they should use the money to improve the city, rather than celebrating the conquerors." Still, in support of community activism, the Garcías went to the parade. *"Cuando ibamos llegado fuimos y nos metimos con los que iban a marchar*—when we arrived, we got in line with those who were marching." She recalled that *"there were policías en carros y* motorcycles, *en caballo, andando*—it was terrible; *lo que estaba mirando,* it was horrible."

That was in 1968 and *"empezaron a pushar los policías y nosotros nos pusharon*—the police began to push people out of the way and they pushed us." Then,

allí enfrente agarraron—no conocimos a mucha gente—a Sal Candelaria, y lo tiraron al suelo
entre un bonche de policías. Lo agarraron como si fuera algo que se les iba a escapar, you know,
arriba de él, y lo agarraron en un paddy wagon *y lo echaron* (she demonstrates how one
throws a sack of something) *pas, ¡tómala!* [They got in the front—we did not know many
people—Sal Candelaria, and a bunch of policemen threw him on the ground. They got
him as if he were something that was going to escape, on top of him, and they threw him
into the paddy wagon like a sack of potatoes.]

For García, such actions were reminiscent of a police state, like those documenta-
ries *"donde entraron los alemanes con el palo en la mano y todo,* like a scene of Gestapos,
'tubo feo, feo." She compared their action to those of German Gestapos armed with their
clubs and all. When it was over, those involved gathered in an open field where the
city was building the Center of the Performing Arts. There, they were asked to attend
"a meeting over at the Guadalupe Church in the Eastside—*en la iglesia."* That was the
beginning of La Confederación de la Raza Unida.[1]

Her involvement in education continued, and whenever García attended meetings,
"we shared *lo que estaba corriendo en* Milpitas," and others would bring information
about "*los chavalos en* Roosevelt, Buchser, Mountain View, Palo Alto, and Gilroy; *por*
donde quiera estaban sucediendo cosas, things were happening everywhere." With a good
neighborhood network or *"los mitotes del barrio*—because it doesn't matter where you
live, you're still part of that barrio . . . , if you haven't forgotten *donde está Sal Si Puedes,*
o si no vives en Decoto, o donde hay Raza, if you have that network and barrio mentality
you're going to find out what happened."

The movement spread, and at Milpitas "we went after the teachers and the principal. They had to apologize to everybody; the school had to apologize." *La Palabra*
newspaper was started; "it was the first newspaper in the *movimiento.*[2] *Allí* is where
you could see that we had that network *para el pueblo*—Fiesta de las Rosas, Chargin."
Then, in Milpitas "we went further—demanded they hire more Chicanos—and Pat
Vásquez was hired as a liaison. He didn't have to work in construction, so that helped
him, he opened the doors, and then I started getting into *comités de la escuela* or school
committees." The parents took on the school for selling Lays Potato Chip products,
since "the Frito Bandito was used to put Mexicans down—we wanted the school to
pass a resolution to take the Frito Bandito out." Milpitas was the first such place in the
nation to pass a resolution banning their sale. Things would become more intense,
and "Milpitas walked out around the same time as Los Angeles because—even *de allá*
había noticias que la Samuel Ayer High School walked out."

In community and school meetings, García continued to observe the *"política, pero*
mi esposo sabía un poco más de esto porque él estaba en la unión, pero yo no sabía ni papa
e íbamos a las juntas de MAPA y oía yo que decían, 'Let's table this.'" One day with her

husband there, García looked under the table. *"Veía que ponían abajo de la mesa,"* she thought they placed something underneath the table and leaned down to see what it was, but her husband explained, "Let's table it *quiere decir que lo van a dejar en paz."* She wondered why they did not say it outright, instead of "let's table it." Meeting by meeting, García learned the organizational culture of Robert's Rules of Order. She became so adept at the rules that she created a story to teach others about them.

> *Este era un grupo de gringos. Entre ellos estaba Robert y el otro se apellidaba Rules. Se agar-*
> *raron y hubo un barullo de la fregada y entonces para que no hubiera barullos allí resultaron*
> *los Robert Rules of Order pa' controlar a Rules y a Robert.* [It was a group of Anglos. Among
> them there was a Robert and another whose last name was Rules. They got it on and there
> was a heavy fight and then, so there were no conflicts there, they came up with Robert
> Rules of Order to control Rules and Robert.] *Para limitar el conflicto y para que no se*
> *agarraran todo el tiempo, sacaron las Robert Rules of Order.* [To minimize the conflict and
> to control time spent on issues, they drew up the Robert's Rules of Order.]

In this way, García incorporated and instructed others in a process that was foreign to her. In her view, *"El mexicano sabe llevarse, no necesita eso, puede llevar las cosas bien. Nosotros sabemos portarnos como la gente y hacer las cosas en orden."* [Mexican people know how to get along, they do not need that, they know how to act. We know how to behave like people, do things the proper way.] To bridge institutional cultures, García learned the rules, advising her children and their friends to build their nascent organizations. *"Poco a poquito aprendí, y así enseñé a mi hija y a los muchachos,* and taught my daughter and the boys what to do. 'Mira, write this letter. We're going to take it to the *casa de* Mr. Houts, the principal.'" In her view, the people in power tended to listen to educated types, and García wanted to ensure their concerns were equally valued.

In her senior year, just before graduation and without any hint about a problem, Samuel Ayer High School expelled Doreen. Excuses were given for the expulsion, including the unauthorized "use of a copy machine, and *libros de la escuela no devueltos*—books that were not returned to school." The family went to "Legal Aid and my daughter sued." Ernestina had to sign because Doreen was a minor, but she won her case. "They had to give her $15,000 dollars." Ernestina says it was not about the money, "it was the principle of the thing *porque* how could you go and not graduate someone for such things?"

She recalled, "With El Comité Pro-Estudiantil, I went after those who discriminated and the more you would dig, the more you would find." She spoke about *"un hijo del señor Mercado"* who brought up an issue with the yearbook whereby students who did not have their pictures taken were mocked. As García recalled: *"A los mexicanitos que no les tomaron retratos—*Mexicans who were not photographed rather than *dejarle* blank—*pusieron un mexicano dormido bajo un nopal y su sombrerito que decía*—they placed a Mexican sleeping under a cactus, with a caption that read: 'Asleep again?'"

This was but one case where she challenged the unequal treatment of Mexicans. Other organizations in the community that excluded Mexicans would also become subject to scrutiny. For example, since "Elks discriminate against minorities, we took on the Elks and Elkettes who held their meetings at Murphy School. *La señora Vásquez y yo decidimos ir a la junta.*" Conceiving of their visit as research, the two women went to investigate.

> So, we went. Didn't know what to expect. But, we went after it started—the room *estaba lleno de puras gringas*—a room full of white women. We entered and sat. The Elkettes looked at each other, and at us, but kept on with their meeting. Again, they look at each other, and looked at us. Finally, *una paró de hablar*—their curiosity was killing them— and said, "Excuse me, would you introduce yourselves. This is a meeting of the Elkettes. We don't know you."

Surprised that "they were kind of hinting it politely," García said, "I'm sure they were just as scared of us as we were of them, but we responded: 'I'm Ernestina García, and I'm Louise Vásquez.'" To which the self-assigned spokesperson said: "Excuse us, but what are you doing here? This is the Elkettes." García said, "We're looking for a meeting that's taking place for Chicanas." "No. Never heard of it. What is that?" an Elkette responded. "What are you all about?" Not waiting for a response, García asked, "How do you join? We'd like to join." Someone answered, "I'm sorry, there's no way you can join, your husband has to be an Elk." Pretending to be clueless and trying to gather as much information as they could, García asked for a contact number. "Well, could you give us the phone number where we could call to join? I'm sure my husband would like to join." Vásquez chimed in, "Oh, especially my husband; he is never home. He's always out meeting here and meeting there."

With the information in hand, each woman called the number several times, until a man finally answered. García asked for "application forms because my husband wants to join," and Vásquez inquired about the status of an application that had never been submitted. That was when the question of nationality arose. "I'm sorry, but what is his nationality?" García replied, "He's Spanish and I'm Mexican," to which the man on the other side replied: "Well, I'm sorry. We don't admit Spanish or Mexicans or Chinese or Blacks or Japanese," ending with an emphatic "that's the rules; we won't allow any minorities."

García and Vásquez took the issue to the school board, requesting that they terminate their agreement and to "*que los echen fuera*—to remove them from the premises." Before the meeting, they spoke to the principal to warn him that "*si no los echan fuera, en la noche venimos a la junta,* and we're going to come with a lot of people de San José—*con todos los que andábamos corriendo*—if you want problems, you're going to find them."

At the school board meeting, the Elkettes showed that they had no clue about who had lodged a complaint. The principal told them, "I've gotten complaints from different people." The media were there. García recalled that "on the school board there were three Elks, *por eso tenían la escuela controlada*—*no les pareció*—that's why they controlled the school—they didn't like it. The principal said, 'I have had a lot of complaints from the community and people are very upset,' adding, 'I'm afraid that they're right.'" Then, "*dijo la americana,* the Anglo woman said, 'I'd like to know who complained on us?'" She added, "There were two strange women that wanted to join the Elkettes; I supposed they reported us." García heard "Mexicanos saying, 'two strange people, who cares? . . . you're not supposed to discriminate.'" The school terminated their use of the building, "*y los echaron fuera . . .* threw them out." Their efforts led to the Elks opening membership to minority members.

That would not be the end of it. More conflict surfaced when the Elks' board "recruited a Mexican man to do their dirty work." This man took the liberty of calling Ernestina's husband. Tony García reported their conversation to his wife: "'Mr. García, you should whip your wife to give her a lesson. Because that woman is just creating problems. Doesn't she know how to behave? Look at these Americans, one should behave well around them, they have all the money, and know much, they're more advanced and because of them we know much. Not what you wife is doing, creating problems. Tell me, are you a communist or what are you? Because those are all tactics they use.'" Not satisfied with that, the caller chastised the Garcías for their involvement in the community, lecturing Tony Gacía about traditional family values: "*La mujer debe de estar en su casa,* the woman should remain at home," and you should wear "*los pantalones para mandar a* su mujer?" The "Mexican Elk"—so nicknamed by the group—admonished Tony: "*A mi esposa yo la mando que se meta en todo eso; las mujeres deben meterse en estas cosas. Si, por eso está el mundo como está, y por eso hay problemas porque hacen lo que les da la gana con uno.*" [I tell my wife to become involved in all of that, women must become involved in such things. Yes, that's why the world is in such a state, and for that reason there are problems and that's why they do what they want with us.] Mexican Elk did the same thing to Señora Vásquez, to no avail.

"Still, life comes around, and we all pay our debts," García added, explaining that Mexican Elk paid the consequences. "*En la high school, la hija del Mexican Elk conoció al hijo de uno ellos. Se enamoraron y empezaron a noviar.*" [In the high school, the daughter of Mexican Elk met one of our sons. They fell in love and started courting.] Despite their differences, the couple got married. Mexican Elk would see the error of his ways, and he left the Elks, dissatisfied with their treatment.

These activist leaders also "had problems with the GI Forum, *cuando le mandaron una carta al superintendent y al principal de la escuela, y al* school board *diciéndoles que no nos hicieran caso cuando íbamos a las juntas,* that we were not like them" [when they sent a letter to the superintendent and the principal of the school, ... telling them to not listen when we went to the meetings]. Considered a lesser class of *"mexicanos que éramos barullentos*—that we were rabble-rousers. However, *el principal de la escuela,* instead of going along with them, showed us the letters and gave us copies—*eran carajos*—they were ruthless." The organization's classism failed to deter those in the Comité Pro-Estudiantil from doing what was in the best interest of their community.

Among members of the comité, "we would discuss *entre nosotros* what we were going to do. Soon, we pushed to get the Cinco de Mayo as a holiday for the school." Toward that end, "we met with the school principal and the superintendent, and we asked for two holidays—Martin Luther King had his holiday, Washington had his—we want two holidays for Mexican Americans, Dieciséis de Septiembre, and Cinco de Mayo." The powers that be did not approve "Dieciséis de Septiembre because school is just starting. Let's go for the Cinco de Mayo." Still, there were "Mexicanos resisting it, you know, our own people—*que* it belongs in *México no aquí*—*este país es de los americanos y este país no tiene que ver con México,*" reminding the parents that this was not Mexico, emphasizing that this nation is for Americans and that it has nothing to do with Mexico. Despite their resistance, "Milpitas became the first city in California to recognize the Cinco de Mayo, and it's the only one where it's recognized as a holiday; it's not a city holiday but it's a school holiday, every year the school closes. It's something to be proud about."[3]

Although their efforts yielded various victories in the community and the school, the comité did not win all its struggles, as was the case with the members of the right-wing, anticommunist John Birch Society. "*Andábamos corriendo* to get things done in various cities, and in Mountain View, *los* Birchers—*traían mexicanos*—*usando siempre a nuestra gente,* always using our people—*que iban hablar against the huelga* who were speaking against the *huelga.*" Because of her organizing, García was the target of their violence. "*Empezó a hablar contra César Chávez, contra la huelga, contra todos los que andábamos envueltos en el movimiento*—*que éramos communistas*—he began talking against César Chávez, against the struggle, against all of us who were involved in the movement, trouble makers, we were out to bring the government down—the American government *y feo que estaba hablando el hombre allí*—that we were communists. And I couldn't control myself."

So, at a meeting, García spoke, mixing Spanish and English. "The man didn't like it—*al hombre no le pareció,*" and one of the Birchers hit her on the head. Security "went up to him *y quiso hacerse vivo,* he tried to act smart, *y lo arrestaron,* and they arrested him." She pressed charges and went to court, "but the district attorney *decidió* to drop the charges, as they didn't want this to be a political thing, because it would benefit César Chávez, and *la huelga*." The case was decided in favor of the Bircher, turning the issue into one against the farmworkers—"*en el* jury—they were all Anglos—*eran puros gringos*," but "we managed to get something *porque*" at least they fined him.

Among her many involvements, and because of her passionate commitment to Raza, García led La Confederación de la Raza Unida and was responsible for filing multiple lawsuits against employment discrimination and for educational rights against various deparments in city, county, and state agencies, and educational entities. García had to put her activism on pause to tend to her frail and elderly parents, but after they passed, García returned to organize on health issues, voting rights, immigration, and educational and language rights.

Others were involved in the struggle for educational rights. José Carrasco worked as an organizer for the town of Alviso, East San José, and other poor communities, a job that gave him great pleasure. So much so that when he went into teaching, "it hit me between the eyes" that it was "something I was stuck with, and then, I was at Roosevelt, I left organizing to be the best English teacher. And I was." It would be a student walkout at Roosevelt that would reignite the passion and inspiration Carrasco experienced as an organizer.[4] He felt alive in the struggle: "When that walkout took place, I found myself alive. I hadn't felt that way for a long time. And although I enjoyed the classroom, it wasn't so much excitement as the final sense of satisfaction about what was happening with the walkout. I found myself fed and nourished, and my instincts were alive again—it was like eating chili." Inspired by the social movement that had begun with student and community support, "at Roosevelt Junior High School, when I walked out in support of the kids, I crossed the line, and I realized that certain motions and principles were more powerful than the circumstances." He was partaking in a revolutionary act, yet Carrasco felt conflicted because "I had just walked out, and my job as a teacher was gone. In my mind, it was all over. I had made a choice to be part of a situation where people who were paid nothing were ready to go ahead and entice these kids . . . nonstudents would be in control, I couldn't let that happen." Carrasco took action, "and in a matter of a moment I was leading them. It was one of those strange things."

Carrasco met Jack Brito and Sofia Mendoza, key figures in this struggle, in 1964–65 when he was organizing in Alviso and San José for the Council of Churches. After he was fired from his teaching job for having participated in the walkout, Carrasco found allies both in and outside the community. There were educational administrators and parents supporting him, and "it was because of Sofie, Jack, and some other parents that I was rehired by the district and offered an opportunity to stay at Roosevelt. But, the superintendent—through the advocacy of Bill Doyle, who came to like me and worked very closely with Chicanos—had other ideas."

Soon, Carrasco found himself working "to develop some way of communicating with parents, and I put together what would eventually become known as 'resource teacher positions' because teachers never respected the word 'liaison.'" As a community resource teacher, Carrasco would "report to the superintendent once a week." At their meetings, Carrasco shared information that would help the superintendent make decisions. "My job was to provide the district with information about things that were occurring or not occurring and enough information to clarify what they needed to do. And, at the same time, without compromising individuals and even activities that might be planned, I provided information." Thus, for a year, Carrasco documented everything he did and even recorded what he thought. He carried a recorder everywhere. "I taped my personal conversations when driving, and I would have them transcribed by one of the secretaries in Doyle's office, which would go to the superintendent, with a copy to me. Much was strictly philosophy, I mean about institutions and how they were, about my views of the children, among other things. After a year or so, I told the superintendent he needed to hire some new people."

All along, additional staff lines were requested, but denied because of the lack of financial resources. Tired of asking for things that were refused, Carrasco decided to leave. Past experience made him believe that he would be the only one hired, having learned "that if you were Chicano, they kept you contained by not hiring or keeping Chicanos in positions, working them hard, and appealing to their sense of duty." For the district, it was a type of political manipulation, especially when they claimed "that we cannot do without you if you leave. What's going to happen to the parents?" Despite becoming a pathbreaker in education, Carrasco resigned. It would be the second time he was out of a job. At his regularly scheduled meeting with the superintendent, Carrasco "let him know how unfortunate it was that I was going to be resigning and wouldn't be seeing him anymore." As Carrasco walked away, the superintendent said, "Well, let's meet again because we can talk about this," to which Carrasco responded, "Sorry, I've already decided."

Educational rights would also inspire Jack Brito, who had become a close ally of Carrasco and Mendoza. Brito worked with the "Community Improvement Center on the Eastside, working mostly with youngsters and against the atrocities of juvenile police, and the California Youth Authority," a path that would later lead him to corrections to deal with issues confronting Raza communities. Brito recalled, "We jumped to organize La Confederación de la Raza Unida; it made for some true representation because it was in fact a group of active organizations that maybe had one or two active members but created an awful lot of power, which was formed outside the Guadalupe Church building because the guy with the key didn't show up."

La Confederación emerged out of Carrasco's organizing efforts, as the idea came up in a meeting with Lenny Fierro, a Chicano activist, in San Diego. Those who participated in the early discussions included Eddie Ramirez, José Villa, Humberto Garza, Jesus Reyna, Jack's brother, and Mario Obledo. They would incorporate an organization premised on historical and cultural presence and their respective specializations. Carrasco added, "Fiesta de la Rosas was already underway, and a meeting had been planned at St. Patrick's Seminary." However, in the process of doing the work, Jack Ibarra ascended into leadership, with José Vasquez as vice president. An autocratic leader, Ibarra did not allow for anyone to say or do anything, and because José Vasquez's daughter was in middle school, "they pushed Vasquez and Diaz to do the lawsuit centering on boundaries."[5]

Brito, like Carrasco before him, was employed by "San José Unified [School District] to stay for just a year to initiate some of the classes that we needed to open up to Chicano teachers—both male and female—and wound up staying three." In that position, Brito closely worked with the superintendent to improve conditions, then he moved on to San José High. There, he set out to educate the superintendent about the San José community and its needs.

Brito said, "I took Charles Knight, who was then superintendent, to City Hall and introduced him to Mayor Norm Mineta, and although they were both San José-born, they didn't know each other." Then Brito "took Superintendent Knight to Williams Street Park to show him why Olinder Elementary couldn't be built back in the same space because of the Silver Creek Fault." Brito suggested they build the school at Williams Street Park, to which the superintendent responded, "I don't think we can do that. Can we?" Brito retorted, "I don't know, but we can sure try." They went to Mayor Mineta, and "I explained what we wanted." The trade-off would be Roosevelt Park for Williams Street, "and we'll have a park for the kids so they don't have to cross the street on the other side and we'll have a park and school over here." Brito met with "the city manager and people in administration, and later with the director of parks and recreation." To build this school, Jack Brito "wrote the ballot measure."

At Roosevelt, Sofie Mendoza recalled, after "we got rid of all those teachers," housing issues emerged. There were "the 193 units of affordable housing that we were going to turn into a co-op—Tierra Nuestra," which failed to materialize. But there were other projects that would be accomplished. For example, among the work carried out by La Confederación was the drive to improve health services in the Eastside. "We got the clinic in East San José—East Valley Medical Clinic." Mendoza was one of the co-founders of the Community Alert Patrol, an organization that monitored the police. "We dealt with a lot of issues; whatever came up and when it was time to go to the City Council, the Board of Supervisors, Jack Ibarra would call all the other organizations, and so everybody from the other organizations supported us. In marches, we had many marches through downtown, marches to expose what was happening in Vietnam—a lot of marches around that issue."

With a coalitional approach to improving the daily life of the citizens of San José, Sofia Mendoza became involved in education at all levels, including early childhood education and day care services, cultural and political life, and alternatives venues to include Raza in the decision-making processes at city and county levels, particularly police community relations. To deal with the many ways in which violence was perpetrated against Raza, Mendoza also worked with the Committee on Public Safety of La Confederación de la Raza Unida and took on the San José Police and Santa Clara County Sheriff Departments.

POLICE COMMUNITY RELATIONS

Sofia Mendoza spoke about the philosophy that drove her work with Community Alert Patrol. "We were teaching people that they don't have to be victims of the cops, teaching them how to do it in a way that was going to create permanent change." As had been the case with affordable housing, where they taught tenants their rights as the organizing principle, Mendoza expanded her efforts not only to "teaching people in the community—but also instructing the city on how to do it right—as a teacher and change agent." A co-founder of CAP, Mendoza said, "we started between 1964

and 1965, but the organization didn't come to be until the late '60s. It took us years. It was easier to organize in schools because it affected our children and our future, but the issues of CAP didn't affect everybody."

Mendoza and José Villa would develop a lifelong collaboration for Raza rights. Villa, who was initially hired to establish the Mexican American Graduate Studies (MAGS) program at San José State, spoke about his involvement in the work against police brutality. This eventually became a source of trauma for him, especially because he

FIGURE 25 Sofia Mendoza talking about the Chicano movement. Courtesy of Karl Soltero, from her memorial program.

neglected his family to organize. He explained, "When I first hit San José, I wasn't home two days in a row. The first year I was here I was really doing my organizing thing, at every damn meeting, at the school district, city council chambers, and board of supervisors, as well as Chicano meetings here, MACSA, casing out the whole community from early morning to late at night, seven days a week." Villa says that it was his wife, Clare, who maintained the family cohesion, cared for the children, and had to make excuses for Villa's absence, as "organizing extracts a terrible amount of time, and energy is taken away from the family, and my family suffered. I suffered." After establishing himself and becoming chair of MAGS at San José State, Villa worked with Ernesto Galarza, a distinguished visiting scholar, during the 1970–71 academic year. "When Galarza hit the campus, he asked to meet with me. He got Chicano students, parents, and teachers to start meeting together in seminars, discussing bilingual education with the idea of institutionalizing it somewhere. He was doing his thing in the bilingual studio lab."

Villa says, "We pushed development of curriculum to where José Carrasco, at that time, started conceptualizing the ISSPA [Instruction for Spanish Speakers in Public Administration] Program, and how to get Chicanos from the community to San José State, and back into the community colleges to become managers." Working with the San José Unified School District introduced Villa to Chuck Knight, "who offered me a job . . . which Ernesto thought was a great idea," because the district "could be the place to institutionalize his concept of bilingual studio laboratories. So, I took that job." Faculty at San José State felt Villa was "abandoning MAGS and the School of Social Work, but the driving reason for my choice was my eight children, and a $14,000 salary that wasn't cutting it; they offered me $21,000." Economic considerations and his association with Galarza inspired Villa to jump ship, and "with [Galarza's] bilingual studio laboratory, we secured funding from Model Cites, and invested in the School of Social Work, developing stipends and programs to train social workers." He was "also was a supervisor of regimental education for San José Unified for twenty downtown schools with mostly Chicano kids." Working in the school district, he created partnerships with the community and San José State. "We developed Project Independence through MACSA—these discussions were initiated before we confronted some of the same problems—Chicano kids need jobs . . . to stay in school, to gain a sense of dignity helping their families with the paying; that issue is always there with large families . . . it was paramount to go in different directions."

While Villa was proud of his contributions to the community and educational institutions, he most valued his work against police violence and the killing of Danny Treviño. In retrospect, that "challenged and extracted the most from me." Those were difficult days; he had to relate to the anger in people and the fear for their communities. Villa elaborated, "On the one hand, the Chicano

FIGURE 26 Clare and José Villa after moving to San José. Courtesy of José Villa.

community was fearful of more police killings, and the police were fearful of going into the Chicano community." "I was able to step into a fearful setting to bring some good into a lot of chaos, a very chaotic situation—a lot of latent anger." Villa believed that "San José could have gone up very easily; it could have gone up like Watts, and the fact that it didn't is very historical." He added, "I kept those fires from burning, and contributed in a historical way to maintaining San José from going up in smoke and prevented many Chicanos from getting killed." The community's efforts created a change in leadership.

> Chief of Police Murphy was fired. Joe McNamara was hired, and he was willing to work with the Chicano community, especially with Jack Brito and Sofie Mendoza. And, beyond, it was breaking down the power of the Police Officers Association, shedding the very racist attitudes, even though it was not easy to change those attitudes. At least those racists learned they could not use their positions of authority as cops to screw over the Chicano community. That was the most important contribution.

Those were very intense times for Villa, and he and his family were constantly harassed. Blaring sirens and drive-bys with high beams aimed at their house were but some of the hostilities they experienced from cops.

Throughout his organizing work, Villa learned, "I was able to speak to different elements of the community—to the gringo community or the Chicano communi-ty—I put their leadership on both levels." Villa was recognized for the work he did on behalf of the city of San José when he was identified as one of the movers and shakers in San José in a 1979 study published in the San José *Mercury News*. He was the only Chicano to be recognized, although he was placed on the third tier of article's hierarchy. The writers, Phil Brownstein and Terry Christensen, noted the personal attributes of those who surfaced to the top, but they failed to document Villa's contributions. He remembered, "They didn't say a single word about why I was not on our report, not only did I stop more police killings for a while, or wanton police killings, I did mobilize the Chicano community to recognize its own power, to influence systems over which they had some ownership. That's what they were not willing to recognize." Villa was more than satisfied with the role he played in the Treviño case. Looked back, he felt the work was worth it, *valió la pena*. "[That case] stands out because that was a biggie, not because of Treviño, but in the way the community mobilized itself and gained the support of the broader community and their struggle to set things right. Treviño gained the press, and the case was used to inform the elite about what was going on and helped to bring about a resolution."

In addition, in this case Villa "developed leadership in the community. [People] struck out on their own and became leaders; the most important lesson was that the community assumed ownership of a process that involved more than Chicanos." Their efforts created alliances and made change. "It took more than Chicanos to resolve that issue. And in that process people like Sofie Mendoza became exposed to the ways of the grand jury" and other power spaces; with "all its parts, it's a big system." As the Treviño case evolved, Villa took pride in educating the community, issuing bilingual reports that explained divergent parts of the system. In his view, "Treviño's death was what started people working with other folks and not just in the Chicano sense, or the health and welfare of the Chicano community, when they engaged support from groups other than Chicano." As organizers, we brought "hope to people that they can accomplish something, and community integration." In Villa's perspective, "the idea was not to segregate into one segment of the community in identity, work, or education, but to apply everything for the betterment and in relation to the broader community." He used his own lived experience to make his contributions: "One of the things about me, my wife and I have an integrated household—I've maintained a very strong identity as a Chicano." He added, "Even in Albuquerque and organizing the San José community, I've worked with Mexicanos. I've worked with Braceros. I've worked developing Chicano programs here, with Ernesto Galarza in bilingual education. So, my whole orientation has been for my people—*de mi pueblo, de mi gente, de donde soy yo*. I've never abandoned that, never questioned the strong identity of Mexicanos." It was that strong sense of self and a passion for understanding other people that allowed Villa to thrive when he left to the seminary at thirteen, "right after my mom died." For him, it was his identity as a Chicano that helped him to excel in the seminary; he felt, "I had to shine because I was the only Chicano—the only Mexican—people were looking at me." He carried that belief to his work with the community, "trying to prove that a Mexican person can confront conditions of whatever nature and do something good with it," that's what has motivated him as an activist leader.

Blanca Alvarado, too, was involved in efforts to improve relations with the police. She worked to prevent the San José Police Department from assisting immigration agents in arresting undocumented immigrants, and she supported youth when they were persecuted for their supposed gang-identified attire and forced to complete Field Identification Cards, the document city police complete to cite youth and keep track of them and their activities. The most recent conflict she had to deal with had to do with the "police review versus police auditor approaches to dealing with excessive force, which is what the [city] council decided to do." Alvarado was invested in resolving the conflict because "there was excessive police force, particularly in our community." Alvarado always tried to carve out relationships with allies. She explained, "I haven't always been able to inject myself in a situation. Too often we still hold back, even when we know that we are called upon to speak out. We hold back because we have been denied an opportunity for expressions [and] there is still a degree of inhibition that takes over from time to time."

From a grassroots perspective, after working with the Anti-Bakke struggle against the dismantling of affirmative action in education, Jorge Gonzalez became an immigrant advocate when he co-founded Raza Sí! with his ex-wife, Elisa Marina Alvarado. As Gonzalez thought back, he recalled, "It was 1980 to 1981, initially, we were doing some work with youth—King and Story Roads, there was police brutality—that's a long time ago, Barrios Unidos and all that kind of stuff. And so, but I think my leadership identity started to develop when we started Raza Si!" The organization is composed of monolingual working-class Mexicans and recent immigrants from Central America. Gonzalez's work reaffirmed his cultural roots and also made visible the many possibilities for the children of immigrants. He pointed out that "being Mexican keeps me from getting swallowed up by Anglo culture. What they [members of Raza Si!] get from me is that I've been here for a long time, and I'm bilingual, that kind of exchange that we get, and a sort of example that their kids can go to college too. That their kids could make it—here's one that has done it."

In his advocacy for immigrants, Gonzalez created coalitions. "Raza Si! was a member of Latino Issues Forum, and related to politicians like George Shirakawa or Blanca Alvarado." In his view, "LIF is a group of people trying to do the best they can, within the system, within the limitations of the system; some of them really believe in the system, and some of them are working in the system" to create change and protect citizens' rights. A key strategy in its organizing objectives is for "Raza Si! to engage in dialogue, and collaborate, when possible, and criticize when needed, in positive ways." As they see it, "we expect Raza to assume its rightful place in the society—to be politically strategic." Thus, "we relate to those people that have power, so as to understand their situation, their point of view, what they can deliver to people, given their situation, their reality. What I bring to that situation is that I have been in contact with grassroots people."

His involvement in San José was framed by his previous student activism and his work as a union and cultural organizer in San Diego. Gonzalez participated in the taking over of Chicano Park, where he was part of the top leadership, and or in a supportive role with the Chicano Federation, in the development of the concept of Chicano studies at San Diego State, and in labor organizing with the Hotel Restaurant Workers Union for a couple of years in Santa Barbara, "my first crack at labor organizing. Like everybody, I had supported the farmworkers, but that was my first paid organizing." With Raza Si! Gonzalez and its members collaborated with Justice for Janitors, organized by the Service Employees International Union. The membership assisted and supported on different fronts. "From blocking the expressway, to sitting down talking civilly with an employee negotiating a contract, using all contacts in City Hall, talking to supervisors, the state, the feds when an employer has a federal contract, there are people you can call, writing letters to question, advocating or clarifying issues—that's why we were successful." In addition to working with grassroots organizations, under Gonzalez's leadership Raza Si! has been "active in the Network for Immigrant Rights and Services and developed and collaborated with different organizations such as the Cleaning Up Silicon Valley Coalition."

As an invested citizen, Gonzalez continued to actively pursue a social justice and social change agenda. He worked for the self-determination of Raza communities, considering their needs and challenging the insecurity of those who are the most marginalized members of society as immigrant workers. He was active in private as well as the public spheres to protect the rights of those who are most marginalized, as was the case with Blanca Alvarado, who got her start working with those who relied on social services and employment training.

POLITICAL ACTIVISM AND POLICY ENDEAVORS: BLANCA ALVARADO

As a divorced woman who had assumed the primary responsibility for parenting her children, Blanca Alvarado was working as a tax preparer, and became an eligibility worker for the Santa Clara Country Welfare Department. But she said that she soon "reached a point that I could not be of much help." It was then that the Opportunities Industrialization Center (OIC) hired her as a counselor in the electronics unit. "My life moved from one arena into another, and focused on people and community service." She added that "OIC-CET was probably one of the most important pieces of my life experience," becoming the venue that launched her on a political path.

After leaving the Center for Employment Training, Blanca Alvarado moved from grassroots to political activism with her involvement in MAPA. As president of the local chapter of MAPA, Alvarado gained "hands-on experience in the dynamics of politics in the mid-1970s, when Jerry Brown was governor, and we had tremendous access to him." Through MAPA's work and in collaboration with Governor Brown, "we were able to get Judge Barrera appointed to the bench in Los Angeles, and we had our first State Supreme Court justice." Also, Governor Brown and Justice Rose Bird implemented the Agricultural Labor Relations Board. Those days were very active and successful for Alvarado. With MAPA, she gained a "dynamic voice in the politics of California," and "I learned how to run a campaign, market our candidate, lobby other constituents through local chapters, form coalitions with other chapters. That's when I really understood and learned firsthand how politics really works."

MAPA placed Alvarado in a prominent position. She recalled that, "as chapter president and as a state officer, we had this massive rally at Roosevelt Park with César Chávez—thousands of people—our community, and the leadership of MAPA . . . it was a very successful rally." That event showed her mettle—that was "when I began to surface as a political leader." With that came the realization that making change has to do "with consciousness, which doesn't begin when you're born; I think it is shaped as you go through life." Clearly, Alvarado perceived herself as one with the community: "Even today I have a hard time looking at myself as a vice mayor, member of the city council. I still see myself as part of a movement." While Alvarado does not pinpoint a defining moment in her involvement, there were many firsts for her. For example, she was the first Chicana appointed to "the Bicentennial Commission, first Chicana member of the city council, as well as the first vice mayor. And the first Chicana on the Board of Directors of the League of California Cities," as well as being a member of the Santa Clara County Board of Supervisors.

Alvarado said that previous involvement established the groundwork to win the 1980 election to city council. The politics in which she engaged were complex—race, class, and gender nuanced. Still, she felt "unprepared, having been elected to represent the poorest and the neediest district, one that has been neglected, and one in which it was difficult to know where to begin addressing the layers of problems." On the city council, with a plurality of women, "there was a great deal of bonding and there was a lot of strength in that, because as women we brought an acceptance that we had a place in this organization—it was a feminist council." There were three men, Mayor McEnery, Jim Beall, and Claude Fletcher. "There was no dispute about the dominant forces on this council . . . it was the first time we represented specific districts."[6] In Alvarado's view, this "allowed each one of us the opportunity to be creative and to address issues which were particular to our district." Gender politics were seldom a problem. "Regarding the Chicano community, I can say with a strong degree of certainty that there weren't more Chicanas versus Chicanos that supported or identified with me, so the gender matter was never anything I experienced."

Having drawn the short straw when she was first elected, Alvarado got a two-year term. In her reelection campaign in 1982, Anita Duarte ran against her. Looking back, Alvarado said she "could legitimately point to years of activism in the [campaign] brochures. People had known of my work with other groups in which we were volunteers, and they were there to endorse the campaign." Still, in her first stint on the council, Alvarado felt "totally unprepared," and it was very difficult that, after having served for just a year, she had "to go right back out in '82; it was a tough race with Anita Duarte." Alvarado won the election.

In her capacity as city councilwoman, Alvarado encountered gender differences in the ways in which organizations were run. For example, "the GI Forum does not exclude women, but it is very obviously male dominated." But "the Latino Issues Forum . . . was an equitable organization, and men and women shared leadership." More recently, with the establishment of groups such as the "Hispanic Charity Ball, . . . men and women are at the table making the decisions." In her view, there is not as much machismo and sexism as in the past. When she recalled the organizational strategies of groups such as the Chicano Employment Committee (CEC), "there were women and men, and more men than women, and . . . males still dominated." However, this "is not limited to our culture, it is across the board," even in the Mexican Heritage Corporation. She pointed out that that "there are more men than women and quite frankly I am at the point now of recruiting women to get a balance of gender representation. Because the mariachi festival is the premier public event, it appears to be and is male dominated." After the last mariachi festival, Alvarado raised the issue of inclusion with Pete Carrillo, then president of the Mexican Heritage Corporation. While the men denied the festival's male centricity, "people see it as Pete Carrillo's or Fernando Zazueta's event." There are women on the board, but they "are not visible . . . or acknowledged as being part of the organization—that's going to change; that has been bugging me, we are going to make some major changes soon."

In addition to sociocultural activism, Alvarado's was involved in various political venues. For her, despite her work with the Confederación de la Raza Unida, the Latino Issues Forum was "the political venue with subcommittees on education, housing, and immigration that was functioning." In her analysis, "the Latino Issues Forum would have been the vehicle to bring all the organizations together, so that even if you have people who disagree with each other, there is still an interest in being part of something bigger than oneself. Hopefully that is something to which we are paying attention in the '90s, there is evidence that in the political climate in California we have these linkages and networks addressing the issues." However, even though LIF was "a model of quality leadership, it folded when it ran out of money and steam." Still, according to Alvarado, when it comes to social justice and social change, "there are really great leaders everywhere, we just have to come together." In addition, "the old guard has been doing all the work for the last ten years. We need new people putting these kinds of groups together; the upcoming generation must take off where we are leaving off." She noted, "We've got some good young leadership; it is just a little bit scattered right now." She is hopeful for the emergence of Raza leadership.

As Alvarado looked back, she reflected on the involvement that launched her. "Whether it was in our church organizing efforts or CET or MAPA, those who happened to be part of a group of people were the pioneering [forces] in those institutions." Now, as part of the Mexican Heritage Project, Alvarado takes pride with its emphasis on art, because the project focuses on "cultural nuances of our community, art that historically displays the cultural contributions or the life of Hispanics, whether it is in California or any place in the country, which have been totally overlooked." She pointed out, "We have a tremendous love for art and for culture and we have incredible visual artists as well as performing artists—our poets and our literary writers—they all have great things to say." In her view, "we are writing the history that has been ignored—through our Mexican Heritage Project, through the Plumed Serpent,[7] and through a sculpture commemorating the founding of the pueblo, with the memorialization of Ernesto Galarza."

The one regret expressed by Alvarado was the absence of women's organizations. "Since the Chicana Coalition . . . there absolutely is a void . . . there hasn't been anyone that has spent the time putting together an organization to advance from where the Chicana Coalition left off." She saw "this is a major weakness, because women—we have so many professionals, we have so many outstanding leaders—are out there doing our own thing independent of each other." Historically, before the Chicana Coalition, Las Mujeres de Aztlán, which was affiliated with the Black Berets and was an arm of La Confederación, organized to take on gender issues and sexism in the *movimiento* and community. Also, many women became active and involved in the Chicano Employment Committee, as did Pete Carrillo.

FROM ACTIVISM TO THE INNER SANCTUMS OF POWER: PETE CARRILLO

Pete Carrillo became a key figure in Alvarado's office. She originally met him at the Opportunities Industrialization Center (OIC), which later became the Center for Employment Training (CET).[8] As Carrillo reflected on becoming politically involved, he pointed out that his activism began "in my high school days, and then here in San José." However, "the most formidable time of my development in leadership was through the Chicano Employment Committee." Its mission was to challenge "the City of San José, the county, and the private sector in terms of their employment practices." Carrillo saw himself as "helping lead the organization," recognizing that "I wasn't the only one. There were several leaders, and it was such that it allowed potential leaders to develop, because there were a lot of different activities to engage." Issues that were successful "paved the way for a lot of things—in the police, sheriff, and fire departments." Because of CEC's efforts, "more Chicanos became employed in managerial positions and directly related to things in which I was involved in 1974."

As an employee of CET, Carrillo was not discouraged to work with CEC, "as everybody was involved with some sort of community activity." Given that he dealt with employment issues, Carrillo became "immersed in an area that I felt very strongly about—employment discrimination," which is how he became part of CET, "a preeminent organization in this county that dealt with impactful issues." Involvement with the organization "enabled me to develop my own personal skills, my own leadership development skills; it was something I felt strongly about." For about ten years, Carrillo "was very passionate about employment, and other Chicano rights," and because of his efforts the media "quoted me pretty extensively. And without, on the part of the newspaper, any real regard to any threat that I might pose to them." However, what would be friendly and supportive coverage quickly turned critical. When "I had electoral potential and interests, then the coverage became different, particularly in the 1990s." From that time forward, especially when Carrillo was tapped to become president of the Mexican Heritage Corporation, the newspaper coverage took "a different slant and relied on different standards." He recalled that when he took on the position in 1992, "I had to get an exemption to the revolving-door ordinance from the city council . . . I was in the Local or B section of the *Mercury News* coverage with a goddamn photo on it saying, 'Key Alvarado Aide Gets Exempt.'"

Still, Carrillo's leadership skills facilitated his election to the West Valley Community College District, having demonstrated that he "had the direct ability and opportunity to change policies and the face of the workforce." He was extremely proud of having been able to exercise leadership and to have learned to work with people from various backgrounds: "I could work with a very conservative majority on the board to get Hispanics and other Chicanos/Latinos appointed to positions within the district. I had a direct impact, starting with the chancellor, when we hired Dr. Gustavo Malander, and when we hired Ed Alvarez to be our attorney for our land development deal at Mission College."

Carrillo took much pride in his abilities to influence others, and he perceived his work on the district board as "the single most important accomplishment and leadership role that I've ever undertaken because that gets to the core of my whole existence." During his career, Carrillo clearly understood that "there's always a political solution." He had long concluded that to create change in City Hall or a school district, one needs to negotiate power and influence. He said, "I had a tremendous amount of influence as a layperson, and you get that influence either by having money at your disposal or having the ability to move people. Or, you get on the governing board to make those changes, or on city council, or county board of supervisors."

As he reflected on his tenure as chair of the Subcommittee on Public Employment of the Chicano Employment Committee, nothing was more difficult than running the everyday affairs. He recalled the committee's first meeting, which was held at MACSA: "There were tons and tons of agendas, unbeknownst to me, and all the people who were involved in one form or another with respect to leadership—Al Garza, Jack Brito, Jack Ibarra, Dan Campos, a whole host of other people." Young and ambitious, "I was about twenty-four years old, and didn't know exactly what was going on, but I knew something was going on, there were all kinds of verbal arrows being thrown backwards and forwards and sideways and everything." This turned out to be the most difficult meeting he ever facilitated, and "it was the most emotionally draining and embarrassing time . . . I felt like getting under the table because I didn't have any control. So, after the meeting, by some stroke of luck, as I was leaving, Humberto Garza was sitting there, sort of like in the dark, almost like *Zoot Suit*—El Pachuco—in the back row." Fortunately, Garza "figured out I was embarrassed. So, he asked, 'You want to go and have a cup of coffee?'" They had an extended discussion about the dynamics of the meeting and explored reasons why Carrillo lost control, reaching the conclusion that many contradictions existed among the *veteranos*—enmities, competitions, and dislikes. Still, Garza pointed out to Carrillo that "the major problem was that you didn't have an agenda. You didn't have the tools in front of you to control the meeting." For Carrillo, that meeting "strengthened my own leadership skills, learning to control the agenda, the room, and the different personalities."

In addition to his involvement with other organizations, Carrillo derived much pleasure from his work with California for Fair Representation and "the whole issue of redistricting, dating back to 1981." As he recalled it, that was "one of the most significant efforts" in which he was involved as a leader. He added that "while it did not noticeably manifest in changes, it enabled change to occur. I feel so strongly about the political process, the groundwork that I helped provide leadership on, in terms of laying the foundation in 1981, because it will bring about much needed change."

Carrillo is very proud of the contribution he has made to the city of San José. "However, there are some things in which I played a very key role but didn't get credit because I was working for an elected official." One issue for which Carrillo was given credit was the formation of the "San José Best Program with an antigang and antidrug focus." His most controversial office was the presidency of the Mexican Heritage Corporation (MHC), which was the umbrella effort for creating a Mexican cultural center at King and Alum Rock Avenue, where the Employment Development Department had been housed, and where some mid-level businesses were said to have been displaced, according to activists that criticized MHC as a memorial for Blanca Alvarado.

Among one of those who opposed the project was Felix Alvarez and other Alum Rock School District members, who ran a campaign in the district against it. Carrillo explained, "Alum Rock decided not to participate [and] it caused other things to be delayed. But then I always try to implement what my mother taught me and that is, 'there's always a good that comes out of a bad.' So I've tried to figure out what is the good that has come out of this bad decision." Carrillo was a key player in the creation of this center in the Eastside of San José a project that had been in the imagination not only of Alvarado but also of earlier cultural activists, and he brought the center

FIGURE 27   Pete Carrillo, on the left, with his father, Alberto Carrillo, his son Patrick, and his grandson Christopher Carrillo. Courtesy of Michal Mendoza.

to fruition. In Carrillo's view, those who opposed it did so because they objected to the use of public funding that could have gone to the poor. For Kathy Chavez Napoli, memories of displacement from her Summer Street home drove her to contest public policies that displaced people or created memorials at the expense of marginalized people, such the controversial statue of Thomas Fallon.

FROM SAL SI PUEDES TO POLITICAL POWER: KATHY CHAVEZ NAPOLI

The only activist leader born and raised in San José's Sal Si Puedes barrio, Chavez Napoli witnessed activism growing up. She recalled that "when I would see things, César Chávez and some of the other things, I would support it, but I never organized it." At San José State, her focus was education. "I was a mentor. They had a service called SHARE, and they would link you up with a young elementary school student, and you would mentor them." She recalled not being visible, and "I would never speak to people that I didn't know. My contribution was to get educated, become a teacher, and help teach other kids. That was my goal."

Displacement and its trauma surfaced in her conversation. "I got involved . . . to show my children that they need to look out for themselves, to speak up for themselves, and their community." In her recollections, the Studio Theater issue—when the city wanted to tear down a popular neighborhood venue—came to the forefront, "because I know what it's like to be displaced." She resided in the Eastside community that was razed to build Highway 280, when "there was no such thing as fair market value [compensation], and my father already had a negative experience because he's Native American, and having all their land stolen, and being treated as a noncitizen." Chavez Napoli elaborated, "My father was a carpenter who taught himself everything. We had the nicest house in the street, a four-bedroom house

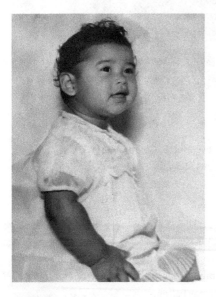

that my father had completely remodeled, and they gave us what everyone else had, and those houses there were thirty to fifty years old, and small, and he went to court to try and fight that, and there was no winning." From a home that was fully paid for, the family relocated to "a two-bedroom house; that's all he could afford, all he ended up with, so that really devastated my father . . . he became an alcoholic, and he never fully recovered."

The Studio Theater became a target issue for her because "it was very close to where my parents live now. They had already destroyed the community—the Guadalupe Auzerais Area—where they put the convention center." Then the city began talking about "extending eminent domain to where my parents live, and I

FIGURE 28 Kathy Chavez Napoli as a baby. Courtesy of Kathy Chavez Napoli.

didn't think they could survive another relocation, another kind of displacement." She asked her parents, "Do you go to that theater?" and when they said yes, she decided to fight back. Confident that she had "some of the skills, and my husband and my business were fairly successful, my children were healthy, I said something because no one was saying anything." No one was involved in this fight. "Nobody said anything. So, I did."

Chavez Napoli took on Mayor Tom McEnery. "Fighting for my parents, from the twenty-some years before—when there was no one there—I really got involved and

FIGURE 29 Kathy Chavez Napoli, on the far right, with her siblings. Courtesy of Kathy Chavez Napoli.

became visible. . . . It wasn't until I had children of my own that I recognized how devastating it had been, and it helped my relationship with my father." It was her involvement that made her appreciate "why he was so against me going to college; he had been betrayed so many times."

Chavez Napoli cut her political teeth when she became involved with the Studio Theater, having served as the president of "the Auto Recyclers Association, four or five times, in a total macho, male-dominated world." With her involvement in the Studio struggle, some people she knew from the Auto Recyclers Association would recognize her leadership, including "my landlord of more than twenty years who came and said, 'I'm really proud of you.'"

A fiscal conservative, Chavez Napoli did not support public agendas that cut into resources that helped the less fortunate, or cases where the city made decisions that adversely impacted them. She took on the powers that be, even when they dismissed her as "a minority woman who dares to speak up, and how dare I?" She brought up the Giants stadium issue (discussed below) to illustrate the ways in which white male power and dirty tricks in San José politics worked. For example, they questioned where she lived, even when there were "six or seven white males who are very influential, extremely wealthy who do not live in San José, but all of those white males want San Joseans to tax themselves." City officials questioned her credentials and interrogated her right to take on those with power, while no one questioned their right to make decisions for the city. According to Chavez Napoli, the media has not been her friend. "None of the media brought up that none lived in San José and didn't pay taxes in the city. Yet, a person like me who has third-generation native San Josean children, went to school in San José, owns property in San José, and maintains residence in San José is questioned. I'm fortunate I maintain two residences, one is in San José, and one is in Coyote Valley—in the county." She has never lived anywhere else but in San José. Still, "they were attacking me on where I lived. When I would go to a debate, when I would go to a meeting, everybody would say, 'Where do you live?' I said, 'Hey, go ask those white males. Don't come bugging me. It's a nonissue." Chavez Napoli pointed out that "the media has labeled me as a rabble-rouser. They use phrases like 'shouting,' and 'complaining,' and 'whining' when we'd bring things up, or 'there goes that Kathy Napoli complaining again.' They don't do that with white people." Other victories she won included defeating "a big, outside company from coming in and competing against the wrecking yards, the placement of the Fallon statue in the Plaza of San José, and the stadium tax."

The first issue she dealt with was in 1986 or 1987 when an "out-of-town [auto] recycler wanted to set up business in San José, they lobbied, and were incredibly political— they artificially created a glut of abandoned cars by paying more than what they were worth, and then they offered to 'clean your mess.'" After four and a half years, "we took it to court and we got neighborhoods to support us against this large out-of-town corporation, and they lost the court battle." Chavez Napoli's first political victory "was hard going all the time, but I'm stubborn, like my father. If you tell me I can't do something it's like saying that I can because I'll prove you wrong." Still, when taking on issues, she would first explore the best approach.

First of all, she does not try to act on her own. Before moving on an issue, Chavez Napoli tries to work within the system. For example, with the Studio Theater, she called Mayor McEnery's office to ask what was going on, but they did not respond. Then, she went to the theater operator to ensure she clearly understood the issue, "because I was reading newspapers, and they asked for her help, to which I replied, 'I'll do whatever I can.'" Interestingly, "all the issues [I've been involved with] have been perceived as a losing battle," but she asserted, "We may not win on this, but we're sure going to fight." Most naysayers, because they perceived McEnery to be "the most powerful mayor that San José has ever had—believe you can't win." Despite warnings, Chavez Napoli took on the struggle. She recalled, "We would meet and we got more and more support, even though it was like a lost cause. We don't care if it's a lost cause, we're still going to try to fight for what's right for this individual, for this community, and we did that on the Studio Theater until we had so much support that the mayor had to back down."

Immediately after winning that struggle, Chavez Napoli said, "I was approached by Javier Salazar; he was concerned about the Fallon statue." She studied the issue and found out "they had not followed procedure. . . . There was no policy for spending public moneys on this . . . pet project of Tom McEnery." Chavez Napoli went after him on policies and procedure, and McEnery had to back down. She says the statute had been but another way to memorialize McEnery by recognizing the "make-believe book on Thomas Fallon, as he was a great admirer, because they shared the same name, and he was Irish."

McEnery would not be the only mayor Chavez Napoli engaged in battle. She would also take on Susan Hammer on building a stadium for the Giants football team—something Chavez Napoli learned about at the mayor's unity breakfast. Once again, following protocol, she investigated the issue. "So, I called her office and asked what was going on, and I didn't get an answer. I went to the community and tried to get information and we did that. We got tremendous support from the community, and we just won with a tremendous margin in the election."

In the issues she takes on, Chavez Napoli's focus is on equality, fairness, and account-ability. She explained, "I was struggling for those issues because of my early experiences in my family where we didn't have a lot of people who would advocate for justice, for equal treatment, for applying the rules equally to everyone without changing the rules as you go along just because you're the wrong color for their standards." What drove her were "the injustices and the lack of equality in being treated by politicians and public agencies." She retold the story about her family displacement, when "we were forced to move out of Sal Si Puedes on Summer Street, when [Highway] 280 came through, no community groups advocated for fair compensation for losing your home, and the reasons that there was nobody there was because it was a poor minority community. The Catholic Church played a very small kind of moral support role, but nothing significant." The message from public entities, including the church, was that people of color do not "belong here and we don't have to pay you what's right. We have so much power and so much money. You're just the wrong color and you speak the wrong language, and so you don't count."

Involved in multiple social change venues, Chavez Napoli was on the board of 4Cs (Community Coordinated Child Care Council) and the Lupus Foundation. She also served on the board of the Alviso Community Organization and was on the task force for the Santa Clara County General Plan Review Committee—a ten-year commit-ment. In her activism, Chavez Napoli challenged those who make and implement pub-lic policies, and instead aimed to create fair and just policies that benefit all, especially Raza and poor communities. This is an approach she shared with Lou Covarrubias. When Covarrubias began his grassroots involvement to bring in and promote Raza into the police department of San José, he went to his base.

FROM THE FIELDS TO CHIEF OF POLICE: LOU COVARRUBIAS

From a rural agricultural background, and as a public servant with decades in the San José Police Department, Lou Covarrubias was the first Chicano to serve as chief of police. He perceived himself as someone who acts on what he believes, and he was instrumental in organizing Mexicano policemen to prepare themselves for promotion. "I was teaching the guys because a lot of Mexicanos weren't getting promoted. So I showed them how to come together as a group, organize themselves, organize the work, and prioritize it, to study the least important things first, and the most import- ant things just before the test. And I gave them homework, and met with them twice a week." With the support of Sofie Mendoza, Covarrubias gained access to the Family Services Association, where he instructed ethnic policemen who desired to advance in their careers. Even earlier, while serving in the military, Covarrubias found himself teaching others. When he left the service, after refusing officers training, he returned to San José, and enrolled at City College. "I did two years, and got my general education, and transferred to San José State, where somebody talked to me about police work. I was competing in judo and had won the Northern California Brown Belt at San José State, and I'd been competing around the Bay Area."

As someone who had always been inclined to help, Covarrubias opted to explore police work "because I wanted to help people, and I could be outside and wouldn't have to sit at a desk job." For the San José Police Department (SJPD), as he did with college, "I applied only to one department, and came out number one on the list. I've always tested well." He pointed out that he has been very successful in reaching number one or two on the applicant pool: "I'm usually one because I can organize my study pretty well, or I'm two because the other person has more seniority points." After he was hired by the SJPD, it took him about three more years to finish college.

To the best of his recollection, Covarrubias was first identified as a leader when he was in the military. "They saw that I was competent in the training that they were giving me. It wasn't long before I was giving directions to the guys in our platoon." He remembered that "they saw that when it came time to getting things down athletically, jumping out of the airplane, planning and packing, and doing all this stuff, I did it competently. So, I was picked because of quiet competence in getting the job done— that's why they picked me."

Now on what he called "the top of the pyramid," Covarrubias had a vision for what was coming his way. For example, after the Rodney King incident he organized his forces. He recounted, "I immediately got ahold of my command staff. I said, 'If we're going to have demonstrations, we'd better prepare for them. I want to make sure we have enough people available to handle them, act with restraint, but be firm. If they start breaking into stores downtown, immediately move in, and make arrests. I want it all videotaped. It'll control their actions and the actions of our officers.'"

The ability to plan and to direct action that protects the community is something valued by Chief Covarrubias. For the community and for him, the priority was community policing, "something to which other people just give lip service." His aim was to do it so well in San José that "other agencies would say, 'You want to find out what it's like, go to San José, because it's happening there.'" In his view, the relational qualities of leadership are central to creating community policing. He said that "when you get to know people and they get to know you, it's hard for them to mistreat you, it's hard for you to mistreat them—these guys are going out to their community, they're meeting with them, they're talking to them, and it's changing the whole attitude." Because of his philosophy in the police department, "my guys sit down with ex-cons. Years ago they never would have sat down with tattooed guys to talk about how to keep kids out of trouble." "Leadership is about bringing both sides together to convince them that this is the way to do the job." What he practices as chief of police came out of the activism he engaged in when working with Lino Lopez at Mexican American Community Services Agency, where he brought youth together "for addressing community and social issues and organizing youth conferences . . . that's where I learned to organize."

Later, his involvement with the Latino Peace Officers Association equipped him to "do special recruiting for minorities, which was very unpopular those days." He learned about other issues firsthand when he served on various boards, including Next Door, a home for battered women. As a Latino, Covarrubias was invested in the Mexican American Command Officers Association, which

FIGURE 30 Lou Covarrubias, chief of police for San José. Courtesy of MACSA.

is a national group. "I've joined different groups where I supported and helped, in terms of leadership in the police department." He added, "I've been instrumental in bringing change, in training that it's more sensitive to the community, and in terms of some of the positions that I've taken, it demonstrates leadership." He focused on the recruitment of gays. "A lot people here were very upset about that and I have received horrible hate mail. But, the bottom line is, I don't care what people think. I felt that it was the right thing to do and so I did it." Another issue was "the Asian mug book—officers were very angry that we gave it up, because we could prove that it was legal, but it was pulled because I felt that it would hurt us with the Vietnamese community."

The most contested situation that he has dealt with was the police review issue. He explained, "I'm not opposed, I just don't want to have that Berkeley model imposed on us, because what they did up there they handcuffed the cops and the cops won't act against a lot of problems because they figure, 'Hey, I can get myself in trouble.' And, you don't want that, you've got to maintain a balance." In his view, the auditor approach was "workable," and he took a strong position against a police review board. Covarrubias explained, "I've looked at them all over, and they're not that effective because the cops can hide stuff—cover for each other—there are a lot of things they can do." The way he saw it, during his administration, he took all complaints seriously. He added, "I've been firing guys left and right to let them know that I mean business, including the officer that cut off that young man's hair, ponytail; I fired three of them immediately because we can't tolerate that kind of stuff. Since then we have not had those deals where they rush into a building and arrest mom and dad and grandma and everybody. We haven't had any of those incidents." Chief Covarrubias tried to take each situation in context, analyzing issues before he acted on them, without stalling or taking too long to make decisions and often opting for the greater good of the community. He said, "I make my decisions based on what I think is the right thing to do . . . I'm not into making *movidas* . . . I'm a straightforward guy." In the final analysis, "I don't play games, so I don't get myself into trouble."

In all the work Covarrubias did for the city and with the community, as chief of police and earlier, he was guided by a "willingness to do the right thing and people recognize that. . . . I try to be fair to people and show concern for them." What guided his work was not the modeling he received at home and among activists in the community, it was "a feeling for other people—concern—so they're not just selfishly thinking about themselves, as I found out, it's just like the Latino Peace Officers Association, either you got it in your *corazón*, your heart, or you don't."

As he looked back, Chief Covarrubias expressed that he "cares about people," guided by "a vision for what I like my job to be," as someone who is "knowledgeable of the work that I do, that I've developed, and the way I've educated and developed myself." Moreover, with "energy and good health, with my communication skills," and as a straightforward person, Covarrubias was not afraid to speak his mind, "although while I may bite my tongue, what you see is what you get—those are factors that have helped me as a leader, and I'm also ambitious." For him, ambition was not something that was counterproductive to his endeavors, since "every good leader is ambitious, and ambition is a part of leadership," but not for self-gain, because "you've got to be ambitious for yourself and for your people."

FROM MIGRANT WORKER TO MENTAL HEALTH ADMINISTRATOR: JOSIE ROMERO

After working in the agricultural fields, and having been married for two years and moving to South Santa Clara County, Josie Romero became employed as a school liaison, becoming "very active in the community of Gilroy." She felt compelled to do this when she noticed injustices or situations where children and youth were not treated equitably. Romero "joined advocacy groups and never stopped." Her involvement in the community was not easy to achieve, since her husband "felt resentful that I was very involved and always being called at home." What helped her was that she and her husband had rotating shifts. "When he was rotating swing and graveyard, I could more freely do things." Still, Romero found herself overcompensating for her absences, with "homemade tortillas with special meals to attend a Wednesday meeting for two hours for a police review meeting." Her husband criticized her for not participating in family events or for not tending to their children. But Romero taught her husband that she "wasn't involved just because I wanted to be away from home, there was a legitimate need," and "to educate him on the issues, I would involve him more and more in discussions." Romero tried to raise her husband's consciousness. For example, "when I was working with César Chávez or the group I would involve [my husband] in situations, so he could see the reasoning behind why people that were educated and spoke English needed to contribute their time to defend and promote equality." Despite her efforts to keep her marital relationship together, Romero planned her exit, "starting when my son was eleven, to prepare myself emotionally." She waited until her youngest child was sixteen to ask for a divorce. She added, "There is less stress and less conflict and less immediate change, I had to buy him off, reduced bills, so I would not disrupt the family, gave him his money—agreed to buy the condo together so he could move in—and then removed my name, and I left him with his condo. Even until then I took care of him." Her marriage ended amicably, and because of their children, Romero maintained a good relationship with her ex-husband. She attributed her ability to make decisions to her family's "promoting confidence, feeling safe, feeling validated, and not having a lot of criticism as to who you are and what you want to become." In her family, she was the only one among her siblings involved in the community. She said, "I have two younger brothers as educated as I am, but they don't get involved, and they don't criticize me for being overinvolved; they respect my space." As Romero saw it, "a leader takes responsibility to advocate for certain issues in that community," which for her includes the church—"*las familias, las agencias que está sirviendo, las escuelas, la vencindad*"—the families, the agencies serving the schools, the neighborhood.

It was when Romero was a migrant worker that she initially noticed gender inequality. "Boys were special and got away without doing certain jobs. Girls did the housework. Roles were clearly different, with the exception that I felt cheated because girls still had to work in the fields." In the labor camp, she became an interpreter and was often called to translate. Translating for a woman who had been abused by her husband, she learned about domestic violence. "I remember being very angry and would always say, 'I would never allow that to happen to me.'" Gender expectations limited with whom she socialized. "If you were a girl visiting another barrio, it was assumed that you were going there to steal the boyfriends, and if you were a boy, they thought you were going to steal girlfriends from someone else, and you weren't very accepted." She and other students also "boycotted the classroom because we didn't have enough books for use."

However, it would be in her work and everyday relationships that she learned "respect for *compromiso*, respect for *valor*, because it's shared—it's the validation that there are other people that believe and feel like me, and their willingness to give, to make a difference." Romero's earliest memory of taking a leadership role was when she was "nineteen and I was working with Levi's doing the hems. There was this supervisor who wasn't satisfied that the quota had not been filled." She recalled, "The production bell rang for us to quit, and the supervisor said we were staying because we had not finished, and I put the scissors down and I went right up to him and I said, 'try to stop me,'" reminding him that the contract stipulated the day ended at five. She walked away saying, "I'll see you tomorrow, and we will talk about it."

Romero did not fear getting fired, and she did what she believed to be the right, when "he could fire me on the spot and probably would've but I caught him more off guard then I expected, in terms of his reaction; he was about forty and I was about nineteen." This was not the only time she confronted injustice on the job. She also witnessed supervisors taking advantage of the women who did not speak English, "those coming from Mexico with very little education, and even though I had an eighth-grade education, I just couldn't tolerate his

FIGURE 31 Josie Romero, at eighteen, in Eagle Pass with her mother. Courtesy of Diana Martinez.

mistreatment of women workers." When these instances happened, she did not leave it there.

When she returned to work the following Monday, Romero approached the supervisor. She told him, I want "to talk to you about your rules. I don't know if they're going to be different than the contract says, and I want to see them in writing, and I want to talk to the boss to make sure we understand each other." She recalled that "the women rallied behind me. This was something that they always wanted to say, but they were afraid." Because she would soon migrate to Washington to work in agriculture, Romero threw herself into the process, "mostly because I felt insulted and humiliated—the way he treated me. When the women supported me, I felt I could complain. So, if there was no toilet paper and the toilets weren't fixed, and things like that, I complained even though I didn't know too much about union type of things then."

In Santa Clara County, Romero began organizing again. In 1969 she mobilized fellow social services paraprofessionals to form a union. We "had been hired to bridge the gap between mental health workers and the community because it was lily-white; there were no bilingual professionals in those years." Forty paraprofessionals were hired by Santa Clara County, with two assigned to mental health and thirty-eight to social services. Romero was the only one hired from Gilroy. She recalled: "When we got together for trainings, we would compare notes, and some had supervisors that were real nasty, controlling, and dehumanizing. I was fortunate enough to be where nobody cared, so it was really open to explore, and because I pretended to know what I was doing, they didn't mess with me."

With additional credibility behind her, Romero "organized a monthly meeting where all of us would do case finding and case consultation, and in the guise of training we did a lot of advocacy." Her aim was to create options for people wherever she found herself. From there, Romero became involved in county politics, careful as to what and whom she picked to support: "I'm very much people oriented and when I see a person whose values I respect, I involve myself to elect them." For example, "I may not attend, but I do a lot of the phone callings and scheduling of meetings," working behind the scenes. Additional endeavors included the Coalition for Hispanic Mental Health Organizations (COSSMHO), where she became involved in drafting and reviewing legislation that would have a positive impact on Latinos. In that position, she is required to travel outside the area. "Two to three times a year, I go to Washington, D.C., to be part of the leadership agenda at COSSMHO, and there I'm very active in what mental health is, focus on ethics, because I firmly believe that as professionals we must be culturally competent and proficiently prepared." Locally, Romero was a foundational part of the Raza Clinical Case Conference, in which she took a leading role in advocating changes in the mental health system. In the beginning, "we analyzed and reviewed our protocols during lunch hours between 12:01 and 12:59 to make sure that there was no conflict of interest." These efforts were carried out in collaboration with Chicano Mental Health Association.

In addition, Romero continued to volunteer. For example, in Gilroy she worked "with migrant farmworkers as well as with kids—gang kids—with probation and all that stuff." Nationally, Romero was involved with the Emergency Social Work Network, which responds to national emergencies or disasters. In all her community work, Romero felt comfortable working in the limelight as well as behind the scenes. "Mostly, I'm in the back doing what needs to be done, the front line is not a priority because I get personal satisfaction seeing what gets done, I don't necessarily have to be in front." Still, her dream was to establish a family institute for Santa Clara County, which she realized several years before her passing in 2004—the Hispanic Institute of Family Development. Josie Romero and others, such as Delia Alvarez and Cecilia Arroyo, would become change agents inside public government and its institutions.

NAVIGATING MYRIAD SOCIAL WORLDS: DELIA ALVAREZ

Comfortable in public and private spaces, Delia Alvarez bridged both worlds of employment. Growing up, she was taught to believe in the American Dream and raised to "always be proud we're Mexicans; we never denied it, but with the notion that 'you've got to be white to succeed.'" In her teens Alvarez experienced racism, hearing people say that "Mexicans were dirty—the stereotype." She explained, "In Salinas you would see a lot of Braceros; you could tell which ones had just come in—they were very poor peasants." Remarks such as "Look at those Mexicans," followed by "Oh, Delia, we don't mean you," perplexed her. "Even though I always have been on the border of identity, it was very difficult because I was raised to believe that we never deny our people, or who we are as Mexicanos. But, at the same time, there was a lot of criticism about all those Mexicans—Market Street—where my dad used to go to the bars; it was a painful time."

In between social worlds, relations such as dating were difficult because "guys weren't interested, and I think a lot of it had to do with being Mexican." Race was not the only issue with which she would contend: gender became central too, which was never clearer than in her pursuit of higher education. She said, "I understood that my brother was the one expected to go to college and not me. I was just kind of the afterthought. He was going to be the man of the house when he married and had a family. So, it was important for him to be economically successful. So, the energy was focused on him." As the firstborn son and a prospective head of a family, her brother was given entitlements that Alvarez did not receive until she expressed interest in college. Even though they made her brother a priority, her parents supported her, but "I wasn't expected to take care of a family. There's a double standard, clearly." She challenged their domestic expectations and learned to do outside work: "I volunteered to work on the car with father or worked in the yard and watered the lawn, because I didn't have to wash dishes," thus freeing herself from gendered responsibilities.

Schoolteachers recognized Alvarez's potential to lead. "In student court in elementary school, and then in the ninth grade I was treasurer, and in Salinas High doing really well academically, I was senior treasurer." From there, she considered community college and "majoring in business. I didn't have a four-year ambition." She wanted to become an "airline stewardess, to travel—to see what the world was all about, but they weren't hiring" people like her. In 1963 she read in the paper that United Airlines had hired the first black stewardess.

As far as leadership goes, "I've been prepared to do that all my life. I'm proud of being a tradition breaker, of growing up in Salinas, where I have a lot of fond memories, of family support, and the care, attention, and love instrumental in providing me with stability." Alvarez added that, as a little kid, she was "always questioning and wanting to be better—I had the motivation and intuitive feeling to do better, not to put them down—I wanted a better life, and there was a world out there to do it."

Filled with curiosity and high energy, Alvarez was "very conscious of breaking tradition. I completed high school. Went on to college—first in the family, one of very few Latinas." Even when it was "challenging and scary because I had no role models, I just did what I saw and wanted to do. I was fortunate to have lived in historical times—the sixties were a big change."

When she entered the career world, "there were very few Mexicanas—that was in '64—one or two social workers in the department, and very few with BA degrees." Because she was comfortable "being around whites, it was an easy transition for me." Even though Alvarez was "comfortable in the white world because I grew up that way, I always had my heart pulled towards what I could do to help Mexicanos because I closely identified with them." As one of the first professionals to be hired by Santa Clara County, "it was pioneering to be able to have a Spanish-speaking caseload, and it didn't even occur to me to ask for differential pay." Language use was one of the ways to make a difference.

The sixties were politically awakening for Alvarez, and she pulled herself "together personally and politically." However, "with the war, it was a whole different thing, being involved and questioning, and still continuing on with my own life." She was initially an observer, but would later become part of the political process. Alvarez explained, "For me, the time when Lino Lopez asked me to speak to high school student volunteers was pioneering. And, then the whole MAYO [Mexican American Youth Organization] thing, and in the late sixties, I came back from Europe and then I slowly got involved in the public antiwar movement, and just getting drawn into it."

Alvarez said that her activism started when she ran for office in junior high and high school, along with her involvement in the Chicano movement during the late sixties and early seventies. As a Chicana, she helped "rally and organize Chicanas to the forefront—Oaxinas de Paz, and the Chicana Coalition—as well as calling for an end to the Vietnam War—that was major."

Her efforts started in 1969 with family petitions. She soon began organizing "a family drive earmarked to bring public attention to prisoners of war; my brother had by then been a prisoner for five years, and the American public has a low memory retention." By this time, "people were jaded by the war. So the petition drive got a lot of publicity." Their efforts drew in extended families, and different people got involved in the antiwar movement. She recalled it was "big organizing," and "I became the core organizer of that. And started the Family Picnic, in late '69. Then, in the seventies it was contacting families throughout the country that had prisoners of war, missing in action, getting organized so that we ended up being on national television." For the families with prisoners of war, the process began by identifying "others who felt the same way that we did, and we were with the other families, and following that network." Alvarez's efforts called for visiting families throughout the country, to recruit them into the struggle. "Hey, let's get together. We feel the same way. We want the war to end, we are opposed to war, and we need to develop a voice." She recalled, "It involved a lot of direct contact and identifying the core leadership. So I traveled. I was in Detroit, I was in Virginia Beach, and in Santa Fe because I had heard of a woman, kind of heard about each other speaking out, because I would go to antiwar rallies afterward, it was just providing that initial leadership. It took a lot of organizing." In this activist campaign, Alvarez created her "own style, which had been developing over the years—that was wild, to be involved in the Vietnam issue and to be involved in civil rights—I was combining both." She, as well as the community, soon realized that the struggles were intertwined: "Even our Chicanos leaving the barrios, brown boys killing yellow boys; that didn't make sense, I incorporated that in my speeches, and, in my personal philosophy, so I was really challenged mentally."

Her brother Everett Alvarez had been captured by the North Vietnamese in 1964.[9] However, in those days there were no protests: "You just didn't buck government." It would be five years after her brother was captured that the family would start a petition drive, "just an innocent thing." However, Delia Alvarez learned how to mobilize "people, the family, and I was always the natural coordinator, director, even with the kids." When she began working for her brother's release, "it was a real new experience to be paid by different organizations to give a speech somewhere in public, creating a national organization." Soon, Alvarez became the personal face of those who struggled for the release of POWs, as well as the image of an antiwar movement that protested the high conscription and death rate of Chicanos serving in Vietnam.[10]

Big changes were taking place during those times. Identity politics were shifting, and on returning from a trip to Europe, Alvarez found out that the term "Chicano" was now in style "where Mexican American has been the term, so it was a real political awakening for me." Yet, she did not immediately join the *movimiento*, because "I don't just jump into things. I'm very cautious." However, the Chicano movement pulled her into leadership. "I was the one that filled the directorship of the Mexican American Community Services Agency." In the antiwar movement, and working as director of MACSA, women active in the organization became a great support

FIGURE 32 Delia Alvarez, on the right, and her sister. Courtesy of MACSA

system for Alvarez.[11] She recalled meeting "Shirley Treviño, Fran Escalante, Ernestina García, Sofia Mendoza, and Armand Sanchez, who was president of the MACSA board of directors." In that position, Alvarez was called "*vendida* [sellout] and communist, and all that stuff, which it was okay for me in a sense because they were accusing everybody, and I knew who was and wasn't—it was the Chicanos' poor way of attacking us." She did not let that influence her direction. "It was difficult to be called a communist and labeled a radical in the papers. And for me, being a radical is trying to do what you think is right, but that's also media manipulation. It was difficult to be called that—not so much the radical, I didn't mind that, because I think radical people are interesting; it was the red baiting, the communist lover, I mean, the country was awful." In 1973, after having invested all her energies in the release of her brother and concurrently working in the Chicano movement, which had consumed her life, Alvarez opted for graduate school. By this time, she said, "I felt I really paid my dues to the community, or to my community at the local, state, national level. I was tired, so I had the instinct to pull back." The distancing from political activism was a survival strategy: "I wanted to take care of myself, to stretch the intellectual; that's why I wanted to go to graduate school, and for the quietness."

However, Alvarez's transition into academia was not as peaceful as she imagined it would be. There, she found herself in the middle of the struggle for the formation of the Committee on Mexican American Studies (MAGS) and the School of Social Work. She went there for peace but found herself "contending with Armando Sanchez—problems seemed to follow me—but I met some good people.'" As a graduate student in social work, Alvarez remained active with the Chicano civil rights movement, which gave her the flexibility to travel. Eventually, she transferred to the urban studies program.

Alvarez took opportunities available to her if they advanced her public work. In 1972 she went to the Paris peace conference; while she was gone, the men in MACSA colluded to remove her from the directorship. "Armand Sanchez pulled the *movida* to make somebody else the permanent executive director. It was dirty," and she was ousted. Males who were there, "many work study students: Tony Estremera, Sonny Madrid, all those guys said nothing for or against me because they were dependent on me to keep their jobs. So it was through dirty politics that I did not become permanent director."

In her community work, Alvarez said she was perceived "as controversial because I've been involved in many things." Among women, she found herself being more respected as a role model, a tradition breaker, and from men there was a distant respect. She had succeeded in a "rough system to work—corporate government—thus, what happened in 1993 [see below] with all this, I think there were those who don't like you who would have said, 'We always knew she was or is a bitch,' that was very painful to recognize."

As a corporate administrator—personnel director and Public Health Department director for Santa Clara County—for self-protection Alvarez had to become more conservative and traditional. But when she was at Harvard, in the Hispanic Health Leadership Program, she reconceptualized her identity. "There, people really talked about their ethnicity. It was a mind-blowing, being challenged, and for a lot of us that just changed our lives. It was then that I realized I went from here, to civil rights, to career executive, and at the same time I was burning out on the job." A more nuanced self-identity emerged during her participation in the program. Her parents had always been aware that she was different. She recalled, "It was just like wanting to go to college, wanting to travel, they never asked me about my break-up with Herman, but what happened is that I fell in love with a woman. And, typical of all families, just as there was denial about my dad's drinking, there was a lot of denial about my lifestyle—no one wanted to know." In her thirties and professionally accomplished, "my identity was okay for my parents, but once I got past my thirties, it wasn't my parents, it was other people." Then the story became that "I was married to a profession, and being viewed as different, being the professional, being accomplished, made it acceptable."

In 1993, while she was director of the Santa Clara County Health Department, Alvarez was outed because of her sexual orientation. The issue of her sexuality contributed to problems at work, which led to her retirement as the executive director.

It saddened her that "the price I paid was that the community didn't really support me when I was being outed, but I mean from the *mujeres* and the male part it's like civil rights but not freedom." Women supporters were concerned about the harm that would come to Alvarez, "but I was so overwhelmed that I was just going to deal with it when it came up, and I was just going to not talk about it, but people who really care were scared to death about me being outed, more than I was."

Her case appeared on the front and local pages of the San José *Mercury News*. Still, Alvarez expressed no regrets, and during the whole process, she said she never felt humiliated. That shocked people. She said, "I didn't do anything.

FIGURE 33 Delia Alvarez. Courtesy of Santa Clara County Public Health Department.

If I'm guilty, I am guilty of fighting for brown people's rights against a very white racist institution, public health nurses. I'm proud of that guilt. So, these are the things I did and fought for. I certainly have my value system. I was very clear about that." It would be the people who were doing the attacking that were "having a hard time. It was a public rape, I was a victim, yet I was being told that, 'for a Latina, I was a role model' because I didn't blame somebody else." She took the fall for the higher-ups. "I didn't say anything. My family value system is you are part of the family, you go down with the ship, and you stay with it—I didn't violate anything; I didn't violate people's trust."

Throughout it all, County Executive Sally Reed, a southerner who Alvarez felt did not understand brown people, did not support her. "She felt uncomfortable with me—had Mexicans as tokens; I know that for a fact because I was director of personnel—there was a cultural gap." Even though she had a long and successful career with Santa Clara County, Alvarez believed her "mistake was staying in that environment too long. The changing demographics . . . had made us more of a threat."

Among women of the Baby Boomer Generation, Alvarez navigated community spaces for social justice in a public bureaucracy that did not always practice equal access or protect its own. Rose Amador, initially employed as support staff for others, became an executive leader in vocational education. Their work would expand options for the most dispossessed.

STUDENT ACTIVIST AND PUBLIC SERVANT: ROSE AMADOR

After working as an administrative support person, Rose Amador would take the helm of SER Jobs for Progress and would become director of Center for Training and Careers, which would be renamed ConXión. In the various positions she held, Amador would interact inside a largely male-centric environment.

Amador recalled that before returning to California she had not felt, even when she was one of only a handful of Chicanas in her community in Pennsylvania, discrimination of any type. But in Santa Clara, in the seventh grade, she and her family had to deal with a racist education system that relied on an A, B, and C tracking system to place their students. Amador was first assigned to the C track. Her mother contested her placement: she "took my report cards, showed them, to which they said, 'Oh, yeah, I guess we made a mistake.'" Their decision to assign Amador to the C level was based on the belief that Mexicans belonged in that group, but "they put me in an A2 track after that."

Amador initially attended De Anza College and received a degree with honors in Chicano studies, later completing her BA. "Involved in MEChA, the grape boycott, campus climate, getting Chicano studies, and things like that," although with good grades, "I got too involved and sidetracked, so I never finished and went a little bit to San José State." Rather than remain in college, she secured employment with the Economic and Social Opportunities (ESO) program, providing clerical and office support, and later at San José State University under the Educational Opportunities Program (EOP). After that she took an administrative position at Service Employment Redevelopment (SER).

With an activist legacy from both parents, at De Anza College, Amador became "involved, and through Richard Rios I learned about the Delano boycott." From there, her activism focused on local issues and political campaigns. "I started with La Raza Unida Party, but ever since that time I've been a Democrat, and as far as campaigns, if Chicanos are running for council, I'll help them. Of course, I've been nominated to the board, and I just try and get more Chicanos elected into office." In 1992 Amador returned to complete her education, since it was "something that was stressed and emphasized in our family—no one graduated from college. So, working at ESO and running one of their programs set me back about five years," until she completed her undergraduate degree at St. Mary's of Moraga.

As an activist leader, Amador said she was perceived as "someone who advises or helps with direction or sets the course of things." For her, leadership means "taking a stance or having opinions on something, and actually doing something about issues." As an administrator, Amador created alliances, depending on where she found support or opposition. For example, with MACSA or Esther Medina, since they do not do job

FIGURE 34 At De Anza College MEChA, Rose Amador is on the left of the women holding the UFW flag. Courtesy of Rose Amador LeBeau.

training, there are no conflicts about that, and Amador can unite with the organization based on shared connections to funding. She was also part of "the Program Officers Association, and I'm their representative to the Private Industry Council." Along with having served as chair of the Chicano Employment Committee, Amador was active with the GI Forum, where she was selected as "outstanding member a few years ago, the Chicana Scholarship Foundation, among things."

Her most difficult experience was with Service Employment Redevelopment (SER) sometime in the early 1980s. Amador was initially hired as a counselor; six months later she was appointed a coordinator, becoming planning director and deputy director as well. "Before we closed down—Alex Delgado was the director, and right before that José Martinez, that's when the FBI came to investigate." Accusations of fraud and misappropriation of funds were at the center of the conflict. Dan McCorquodale and Zoe Lofgren were representatives of the county board of supervisors, and "there was dissension between the GI Forum and LULAC," co-sponsors of SER. Amador explained, "The board of the organization was very supportive of Alex—Lupe and Gil Rodriguez were very active—Lupe was on the local board and Gil was on the national SER board. And, then Esther Lopez . . . so, overnight the board of supervisors was going to defund the organization unless they got rid of Alex." This all happened within a matter of days. "Two factions connected to Alex Delgado when he was selected over Victor Garza, so there was always this division." People took sides with whomever they supported. She remembered, "It was a mess, even though the organization did a great job—it was a good, good training program; I ran the operations, and John Cunningham ran administration."

To deal with the conditions imposed by the board of supervisors, the organization had to replace the director. Amador elaborated, "Well, SER being a Mexican organization, they couldn't choose John Cunningham because he was white, and they didn't like me; this started before I went into planning; . . . it was a mess, and they put me in there to clean up." Since Amador successfully carried out her duties, she was transferred to the East Court facility. "Many SER people had been there forever, took the agency for granted, and came to work late, when they came at all, and for me it was 'if you're late, I want you out.'"

In the Planning Department where she had been placed, much pressure was put on her in regard to proposal deadlines. Demands such as "we want this proposal by tomorrow" became the norm. So as not to experience retaliation, Amador "stayed up all night, but I'd do it just to show them." According to her, "there was a lot of dissension, so many things happened those days." For example, "they had this auditing firm come in; I think the county board of supervisors either ordered it, or they asked for a review of the program to make recommendations." The staff were uncooperative, because they were aligned with the administration. By that time Amador had had enough, and she was considering a move to CET in Reno: "I had decided to leave. And Pete Carrillo even had a going-away party for me and everything. Then Victor Garza didn't want me to leave, he wanted me to stay." So, she agreed to stay. This would not be an easy transition for Amador, since staff accused her of being an inside informer. The climate became more hostile, and Amador contemplated resigning. However, she decided to stay and sent a mailgram to that effect. "Thank you for your offer. I accept. And, I'll be there Monday morning, copying everybody in the world."

A game of cat and mouse ensued. Amador would show up to work and "Alex wasn't there. So, I would tell the staff, 'I'll go home and you tell him to call me.' I'd show up, and state, 'I'll be here again tomorrow.'" So it went on until Delgado agreed to meet with her. She arrived armed with a recorder to document their meeting, at which he said: "Well, yeah, we're looking forward to having you in Planning," adding, "Nothing ever happened, right?" She responded, "Okay, fine. I'll be there tomorrow. Yeah, right." Soon after this exchange, "they removed Alex—moved him out—and had no choice [but] to put me in. Most of the board didn't like me because they supported Alex. So, they were stuck with me, and I mean stuck, because they didn't want me." A hostile climate pervaded, and snide remarks were bandied about by staff: "Lupe Rodriguez would say, 'Oh, we have to get a nice strong Chicano in that position, in a permanent position.' Or, others would chime in, 'We'll get our funding and then we'll worry about getting a male in there.'" While it was hard to work in a hostile environment, the most difficult part in her negotiations would be obtaining a fair salary and administrative authority. In that regard, Amador got the runaround. "They were going to give me the same salary, which was lower than Cunningham, without hiring and firing authority, because they knew I'd fire everybody, which I would have." Without a resolution, Amador went to the board of supervisors and met with Zoe Lofgren, who told her, "You've got to clean house." At the public county board meeting, there were "individuals and organizations willing to help SER and gave it all the support." The board of supervisors voted to continue funding. "Meanwhile the organization's board had daily meetings with John Cunningham, not with me; they were meeting at his house to work out the budget and everything."

Even though Amador had been appointed to the position, Cunningham had taken the reins of the organization. Amador remembered, "He was running the show. So I went to address my concern's with SER's board, taking a stance that, 'No, I won't deal without both those issues,'" and warning that "if I quit, they'll probably defund this organization." Those who opposed her placed their bets on the support of SER National, which had not helped in the past. Once again, Amador restated the conditions under which she would remain in the position. With the expectation that she would not be listened to, "I wrote my letter of resignation and made copies, just in case." With copies of the letter in hand, Amador once again tendered her "resignation, and they went back and forth on the salary, and finally agreed on it." In response to her request for administrative authority, because they knew she was going to get rid of many people, "they voted no. So, I refused the position. 'Fine, thank you. Here's my letter,' and I left the board meeting. I went to the newspaper, to city hall, and took my letter to the board of supervisors." And "the next day there was a big ol' article in the local section 'SER Director Resigns, Berates Board,' using the letter to make their case."

FIGURE 35 Rose Amador and Victor Garza. Courtesy of Rose Amador LeBeau.

The conflict did not end there. The SER organization sent "a letter to the board of supervisors saying that the board was going to run it. 'No. No. Boards don't run organizations.' So, then they appointed the management information systems director, Art Aldama, as interim." At the board of supervisors' meeting, after the organization had made that decision, "SER people were there with their signs and everything, and all the community organizations said they were withdrawing their support," except for the national organization that claimed to support the local SER. According to Amador, "They played so many games. The national SER deposited funds and took them out, and never provided a penny, and with empty promises of, 'Oh, yeah, we're going to make sure it survives and we're going to support it; they never did.'" After the conflict, the board of supervisors voted to defund SER.

After that, "the GI Forum had hearings at their office, and many people were called in—there were fights in the parking lot; it was a disaster." Amador "stayed away from things for a while, although involved with GI Forum, and was [on] unemployment for five months." Around 1982, Chair Zeke Garcia approached Amador to apply for the executive position at CTC. With reservations, because of LULAC and SER's ties, and despite potential conflicts, Amador applied, and "a couple days later the board chair called—my unemployment was supposed to end that Friday—to start on Monday." At the interview, she was told that the board "was thinking of merging with CET." There were other problems. For example, "the Commission on the Status of Women had a lawsuit. They had a mess. A monitoring report was due. However, after the first six months, with all the audits cleared up there really was no more talk about merging with CET." Emotionally, all of these crises imposed a toll on Amador. It was traumatizing to make her people look bad, but still she carried on because of "guilt that I made Chicanos look bad, because it was a big public thing. It was all over the papers and everything." While she recognized it wasn't her fault, "I felt bad because SER was gone, catapulting CET into the organization it is today."

In most of her work, Amador focused on employment-related issues "through the GI Forum or the Chicano Employment Committee." For her, "it was about getting someone hired, or someone got fired, or accessing a particular position coming up in different departments. So, it was always about affirmative action." Along with that, Amador was active at different levels and with various issues. For example, she was a member of the Economic Development Board for the City of San José, on which "mostly CEOs of banks serve," and the San José Development Corporation Board and the Private Industry Council. Nationally, "I'm active with the National Council of La Raza; we're an affiliate of theirs, and on the San José Job Corp Advisory Board," and since her SER days, "I have been involved in the GI Forum, and with the Hispanic Chamber of Commerce. Through the National Council I have had excellent exposure to many people I would have never had the opportunity to meet, such as the secretary of labor."

At the community level, "I put on a great menudo cook-off. In co-sponsorship with Kiwanis and the Hispanic Chamber, we had 10,000 people; it was a lot of work and a lot of fun, quite an accomplishment." For the GI Forum, "I took over what had become a scholarship pageant, not a queen pageant, but I made them change their rules." In addition, Amador chaired a national GI Forum convention. "Something I had never done before and would never do again. I started out co-chairing with Ike Hernandez and then he dropped [out]. We had it in San José and Senator Feinstein was our speaker. It was a real successful convention—I tended to a lot of details and scripting everything that's going to happen, all the way through the lunches, through everything—so it went very smoothly."

At the time of our interview, there were community climate issues and a so-called cultural war among Latinos. As Amador saw it, "The report of factions in the community is fictitious on the part of the San José *Mercury News*—yes, there are differences in the community, not all agree on everything." For example, on the Mexican Heritage [Corporation] or the Cultural Gardens and the displacement of residents, "there are a couple of white-run businesses, but it just boggles the mind that activists are concerned, and the people who are renting aren't complaining because they're going to get moving money." For her, this conflict is about personalities and divisions between "the Latino Issues Forum, Blanca Alvarado, and many active organizations constructed as a conflict of sides—you're on this side, I'm on that side, but they're not on opposite sides." The same issue of community needs surfaced with the argument over the Fallon statue, and activists have yet to realize that "redevelopment money isn't going to the homeless anyhow. It's going to go to another building downtown. So, let it go to our community, for a cultural center for us." Then there is the issue of a citizen review board for the San José Police Department. This is a burdensome issue, Amador said, because for the first time there is a chief of police who brings a community policing perspective, and "they want a citizen review board. Why didn't I hear this when McNamara was chief? We were always trying to get Chicanos in this position, and activists are actually making his job more difficult." Invested not only in the activism that comes with her job but also in the cultural life of the community, Amador is involved with La Raza Roundtable and hosts an Indigenous television community program that features the life of Native Americans in Northern California. Her goal is to see "Chicano kids help other Chicanos rather than be in competition . . . to help each other get through high school, college, and different levels to just keep pushing representation."

CONCLUSION

In the daily life of San José's community, Chicanas and Latinos/Chicanos have contributed to the greater good, with their investment and involvement to improve the conditions of those who are most marginalized, particularly people of Mexican descent. Whether from the Depression or Baby Boomer Generations, the participants in this study have accessed multiple points of entry. With the intent of creating change, they have fought for the rights of those most affected by the lack of access to resources.

They have contributed to the cultural, social, political, and work lives of Raza, as they gained insight about and confronted race and racialized ethnicity and classed and gendered structures of inequality. For Chicanas in this study, even when gender restricted their involvement, and prevented them from advancing in their educational pursuits, they later sought higher education as nontraditional students—a problem not experienced by Latinos/Chicanos. The next chapter narrates the lived experiences of Latinos/Chicanos of the Depression Generation. In their own words, and in the context of their families and communities, they share their sociocultural lives.

7

· · ·

LATINOS/CHICANOS OF THE DEPRESSION GENERATION

FROM BRACERO TO EMPLOYMENT TRAINING AND GRASSROOTS COMMUNITIES: ANTONIO SOTO

Antonio Soto traced his roots to Arizona when it was "still Mexico and even Spain." He said, "We didn't come from Mexico. The United States came to us." Both sides of the family have been here since the mid-1800s and have "resided in Arizona since it was Sonora." The Ortizes, on his maternal side, also originated in the region, "my grandfather being born in Sonora, in 1847, and migrating to Tucson in the 1860s." The paternal side of his family established the "Sierrita Ranch south of Tucson." However, they moved out of the area during hard times. The 1900 drought forced his grandfather to sell "his cattle and move into the city," but he later "moved back and built a dam." On his maternal side, Soto's "grandmother was born in 1856, before the Mexican troops departed, when Tucson was still Mexico." Soto said his family "was doing ranching and a little bit of farming because it doesn't rain there, so in that sense, we were not migrating." He continued, "It was the time of the Homestead Act, and Ramon Soto established a ranch in the middle of the desert. Because that's where Tucson is—southern Arizona is all deserts not farming—all desert. From the previous hundred years when the Mexican people and Spaniards were there, cattle were the only industry." Soto added that "we spent as much time at the ranch as we could—cattle, horseback riding, the whole thing. The ranch is still there." In his experience, "there was leadership among Mexican people, Anglos too." However, by the time he was born, the 1920s, "there were two towns: one Mexican and one Anglo. And during the '30s it continued to be that way, with the Mexican section in South Tucson." Still, even when Tucson was separated by race, "there were many Mexican-origin political leaders."[1]

Soto took pride in being one of the Descendientes del Presidio de Tucson on both sides of his family,[2] pointing out that "they still have meetings and my sister belongs to it," even though members of the organization, as a result of mixed families, consist of about 60–70 percent people with Anglo surnames aware of their Mexican ancestry. Without focusing on class or racial distinctions, Soto pointed out that most members of his family were "business and political people, ranchers, and they weren't farms— Arizona didn't have farms in those days, so you didn't have farmworkers."

In addition to his parents—Ramón Soto and Artemisa Ortiz, who married in 1917—the family included one brother and two sisters. Antonio took pride in their educational achievements: "My oldest sister finished high school, and she still lives in Tucson, seventy-three, very active." In his "very close-knit family, there are two cultures—the Soto and the Ortiz—nuclear family as well as extended family." He was proud to point out that "on the Soto side, there were some values that were paramount and reinforced that they taught us—those ways—by the kinds of tasks that were given to us. As we were growing up, they were put on the table for us, by the kinds of rules we were expected to follow."

These values were very important, because they came with "responsibility as the uppermost value. That is, how one learns to be responsible for one's behavior, and for other obligations." For example, Soto spoke about one time they opted to miss school. "It was winter; a lot of snow, and, for some reason we went to school, but we didn't get there. We came home with the excuse that 'there was no school.' When our parents found out that there was school . . . they sat us down and told us that school was of the upmost importance, so you don't miss school unless there is a serious reason for missing." Soto's parents placed a high value on education and were present when their children were doing their schoolwork. "It was a ritual after supper. Everybody sat down around the dining table and did their homework; the homework was reviewed by them—that was standard everyday practice." Education was a precious commodity for both ancestral lines, and it was particularly coveted by those who were of high socioeconomic class.

His definition of community is associated with belonging, and includes geographical areas such as neighborhoods—Westside, Eastside—and his involvement at Guadalupe Church. "We had a community, which did not consist only of people living five blocks away. In fact, some of those people never went to church," he said, referring to the way in which La Comunidad—the spiritual community that emerged from the work he did with Chicanas and Chicanos—began as a site of "belonging" and they met "in various houses without connection to geography." He continued, "Some live in South San José, others inside Sunnyvale," pointing out that "La Comunidad emerged from the secretariat of the Cursillo movement, people who became alienated from the church when they became conscious that Chicanos had almost no role" in its structure.

By the time La Comunidad was organized, Antonio Soto and Reynaldo Flores, another Chicano priest, had left the church, and Soto had married Phyllis Armas. Although there was a newly ordained priest, Richard Garcia, who was helpful to them, there was no place in the church for those who were interested in practicing a liberatory spirituality. Activist leaders set out "to start our own house churches where we broke bread and wine with no need for an ordained priest. If there was an ordained one there, he came as one of us—comunidad." For Soto, "La Comunidad is a spiritual alternative that has continued since 1977—no structure, no hierarchy—some of the people in it go to church, some don't." In his view, the quest for participants was to seek spiritual fulfillment, not fight the church, or start a new one. "We're simply doing what is necessary to nourish ourselves spiritually," he said, noting that "when we do go to church, we sit there as spectators, and there is a big difference between that and sitting around in a circle in a room and creating community."

By this time, Soto had reached the conclusion that ordination was not important to linking the spirit, which "might seem kind of radical, but in early Christian communities of the first centuries, they did not have ordained priests." Still, it was never the intention of Soto or other participants of La Comunidad to persuade anyone not to go to church, "because that is their structure . . . the church gives meaning to their lives, and if you take that away from them and put nothing in its place, you're doing something really bad, because you're taking away the *muleta*—the crutches to walk. So, we never persuade or dissuade people from going to church."

While Soto attributed their efforts to changes made by the Second Vatican Council, he offered that "the church officially blessed that approach," emphasizing that "the bishops didn't know what they were voting for," and it "didn't have much of an effect, it was on paper . . . the evolution from a cold, legalistic, formal approach to religion, to a personal, communitarian approach. La Comunidad laid the foundation for what I did in the 1970s, which was to leave the structure of the church, get married, and continue to reform it outside, rather than from the inside."

Thus, instead of continuing to practice his spirituality within the institution of the church, Soto joined with La Comunidad in creating an alternative venue. He communed with people without the trappings of being a cleric, the priesthood that he felt had distanced him from any community. For Soto, "being a cleric means one who's separate from the people. The way you dress with the Roman collar, where you live, the rectory, the Mass, everything is hierarchy and separation. There's no way that you can be part of the people as long as you are in the structure of the church. No matter how good your intentions are, there's no way."

There were other ways Chicano priests attempted to implement the ideals of the Second Vatican Council, Soto said, beginning "with a Chicano deacon program. If the priests couldn't get married or go out into the people, we would simply take married men and have them ordained as deacons, which is next to the priesthood." It was after that that the notion of *comunidades*, little communities, surfaced. "It was an *alboroto*, a riot, I mean it was really dynamic. In this *alboroto* the priest was now being with the people and one of the people; we stopped wearing our Roman collars." With that came other changes. "Without the archbishop's permission, we allowed the people to take communion in their hands, which was strictly forbidden. Women took communion to convalescent hospitals; there are a lot of them around here." But those small steps would be challenged by the church. "I started getting letters from the archbishop: 'You can't do this. You can't do that. It's strictly forbidden.'"

It was during that time that Soto realized he was attracted to church activist leader Phyllis Armas. He said, "There was a dynamic between her and me. However, because I was completely and totally committed to my work, to the priesthood, and to the laws of the church," neither party acknowledged it. By this time, "priests had left but not me. There was no way I would ever acknowledge human love—love of God is the only thing." During ten years of working together "*congeniamos,* there was something congenial between us, I had denied it all the way through, until 1970, when we went up to the archbishop's new cathedral."

In his recollection of clergy activists, Soto spoke about the Chicano Priests, who met at Sacred Heart Church. He recalled that "when the archbishop announced he was gathering money to build a $15 million cathedral, we asked for money for the poor, for civil rights, and all sorts of thing. He didn't give us anything." However, some minimal support came from the institution for their community work. "Maybe little crumbs here and there. So, on May 5, 1970, at the dedication of this $15 million cathedral complex, not just a cathedral but also the high school, the rectory," and other amenities, the Chicano Priests took a stand. "Father Casey and Jim McEntee, Reynaldo Flores, and myself and a few others, mostly Anglo, by the way," protested the bishop's lack of support.

Since his arrival at Guadalupe Church, Soto had been involved in the community, attending meetings, joining boards, and advocating for social rights. "The most troubled times" of his life would begin when he left the priesthood. "Living in that trailer. Moving out of the parish. The trauma of deprogramming myself from thirty-eight years. I had never known any 'secular' life." Being on his own, the change was "a very traumatic experience," even though "I still kept active with CET," where he had been an inaugural board member since 1967. In addition, "I was elected to be on Leon Sullivan's national Opportunities Industrialization Center (OIC) [board] because they were all black and they needed a Chicano, so I would go to Philadelphia. I was teaching at San José State part-time, full-time. So CET was my new ministry." Soto became founding chair of OIC-CET's board. During the 1970s and 1980s, he continued his work with La Comunidad, "although I was not a leader, my wife was; the women started this movement." "In the early '60s, Phyllis was a leader in the Cursillo movement, became a rectora, the leader, and we would have women's cursillos." These cursillos became foundational "for leadership in Santa Clara County. So many men and women leaders came out of the Cursillo movement—that's the women's cursillos."

When Soto left the parish, "I was kind of burned out, school, so on, I was kind of staying aloof, but Phyllis and my friends were still leaders of the Cursillo movement." He added that "by this time, they were disenchanted with the structure of the church and decided to have a cursillo without a priest, which was unheard of, maybe in the world." He took pride in pointing out that "there was no such a thing, anywhere. But they did it, and it came out beautifully. Then, at Asilomar—a large group of people at a retreat house—we decided to form small communities, not in opposition to the church as such, not separate from it, but simply alternative ways of doing it, and that's when La Comunidad was formed." Interested in providing this alternative practice to others, La Comunidad "started *Encuentros,* meetings, based on the Cursillo—three days, Friday to Sunday—focusing on leadership, liberation theology, and liberation from the structures of the church."

Given their disassociation from the church structure, there was no place to gather, so "we had to meet at Job Corps Center, Center for Employment Training Center, and so on." Their organizing efforts faced opposition. For example, at "the Franciscan retreat house at San Juan Bautista we used a separate *casita.* Sunday mornings we had our own liturgy, sharing bread and wine." But "once in a while I noticed one of the Franciscans coming around, trying to see what we were doing. With the first *Encuentro,* we were going to have it at the same place." Five days before the event, however, Soto was called and informed that their reservation was canceled. He knew it was because they were independent of the regular church structure. So "we went to CET in Mountain View, where those *Encuentros* continued for a couple of years. But, fifteen or sixteen years later, La Comunidad is still going." It has not been for a lack of trying, but "we have not been very successful in getting other, independent Comunidades going," possibly because "it's more comfortable for people just to show up in church once in a while."

Upon reflection, Soto added that "the people we had been dealing with were not churchgoing people; they were alienated people who might not have felt capable of starting their own Comunidad." In Soto's view, La Comunidad has had an impact on the church nationally and internationally.

Nationally through our membership in the Federation of Christian Ministries, which is a federation of small, independent communities, almost all Catholic, but ecumenical, we've attended almost all the national meetings, wherever in the United States. I was elected vice president for the west of the Federation of Christian Ministries. Now, the national vice president for the west is Linda Gonzales, who is a member of our community here in San José.

Internationally, "Jerry Grudsen and I went to Oxford, England, to an international meeting of small communities, both Protestant and Catholic," and "Phyllis and I went to Central America to visit the *Comunidades de Base*, both Protestant and Catholic." Reflecting on the Federation of Christian Ministries for Church Reform, Soto said, "This was kind of a radical group of mostly priests in the beginning, and later men and women not ordained, in which we basically had home meetings from liturgies, with or without or a priest. It didn't matter, which was a radical thing for the church." Soto concluded that the work he had done in the community, not only in social justice but also in the spiritual lives of individuals and La Comunidad, had served others well. But he also became involved in secular areas as well.

As a nascent academic, Soto became involved with the Mexican American Graduate Studies Program and taught at the School of Social Work at San José State College (SJS). At SJS, he began at the bottom of the pole as a lecturer, "but I was very active, very loyal, fully committed to Chicano Studies, and I saw that maybe things weren't going too well, so it just occurred to me, why not put Chicano Studies under the School of Social Work because it is oriented towards Spanish speaking, and eventually they might abolish Chicano Studies." With the idea of merging the two new programs, Soto wrote a memo to Armand Sanchez, dean at that time. He recalled the conversation. "Why don't you consider taking in Mexican American Graduate Studies as part of the School of Social Work?" Sanchez invited Soto to "have lunch and discuss this." At a Story Road eatery, Sanchez asked Soto to consider a tenure-track position, which he did not expect. "So that's when I got into the School of Social Work and surprisingly enough, ten years later, ten years—it took a long time—Chicano Studies was revived and brought into the School of Social Work."

Another type of activism that would evolve for Soto when he left the priesthood would be his writing. "During the '80s, basically teaching, and writing articles—a form of leadership, all during the '50s, '60s, '70s—articles on farmworkers were published in various magazines, so I continued that in the '80s." He noted that "I have about twenty articles that I have been writing and one book, *Chicanos and the Church*."

In November 1985, Soto was diagnosed with colon cancer, and he "was scheduled for an operation on December 21, the last day of the fall semester." With the belief that he had accomplished all he could have, he recalled telling Phyllis: "Well, I've had my turn; I've done almost all the things in my life that I wanted, and if this is the end. Well, I'm grateful for that." She challenged his fatalism. "No, no, no, that's a terrible attitude.

That's a negative," and "she turned me around with, 'You will keep on going. You have to think positively, and you're going to keep on going.'"

Soto handed in his graded exams on "the 21st of December, and within half an hour I was in the hospital, being prepped for the operation which took place the next day." When spring 1986 came, he was back in class "with a lighter load." Soto continued working until he retired from San José State University in 1988, when he was sixty-seven. For Soto, "the '90s have been very happy years, full years, full of good experiences because I've done a lot of the things that I wanted to do."

Reflecting on the previous ten to fifteen years, he thought that the core of his involvement was the Center for Employment Training. Even after retiring from SJS, Soto remained active on the CET board, and became an emeritus member in March 1991. In addition to tending to his health, Soto's objective was to take care of his family, which included his step-grandson born to their daughter in 1976. For Soto, "that was a very big objective in my life that he was going to get the best in thinking and values." Thus, in his personal and community life, Soto continued to focus on the welfare of his people, including their spiritual welfare.

FROM THE BARRIO TO IBM: GEORGE CASTRO

George Castro was born in Los Angeles, California. His mother was from El Paso, his father immigrated when "he was seven years old" from Nochistlan, Zacatecas, and his grandfather "was born in Juchipila—two little pueblos about twenty miles apart." Castro's parents did not have much education. "My father I think went to the ninth grade and my mom went to the eighth grade." Later in life and through night courses, his mother "took an algebra course to become a controller." Both his parents worked.

Castro described his family as poor and as constantly on the move, albeit "poverty was kind of relative." Their circumstances were similar to other Mexicanos, "but when we moved near whites, it was clear that we were poorer." His family's geographical migration was a strategy devised by his father "to keep us out of gangs": he believed that his children would not join gangs if they "kept moving out of the neighborhoods, from East Los Angeles, the suburbs of Norwalk, El Monte, and other parts of Southern California." His mother was "hardworking, very strict," and both Castro's parents were employed "most of our lives, so we learned to take care of ourselves." When they were children, his parents received help with their care, but by the time he was nine years old, the siblings tended to the babies. "All three brothers were close together, the oldest, and then there was a big gap between a girl and another boy, seven or eight years. So, we learned to take care of each other." Castro is the second-oldest sibling.

Castro's paternal grandfather kept a journal about his life in the United States, where George learned that his reason for immigration was to get work "in the railroads," but he also had other compelling reasons for leaving Mexico. For example, an enterprising person, his grandfather had started "various businesses in Juchipila and he got ruined twice." He documented two instances of thievery. The first time it involved thieves coming to "his little store, and they stole everything." The second time, "ex-soldiers, more or less bandits, came through and wiped out everything." That was not what pushed him to immigrate, however; it was his involvement in politics and becoming a judge, and during that time "something happened and he had to get out of town, warned by his father that 'they're going to kill you.'" So, he went to *el norte* and left the family behind until he could send for them. His grandfather never returned to his place of birth.

George Castro and his sister shared a love for social justice that made them different from their siblings, because, he says, the "two of us are much more committed to *la causa* and the Mexican people and the culture than the rest." Skin complexion and the consequences of colorism are at the center of his explanation. Castro and his sister were perceived as different "simply because we're darker. The other three in our family could pass for white." Two of his "brothers married *gabachas* and they look like *gabachos* [whites]. And, my other brother, *también güero, güero* [also light, light]; they just don't feel the way my sister and I do." To the best of his knowledge, "in their lives, they have never felt prejudice the way we did, or there was no mistaking my sister and I—we're clearly Mexican—there's no confusion about that." Still, those siblings, even though they lived inside the privilege of color, "were not ashamed of being Mexicanos, they just are not involved, while my sister and I are completely involved; we want to make a difference."

Castro's parents were not activists or leaders, although they were involved with union issues. He said, "My folks were extremely liberal—very left-wing kind of politics." A garment worker, "my mom was always a part of the International Ladies Garment Workers Union. She worked in sweatshops in LA where they make dresses."

Throughout his upbringing, Castro understood what it was like to live in the midst of poverty; the family experienced difficult times, but we "always took care of ourselves, and when times were hardest, we'd get a little help from the church." From his own experience, Castro developed a commitment to the less fortunate and to those who have to work for a living and strive to make ends meet. This awareness inspired him to create educational options for Raza. The church was always there when they had to deal with difficult times, such as when his father got in trouble, when "he was shot by a policeman; he was in the hospital for quite a while, and my mom wasn't working." Besides help from the church, "an uncle would come and give us five bucks a week and we'd go get day-old bread and the priest would come by and give us a little money."

He was proud to report that "we were never on welfare or nothing like that. Never." A self-reliant family that dealt with scarcity and poverty on their own, without relying on public assistance, they were like others of that generation who would also show the tenacity of self-determination and self-reliance. They upheld an ideology of activism that was inspired by their family background.

COMMUNITY ACTIVIST LEADER TO HIGHWAY COMMISSIONER: JACK BRITO

Born in San Diego, California, Brito's mother "was part of the clan that saw the Mexican Revolution taking place." His maternal family left for the United States when his mother was six years old. Brito's father was born and raised in El Paso, Texas, and did not know his dad until he was about twelve. Brito took pride in the fact that his father was a self-taught man who became a catcher in the minor leagues: "When Chicanos and Negros could not make it to the major leagues, he played Triple-A ball—that was something. I remember him telling me that in the 1920s he was making $300 a month. That was a lot of money." In 1922, "my father got hurt and quit organized baseball. . . . He moved to Los Angeles in 1923 and met my mom—my dad was a plasterer—and my parents got married in 1924." For Jack, the Brito family was unique, with their investment and activism in their church community, for example, although he did not recognize it at the time. "I had a father, a mother, two older sisters, and two younger brothers." As the eldest boy, he had much responsibility. He recalled that when he turned thirteen, his father had a talk with him, and told him, "I'm really proud of you, you're my oldest son and I love you with all my heart. And so, on your thirteenth birthday, I'm going to give you, as your father, permission to do anything you want, anytime you want, wherever you want, with whomever you want, as many times as you want for whatever reason that you want. I don't care. I give you full permission." Brito's parents were a spiritual couple active in the Catholic Church. "They were both involved at La Soledad on Brooklyn Avenue, now César Chávez. That was my church when I was young," and he went there until the age of thirteen, "when I got in a beef with a French priest called Father Gauvette who accused me of something I hadn't done, and then condemned me to the gates of hell, or something." Brito did not allow the priest to intimidate him and "told him where to go." Still, his father was an usher at church and "part of La Sociedad del Santo Nombre or the Society of the Holy Name." On Sunday mornings, Brito's father "dressed up real nice, sat the people, and collected the money, and by three in the afternoon they were all down in the cellar drunker than skunks."

The men also participated in the rituals of the church: his father was in "the Passion play and the Christmas play, every year," and during Lent "he was Judas Iscariot, and

I had to go through the misery of seeing him hanging there with lightning and thun-
der. He was a beautiful singer and he played the guitar." Even though Brito's father
only went to the third grade, he "spoke English and Spanish fluently; he could pick up
any newspaper in English and read it to you verbatim, translating as he went along."
His mother "went up to the fifth grade in Clifton, Arizona, to a kind of a rural school
because it was a mining town, and she had difficulty speaking English, but—*se daba a
entender*—she made herself understood." He recalled "mom as the disciplinarian, but
I could run away from her."

In his own education, Brito went to the tenth grade, but "my oldest sister set a per-
fect example. She finished high school and started just a little bit of City College, at a
time *que no habían Mexicanas en* ELAC [East Los Angeles College]." When the family
moved to Santa Clara, "she got married, but she's the only one that graduated from high
school." His sister Sally, "who died at age sixty-six, went to the eleventh grade." One
of his brothers completed ninth, and the other did "most of his education in reform
school—at Ione."

When the family moved from Los Angeles to Santa Clara, Brito attended "Santa
Clara High School, where they were still studying about Christopher Columbus. I'm
all ready to get into calculus, and I thought to myself, 'Boy, I'm not going to make it
here.'" It was no different than it is today. In his view, "our gifted kids are caught up in
classes where youngsters who have not had the same opportunities hold the smarter
kids back, which I think is a crime." Before long, "I left school and I went to work for
Pick Sweet—one of the canneries in the area—at a time when the truant officers still
chased you. So, they got me, they made me quit." In an institutional setting that failed
him, Brito sought alternatives to become self-sufficient, and the military became his
way out. It would also become an access point into home ownership and some college
education.

FIELDWORKER TO ORGANIZER AND
ACADEMIC MENTOR: JOSÉ CARRASCO

Of first-generation Mexican descent, Carrasco was born in Fort Morgan, Colorado,
and grew up in Santa Clara, California. His father was from Camargo, Chihuahua, and
his mother from Torreon, Coahuila. As a Chicano, growing up in Santa Clara was, he
said, the "worst thing that could have happened to me—the book *Pocho* kind of shaded
my memory." *Pocho,* a book by José Antonio Villarreal, focuses on Depression-era California and documents anti-Mexican sentiments and the cultural conflicts of living
in two worlds, exploring the contradictions confronted by descendants of Mexican
immigrants in U.S. society. For Carrasco, that book "was almost like a blueprint of my

experience, all the way from my interaction with the Spaniards, Italians, and then my encountering with the Chicano—with the Mexican *pachuco*—it's almost like déjà vu." From Carrasco's perspective, "Villarreal really captured much of what it's like to grow up in a place like that. Even today to a certain extent it still yields you that experience."

Among his siblings, Carrasco was the middle child. In addition to himself, he said he had seven brothers and sisters. "One brother was the one just before me; he was two years older. My oldest sister was Grace. She would have been maybe about five years older than me. Then my next sister Isabelle, then my brother Isador, then me, then three younger sisters after me. So, we were all within a year to a year and a half apart." His upbringing in the family "was unlike today; there were no rules and regulations of what family was to be or not supposed to be." The family came out of the sugar beet fields. "We were farmworkers when we decided to settle down in Santa Clara." His parents "had to work two jobs—daytimes in the fields and then at nights as custodians or whatever they could find." This meant that the children's upbringing was the responsibility of "my older sister, who herself was working full-time by the time she was in the sixth grade." For him, "growing up was a lot of fun and then there was a lot of pain."

His schooling did not include the most sophisticated of educational institutions. He recalled that education in Santa Clara was "still evolving from the 1800s . . . operating on an antiquated curriculum—a normal school—everybody got the same stuff . . . tracks were not solid like . . . schools in the cities—that missionary zeal was still operating." He recalled that "the vast majority of teachers were women, but only two were married. The rest were spinsters; it was its missionary zeal that prevented it from being a strongly racist place." With no clear demarcations as to racial or class barriers, "both whites and Mexicans crossed over them." Carrasco said that "among elders there was discrimination and bigotry, but *gabachos* defied their parents to hang around Mexicans." However, for him, the equalizer became "sports, because I was quite good." Yet, he could discern invisible boundaries: "There were times when you'd go play baseball and you got the wrong time, the wrong group of people, they wouldn't let you play." So he learned to understand the spatial dynamics of his neighborhood.

Carrasco's parents were involved in the community. José did not recall how they became active, except for the mutualistas in Santa Clara. But he associated their involvement with "when my brother and I first got into trouble. Because we were both, at least myself, I was in and out of jail since maybe eleven years old or maybe ten, somewhere around there." He also remembered his parents' involvement with the "Comisión Honorífica Mexicana, led by José J. Alvarado; he and my father were very close." His father was very fond of Alvarado, and "in Santa Clara my father was sort of the leader of a lot of the Chicanos; a lot of them came from the same region."

With regional associations in common, because they came from same areas of Mexico and Colorado, his father and Alvarado "would sponsor dances and stuff and raise money sometimes for legal questions, but the legal things normally came from the central kitty, and what little I recall is that they would try to participate." His parents "attended the meetings together." Carrasco noted that "my mother, like a lot of the other women, did a lot of the work ... with preparation such as cooking. They couldn't cater, so they cooked a lot of stuff." These activities, along with dances and other social affairs, were part of their socialization. "Because dancing was part of the culture, they could not get a baby sitter. So, whenever they had a dance, we all went. The babies, my little sisters, would be under the bench." It was an unspoken expectation that as soon as his sisters were old enough, they would become involved and help set up dances, "getting the hall ready, and afterwards cleaning it up, it was just sort of a family thing. Along with certain other families that were just very close at the time, that was kind of the extent of it."

His paternal side of the family was very Catholic—he had an aunt who was a Carmelite nun and an uncle who was a Franciscan priest. On his maternal side, they were Protestant. "I'm a product of both of those. Evangelicals. My brother and I, and my sister would go to my uncles on my mother's side. We were caught between those circles too. But yeah you could see the distinctions evolving already, color was a distinction, and the other was definitely one of class." The structural forces that Carrasco had to contend with, such as race and class and religion, informed his involvement in the struggle for social justice and social change. Lessons learned from a silent mentor—his father—and others who came into his life, made it feasible for him to become involved.

COMMUNITY AND ACTIVIST AND ACADEMIC LEADER: JOSÉ VILLA

In 1916, during the Mexican Revolution, José Villa's family immigrated to Clovis, New Mexico. "My father, all of his family—his father and mother, widowed sister with two children, a younger brother, my mother, and my two oldest brothers—*vinieron de Mexico*—they came from Mexico," and set roots in Clovis, building a "little adobe house out there in the barrio." His father had scouted *"a ver donde había trabajo* [to see where he could work]. He knew the *ferrocarril*, the railroad, where there was work. So he had spotted a place where he could set up a base to work in the railroad." With their meager resources, the Villa family bought a parcel of land. To do that, they lived "with *compadres*, or someone, until he got a room built, and we were crowded, and he kept adding rooms the way that, you know, families do, but it was just surviving."

Throughout all of this, Villa learned that his father's aim was "to protect his family, his culture, his religion, his language, and everything that he valued. That was very symbolic, so I learned." Villa's mother was religious, and she readily assumed the responsibility for taking them "to church every Sunday," ensuring that they wore clean and ironed clothes. There came a time when Villa questioned his father about not attending church with family. He asked, *"Pos' uste' ¿por qué no va a la iglesia?"* Villa's father retorted: *"M'ijo. La vida es la religión y también cada persona en tu vida es parte de tu religión."* For his father, life was religion, and every person that is part of your life is part of your religion, thus there was no need to go to church.

His parents were not formally educated; neither learned to read or write. They met when they were very young. "My mother was fifteen and he was twenty. She started having kids right off." However, in time and with the help of a *comadre,* his mother learned to read, using the Sagrada Biblia, the Spanish Catholic bible, as her text, biblical lessons she would impart to her children: "She was practicing, but also delivering a message that it was very important to have something. In a teaching lesson she transmitted her will to become literate and to be a teacher to us too. Those were very important things we didn't figure out at the time."

Villa's mother gave birth to fifteen children, several of whom died. Among his surviving siblings there were "eight brothers and two sisters that I grew up with." There were eleven siblings when his youngest sister died. He said, "I remember her death, and her burial. Serafina, named after one of my maternal grandmothers, was six months old." According to family lore, "a big police dog had come and barked and stood on my mother, you know, and she was protecting the baby with it, and that's the *susto,* the fright—that's what she attributed the death to." He added, "My oldest brothers and sisters died during and after World War II . . . influenza that killed two, and one died a stillbirth—that's three sisters and one brother—two were miscarriages or stillbirths, and two died of the flu." As for José, his frail health ensured special care from his mother and father, who favored him. "They took special care of me, I became someone special." His brother who was third in order of birth and Villa, twelfth in rank, were the only ones who graduated from high school and pursued a higher education.

In the United States the Villa family migrated as agricultural workers. His father and older siblings worked the fields to augment the income he made from railroad. Villa said, because "my father couldn't earn enough just holding a railroad job, we migrated. So we worked in *los campos de algodón, las escardas,* in the cotton fields and pulling broomcorn, and all that sort of thing. We had to help out. And so we did." To augment their contributions, one of his brothers bought a truck, and "he contracted labor, or gave rides to people to get out and around the Texas Panhandle—Littlefield, Middleship—and all that." Still, the scarcity was such that his mother had to make do and get by with whatever was available. For example, "when my father was laid off of work, we were so poor we used to be able to cook beans, but we didn't have a nickel to buy the salt. I mean, we had sacks of beans we'd save, in *botes* or cans, you know *y hasta la harina* even the flour. But, I remember my mother being so ashamed that she didn't go across the street to ask the *comadre* or anybody *por un puño de sal*—for a pinch of salt." Despite their neediness, the family was very proud. Villa said, "My mother made all kinds of excuses not to ask for help," and because "*era tisico*—we were very poor and we couldn't afford much, my brother John, who was going to college at the time, took me with him." Thus, at the age of eight, Villa had no choice but to become independent. He learned, he says, "to hold my own ground, to play the violin, and unconsciously my brother taught me to assume leadership and responsibility for my own life and my own decisions." At that time, "my brother John was twenty-four." Villa reminisced, "At New Mexico's Normal Teachers' College—now Highlands University, in Las Vegas, New Mexico—I used to follow my brother around to classes. When I was not going to school, he would pick me up and we'd go to his classes; I became sort of like a college mascot." In school he would learn to find the differences and similarities among his people and the environment in which he lived. He learned to become a critical thinker among the college students and found differences even within his family.

For Villa, his parents were different. "My father *era muy Indio él, and mi mamá era muy güera*—more the Spanish background—that background reflected some of these very strong cultural kinds of behaviors." A traditional man, his father was a stern disciplinarian, and "he kept my mother in check because he thought it was his duty." An honorable man, "he was very faithful to the family, and very demanding in how we all showed *respeto*." For example, "we would never take a glass of water, and would never take a sip of water, before offering it to our mother, to him, or our elders." Villa's father was not involved in unions or any community activity. "At that time, they practically dragged you out and shot you if you even thought about joining a union." He was so busy taking care of the family "that my father didn't have time or energy for anything else." Focused on survival, Villa's parents nonetheless instilled in their children the passion for making a difference and creating change, even if it was limited to church involvement.

FIELD WORKER TO CHIEF OF POLICE: LOU COVARRUBIAS

Born in Irvington, California, Lou Covarrubias was raised by his paternal grandparents after his mother passed away when he was three. After a stint as transient agricultural worker in the local area, Covarrubias's grandfather found employment at "Lesley Salt and stopped following the crops, and found a degree of stability." But Covarrubias believed that "my brother and I raised ourselves because our grandparents had no concept of school." They "were fortunate in the school-oriented friends we found because we were able to complete school." No one pushed them to succeed. Even though "my brother was a great athlete and I was a pretty good student, the home itself was very harsh because my grandfather was very critical, but in spite of that, I have tremendous love and respect for him." Covarrubias's drive was inspired by his grandfather, who espoused the belief that *"nosotros no le pedimos nada a nadie,* or we don't ask any person for anything—the way I try and live my life." As a result of such harsh expectations, his grandfather "never owed anybody, and he never had anything." On the other hand, "my grandmother was a very loving person, although she wasn't demonstrative. In spite of the poverty aspect of it, we had a pretty good home. My grandmother never worked. She was home. So that was good."

In Irvington, "there was prejudice. We were the people who lived on the wrong side of the tracks—looked down upon. I was embarrassed by some things that my grandmother did, like kiss the ring of the priest." There was also the issue of dating outside your group: "When you liked a girl, she had to sneak around because her parents said, 'Don't be hanging with them Mexicans.'" The prejudice he witnessed was "very subtle," though. For him, class was more of an issue than race. There was bias, and those educators who taught him "would make it clear that you were inferior."

When Covarrubias turned fifteen, his grandfather told him he was too old to be carrying those books around and sent him to work to help the family. *"Mira, tu ya eres muy grande; deja esos libros y ponte a trabajar, ayuda a la familia* [Hey you, look, you're already grown up; leave those books and go to work, help the family]." He was fortunate that his grandmother understood the value of an education, and she opposed his grandfather. *"No, Pablo déjalo estudiar, le gusta estudiar"* [No, Pablo, let him study, he likes to learn]. It was those words "that kept me in school, and because of that we graduated." Even though his grandfather relented and allowed them to remain in school, he would send the brothers out of the house with instructions not to return until they found a job. "So, we would go out and, you know, we would go down the road. I was really embarrassed and shy, and I would see some farmer and I'd ask him for a job, and my brother who was little, the farmer would inevitably say, 'What'd he say?'" His brother would respond, "He wants to know if you've got a job for us." His brother's personality would open the door, and "some farmer who would feel sorry for us, because like I was only eight and my brother was six, we'd find something, pulling some weeds and they'd give us a couple of dollars, and I could go home." As expected, "we always turned our money over to our grandmother, and she'd help us buy the clothes we would wear to school." Thus, non-Mexican and middle-class families were an "ideal and you always wished, man, I'd wish I had a family and a home like that." He recalled going to a kid's home where his foot "made a half-inch indentation in the carpet, and we didn't have a heater, even yet—we had to run into the kitchen to the wood stove." Covarrubias "never even dreamed that I would have any of that." He added, "When I built my home over here, I didn't feel comfortable for about ten years after . . . I always felt sure somebody was going to come and take this away from me. And I was a lieutenant or something by then. But you never get away from that,

I guess, you know thinking about it. But that was it was more like I said, the house, being ashamed."

Covarrubias recalled his grandmother being "involved in the church and joining Las Guadalupanas," a devout women's religious group. On the other hand, "my grandfather didn't join anything. He was not a joiner." His grandfather was an independent person, and "the worst insult you could give my grandfather, if in any way, was to insult his integrity."

Growing up, Covarrubias "was influenced by my *nino* or godfather, one of the founders of the Honorífica," the Comisión Honorífica Mexicana. It was he who warned Covarrubias to stay away from Anglos, because if you became careless with them, they would hit you: *"Cuidate de los gringos porque con un descuidazo te pegan."* His *nino* would always urge his grandfather to join the Honorífica in order to defend their rights. "He would say, *'No, Don Pablo se tiene que meter a la Honorífica porque tenemos que pelear por los derechos nos han fregado ya muchos años'* [No, Don Pablo has to join the Honorífica because we have to fight for our rights, they have taken advantage of us for years], and things like that—I used to listen. So, that was my first taste for understanding that we have to join, stick together to speak out, and act out." Covarrubias attributed his grandfather's distrust to having "left Mexico because of La Revolución." He also gained an understanding of his grandfather as just a cowboy. Covarrubias realized that, in his harshness, his grandfather was trying to teach them how to support themselves. He attributed his own "never ever being out of work to those lessons," adding, "I always worry, in a sense sort of like the Depression people, that I may lose everything, I've always got that little fear." Clearly, those early life lessons taught him that if that ever came to pass, "I can always work in the fields again—I'll manage to survive, because I've been there—I've picked cotton, prunes, and all that stuff."

As far as his educational legacy, Covarrubias said his "grandmother had about a sixth grade education. So, for Mexico at that time, she was considered highly educated." They had status in the social structure in which they lived, his maternal great-grandfather who was the foreman at *la hacienda, "era más—bueno—*he was more on the Spanish side, *parecía más güero y español* and my grandmother *se parecía muy India; era Mexicana."* In other words, Covarrubias attributed this to his grandfather's status and position at the hacienda. And, to his light complexion, which identified him as better, looking like a Spaniard, while his *abuela* was Indian looking, a Mexican. As the *"mayordomo of hacienda,"* his great-grandfather "had a house and a little ranch area all to himself." However, his great-grandfather "didn't like my grandfather because he wanted my grandmother to marry better."

Still, during the Revolution, "my grandmother was worried that my grandfather was going to take off and leave her to join, and her father, sensing that they might have some real problems, hid a good horse." But the rebels found it "and actually put a gun to his head and cocked the trigger," telling him *"si otra vez nos escondes algo y nos mientes los matamos,"* if they hid something from them again, and if they lied, they would kill them. Rather than risk death at their hands, his great-grandfather suggested he "take her and get out." Covarrubias learned from his grandmother how "they took the horses and they took a lot of stuff *porque se va a poner muy feo aquí*—it was going to get ugly here."

His grandfather "started school in Mexico." He worked at the hacienda where his great-grandfather was the mayordomo and *"siempre lo prefería y él quería andar así con los vaqueros, y el ganado;* the guys at the hacienda liked him, and they brought him in as a house servant, and were always telling him, *'que se tenía que educar.'"* Since he was a hard worker, the hacienda owner hired him as the overseer and often reminded him to get an education, although later in life he did not support education for his grandson.

It became a point of contention for Covarrubias's grandfather that his grandchildren knew how to read. "When he had a few *tragos* or a couple of drinks he'd say, *'ustedes se creén muy grandes porque saben leér. No son nada, son unos malos pa' nada,'"* deriding them for believing they were big shots because they were able to read, reminding them that they were good for nothing. Later, after telling them that they were worthless, he would show that "he was very proud of us." His grandfather could be very critical. "We couldn't do anything right, and like he'd say, *'Agarra esa hacha y corta esa leña'* [Get that ax and chop that wood]. To later state, *'Deme esa hacha. Ustedes no saben. Mire como se hace'* [Give me that ax. You don't know anything. Look at how it's done]. I mean really kind of harsh too." Covarrubias could not win for losing.

The biggest conflict he had with his grandfather was over his desire to get an education rather than opt for a job: "He just felt that at a certain age you were not a man if you kept fooling around with those books." On the other hand, with his grandmother, "the conflict had more to do with those stories: *'es mas facíl para un hombre pobre pasar por el ojo de una abuja, que un rico'* [that it was easier for a poor man to go through the eye of a needle than for a rich man]. She was *muy humilde,*" very humble. In that vein, she urged them to not set their sights too high, because "she didn't want me to get hurt, I guess that's what it was." Many of Covarrubias's conflicts with his grandparents had to do with becoming an "acculturated American as compared to following Hispanic traditions." When he and his brother learned the "American ways, you know, then it was a conflict between that and what they did."

The way Covarrubias understood it, his life had not been all about dealing with contradictions, it has been about learning lessons from his experiences. From his grandmother, he gained an appreciation for an education and learning, and from his grandfather the pride of never asking anything from anyone and knowing how to work and how to find work when you needed it. Speaking as an adult, he said, "In my immediate family, my wife provides stability and it's nice to go home and have a place of refuge because sometimes you get battered. When you're out in the front you get battered and you go home bleeding sometimes." A self-determined man with the aspiration to become a change agent in his community, Covarrubias worked to improve his community's lot, knowing that if the lives of his people improved, so would his.

FROM MIGRANT WORKER TO SOCIAL ACTIVIST: VICTOR GARZA

Victor Garza was born in Eagle Pass, Texas, in 1937. His father had immigrated from Piedras Negras, Coahuila, Mexico, and was raised in Eagle Pass, while his mother came from Eagle Pass. Other family members were born in Texas, "because during World War I my paternal and maternal grandparents migrated." A binational family, they traversed the international border; "some were from Mexico and others from Texas." His "dad never went to school and my mom went to third or fourth grade." In his family, Garza learned that "when you don't know anything aside from your immediate surroundings, you feel that you have the world in your hands." He grew up in a family that relied on agricultural work for their sustenance, following migration paths to various parts of the United States. For Garza, working in the field "as a member of the family" began when he was "five or six years old," and by the time he was around eleven, he found himself supervising a hundred people. Because he spoke English, Garza "was the foreman, and the others were adult workers," and he earned the same two dollars an hour.

The family's economic status was extremely precarious. However, his "mother did not impart an ideology of poverty," instead teaching them that they "were just as good as anyone else." Garza explained, "Even though we may have been the poorest of the poor, somehow my mom and my dad, especially my mom, always led us to believe that we were not poor." There were times that their economic situation was so desperate that "we were sometimes barefooted and we'd have raggedy clothes, those she bought at the secondhand store, or made for us," but she always taught her children that they lacked for nothing. Garza saw his mother's efforts as a strategy to protect them from the stigma of poverty. He said his mother "was probably inciting something inside us to feel that we were just as good as anyone else," adding that "we were farmworkers all our lives. In fact, I worked in the fields until I was twenty-six years old, even though I had already had been in military service for four years."

Garza was the second of ten children, seven boys and three girls, "so we were a large typical family from the old days." In spite of the difficulty of agricultural work, for Garza those times were extremely happy years. That was all he knew. Garza recalled a school assignment where the students where asked to describe "what you did over your vacation." He had never taken a vacation, so he did not understand the term. For him, the meaning of the word was associated with the times when they did not attend school, "when we went to work again in the fields and had fun. To me that was vacation. I often reminisce and miss something about those happy days."

However, not all was happy in the family. Garza recalled that his father "had a lot of negatives; he would get drunk and occasionally beat Mom up, and I grew up to fight him about it, and would literally knock him down." Soon he would not be the only one defending his mother. He recalled that, as a very young boy, his brother Humberto would ask, "'Dad, you want us to be afraid of you? Or do you want us to respect you?' My brother explained the difference to Dad, 'because there's a difference between being afraid of you and respecting you, . . . and if you want us to respect you, you have to earn that.'" Without judgment or blame, Garza understood that his father was not raised to behave differently. His upbringing was traditional, and so he reproduced the experiences he knew. Garza explained, "So we really couldn't blame him for the things he was doing . . . that was his life experience. How could he get any other thing? He has never seen anything different. So, it was hard on him." Still, they challenged him to the point that "we made him change, we talked to him, and argued with him, and fought with him, until he finally changed. And, to me, there were a lot of conflicts in that sense."

The family environment was volatile. Garza mentioned the time he took "a gun and waited for him, to kill him; I was around fourteen or fifteen, but my mom and older brother finally convinced me to give them the gun." Garza's wanted to teach his father a lesson, "because my dad had beat up my mom. No way am I going to allow this to happen again." When family members took the gun away, the conflict was diffused, and "my dad realized his mistake." After that, many a night he recalled hearing his father cry: "He felt badly about being short, and believed he was half the man he wanted to be, and desperately wanted to be handsome for Mom, and he was extremely jealous of her." The relational tensions Garza experienced at home were mostly with his dad; there were no conflicts with his mother. "Always able to communicate, I saw her as a friend, a mother, and a sister—conversations that I had with her, I never had with dad or my brothers."

Garza's schooling took place in Eagle Pass. Coming from a migrant family, he had an itinerant education. "In March we would drop out of school and go up north and work in the fields, then late October or early November, we would reenroll. We thought it was fun but we didn't know better." As a result, the children had to work doubly hard to catch up with the work they missed: "We were only attending about three or four months but competing with kids who were there nine months out of the year." They were managing, but it was difficult. Garza dropped out of school when he was in the eighth grade—no one asked him to do it, he just did. "My parents never requested that I drop out. In fact, they encouraged me to stay." When he told them he had "made up my mind, they said, 'Okay, then you want to work?'" So he started full-time in agriculture, a decision he would later regret. "My oldest brother got married when he was seventeen and only went to the sixth grade." In "those days, it was a challenge to graduate from high school."

Although Garza was not identified as a leader at school, he became one at work. He earned a reputation standing up for others' rights. "I didn't like people abusing others." He learned to fight back as a child. "My parents were always spanking, hitting, and otherwise abusing me." He shared an example: "I was made to kneel in front of the street, arms crossed as punishment . . . because brothers didn't stop me, they joined in . . . it was for those who drove or walked by" to witness our rebelliousness. Still, fighting against all he perceived as unjust, Garza continued to get trouble, and "because my brothers would not stop me, they continued to get it."

Most of the punishment he received was because of the fights he got into. "My parents didn't want me fighting," nor did they care that Garza was defending someone. His practice was "to immediately jump on the side of the weaker person, even though the other person might have been bigger," emphasizing, "I would always side with the underdog—younger ones, or weaker ones, even in the navy." In the service, he recalled "bullies picking on the weaker ones, but not the Mexicans, four or five of us were always together, but they would pick on the weaker white people." "I would step in, defend whoever was being picked on—Anglos would get angry and Mexicans said not to." His urge for justice was so strong, it took over. "I did not like people abusing others, so I'd get into the middle." With a strong sense of integrity and support for the underdog, Garza was always ready to fight for justice and equality.

CONCLUSION

With the exception of Antonio Soto, who grew up in a middle- to upper-class community in Tucson, Latinos/Chicanos of the Depression Generation participating in this study dealt with scarcity, navigating poverty in marginalized communities and being part of family work crews to make ends meet. Still, having worked under the tutelage of their fathers, all gained a strong work ethic and an appreciation for work. From their mothers, and less so from their fathers, they inherited an ideology of responsibility to work for the betterment of the community. They were raised to be self-reliant and shunned whatever public assistance may have been available, except for that which the church might have provided them in time of need. Among the oldest of the generation, Latinos/Chicanos revered their mothers, and most spoke about the traditional behavior of their fathers in the home, relying on traditional values to keep their spouses in check. Some spoke of intervening and identified that as the reason that those domestic relationships ended.

While all confronted racism and classism in their daily interactions, these activist leaders relied on the values and beliefs espoused by their ancestors, based on a philosophy of service to improve conditions and advance the betterment of their community. The GI Bill gave Latinos/Chicanos of this generation access to higher education and housing. The only exception was Jack Brito, who dropped out of school in the tenth grade and later attended community college without completing a degree. The next chapter documents the experiences of Chicanas of the Depression Generation.

8

● ● ●

CHICANAS OF
THE DEPRESSION GENERATION

SOCIAL, CULTURAL, AND POLITICAL ACTIVIST: BLANCA ALVARADO

Born in Cokedale, Colorado, a mining company town of about two hundred families where everyone knew everybody and "all kids went to the same school," Blanca (Sanchez) Alvarado traces her origins to New Mexico. In her community, fathers and mothers did the same things, and all went to "the same company doctor, the same company church." According to Alvarado, among the town's residents "there was a sameness that was pretty inclusive." She had nine brothers and three sisters, and even though her family was large, she grew up lonely. From the beginning, Alvarado found comfort in books. Books gave her companionship; she loved to read, "sitting behind the stove, and under the tree all by myself." Knowledge was important for her. One memory in particular was that "I was the county spelling bee champion, and it was pretty impressive." She attributed her isolation to the Great Depression and her father's emotional distance, since he was "an orphan . . . and grew up very much alone."

Although he had only a first-grade education, her father was an avid newspaper reader, and "he was very active in the mine workers' union; he was the treasurer." She recalled, "Dad was the one that was involved with the union. But I can remember discussions, and so it's not as if Mom was very meek and humble, she was a hardworking woman . . . she always, from what I can recall, had a mind of her own. She was always very outspoken. And she was not timid by any stretch of the imagination." Both parents were very involved with elections, and Blanca credited them with her political formation: "it began with my dad and with my mother," and because of them "I grew up knowing that role models play a part in our lives."

About 1947, when Alvarado was about fifteen, the mines closed and workers lost their jobs. Most of the miners migrated to various parts of the United States, while her family traveled to Los Angeles, California, with $2,000 dollars her father had squirreled away. Not unusual for the times, this migration paralleled the experiences of those families who moved west during the dust bowl. "We came in one car; our meager belongings in a truck covered with a canvas. I remember riding in the back with all the furniture." Their move was a positive experience, and "one of my most precious memories, too—I remember a lot about the hardships of that trip—we came across the desert and it was just so hot . . . but as we came out of Barstow I had my first look at palm trees." This made such an impression on Alvarado that she has "always loved palm trees, because as we came into California, there were the glamorous palm trees." This move would be a separation from all they knew.

The family remained in Los Angeles no more than two months, and "we came right up to San José to the harvest with our uncles, I mean, with our *primos*, and ended up at the McClay Ranch located on Quimby and White Roads." In the new community, "we worked. It was this whole thing that work was an important part of one's life—we certainly got that from our parents, but we also got that from our individual desire and need to work." In San José, daily life mirrored their experience in Colorado: "It was the same thing as the mines. We got up very early and worked until almost dark, barely get home and wash some of the dirt off and eat a quick meal and get right into sleep for the next day." Their life was difficult, "but there were beautiful times too in many respects because where we had been transported from a very united community in Cokedale, we ended up in a camp of farm laborers where the same sense of community developed." She recalled the family "had planned a return to Los Angeles, but that never came to pass."

It was arduous for Alvarado to recall the everyday experiences of those early years. However, "my years at San José High School" were the best, as "we were a very, very small group," which included Bobby Zamora, the musician. She added, "He was part of our group and because we were such a small group in this institution, of course, we gravitated toward each other." Among her early mentors,

FIGURE 36 Blanca Alvarado at San José High School. Courtesy of Blanca Alvarado.

Alvarado identified "a woman who played a strong role in our lives—Mrs. Crist at Catholic Social Services, which was across the street from the campus on San Fernando." No one sought her out, "but she took us under her wing and helped us organize Club Tapatio." Without her peers, Club Tapatio at San José High School, and Mrs. Crist, Alvarado's life would have been a "dismal, boring place."

At San José High School Blanca met José J. Alvarado, who would become her husband. He was "a well-established businessman in San José, with a radio program on KLOK, and a record shop called Jay-Jay's in his broadcasting studio right on Post Street, at First and Market." His social and political activism inspired her because "he had a great deal of interest in the political life of our community," and he demonstrated a commitment to youth. For example, "he put together a youth drop-in center right in his office and a juke box, with little checker tables, ping-pong tables, and the Coke machine; it was a place that we used to go and hang out."

That mature and sophisticated man "was an inspiration to us, probably, because he cared about us, too. By that time, he was creating his own revolution in San José by being outspoken on some very major issues of the community, police brutality being one of them." It came to pass that "hanging out there, before I knew it I was working in the record shop, selling records." The shop became a cultural beacon and José a cultural broker for the Mexican community. According to Blanca, José "had tremendous popularity . . . and he was doing his own activism on social issues, he was also a dance promoter." This gave her the opportunity to attend events he organized, which did not go well with her mother. "So, my poor mother, if I have any regrets about what I did to my mother, I must have given her heartache after heartache, because I used to just take off with him; I was disobedient, *muy desobediente*." "I remember going to Salinas, to Sacramento, to Stockton, to Tracy, and met such famous people or *luminarios cómo* Jorge Negrete, Pedro Infante, Lalo Guerrero, and Maria Victoria, whom he brought from México."

José J. Alvarado was in his forties and Blanca Sanchez about twenty-two when they married in 1953—the first and only marriage for her and the second for him; Lina Manriquez, a local businesswoman, hosted the ceremony at her house, "a very nice backyard wedding." With her marriage to Alvarado, she found herself in an enviable position, because "people, especially the women, just adored José—he had women all over—he was popular and very much in demand." As a married couple, they moved to the Sunset Avenue house in East San José, where their five children were born—Michael, Trish, Monica, Jaime, and Theresa—their home became a meeting place for activists.

Marriage to José brought Blanca into the world of community involvement. She recalled, "Good things were happening around Sunset Street, when we were very involved with Father McDonnell at Guadalupe Church, when César Chávez and Herman Gallegos began organizing, the people who founded CSO [Community Services

FIGURE 37   Blanca and José J. Alvarado's marriage, by a justice of the
peace. Courtesy of Blanca Alvarado.

Organization] in the Mayfair area; I mean we were all part of that. I remember having
meetings in our little garage on Sunset." That was when the first Chicano attorney
arrived on the scene, "and going up to his house above the country club when Ed
Roybal was still a councilman and he came to raise money for his congressional race."
In addition to the time she spent with her parents in Cokedale, "I experienced real
Mexican culture and traditions and activism through the work that José did." It made
her feel a strong part of the work that "César Chávez, Manny Gomez, and those other
folks did." She said she felt as if her trajectory had been predestined. For Alvarado, "life
has taken on its own shape and its own form and I have been in places and a part of a
collective that continues even today."

But with marriage came heartbreaks, betrayals, and opportunities, given a husband that was a recognized businessman active in the community with sociocultural

FIGURE 38 The Alvarado family: from left to right, Jaime and Michael; Terry, Trish, Blanca, and Monica. Courtesy of Blanca Alvarado.

connections in Mexico and the United States. Alvarado noted that "before José and I got married he had his clashes with the status quo." For example, he wrote "for the *Mercury News* blasting the chief of police." With access to the airwaves, he also instructed listeners to fight for their rights and become invested citizens. "On the radio program, he would exhort his listeners to civic involvement, to being citizens, to looking at education as a means towards an end, so I used to hear his features." He challenged the status quo in the United States, but he also took on the Mexican government. For instance, "as member and president of the Comisión Honorífica Mexicana, there was a time when he gathered hundreds of people to write a letter to the Mexican president," in which José charged "the Mexican consul with interfering in local affairs," stressing that the consul "had no business telling Mexican people who were born here that their allegiance was owed to Mexico." This effort riled up "members of the Comisión Honorífica, conservative people dedicated to Mexico first and the United States second, and he began to get attacked." The organization not only complained about him to the radio station manager but also went to advertisers of his program and took their grudges to court. "They challenged him in the courtroom when he was going for his citizenship." His critics went as far as accusing him of being a communist.

José Alvarado thought his fans would support him in the struggle. Blanca said, "He was so convinced that his community, his following would stand behind him and that they would mount a campaign to defend him, but that never happened." Despite these setbacks, he continued to participate in the sociocultural life of San José, with the creation of other groups, including "the Club Gardenia in Gilroy," an organization in which Blanca Alvarado participated. What brought an end to those struggles was his dismissal from KLOK, which forced him to travel to San Francisco, KOFY radio, thus losing face with the community because of his activism. Blanca Alvarado recalled that it was a very difficult time for them in their marriage, citing her "own lack of maturity" for a divorce in 1968, after fourteen years of marriage.

Alvarado recognized that her political activism began with her husband, and with such leaders as César E. Chávez, Edward Roybal, and Manny Gomez, the first Mexican American attorney in San José. She credited those years with building a foundation for her work as a leader: "Those years I experienced real Mexican culture and traditions, and activism through the work that José J. Alvarado did. I feel a strong part of the work that César Chávez did, Manny Gomez and those other folks. Still, my life has taken on its own shape and its own form, and I have been in places and have been part of a collective that continues even today." From her involvement in the politics of Sal Si Puedes, Alvarado became active in her children's school, as a member of the PTA, and then with Most Holy Trinity Church through its new school, its lack of Spanish-language masses, and the projected removal of a priest by the diocese. Through the efforts of a parish organization, called Los Amigos, they "formed a coalition that picketed Most Holy Trinity, and the archbishop at the diocese in San Francisco." Alvarado spoke of the tensions for cultural rights in the Catholic Church, as "its parishioners, no different than today, experienced conflict and took it upon themselves to make changes that were very important to us."

As a single mother of five in the 1970s, Alvarado found herself employed with a certified public accountant, her work related to duties she had discharged in her ex-husband's business, in addition to taking a position as a welfare eligibility worker for Santa Clara County. It was then that she found employment at the Opportunities Industrialization Center (OIC), which would later become the Center for Employment Training (CET). In retrospect, "my work at OIC-CET was probably one of the most important pieces of my life experience." For Alvarado, OIC-CET "was an environment of nurturing, of learning, of giving, and part of a movement that really stood up in support and in defense of the less fortunate of our community."

In her position, Alvarado found herself working with a population of people whom she understood. Still, she would challenge "the institutional sexism of an organization" for which she had "tremendous love and respect." She elaborated, "It was a system that was very noble in some respects, but it was also a system that was very oppressive in its expectations for those who were employees." She recalled that "it was a very heartbreaking thing for me to have experienced male dominance in a place I literally worshipped." The conflict that emerged in an environment that she had perceived as "my heaven, my calling" would become discouraging because of its hypocrisy and the double standard whereby she "was told that I would never get a job as a manager." For the first time, an in-house group began organizing, since "there had never been a process for grievances; there was no one you could take your issues to." One employee, also a recognized leader in his own right, was dismissed during this time, which inspired workers to continue organizing, while CET strategized to undermine the workers' efforts with extended meetings or individual negotiations with employees to sabotage their efforts. Alvarado recalled that "Russ Tershy and a manager invited me out to lunch one day, and Russ was very clear, and he said to me, 'Blanca, where else but at CET—you've only got a high school diploma—would you have succeeded as much as you have?'" The statement showed her "that Russ had no interest in listening to what our concerns were, and I felt very much insulted to have been demeaned in the manner of saying, 'you're only a high school graduate.'" It was after this and much soul-searching that Alvarado resigned her position.

When she left CET, Alvarado reestablished her business and advanced her political work through the Mexican American Political Association (MAPA). She explained: "As president of the local chapter, not only did we have to deal with issues of the local community, but also pursued issues of concern to MAPA. That was where I had my real hands-on experience with the dynamics of politics, that's when I really understood and learned firsthand how politics really works." It was during that time that Alvarado emerged as a political leader when Janet Gray Hays "appointed me to the Bicentennial Commission." Also, Councilman Al Garza was running for mayor, and because of her visibility and activism with his campaign, Gloria Molina, a Los Angeles County supervisor, "assigned me as Northern California Carter chair." In addition, "because of increased visibility and recognition as a political leader within the Hispanic-Chicano community," Alvarado was appointed to the San José Charter Review Committee. Out of that effort came the recommendation to eliminate at-large elections in San José, which went to the ballot in 1978 and passed by "a very narrow margin." For Alvarado, "the 1979 elections for District Council was the most prominent community issue of the time, and the '70s were truly formative" in her leadership.

Alvarado said that her passion for helping others and righting wrongs dated back to early childhood. It was this lifelong sense of justice and fairness that sharpened her notions of gender inequality when she "defended myself and other women, not only at CET but even throughout MAPA, because MAPA was another male-dominated organization." Inequality was not only found within political interactions, since "even within the Chicano movement, women were denied their rightful role or the respect that we deserved." She recalled always contending with issues that focused on fairness, equality, and justice, elaborating that "this social conscience has always been a part of me."

Alvarado said her life was "enriched by my family and the community—whether it was MAPA, Tapatio Club, or Los Amigos—they made me feel part of something bigger than myself." Lack of solidarity is what she identified as the problem confronted by the younger generation. In her view, "they haven't had those institutions; they haven't had those support groups to give them a sense of belonging, and to put them in a place of giving." In the end, she could provide "an aspirant frame to gain an understanding of themselves and their communities." Alvarado said, "I want my children to value family and each other as much as I have. And above all, I want my grandchildren to feel that."

Even though her mother lacked an education and her father only went to "first or second grade," Alvarado graduated from high school—a tremendous achievement for a Chicana of her generation. In school, there was a sense of not belonging. "I had good teachers; I had indifferent teachers," but "there was the feeling of looking down on you. I don't recall a single teacher during my years of high school—very different from my years in grammar school in Colorado—there wasn't a single teacher that stood out as having an interest in me. Because I have my own intelligence, I learned what I learned and I moved on." In her view, educational access "may have changed a little today, but still at that point people like myself weren't even expected to be in high school, much less to go on to college." Among her siblings, Alvarado was one of the first to graduate from high school, paving the way for the younger ones, unlike her older siblings, who did not graduate. Alvarado underscored that despite "the largeness of my family—ten siblings—I can count on one hand those nephews and nieces that went to college, on one hand, and that includes my children."

As the first Chicana elected to the San José City Council, Alvarado made her mark in city and county governments. She still had much more to contribute to a community she embraced as her own. In the context of an anti-immigrant campaign that emerged under the auspices of Governor Pete Wilson, she continued to call on the people to struggle for their rights. The way she saw it, those with "the strongest voices need to understand the influence of politics, and in instances where Governor Wilson is calling for so-called immigration reform, we ought to have college students, mothers and fathers, people from all walks of life in our community calling their legislators, because a phone call can make a difference." However, "there aren't enough people who are willing to say, 'Hey, I'm upset about what is being proposed and I'm going to let my representatives know about it.'"

GRASSROOTS ORGANIZER AND POLITICAL ACTIVIST: ERNESTINA GARCÍA

Born on an agricultural ranch in Tollison, Arizona, Ernestina García recalled that her parents were born in the northern states of Sonora and Sinaloa, Mexico: *"Mi mamá nació en Ciudad Obregón, and mi 'apá en Culiacán"* [My mother was born in Ciudad Obregón, and my father in Culiacán]. Her father "was active during the *Revolución,* and after that *trabajó en las minas, y después en el rancho, pero no les pagaban mucho*—he worked in the mines, and then on the ranch to support all of us, but they didn't pay him much." In agriculture, her father sought seasonal work contracts that would soon come to an end. One positive aspect was that the jobs came with housing. However, nothing was free, since the owners deducted the cost of living arrangements from their wages.

Describing her upbringing, García spoke about being "very happy in a crowded house because we were many—seventeen of us." Yet, while her home environment was happy, her schooling experience was not, because "we went to a segregated school." A memory she was not able to erase was "how we were treated as Mexicanos." With age, Ernestina's memories of being marginalized by race and class have become more painful. She said, "For some reason as I get older, I seem to feel and think more about it because me *da mucha tristeza*—it overwhelms me with sadness." School and work were linked with García's memories of living on the ranch in a dilapidated home that belong to the rancher where the family worked. She explained, *"Vivíamos allí, trabajaba mi 'apa para el ranchero, y nosotros,* as we grew up of course we helped *trabajar en el algodón* or worked the cotton or whatever." Her father received the family wages, even when her mother also worked doing domestic duties for the owner's wife while also meeting the domestic needs of her own household. Their mother washed clothes for the rancher and his family, but it was her oldest sister's responsibility to clean their house: *"Mi hermana,* the oldest, *trabajaba limpiándole la casa a la señora."*

Those experiences taught García many lessons at an early age, not only about their worker status but also about the racialization of the spaces in which they resided, both in the school and in everyday life. She spoke about their segregation in school, demonstrating a cogent understanding of oppression. García recognized the inequalities "at an early age, *pero no podía entender porque es que los hijos del ranchero podíamos jugar con ellos mientras que estábamos allí en la casa, pero cuando se trataba de la escuela no, no podíamos"* [but I could not understand why we could play with the rancher's children while we were at home, however when it came to school we could not, we could not]. This racialization was evidenced in the separation they experienced at school, having to ride a different bus from the white children, even though they played with them at the ranch. *"Venía un bus a levantarnos a nosotros los mexicanos, y otro a los gringos."* García could not fathom why the two groups of children traveled separately event though they were going to the same destination. In school, too, they were in complete segregation, with cyclone fences that kept them apart. Worst of all, *gringo* children had brand-new playground equipment, while Mexicans were left with a bare desert landscape that had nothing they could play with; gringos had swings, slides, and Mexicans had nothing: *"tenían columpios y tenían el slide y nosotros nada."*

Proud of her family's work ethic, García said that her family never received public assistance, despite difficult economic times. She said, *"nunca me acuerdo being on* welfare because *ellos no creían en eso.*" She did not remember receiving aid, even though there was one time that the family sought medical care at a public hospital. It happened during the cherry-picking season in San José. To cook, her mother relied on a modified barrel that looked like a potbelly stove. They fired it with the kindling and lumber they found at the ranch, and her mother would make tortillas and coffee on it. *"Mi amá le ponían leña por debajo y andábamos todos corriendo y en una de éstas se arrimó la chiquita* toward where mom was cooking *y jalándole la ropa, en una vuelta le cayó café y la quemó*—it burned her." With tears in her eyes, García told the story of how the children used to run circles around the stove. In one of their rounds, her little sister got too close and when she pulled at her mother's apron, the coffee pot fell on her and burned her. Her sister received serious burns, and the family rushed her to the hospital. "At the hospital, they wouldn't take us," and they had to drive to Oakland, where her aunt passed her off as a daughter and had her admitted to a hospital.

Once settled in Decoto, California, her father started work at a foundry, *"en una fundición que estaba allí."* Still, because theirs was a large family, they all contributed financially. When the children worked, their wages also went into the family fund to be doled out later for whatever expenses arose. *"Aquí está el cheque—ellos nos daban si necesitábamos pa' los gastos*—our parents would give us money when needed for our expenses." Soon, with the size of family they had, her mother was able to ease her way into work. *"Mi 'amá, poco a poquito, empezó a trabajar en una* nursery *que esta allí en* Niles." It was then that her mother began to work in a nursery located in Niles. Most of her life Garcia didn't work for pay, since there was too much work to do at home. *"Pero si trabajaba* [But I worked] on and off, seasonal work, and then we started growing, and *yo no mire mucha escuela.* I didn't see much school, except that I did graduate from the eighth grade."

In 1948, when Ernestina was seventeen, she met Tony García, and after a two-year courtship, they eloped to Reno. The couple would later divorce and get married a second and then a third time by the Catholic Church: "We went to divorce court and began courting again, married again, then we got married by the church, so we had three marriages." Her marriage would be one of constant change and struggle that

FIGURE 39 Ernestina Garcia as a young woman. Courtesy of Doreen Garcia Nevel.

lasted a lifetime, but with a strong commitment and partnership in the struggle for social justice.

To support their growing family, Ernestina and Tony García migrated throughout Southern and Northern California. She recalled that the circular migration pattern began with her marriage: "*Cuando nos casamos vivimos en* Oakland *y luego* Berkeley *y pa' atrás en* Oakland, *y en* Oakland *fue cuando nos fuimos pa' atrás pa'* Berkeley *y* Hayward *y de allí nos fuimos pa' atrás, pa'* Oakland, *y allí vivimos más tiempo. No espérate, se me esta pasando, nació la* Doreen *y nos fuimos a trabajar para* Oxnard, *y luego nos movimos para* Santa Maria." García detailed migrating up and down California towns: Oakland, Berkeley, and back and forth to Oakland, Berkeley again, Hayward, Oakland, and Oxnard. The couple regretted leaving their firstborn daughter, Doreen, behind, under the care of her maternal grandparents, so they could work. Finally, they returned to Decoto, "*pa' atrás, y yo estaba muy triste esa época de nuestra vida, porque estábamos muy, muy pobrecitos*" [I remembered feeling extremely sad during that period of my life, because we were very, very poor]. The Garcías were so poor that they found themselves sleeping on sacks of beans. "*No teníamos cama en un tiempo y dormíamos arriba de sacos de frijol porque el hermano de él tenía tortillería y parte restaurante. So, dormíamos arriba de sacos.*" Her husband's brother had a tortilla-making business that was part of a restaurant, where bean bags became their mattress.

Still, the poverty was less difficult than the sadness of not being with her daughter, Doreen. Before too long, more children arrived—four girls and a boy—and García went to work to pay tuition for Catholic school. When both parents were working, they alternated their children's care, switching day and evening shifts; she took care of them in the daytime, while her husband took the evening: "*de día yo cuidaba las criaturas y él las cuidaba de noche.*" Tragedy struck when one of their younger girls got a hold of some matches, which she inserted into a socket: "*la niñas se agarró una mecha y la metió en el ese, tu sabes donde esta pa' prender la luz.*" A dilapidated house, "with exposed wires *se prendió, y mi niña se quemó y la más chiquita se estaban también quemando los ricitos. Tu sabes, yo agarré una sabana y la agarré hacía me, y yo me quemé poco la mano—todavía traigo cicatriz—y la niña se fue.*" Her fourth child perished in the fire. "*Fue the fourth—* Dorinne, Curley, Gina, and Teresita, next Dianne—Dianne is the baby." This situation was so traumatic for the youngest child that she experienced a lifetime of problems, "*a la más chiquita se le grabó tanto que por mucho tiempo tuvimos problemas.*"

A settlement of $1,000 gave the Garcías the option of buying a home, which they built in Milpitas in 1967. That was when the children's Catholic schooling ended, and their public schooling began. Ernestina explained: "*Ya no podíamos mandarlas a la escuela católica porque no había aqui,*" there was no Catholic school in Milpitas. The children started attending public schools, which compelled Ernestina and Tony to become active in their children's schooling: "So, *tuvieron que ir a la pública, y de ahí es donde empezamos a meternos."* Up to then, her activism had focused on teaching catechism because there was no Catholic church there—so *"daba catechism en la casa porque no había iglesia."* Then, *"me metí en ir a la escuela con mi muchacha."* She intensified her activism when García learned from her daughter that students were not treated right at her school and she did not want to attend anymore, expressing dislike for the teachers and their treatment of the students. Mexican-descent students who spoke English did not have to clean the school but served as translators for those who were assigned these tasks.

García also spoke about the everyday racism they confronted, *"había mucho racismo porque la gente, los maestros discriminaban a los mexicanos."* The environment became so hostile that students demanded the establishment of Black Student Union and a Chicano Student Union.

In García's memories, school was not a very happy place for her growing up; she only went because she had no choice. She recalled having to learn through rote memorization, since the teachers were not interested in instructing Mexicans. García equates her schooling with brainwashing. They would "teach us to memorize material for the day." She said, "As I got older, I started thinking 'they were really brainwashing us.' *Porque lo que ponía en el* board *la maestra era* 'land,' *y* aprendieramos 'land, America, beautiful' *y luego* 'red, white, blue' *y* 'President Washington.'" Ideological concepts were written on the board to Americanize them and their views about the world. She resisted and to this day has difficulty accepting ideas at face value.

García felt she gained limited knowledge in school, since memorization was an ineffective teaching tool. She recalled experiencing difficulty learning—not to write, nothing. *"So, yo no aprendía nada—ni escribirlo, ni nada. Cuando aprendía,* it was to memorize things, *pero de saber de que se trataba. Amen."* Concepts were never explained, but children were pushed to learn *"el Preamble, y el Preamble lo aprendí yo, pero por memoria, y lo aprendí* saluting the flag, *porque decía el maestro 'él que aprenda esto no se tiene que quedar pa' la tarea, después de la escuela.'"* She learned her assignments because it kept her from having to stay after school. She did not understand the material, yet *"lo aprendí de memoria, pero no te creas que entendía yo*—I just got the gist of it ... but liberty and justice for all—that I couldn't get." She added, "There was no liberty. There was no justice for us, not for them, not for poor people ever, or Mexicans."

She spoke about annual activities where those who had more resources would donate their discards to the poorer children. That was something that would stay with her for the rest of her life. For example,

Un Christmas—eso nunca se me va a olvidar—el único Christmas que nos llevaron a todos los Mexicanos al auditorio del otro lado de donde está la escuela. Tenían ahí un bonche de criaturas Americanas sentadas en un lado, enfrente, y tenían una caja de presentes, y way up

on the stage, tenían una caja grandota; era cómo un acto donde abrían la caja y salía una muchacha vestidita cómo la Shirley Temple tap dancing—*era la hija del ranchero.* [One Christmas—this I will never forget, the only Christmas that—they took all the Mexicans to the auditorium at the other side of the school. They had a bunch of American kids sitting in front on one side and they had a box of presents, and way up on the stage, a big box—it was like a one-act play where they opened the box and out would come a girl dressed like Shirley Temple dancing tap—it was the rancher's daughter.]

García continued:

Yo miraba todas las criaturas como iban muy vestidas, con sus patent leather shoes *y todo.* I wondered *¿por qué?* You know, *pos uno pobremente vestido, ropa que mi 'amá nos hacía en la casa, zapatos—cuando tenía zapatos—no estaban nuevecitos.* So, *yo nomas hacía así* (tucks her feet under her not to show the holes on the soles). *Tú sabes cómo querer esconder mis pies 'pa que no me miraran mis zapatos con hoyos. Luego venía el Santo Clós. Yo no entendía "¿Por qué tienen Santo Clós?" . . . También ese día nos llevaron a la cafetería— nunca podías tú comer en la cafetería, nunca, nomás ese* holiday. I mean, *eran cosas que le hacían a uno en la escuela.* [I would look at all the children who were dressed very nicely, with their patent leather shoes and all. I wondered why? You know, we were poorly dressed with clothes made by my mother at home, and shoes—when we had shoes— were not new. I would, you know, attempt to hide my feet so they wouldn't see my shoes with holes. Then, Santa Claus would come in; I didn't understand why Santa Claus—in our house, Santa Claus didn't come—the Magi came. We would go home, and I became happier because I didn't like any of that stuff. They also had a cafeteria, that day they took us to the cafeteria, but you could never eat in the cafeteria, never, only that holiday. I mean, those were things we did because we went to school.]

She recalled one time when an English-speaking woman came to the house seeking her mother. "*Pero 'amá no entendía inglés y, pues, menos nosotros,* but there was someone at the ranch who spoke English and translated for *'amá, 'viene por las muchachas porque les van a dar zapatos*—they had come for us to provide us with shoes." The children piled into the woman's car, and they went from ranch to ranch, picking up Mexican children along the way. When they arrived at their destination, the school, "*nos dieron unos zapatos*—they gave us shoes. Man, you should've seen *esos zapatos.* I noticed that the styles come back—*vienen pa' atrás los estilos que usaban las viejitas,* with the buckles, *y esos otros de tacón.*" Those were not girl shoes, they were for older people, and "*los míos se me salían,* they were too big." García showed the woman the shoes did not fit, and the woman promptly gathered up "*un bonche de algodón* and stuffing the shoes with cotton, she said, 'They'll be all right, you know.'" Apparently, the woman's only interest was to get them to school, *"que fuéramos a la escuela,"* not to teach them but to generate attendance funds. *"Fuimos de la escuela con esos zapatos que se salían y* when we returned with our floppy shoes, *'amá miró los zapatos y dijo, '¿Cómo que? Dame. Quítate esos zapatos'* [my mother looked at the shoes and said, 'What is this? Give me those. Take off those shoes']." Her mother took away the shoes, stating they would not be returning to school because she would not allow those who had nicer things to mock her children because *"mis hijos no son burla nadie."*

When her father returned from work, their mother showed him the shoes, and he promised that his children would remain home until he was able to buy them shoes. *"No van ir a la escuela hasta que yo pueda comprarles. No van ir y esos zapatos si viene la mujer tírenselos en la cara."* Of course, no one was actually going to throw the shoes in the woman's face, but García *"was happy que no iba ir a la escuela."* Still, the rumor spread that they would be throwing the shoes in the woman's face, and the children at the ranch excitedly awaited the impending shoe showdown. "Sure enough, *a los cuatro días* after *llegó,* and *mi 'amá agarró los zapatos y estábamos gritando 'Ahí viene en el carro.'* There were few cars, and we knew who was coming into the ranch." Enthusiastically, all the children ran toward the car, and "amá got the shoes and threw them at the car, instead of at the woman *antes de que se bajara del carro, y no, no volvimos ir a la escuela;* she just took off." García wondered how those people gave themselves license to treat Mexicans that way. *"¿Cómo es posible que nos traten así? ¿Por qué razón?"*

She carried vivid recollections of life at the ranch: "We looked for work, to see how we were going to survive at the ranch; *no íbamos casi nunca a la escuela porque íbamos de allá, para acá, a trabajar en los files,* up and down California, *y luego pa' atrás y el siguiente año a trabajar en el* Valle Imperial, San José, *y luego pa' atrás,* Walnut Creek *y pa' atrás.* It was a time when we all lived the same way: *¿Cómo te dire? Era una época de que todos vivíamos igual."* Throughout her life, Ernestina García experienced and witnessed poverty all around her. "All Mexicans experienced the same thing, and for me, poverty, that type of poverty—*esa clase de pobreza—yo no la miraba triste, pero la miraba de que,* something's wrong."

Despite the poverty, their parents raised them to know better, to behave so there would be no doubt about their education. "The way *'que nos crearon, nos crearon en modo de que todos tenemos que respetarnos uno al otro, y todos tenemos que ver por el pro-jimo y no hay distinción,'* that we have to respect one another and that we have to treat our neighbor as we want to be treated." Even though she honored the family's philosophy of equality, García recognized differences among people, such as *"la tienda era de un Chino, había negros en* Phoenix *cuando venía uno u otro a la tienda, pero no había vecinos de otras razas, nomás el ranchero que era gringo y los mexicanos."* García talked about the ways her father kept them in line on Saturday and Sunday when there was no work or anything to do. So, he would have them march with a stick. *"Bueno, vamos*

a marchar. Cada quién agarramos un palo," singing *"mexicanos al grito de guerra . . . alre-
dedor de la casa,* until we were tired—it was our entertainment."

The English language was hard for García. She illustrated her point with a story
of the time she repeatedly asked the teacher for a "slip," thinking it was the word for a
"clip." It didn't take long before the teacher lost her patience, and she shoved García,
saying, "What is it you want?" "'Slip,' *y de slip no salía yo."* Soon, the teacher began
pushing and shaking her, telling her: "I'm tired of you people. You don't know how to
speak the language." If it wasn't for the teacher's helper who came to García's rescue,
the situation would have escalated, but "Helen *fue pa' allá* and told her, 'She wants a
clip,' saying 'she doesn't know English very good,'" to which the teacher retorted, "Why
doesn't she learn the language?"

García's most painful recollections were about the treatment of students who did
not speak English. They were placed in a closet. *"Aquel que no aprendía y no sabia el
inglés muy bien nos metían a un closet."* This she viewed as unjust. "It was unfair. *Pero
que injustos. La mentalidad que ellos tenían*—they were afraid of us, and I was afraid of
them." She recalled, *"El miedo que yo les tenía era porque eran malos. I'll tell you eran
malos, y no podía ver como se ponían a gritarle a los mexicanos como si fueran basura,* you
know, it was sad; *fue muy triste. Nunca volví pa' la escuela*—I never returned to school."
Her fear was exacerbated by her dread of the English language, because "it is not an easy
language, *el inglés pa' mi no es un idioma tan facial. Yo nunca lo pude dominar. Nunca."*
She could never master it, but on the other hand, at home she learned *"el español"* from
her father. He taught them to become literate with the newspaper: *"Mi 'apa agarraba
el periódico y él lo leía, y nos decía 'Léeme aquí' en los* funnies—the comics—that's how
we learned, *así aprendíamos. Allí en la casa es donde aprendimos."* In her narration of
the experience, García illustrates the ability to understand both languages, imparting
complex notions of her experiences in school and with language.

While most people would regard her education as too limited, graduating from
the eighth grade was a source of pride for García. She pointed out that she attended
meetings with educators such as President Locatelli at Santa Clara University. "For
example, at Santa Clara University *estaban cobrando cien dólares, y dije cien dólares
¿para qué?* It was a good thing they told me, 'You're going to go in free, just tell them
your name—you will be on the list.'" At the door, however, García was refused entry
because she could not pay fifty dollars. She told the person at the door, "Well, then,
I'll just go home, I'm not going to pay fifty dollars for that." A black woman *"se arrimó
y dijo,* 'What's the trouble?' *Le dije,* 'Well, I'm not going in.' I didn't even know *quién es
esta negrita.* 'I'm not paying no fifty dollars.'" The woman asked her, "'Wait a minute,
what's your name?' *Le dije mi nombre,* 'I'm with the Confederación de la Raza.'" With
that, García gained entrance, and she listened to "very good speakers. I loved some of
the things that were said there."

During lunch, they had discussions at the table. All of them proudly displayed their titles, "'I'm so and so, with such and such.' I was the only one at that table who didn't have a degree. Santa Clara Mayor Souza was there." She pondered what she would say, and when her turn came I told them, *"les dije,* 'I am Ernestina García, and I graduated from the eighth grade and I'm very proud of it.'" She understood the sacrifices her family had made and recognized that not many Chicanas of her generation graduated from high school, and that most were lucky to have finished elementary school.

SELF-MADE BUSINESSWOMAN AND COMMUNITY SERVICES ACTIVIST: ESTHER MEDINA

Esther Medina was born in 1936 "in Rancho Cespe, which is in Fillmore County, on a ranch in Orange Grove, which was a community of families that lived there." Her father was an immigrant who could not read or write; both parents came from Jalpa, in the state of Zacatecas, Mexico. Her father came because "of the killing. He had fought in the Revolution, he witnessed a female cousin get killed." As agricultural workers, the family migrated "all over, settling in San José, when I was about four years old," and "I have been involved as long as I can remember." The youngest of four female and four male siblings, none of her sisters were activist leaders but most were active in the church.

Medina has memories of life before coming to San José. She was about two years old when they moved from a camp at Santa Paula. She does not recall how long they lived there but remembered going to "Lindsey, California, to pick olives," where they were "promised a real nice place to stay" but instead were given "a shack, a one-room shack with a dirt floor and the boards in the so-called walls had gaps, about an inch and a half between them. That's where we were supposed to live." In San José, after residing in several houses, "we went to a big old Victorian house. I remember feeling very at home. It was a good childhood, but I remember being very unhappy in school."

In her relationship with her parents, Medina perceived her mother as exceptionally supportive of her and quietly nurturing her goals, while she and her father "clashed big time." Despite their disagreements, Medina "listened to his ideas. He upheld the responsibility to make things better for people." He thought that "I asked too many questions. I was not what girls should be like; he was very traditional, and I was too opinionated." She said that "the rest of the family was used to getting a no, and I had to find out why he was saying no."

Medina graduated from high school in 1955 and, like other women of her generation, was not encouraged to pursue a higher education. Her option was a "beautician career because it was a way to make money." To get the necessary funds to attend vocational school, Medina worked full-time in a nut-shelling place, and "I saved all my checks to pay for beauty school." As a beautician, Medina was valued for her skills. She recalled, "I did very well. I was able to take care of my parents. And then they passed away six months apart."

In between high school and graduating from beauty school, Medina married her first husband, whom she met at the Rainbow Ballroom, a dance hall that catered to the Mexican community. Once they were married, though, she learned that "he wanted money, he was a very materialistic person." Over time, Medina realized they had "different values, and so we weren't compatible. He saw me as a person that was to be used for whatever skills I had to make money." Their marriage lasted fourteen years.

In her adult life as a businesswoman and an activist leader, Medina's investment in the community was built on a philosophy she learned from her father and her family. Her father helped homeless or displaced Raza as ethnic brothers, explaining that his own children might find themselves in need of somebody's help someday. Her mother supported his altruism, and her father also taught her that there were many ways of helping the community. That was their way. "We just made room for them. It was kind of a natural thing to do." Moreover, during World War II, Medina recalled that her father brought "Latino soldiers to our home" because it was a sort of social insurance that maybe someday other people would take in his sons who were at war. "He would invite soldiers that looked kind of lonely out there and brought them home." She explained that although "the family is very aware of giving," she and her father were the only activists. Medina added that her father "was a very political man and a labor organizer." "One of the reasons that we were, in a sense, evicted out of the place where I was born was because they organized a strike; they were asking for thirteen cents an hour instead of ten. And we were buying food from the company store. It was a big rip-off. And my father and some of the men organized a strike."

The economy and employment sectors were weak during the Depression, and competition for the few jobs available came from those migrating from the blighted state of Oklahoma. She remembered them arriving in "little rickety-dink cars and trucks, real poor-looking people, as poor as we were, but blond and blue-eyed." They displaced Mexicans from their jobs, "and we were basically thrown out of our home, evicted and our furniture was put out in the front yards, then we were put in a camp—a federal camp, I think." According to Medina, agricultural interests were "concerned only with keeping the wages low and minimizing the cost of labor. The company threw us out." She was not certain if there was government intervention in that strike, but "I think it was some kind of state or federal welfare thing. According to the size of the families, we were given tents. We would stand in line, and we would get milk. I remember eating a lot of applesauce." During that time, the children went to school in one huge tent.

"They had like childcare there and stuff." Although those memories are sharp, Medina did not "remember exactly how long we lived in this tent." She was certain that their displacement "was as a result of the company throwing us out because our fathers were trying to better conditions for the workers."

"I remember my father being involved in many things. He was part of the people that started the Comisión Honorífica Mexicana in San José and also among those who started the Fiestas Patrias; he worked hard on getting them started. So, he was pretty involved." From her family, and her father in particular, she learned to stand up for herself and her people, upholding the responsibility to try to make things better. As a result of the marginalization and discrimination Medina experienced growing up, for her the notion of social justice "is so strong" that she imagined at ninety years old "still being like that."

Culture was central in their lives too. For example, in Santa Paula, despite lacking a formal education, her father organized the parents to pool their money together to bring a teacher from Mexico. Although Medina did not recall the teacher's first name, she could still picture her face and would never forget her surname—la Señora Ortea. However, not all of the children were happy about the additional schooling. For example, her siblings "used to gripe, because they'd get out of American school and they have to go to Mexican school." Yet, if it were not for that additional instruction, her older brothers and sisters would not speak Spanish fluently. Education was very important to her parents. "I remember my father putting on whole plays and knowing everybody's part and teaching it to people." Unable to read, he relied on memorizing the stories he narrated to children in the neighborhood. "I remember when I was a kid, kids came to my house and sat around my father, and he would tell us stories—I mean they were great stories."

Still, Medina does not have such fond memories of her experiences with educational institutions. She said that they walked to school, and "for some reason they never sent buses after us." They lived in a berry camp—*campo de la mora*—with many families. "We all went to school with these kids that had money. Their fathers were presidents of banks and all that stuff. And the teachers treated us differently." Shunned because of race and socioeconomic status, Medina recalled her early schooling experience in San José. If students did not meet hygienic standards, they were kept "out of recess and play," and "you had to stay indoors and put your head on the desk. So, the kids would come in—every day—these kids would laugh" and called them names "when they returned to the classrooms." Sometimes this separation affected whites as well, when "the rich kids would end on our side because there were less of us, they would become angry with us. I remember that happening a lot." So in addition to dealing with the isolation of separation, they had to contend with the anger of the white children who, because of their poverty, were assigned to the Mexican side.

Medina never raised these issues with school personnel. Instead, she took her concerns home. "I remember telling my parents, and my father and mother sitting down and would tell us: 'You know you're worth a lot. You come from this culture,' and they'd talk to us about the culture and how ignorant people were." In their wisdom, her parents gave lessons in compassion. "They'd tell us not to hate them, because they were ignorant people and that we had to remember what we were worth, and they would counter all this negative stuff that was going on at school." She could not emphasize enough how helpful it was to have the support of her parents. "I am sure that if they had not done this, I would really be messed up. I remember being very depressed in that school."

It was these and other childhood experiences that inspired Medina to help her people. When she entered high school, Medina organized the Latin American Club, since students of Mexican descent were not included in other school organizations. She explained, "I remember all these little sorority clubs. Even though by the time I got to high school I had enough clothes to pledge to one of those little clubs," her interest was more "in forming my own." "Unless you came from a wealthy family, you didn't belong to any of the clubs." Thus, she began to strategize a way to create "a support base, to have a feeling of belonging. It's kind of, if you don't let me in your circle, I'm going to create my own." Her interest was not only in creating a social club but in doing "social stuff and good stuff for people." Medina wanted "these people to know about us." By "the end of the year, the school gave the club a trophy for all the things" they'd achieved, and the Latin American Club "was selected club of the year."

In recalling her dream of pursuing an academic education, Medina pointed out that "in the 1950s, there were few opportunities for Latinos, in terms of jobs or any kind of policy-making positions." "When I was a teenager, it was unusual to even know any Chicano issues." To the best of her recollection the only educated individual who was organizing around education "was Ernesto Galarza; he was the one that anybody would listen to," since there were few Chicana/Chicano educators, "even teachers were

FIGURE 40 Esther Medina, in high school, photographed at the Santa Clara County Fair. Courtesy of Cameo Burton.

unusual, a lawyer was unusual, and they weren't very involved; they weren't giving back to the community." And those who were there did not see the need to involve themselves in improving la Raza: "It was kind of like getting away from their culture." While not speaking directly about Americanization, Medina emphasized the assimilation of those who left their community to become part of the dominant group.

After achieving financial success, Medina would sell her businesses to work for the public good as an activist for women's rights. From the Santa Clara County Human Relations, Medina landed a position with Economic and Social Opportunities as the founding director for their Women's Program, and later she was head of the Mexican American Community Services Agency. At the peak of Medina's career, for her work and contributions to the community and for advancing the educational options for Mexican Americans, she received an honorary doctorate from Santa Clara University—a recognition in which she took much pride.

EDUCATOR, ORGANIZER, AND ACTIVIST: SOFIA MENDOZA

Her paternal family origins connect Sofia Mendoza to Arizona, although the family's ancestral roots link them to the state of Jalisco, Mexico, where her father was born. A transnational family, her paternal grandfather owned "a lot of land in Arizona, a lot of cattle, a lot of goats," with "several boarding houses, a bakery, and a store—two or three stores; all of his businesses were run by his children." Her grandfather had "nineteen surviving children." Her grandmother, from Chihuahua, was a "Tarahumara who spoke the language, a language we often thought she was making up." It took them a while to figure out that "Valentina really did speak Tarahumara." A fighter, Mendoza's grandmother was involved in the Mexican Revolution with "Pancho Villa, of whom she used to tell us all kinds of stories." Her grandmother came "from a family of conviction; she married a widower with thirteen children when his first wife passed away, and my grandmother had eleven children. So my grandmother raised them all—that is, his and theirs." Mendoza added that "some of those children were older than she was when she married my grandfather. And so there were nineteen surviving children." In addition to assuming responsibility for all the family members, "grandmother used to wash clothes for boarders, cook, and clean house." Her dad worked in the bakery and would go out and sell baked goods, while other siblings worked in the store. Mendoza said that "my dad, because he was one of the younger ones, used to have to go out and tend to the goats and the cows."

Her father's side of the family had money. "According to dad, their financial security prevented them from suffering during the Depression, but he gave away a lot." Mendoza explained, "I mean they tried to help in any way that he could, and during that time, my dad got very active with organizing efforts. He said there was a lot of activity, a lot of stuff going on in the '30s, and he was involved in all of that."

Sofia Magdaleno, later to become Mendoza, was born in Ventura County in a town called Fillmore. At that time, her dad was in San Diego "involved in something historical. In the [1900s] he organized a strikeout of fruit pickers in the biggest ranch in California." After the strike, they evicted everybody. Mendoza "witnessed the displacement of farmworkers from the agricultural fields." In San José, she would learn that Goyo Medina, Esther Medina's father, was also involved in that strike. "I was just a child. I was really young. I might have been, maybe like, three years old. I remember a lot of tents—what they called a tent city—and then they took all of these strikers and housed them."

According to Mendoza, "the unions were supporting the strikers. It only lasted six months, but it was one of the longest strikes. It really was." When the strike ended, it was the onset of the Second World War, and the family migrated for work. "From there, we went to a little town called Sonora. Yet another company town, and my dad got a job in the mines, started working, and called for a strike. What happened was that the Second World War started, so they had to settle with the strikers because they needed the copper for the war." Mendoza did not recall how long the family stayed there but remembered moving to San José. While her father was engaged in the strikes, her "mother was always involved in helping the striking families." Often, her mother would say she wanted "one of my kids to be just like me," which influenced Mendoza's decision to eventually become an organizer and leader for the betterment of her people. The family finally settled in Campbell, California, "where my dad bought an acre and we were just out there by ourselves." In that new place, "it was just our own family, so our parents would do all they could to keep us kids together, saying, 'they got to mind, they got to make life better.'" As the oldest child, she saw herself as the "sergeant with my brothers and sisters." Amid all of these activities and struggles, Mendoza realized change "started with me. I took my responsibility very seriously when my parents weren't home."

Sofia and Gilbert Mendoza married in 1954. "When I married him, my father got very upset." She dropped out of school with the promise to return, even though her dad warned her that if "you get married, I'm going to have that marriage annulled." After her marriage, "my dad didn't speak to me for a long time," and he warned her that she was "going to change. You're not going to be the same person." To which she retorted, "No, dad, I will be." It would not be long before they reconciled. "After my son was born, he came over commenting, 'I came to see my grandson, not you.' So he came in with gifts and after a while we started talking. Then he met Gilbert and absolutely adored him."

Mendoza saw her parents' family as "a very stable family," adding that "I've been married for thirty-eight years. We've never been separated one day. My husband and I have a good, good marriage." With the belief that "organizing starts at home, and then it goes from our family, to the community," Mendoza spoke about involving their children in their activism. She stated, "My children are not like other kids, they are committed. I think my kids have very good values, a lot of respect. They love people and they interact very well with people, and I think it's because they grew up being involved with everything that I was involved in." In her organizing philosophy, Mendoza believed in having your own house in order, "because if I can't organize my family, I have no business organizing out in the community." Moreover, she perceived her organizing and leadership as linked with her domestic responsibilities, valuing both in equal ways. Mendoza clarified: "That's why the role I play at home is important. The other thing is that when you hold a position like I do, my house—looks like an office—I have papers all over the place. They have to learn to live with them. I have stacks of paper. I have books I mean everywhere. Phone calls all the time. People just dropping by, and, so my house is like my office, that's the way it's always been." The work of organizing and taking on leadership was not a new endeavor for Mendoza. When "I was living in East San José, 'cause my husband made me leave Campbell, I became involved in educational rights," focusing on children. "The first thing I got involved with was starting a preschool program; we had a house with sixty children, all poor and minority." With the preschoolers came the mothers who would be taught how to instruct their children. "It was a wonderful program." She explained, "When I organized the preschool—sometime in the early '60s—the antipoverty program, Model Cities, came into town and we tried to get monies for our preschool before Head Start, but they didn't know what they were doing."

Throughout their relationship, Gilbert Mendoza supported his wife's activism, as did their children, who took part in her work. Mendoza said, "If I didn't have a husband that understood, we would have had problems a long time ago. He was very receptive. I'm out there by myself, but it's like my whole family is there." Throughout her years of activism, Gilbert Mendoza was central to her work. "My husband was really, really, helpful to me." Both shared the consciousness that in activism "you've got to play all of these roles."

From her parents, Mendoza learned "that organizing starts at home," believing that "if you're a social worker, you start your social work in your home with your family. If you're a leader, you provide leadership within the family. Everything starts at home." Informed by her dad's values and beliefs, she articulated that "if you can't get it together at home, you got no business trying to go out there and tell people how to do it. If you haven't done it at home, that means you don't know how to do it right."

Her work with preschool children brought Mendoza recognition. "We became more and more well known, we were dealing with a lot of people that were minority, low-income people, and their kids were going to Roosevelt Junior High School and facing a lot of discrimination." In 1965, middle school students began to talk to Mendoza about

FIGURE 41 Collage of Sofia Mendoza with her husband and children, flanked by her inspirations: Dolores Huerta and César E. Chávez. Courtesy of Karl Soltero, from her memorial program.

their daily experiences in school. "The kids, they would tell me this happened and that happened. I didn't believe it, so I said, 'Oh, okay, come on, let's go see.'" She brought her concerns to her husband, who believed that they were telling the truth. He said, "They're telling you the truth because that happened to me." Armed with his support and the information she had collected from students at the school, Mendoza went to the principal. He responded with, "Well, you know these chongs and these surfers." Not familiar with those terms, Mendoza asked for an explanation, to which the principal said, "Well, the changos are the blacks and the Mexicans, and the surfers are the white kids." She could not believe the principal was speaking that way about the students.

This was her first big organizing effort as an adult, where she partnered with parents and youth in the community to address the mistreatment they were experiencing in school. Mendoza explained how she went about organizing, focusing on youth. "So then, the kids used to tell me, in fact one of them became my, I had several foster kids, one of them that I picked up at Roosevelt is living with me and is forty some years old now, and he's still living with me. He used to tell me, 'Oh, so and so, the teacher hit so and so in the classroom.' And I used to tell the kids, 'Don't do anything, just write it up and tell me.'" Soon, Mendoza had gathered "sixteen complaints, very well documented. The kids were continuously getting thrown out of school or sent to juvenile hall." She invested her energies in the students and convinced them of their leadership responsibilities, and sooner than she expected, students brought "all this stuff and what I did is that I got about half a dozen parents and all this documentation." Mendoza wasted no time exposing the mistreatment and inequality experienced by students. "I called the newspaper and I walked down the halls, went into the classrooms, and I confiscated sixteen paddles." They "were exactly where the kids told me. Exactly right on the spot where the kids told me." As a result of their organizing efforts, Mendoza "was able to show that there was discrimination in that school." Moreover, she uncovered a tracking system that targeted ethnic students.

Even after exposing the inequalities and mistreatments experienced by student, Mendoza "organized parents for a year." She went house to house and instructed children to "tell me if somebody else gets in trouble." Then that person would send her to another kid, and she would request that they continue sending students who were mistreated to her, so they would "send me to somebody else that gets in trouble. I did this for ten months. I have a big stack of documentation," which she used "for the removal of thirty-six teachers and the principal and the vice principal." We got a lot of publicity. Then, "in 1966, things started happening at San José State, and the students joined us. We joined the students, 'cause by this time they organized—they had an organization called Student Initiative. And then after that came MEChA, and then the EOP Program. So the community and the students from the school got really, really, really, well organized." With the new communities of interest—students of all ranks, community activists, and others who wanted to make a difference in their community—Mendoza continued her work for social justice. An activist leader who began her involvement at the grassroots, Mendoza collaborated with students and their parents to bring about social change at Roosevelt Junior High School.

In all her involvement, Mendoza relied on the ethics of compassion and notions of equality she learned in her parents' household. She remembered, "My dad would come home at night, and if we had been too busy and if the dishes had not been done, my dad would go straight over and do the dishes." He taught his children that regardless of gender, "you do work because it needs to be done, not because you're a man or a woman." Her father was a progressive thinker who was impacted by the "Depression—there was a lot of organizing during the thirties. I mean that's when unions were organizing all over. People were having hard times."

From her parents, she learned to help others. They were both very compassionate, helpful, and "believed in helping others. My dad would bring people in, then my mother would find them a place to stay, or she'd find, if they needed furniture, she'd go out and find them furniture." They made a great partnership, "so there was a combination between my mom and my dad. My mom was more like the social worker, very resourceful, she just knew where to go get things." She recalled her dad bringing strangers to the house. "I just ran into this man, and he just arrived from Mexico with no place to stay," then "my mother would go and set him up, and if people needed help they knew they could come to the house." The lessons she learned, such as self-sufficiency and self-help, she passed on to others. From her mother, she learned to sew. "She taught us how to knit, how to crochet, how to cook, how to do, I mean, everything." Mendoza's father would also instill self-reliance. "My dad, because we lived out in the country, said, 'If you're going to drive, you're just not going to drive you are going to have to learn to fix a flat tire. If a car doesn't start, you're going to have to learn why the car doesn't want to start.'" Her parents taught them they could rely on themselves as well as help others who were less fortunate.

Power and education are two concepts that guided Mendoza's work in the community. She said, "My whole thing has been to show people that they have political power, and my main goal has been to convince people that they are intelligent." Mendoza believed that "intelligence comes from birth, not from education. Once you begin, it's part of that empowerment, not just political but people have to know that they're intelligent. They are creating something they have, but yet somebody's been trying to take that away from them." Mendoza regretted was that she could not always "convince people that they are intelligent because they're born with it; I mean people have been taught that if you're not educated you're not intelligent. I know a whole lot of educated people that aren't too intelligent," pointing out that there are "just as many uneducated people that are super, super intelligent," and "that intelligence goes hand in hand with political power." Her "goal is to show people that they do have political power in numbers, and that they can together have a voice."

Mendoza said: "We turned this town on its head over, and over, and over again." However, nobody has given their efforts credit. "I hear people talk, 'Oh, our housing department.' They never say, 'Chicanos made us work to have this housing department.' They never say, 'We have ten people on this council because Mexicanos were the ones that had an initiative on the ballot.' Never do they say that there was a turnaround in the police department because of Chicanos. They don't tell us that, and these are major, major, policy issues." For Mendoza, changes have been brought about as a result of Chicana and Chicano activism. Many positive changes were realized because of Raza's investment in improving social conditions in their communities.

Throughout her life, Mendoza was perceived as someone with the capacity to get things done and to enlist others in whatever endeavors are necessary to create change. She explained that "as the oldest girl of five children, I was given a lot of responsibility for my siblings, and I always used to boss everybody. I wasn't much older than them but I felt that I had a handle on it." In high school, she noticed that "they had all of these clubs, but no Spanish Club." So, she organized the students in the different Spanish classes and got a Spanish Club.

That was her first organizing effort. In retrospect, she said, "I'm very happy to say that everything that I have organized people around have been winning issues." In her efforts, she felt confident in launching an organizing campaign because she trusted her intuition and rested on the assurance that others would become involved in righting the wrongs they saw. Mendoza continued to become active with other issues, and high school became a time for sharpening her organizing skills. She recalled,

> I had a Spanish teacher who had an accent; I saw him more as a Chicano, and, at that time we didn't have Chicanos or Latinos—Chicanos that went to school there. Encouraged me in the classroom and because of him I was on the Awards Commission. Volunteered for everything, anything where you had to take responsibility. I was always there, and I worked beyond what was expected of me, and was always told that I could do much more.

Although Mendoza did all she could to improve her school, she could not become involved in everything, recalling that her dad always told her to pick her target. This was in reference not only to the issues she confronted but also to her performance as a student. He would say, "Pick your targets—look in the classroom to see who's getting what grade and that's your target. You do better than that person." Her father inspired Mendoza to aim for the top and to achieve her best. "Don't ever be satisfied. We always have to make it better." She followed his advice and was able to graduate from Campbell High School a semester early, because "I took a whole bunch of classes—seven or eight classes—I liked a challenge and I got my credits early on and graduated." Through a friend's encouragement Sofia went to San José State. Her friend's father used to say, to this other Japanese girl and myself, "you go to school, you got to become a teacher." He had a dream of becoming a teacher and moving to Trinidad. "We had big plans when I started San José State."

The passion to achieve became foundational to her education and was also the guiding principle by which she would carry out her community work. "I guess I'm somewhat of a public figure. When I'm out here, people see me, and recognize and acknowledge me," Mendoza said. "I come from a very, very, humble Mexican background," yet "people expect me to tell them how to do things, tell them what to do." But "when I go home, I can't impose my will because I have to be an equal," underscoring that her husband comes from "a very, very, tough background. He grew up in Westminster, went to a segregated school, so he came from a different background than I did. His experience has been very different from mine." Based on that, "I have to play a different role with my husband. So, when I'm at home, I'm no leader, I'm no organizer." Still, it is sometimes difficult to negotiate interactions at home. "It's so hard because you want to push at home, and you can't." She noted, "You can't complain to others, not in a Mexican family you can't," even though there are times she wished she could talk to others about conflicts that arise.

Sofia Mendoza's community investment and involvement continued until she passed away in 2015. She would be recognized for her contributions to San José by all whose rights she had fought for and protected.

DOMESTIC VIOLENCE ACTIVIST AND POLITICAL WARRIOR: BEA VASQUEZ ROBINSON

Bea Vasquez (Vasquez Robinson after her marriage) grew up in a two-parent family of six brothers and three sisters. She had a sad and dysfunctional childhood, with much poverty. She grew up with an "abusive and alcoholic father," and a mother who was "very timid and afraid of being sent back to Mexico" because of her legal status. Vasquez Robinson's memories of childhood were painful and traumatic.

Her parents came from Mexico. Vasquez Robinson was born in Ventura, California, and the family later settled in Gilroy before moving to San José. While they were living in Gilroy, her "brother died from a burst appendix." Because the family "didn't have a regular doctor, medical insurance," the only recourse was "the county hospital, as they called it, and so by the time that he was brought in an ambulance, the appendix had burst and he died."

Her mother, Francisca Vasquez, went to school as far as the third grade. "An interesting woman," Vasquez Robinson said, "she loved classical music, poetry, and flowers. She had a green thumb and a lot of attributes that don't usually come without an education." Her father never went to school. "He was totally unlearned," even though both parents "read and wrote Spanish." Their English-language skills were very limited: "neither one of them learned how to speak it well." She and her siblings "were brought up having to translate for them all the time—that was my parents."

Vasquez first married at the age of seventeen, and she acknowledged that this was her way of escaping the home environment. "I was just trying to get away from the home situation and stupidly married and promptly got pregnant. And before you knew it, there were two children and a third on the way." When she came to terms with the fact that her marital relationship was not good for herself or her children, "I finally left him because he was a batterer. I feared for my life. Then, after that I had to raise and be responsible for [my children], emotionally and financially." At the age of twenty-four, divorced and with four children, Vasquez had to seek employment. "I had to hurry and find a job, and so I did."

Vasquez met her second husband when "I went to work in the sheriff's department; he was a captain of the civil division, and after about a year we got married." She added, "I married because I was looking for help in raising these children." Mr. Robinson was "sixteen years older, so that put him in his forties" while "I was twenty-five. So, we married, and he adopted my children. We subsequently had two for a total of six children, who are now all grown and gone."

FIGURE 42 Bea Vasquez Robinson, on the left, with her brother Manuel and sister Frances. Courtesy of Bea Vasquez Robinson

During her marriage, Vasquez Robinson "became active. I did it through the home and school, the PTA, the Boosters' Club." With the building of a new high school, Vasquez Robinson "became involved in the Boosters' Club and in just about everything you can think of . . . and much to my surprise I found could be in charge of a fund-raiser." Her first fund-raiser netted $600 dollars. "I was in shock that I had been able to pull this thing together and was amazed that I could function in a world in which I had never been involved."

She gave credit to her husband for the support he provided in the children's schooling: "I think that in the beginning because I was young myself I was grateful for his assistance and his support, I felt that that was okay." When the marriage was faltering, Vasquez Robinson continued with it for the welfare of the children. "If that was the price I had to pay, that was okay. As the children got older and as I felt stronger, not

FIGURE 43 Bea Vasquez Robinson's school picture. Courtesy of Bea Vasquez Robinson.

so needy, I began to change, then things changed in and of themselves." Her initial involvement in her children's education gave her the self-confidence and fortitude to believe she could make a difference in the lives of others. It was this community activism and Vasquez Robinson's divorce that opened up new venues of involvement for her. Still, she attributed the break-up of her family to the times and the age difference between her and her husband, adding, "I could have stayed with him except that I was sixteen years younger and the women's movement, the sexual revolution, all those things that were happening in the late '60s and '70s, and with it I changed."

As a woman, with a different notion of herself than she had when she entered the marriage, Vasquez Robinson said the "relationship began to change, and he couldn't change with it." Yet, despite her personal and emotional growth, she felt pressured by her husband "to be the way that I had been and I couldn't." So rather than stay in a marriage that no longer worked, Vasquez Robinson returned "to school, and I read and I became involved and I no longer was the person that was so needy." For her, it was unsatisfying to remain in a marriage that failed to give her personal support, even when it provided for her children. She searched "inside myself for strength, and our relationship got lost. He since has died, and I have been divorced for about eighteen years."

The mistreatment experienced by women, and the secondary space to which they were relegated, awakened the consciousness that compelled Vasquez Robinson to fight for social justice. She created a space for women in San José and the county of Santa Clara, founding the Women's Alliance, or WOMA, to provide services for women who experienced domestic or personal violence—a place that is now called Next Door. "Once I separated from [my husband], I became involved in a women's organization that was forming at the time," remaining "with that organization for fourteen years." Not only was the creation of such an organization a life-changing venue for women who needed the service, for her it was a new start. "It was the beginning of a whole new experience, and it pitted my skills, skills I didn't even know I had, against overwhelming obstacles in terms of having this organization succeed and get a name for itself in this community. I think I succeeded." Little did she realize that her drive and determination would compel her to create options that had not previously been available for Mexican American women: WOMA became the first bilingual domestic violence program in the nation. Vasquez Robinson readily immersed herself in work that "was probably the most dominating force in my life. We were expected to work and to be productive, and so, as a consequence, I have a very strong work ethic. Everyone in my family does." Free from the responsibilities that came with marriage, Vasquez Robinson moved on to create women's consciousness-raising groups.

Personally, this was a difficult time for her. Her ex-husband discouraged and sabotaged her involvement, counseling their children to turn against her. "He was totally against it and would really [try to turn] my kids against me." He demonized her activities, suggesting that "I was a loose woman who would likely become a lesbian—all these horrible things that frightened them. So, my relationship with my three youngest became a little bit weird." After much thought about what would be best for her children, Vasquez

FIGURE 44 Bea Vasquez Robinson, when she was as director of the Women's Alliance. Courtesy of Bea Vasquez Robinson.

Robinson agreed to let them stay with their father. As she saw it, it was best for all concerned, "for me to go because I did not want to disrupt their home life. So, I left them." This decision allowed her to "devote night and day to the organization," although she had limited income. Her commitment to the movement against violence toward women did not come easy. Financially, there were many sacrifices. On average she had "about $200 or $300 dollars a month to pay my rent," and she was only able to survive because "a lot of people gave me donations." While the services filled a need and provided her recognition, her commitment to her community brought much heartbreak for Vasquez Robinson.

A graduate of San José High, Vasquez Robinson began to take courses at San José City College, which gave her an honorary associate of arts degree. She would later take professional development courses at San José State.

Vasquez Robinson spoke about her early years in school. "When I first went to school I didn't speak English. Isolated, I was very scared because of that language barrier and because we were extremely poor. We dressed accordingly. Neither my father nor my mother had any idea of kids wanting to be like their peers. That was very far removed. We just dressed horribly." Things were no better "when we settled down in Gilroy—Gilroy was a bad experience. We always looked like nerds." However, "when we moved to San José things got a little bit better but not much." She recalled going to school with "my shoe soles flapping. I only had two or three dresses and no coat. I just always looked awful and braids, braids, braids—I wore them until junior high school." Despite the poverty and the language barrier she had to overcome, "I seem to have done okay in grammar school."

Still, poverty was not the only difficulty she confronted in her school. Vasquez Robinson's creative genius was not appreciated or nurtured at school. For example, when she "started writing poetry in junior high school a teacher really stunted me because she caught me—I mean my grades were fine—writing a poem rather than doing what I was supposed to be doing." She spoke about the humiliation: "She grabbed the paper from my hand and she proceeded to read it to the rest of the class. I misspelled *walked* and she pronounced it as *whacked*. The whole class laughed. So that stopped me from writing poetry for many, many years. I had a writing ability that was stunted."

The injuries of class and race did not prevent Vasquez Robinson from recognizing her abilities to critically view the world and to learn. Her grades were good in junior high school, but her social status was evidenced in her presentation of self. "I was not a popular child because I dressed horribly. I didn't have any of the social graces of the other kids." Moreover, the limitations imposed by her mother, who "was extremely strict," kept Vasquez Robinson from developing friendships. She added, "She really was the one that raised us and she didn't believe in us spending the night with our friends. We didn't go to movies like everybody else did." Thus, the activities in which they participated as children centered on the family, such as going "to the Mexican movies," attending "church all the time—Catholic Church." With a life of deprivation and social isolation, "we just didn't do things like other kids. We didn't have skates or bicycles or anything like that. It was a hard life." In the end, the strict and controlling environment imposed by her father and maintained by her mother pushed Vasquez to leave home, so when it came time to apply for college as a way out, she did. She took the entrance exams for San José State College and was accepted, but her mother, who needed her to work in the family restaurant, La Rosa, expressed disappointment: the family expected her to "work full-time at the restaurant." Without support and encouragement from her family, instead of going to college "I just ran away. I eloped instead." Only one of her siblings, José Vasquez, attended college, the University of Bridgeport, thanks to the GI Bill, although without completing a degree; none of her other siblings pursued higher education. However, one of her sons, Victor, graduated from the University of California, Santa Cruz.

In her activism, Vasquez Robinson focused on bringing people together. All of her lived experiences and social isolation were a consequence of her economically, racially, and sexually marginalized social position. As a result, these experiences framed her notions of fairness, equality, and justice and became foundational to her role in the struggle for women's rights in San José. She explained, "Because I know what it feels like to be on the fringes. Because when you're a little child there's nothing you can do about that; that's just who you are, that's your place in life. So as an adult, it was really important to me to bring people into the circle, so that we could all have a better life. I think that basically describes me as a person and why I have done what I've done."

Even with this philosophy, Vasquez Robinson carried injuries that still hurt when she thought back to her youth. She recalled the classism and racism she experienced at San José High, which profiled her to be picked on or marginalized by others. Still, "I was always a good kid, a goody two-shoes." She spoke about a traumatic experience that happened during physical education class. "I was in swimming, and I never learned how to swim but I was in a swimming class, and I was second to last. I was always late getting out because I was horribly embarrassed about taking showers. Those days you took showers; it had just changed from private showers to double showers." She did not like exposing her body, so it was difficult for Vasquez to comply with the change. She explained that "we were raised to be very private about your body. I was always waiting so I would not have to shower with somebody—the last to leave the area." So, one fateful day the dean of girls called Vasquez into the office and accused her of stealing a girl's watch. Taken aback at such an accusation, all she could say was, "What?" They blamed her because she was "the last one there." All she could say was "I don't know." The accusations were repeated: "They would call me into the office and keep me there. It was horrible. I cried, and cried, and cried." Finally, when they could not get a confession of guilt, they warned Vasquez that if the watch was not found, they would tell her mother.

When the watch was found, she was called to the dean's office. Without hesitation, Vasquez asked for an apology: "Well, I think you should apologize to me." But, no apology was forthcoming. "They refused, of course." For Bea Vasquez, nothing hurt her more than being blamed for that theft. To this day, she said, it is "the most horrible, heart-wrenching thing that happened to me." "As it was, I was already shy, and then to have this happen, it just felt so damning. It was saying, 'You are no good.'"

These early childhood lessons taught her to create community. While she could not do anything about the feelings of exclusion she felt as a child, as an adult she made it her objective "to bring people into the circle to create a better life." In her view, the insight and awareness she garnered set her course as an activist leader. Vasquez Robinson spoke about her activism "at the national level, organizing women's centers," as the co-founder of the first National Association of Women's Centers, and her work with the National Coalition Against Domestic Violence. Yet, her involvement was not restricted to gender issues. She became active with the Bay Area Construction Opportunity Program (BACOP), "which in the '70s brought minorities and women into apprenticeship programs." She was one of "nine county board members to help

FIGURE 45 Bea Vasquez Robinson is in the front row, fourth from the right. Courtesy of Bea Vasquez Robinson.

make that happen." For her, this was an "important but intimidating and scary experience." Vasquez Robinson explained: "BACOP consisted of developers and these huge nationally known construction firms, and I'm sitting there at the meeting, and they talked about women as girls. In fact, they referred to them as girls, even as they brought them into these apprenticeship programs." Extremely invested in the project because it stood to improve the lives of single women who were heads of households, when she first joined the group, she waited to speak. She observed, took notes, and gained insight on the men who made up BACOP. "It was at my third meeting when I first spoke because I wanted to make sure I knew who everybody was, what the agenda was, so I really studied everything, and I was well prepared, but I didn't speak until the third meeting." Rather than address the issue under discussion, she gave the board a lecture "on what they were doing and why it was so wrong and why these programs would fail," informing them that "from this day on, I don't want Indian women referred to as girls." Soon after, she became the first women elected to the executive board.

Yet, she felt that the "work she did with the women's movement was more important." Her endeavors emerged at a national conference where the idea of starting a women's organization would take hold. They wanted "a National Women's Centers Association . . . and set a date to further discuss it—most were from the East, I was the only one from the West. I think as a result of my being involved, there was an awareness of the need for bilingual services that was just never there in the women's movement." Vasquez Robinson began her involvement in women's rights in the early 1970s, inside a movement with "a middle-class focus where I raised the issue for bilingual women's services nationwide."

The issue of language and culturally informed services was central. However, it would be at another conference, in Denver, that she would have to call out these activists on their preconceptions:

> I've been coming to these conferences and talking, trying to convince you all, but I'm not going to try any more. I give up. But, I'm never ever going to quit believing the way that I do. If you don't want bilingual services, it's all right with me, because every time there's a grant available at the national level, I'm going to go for that grant. And I'm going to get it and you're not because I'll offer bilingual services and you don't see the importance of it and that's fine with me.

Up to then, all her words had been for naught. Until she hit them in the pocketbook, she was ignored. "So, I brought an awareness of the needs of minority women to the Domestic Violence Association, the national organizations, and women's centers; I can't believe they were so *atrasadas* or backwards." Vasquez Robinson founded the first bilingual program nationally and in California. "It was one of the bigger programs; most of the programs had budgets of less than $50,000, but I used a lot of political muscle to get where I was."

Despite her efforts to confront domestic violence and violence against women, the media coverage that Vasquez Robinson received did not help her cause. "I remember an article, I can't recall the newspaper, but I was quoted as saying, 'No woman deserves to be beaten.'" Criticisms and comments came from all sides, with statements such as, "'If she acts up, she's going to get kicked.' Those days, it was a very radical statement. And for a Latina to say that was even more so." Sexism and gender issues complicated the ways in which domestic violence was understood. She recalled that women of color at conferences would readily caution each other "to be careful because we don't want to get our brothers upset," and she would retort with, "I think you're wrong, you're wrong! They abuse a woman, it doesn't matter what color they are. You can't protect them because you're hiding behind color." She would eventually move out of her work in domestic violence and "turn my energy into Latino issues."

Her strategies to gain the attention of the politicians knew no bounds, and often caused her trouble. One time, Janet Gray Hayes, then the mayor of San José, expressed

FIGURE 46 Bea Vasquez Robinson with Governor Jerry Brown. Courtesy of Bea Vasquez Robinson.

her displeasure when Vasquez Robinson jumped a guard rail to speak to the state governor. "I got right up to Governor Jerry Brown, and before the guards could come I was already talking to him, and I got what I wanted. I got his agreement on something I wanted. But I would do spectacular things to bring great focus on what I wanted." Her challenge to social conventions antagonized Mayor Hayes and other women leaders— white women leaders. This happened not just at the local level, but nationally as well. She recalled getting into a horrible disagreement at an international conference in Mexico City. The argument "was with Betty Friedan [because she was] totally against having the idea of caucuses, and I had called for the formation of a Latina caucus. It was very simple. That was an argument too: all I did was to write Latina Caucus with a felt-tip pen on 8½ x 11 [sheets of] paper and posted them around everywhere with the room number to attend." Her efforts resulted in the recruitment of 250 women, although "I thought it would just be maybe ten or twelve, and we'd sit around in a little circle and decide about all these things that were going on. No! There was this huge crowd." Instead of trying to understand the politics of power for women of color, "Betty Friedan was really upset. So I went to look for her where I knew she was going to be, and confronted her. We had told the news media that this was going to occur and they came." *Time* magazine covered it. Freidan attempted to educate Vasquez Robinson on the divisiveness of her organizing strategy, explaining that "it was divisive for Latina women to get together, and we were arguing, and she was raising her fist, and I was yelling at her."

The media and women's community focused only on their struggle because she took on Betty Friedan. "The things that I was doing, to bring Latina women together, and not just Mexicanas—Latinas from over here—I was crossing a lot of barriers, and it was amazing! These women all wanted to do it. Every single day we held meetings, and I had reporters trailing me everywhere. The conference organizers realized that they couldn't stop it, it mushroomed; we were getting a lot of attention." In the end, Vasquez Robinson's efforts resulted in the formation of a committee, and they started working with Chicanas/Latinas, but by then the conference was almost over. However, "things that we had written got included in the report, and we made presentations, and even though it was done in a confrontational way, it was very, very important. But that's the way you got things done."

In the fight for inclusion, Vasquez Robinson would antagonize women organizations such as the "National Women's Political Caucus, because I'd go to their meetings to tell them how wrong they were, and I did the same with the National Organization for Women to the extent that we formed the Chicana Coalition." In its day, the Chicana Coalition was very powerful; it eventually died because the need for it fell away.

Vasquez Robinson regularly confronted gender and sexism, but she also dealt with racism and its sexist notions. She recalled that "some Latinos were really upset that I had married a white man and so I had to get past that. That was disconcerting. I mean I'm not a racist, but that was really offensive to me. But I got past that." Vasquez Robinson would insist upon being taken seriously at meetings, by men and white women. She explained that "in the late '60s or early '70s Chicano men were just as patriarchal and as offensive as anybody else toward women. It took a long time for them too; number one, they just never let a woman speak, not because women can't speak, but because they always had their hands up and they were always recognized and spoke loudest. So, it was really hard." When she spoke, she found herself being "forceful and aggressive and was seen as a bitch. Those were the words. 'She's a bitch,' if you stuck to your guns and made motions and were forceful; you were a bitch." Men tagged her as aggressive, and most women agreed with their conclusion. She remembers being "at a board of directors meeting and actually having men publicly call me a bitch. They accused me of sleeping with the board president, just because I was forceful in something that I thought needed to be done; it was some organizational work." In the nonprofit world, she said, women are the ones that carry the load, while males fail to pay attention to details, adding that "women are not taken seriously, are put down, and are made to do the work that's really difficult." On the one hand, they are devalued as women, or "they make you do all the work without advancing you to an executive position or recognizing your achievements." In the private nonprofit world, it was all about "men, men, men. But times have certainly changed. That's not the case nowadays." Back then, there were slights from Chicano males but also from women. She added, "I don't know if this is true or not, but it seemed to me that it took Latina women longer to come around to the feminist perspective. A lot of them would tell me they felt that if you were a feminist you were against your own culture, because you were against men and it was hard to get past all that."

Influenced by Chicanos, Latinas claimed "that because of my feminist positions or ideologies that I was getting too close to whites, I was getting too white, so I had that to overcome." However, "the most difficult part for me was when we had a political upheaval at WOMA and a Latino was amongst the instigators that ousted me from this position." For her, "that was hard to understand. A Johnny-come-lately, so to speak, who felt he was going to make his name based on getting Bea Robinson, sought a lot of power in that for himself. I can look back at it now and see that that's what was going on, but it was hard to do." Still, despite the difficulties of having had her reputation soiled and her name strewn about in the local newspaper and the community, Vasquez Robinson took pride in having relied on her "ability to get things done, having many resources at my fingertips, and knowing a lot of people. Also, my thinking, my ability to strategize and to do long-range planning was appreciated."

Vasquez Robinson accomplished much: "I was on the BACOP Board, the Chicana Coalition, the National Association of Women's Centers board, and on the Legal Aid Society's board for six years." Also, "when WOMA received a $100,000 grant, and I signed to purchase the shelter—that was a historical moment." Another highlight of her work was the time she was asked to go to Morelia, Michoacán, to retrieve a little girl who had been kidnapped by her father. (For a full account of this event, see the appendix to this chapter.) Still, she is most proud about the "redistricting victory that benefited Chicanos most; that was historical. The first time anything had been pulled off by a Chicano group. I was very involved in that victory."

CONCLUSION

Chicanas of the Depression Generation followed their parents' paths of involvement in their communities. Ideologies of equality, fairness, and justice, pursued with a collective and collaborative approach, informed their involvement, despite or because of their early experiences of trauma. While both Chicanas and Latinos/Chicanos of this generation focused on race and class in their efforts to create social change, Chicanas also had to challenge the power of gender, which directly excluded them from equal and fair employment and access to education. Chicanas were involved in creating employment, education, and policy options that gave them access to opportunities in employment, as well as fighting for fair and equal treatment of Raza in their neighborhoods and the larger community. They worked to create employment policies designed to open up cultural, political, and economic options not previously or readily available to them.

Chicanas challenged and opened spaces where they were previously excluded, creating venues for services and improving their quality of life as women of color in a community that had disregarded them. They contested and challenged the ways in which their gender limited equal access or fair play in the marketplace, engaging everyday expectations in their families and communities, beginning with the recognition that poverty and race were limitations.

Chicanas also entered political arenas and created culturally affirming services not previously available to them. These activist leaders contributed much to the community. For example, the first bilingual and bicultural domestic violence program was founded in San José. As well, Chicanas of the Depression Generation organized campaigns to improve education at all levels of access, created anti–police violence programs, engaged in antiwar activism, and fought for affordable housing options not previously available to Raza. Most of all, Chicanas—along with Latinos/Chicanos—worked to improve the everyday life of their community. The following two chapters address the experiences of Chicanos (chap. 9) and Chicanas (chap. 10) from the Baby Boomer Generation.

APPENDIX

Just as Bea Vasquez Robinson was being pushed out of WOMA, she had an unusual opportunity to fight injustice when she was asked to go to Mexico to retrieve a little girl who had been kidnapped by her father. One of her clients at WOMA came to her for help. As Vasquez Robinson narrated the story, woman said to her, "Bea, you're the only one who can help me. I'm certain *mi esposo se la robó y se la llevó a México*, my husband has stolen my daughter and taken her to Mexico."

"Poor woman," Vasquez Robinson recounted during our interview, "she didn't know what to do. Even though she lacked evidence of the kidnapping, since she had escaped an abusive relationship with him, she was sure he most likely took her." The woman had proof that she was the child's mother, and she had a secure job as a janitor at a local hospital.

Vasquez Robinson continued in her client's words. "*Estoy segura que usted puede ayudarme a traerla. Si alguien lo puede lograr es usted.*" She was certain I was the only one who could help her. If someone could do it, as she saw it, it was me.

"*Usted me ayudó* when he mistreated me *y mejoró mi vida. Usted y* WOMA me *ayudaron* to get out of that abusive relationship." Once again, the woman reiterated, "You're the only one that can help me."

With little prodding, Vasquez Robinson decided to join the aggrieved mother on her quest. Before their meeting was over, they began their plans. With guidance from anyone from whom she could seek assistance, Robinson amassed the materials that would validate and affirm her association with the woman. Congressman Norm Mineta, a friend, provided a letter written on congressional letterhead to vouch for Vasquez Robinson, lauding her as an advocate for women survivors of domestic violence.

"You know Norm, he would help anyone who sought his assistance."

Meanwhile the mother "arranged for time off from work and secured the necessary resources to get to our destination, including a flashy red wig and oversized dark glasses, along with the address where the child could be found."

In Mexico City, the women rented a Volkswagen bug, thinking it the most unobtrusive and economical way to reach their destination, Morelia, Michoacán.

"We found a hotel near the address where the suspect was supposedly keeping the child." With lodging secured, the women kept daily surveillance until they confirmed the daughter was there.

Roaring with laughter, Vasquez Robinson recalled that they "initially parked the car across from the suspect's home." Soon, they had second thoughts about that strategy and parked some blocks away, on the opposite side of the street. Once they spied the child getting off a souped-up truck, Vasquez Robinson and her client made their move.

"In our manual Volkswagen, with the mother of the kidnapped child in her screaming-red wig and Elton John glasses, we went to the truck and grabbed her daughter, rushing back to the car—with screaming daughter in hand. And so it was done.

"Of course, the child was petrified. She did not recognize her own mother. The girl was screaming at the top of her lungs, asking her father for help: '*Papi! ¡Socorro! ¡Ayúdame!*'

"The girl's shrill and frightened voice blared in all directions. And my partner in crime did not make matters easy, as she failed to shed the wig and glasses. She wanted to remain incognito.

"Suddenly, with a gun in hand, the father rushed out of the house, shooting in the air and in the direction of our rented car. He rushed to respond to his daughter's call." Luckily, the two women were able to get away. But the police quickly stopped both cars.

"We were surrounded. The man, who had chased us with a barrage of bullets, stepped out of the truck, and rushed toward me." In a high noon scene, the kidnapper approached, "attempting to intimidate me," Vasquez Robinson recalled. Cursing snakes and toads, "*pinches, putas, and cabronas*," were bandied about. Rather than retreat, Vasquez Robinson assertively advanced toward him, saying, "I'm not afraid of you." Her statement disarmed him more than the presence of the police.

The conflict brought out more spectators to witness the exchanges between the policeman, the women, and the kidnapper. Sides were taken, mostly in favor of the women and child, with cheers and applause coming from all directions. Some in the crowd even dared to tell the police let the women go. Despite the public support, all were taken to the command post, where the person in charge let them have their say.

"*Viejas argüenderas, hijas de sus putas madres*," the kidnapper continued to hurl insults. But the kidnapper lost his bid, as the commander sided with the rescuers because they had proof of custody rights.

"He stole her. Took her in the middle of the night. He lacks the papers that authorize him custody," the commander said in Spanish.

"Let them be. *La niña debe estar con su madre. Déjenla ir.* They're not doing anything wrong; the child belongs with her mother. He had no right to take her."

But while the commander sympathized, he informed the women that his duty was to refer the case to the district attorney: "*Esta decisión está fuera de mi control; la decisión resta con el fiscal del distrito.*" He arrested the alleged kidnaper for having disturbed the peace and sent the women to an office nearby.

At the new venue, the women retold their story. They showed their papers and pleaded their case.

Finally, with a decision in their favor, and with the kidnapper under lock and key and their true identities revealed, the women left Morelia for San Francisco. Still, their troubles were not over. The airline would not allow the women to purchase a ticket for the child.

However, there are many ways that all can be fixed in Mexico, and angels come in many forms. "We found a janitor who worked on our behalf. With instructions not to speak to anyone, she brought us a ticket, telling us: '*No digan nada.* Don't say anything, just show your tickets to the airline staff and make your way onto the plane. *No hablen. No digan nada.*'"

Without a word, the two women boarded the plane and made their way home, leaving behind a bullet-laden VW bug in the parking lot. They were all safe. And the women had no regrets, even though they had placed their lives on the line. As a Chicana activist leader, Vasquez Robinson took many chances for the greater good of her community.

9
• • •

LATINOS/CHICANOS OF
THE BABY BOOMER GENERATION

Members of the Baby Boomer Generation were born in the years from 1946 to 1964, after many Mexican Americans had served the nation during War World II and the Korean conflict. It was a turbulent time: a time of mass genocide, and the atom bomb. A time of space exploration, and a time of unrest. A time when the challenges of Jim Crowism and racial segregation fanned the flames of a nascent civil rights movement. The war in Vietnam was the backdrop against which Baby Boomer Chicanas/Chicanos came of age. It was also the time of the Bracero program, which lasted from August 1942 to 1964. And in August 1964 the Department of Justice launched Operation Wetback, deporting anywhere from seven hundred thousand to over a million Mexicans, including U.S. citizens and their children (Acuña 1988; Grebler, Moore, and Guzman 1970).

With a legacy of struggle and self-help organizing, Mexican Americans continued to challenge unequal treatment, although only those who spoke English and were citizens of the nation would have a part in the League for United Latin American Citizens (LULAC), later to be followed by Americanist projects such as the American GI Forum, and thereafter by the Mexican American Legal Defense Fund (MALDEF). Other political activist organizations that promoted civic and political participation in the community, such as Community Services Organization (CSO), emerged in the political lives of Chicanas/os in the United States. At this time, despite countless efforts to organize agricultural workers, a protracted campaign for workers' rights in the agricultural fields in alliance with Filipinos became the precursor of the United Farmworkers of America (UFW), formed to fight for the rights of farmworkers, alongside the struggle for equal rights and equal educational opportunities for Mexican Americans and their children.

With a legacy of struggle from their own families and their participation in cultural organizations and mutualistas, the Baby Boomer Generation made space and created options to improve the lives of their people. What follows are narratives of Latinos/ Chicanos of this generation and the story of their involvement in the struggle for Raza rights.

CULTURAL WORKER TO COMMUNITY ACTIVIST: FELIX ALVAREZ

Born in McAllen, Texas, Felix Alvarez traced his beginnings to South Texas, where his father and mother were born. He grew up in a large family with five brothers, two sisters, his parents, and one set of grandparents. Alvarez said it was "a big close-knit family because we always lived together." However, it was not "a Brady-bunch type of family. I grew up in a two-bedroom house, one bedroom for my mom and dad and the smaller siblings that grew up literally in their bed, and the other bedroom was for my grandparents." Despite limitations, Alvarez did not feel deprived. It would not be until he graduated from high school and moved to college that he would understand what it was like to live in poverty. He "grew up with was a very supportive family. There was a lot of love. There was no domestic violence or anything like that; it was very nurturing." His early schooling took place near their home. "I went to kindergarten; I went to elementary and junior high, and went home and had lunch, because my grandmother would be there making tortillas *de a mano*, and that whole home environment always being there for me." It would be as a young adult that he recognized "what a strong thing that was for me to have grown up with."

His father "always was working; he was a cook and then he became a chef, having literally grown up in a kitchen." During the Depression, his paternal family was repatriated to Mexico, even though they were citizens by birth. At the age of ten and eleven, respectively, his father and uncle returned from Mexico to the United States. Alvarez said his "family had been victimized when the United States kicked out a lot of supposedly undocumented illegal aliens," even though they were "Raza born in this country." "My father and his brother had been part of that whole shuffling and had been carted off. When my father and uncle realized they were American citizens, they came back on their own."[1]

Despite language discrimination, with the support of the extended family Alvarez "grew up bilingual. At home we spoke mostly Spanish." Because of daily interactions with his maternal grandparents, "my brothers and sisters to this day are bilingual." Alvarez believed that where he grew up had much to do with how he and his siblings ended up as adults. Transcultural and transnational citizens because his "paternal grandparents lived in Reynosa, we were comfortable going back and forth." As a

FIGURE 47 Felix Alvarez as an adolescent. Courtesy of Felix Alvarez.

U.S. citizen, Alvarez grew up with much confidence, shored up by an extended family and the community in which he was raised.

Alvarez's maternal side of the family was "community oriented and socially minded, and involved in what was going on in the community." His mother worked as a part-timer at Penney's. As a Mexicano, he was influenced by a strong work ethic and commitment to the community. Alvarez spoke about the knowledge he gained about being of Mexican descent. "I grew up with that kind of a consciousness. From my mother and my maternal grandfather, I heard stories about Texas having been part of Mexico, that the land in Tejas had been stolen by the Anglos who had come in from the South. I had this historical perspective about who we were as a people." Taught to be "proud of being Mexican," he would not be introduced to Chicano as an identity until much later. "We were proud of being Mexican, and when we say Tejano, you really mean Mexicano; it's Tejano-Mexicano identity, not Mexican American." With multiple identity options, the family was proud of their ancestral roots.

Alvarez was the oldest son, and he proudly shared that one sister and one brother are "involved in some aspect of community service where they're doing something." Although his father was not active in the same sense because "he was always working, but he'd help when he could." On the other hand, his mother was an activist. His mother "got Raza to vote back in the '60s and was also involved in many community issues at the neighborhood level. An activists' activist, she organized at the grassroots level where people would just be drawn to her in the community." This was not something she was pushed into; "it wasn't like she was out there trying to do that, because that is her," she "would stop and help people." Thus, when Alvarez went to college, "it would not be out of place to find somebody living at home staying with us for a couple of weeks. That's just the way we were." Because they had more than most people, his mother helped others, but she could have not done it without her husband's support. Alvarez said, "My dad was consistent. He was there. He wasn't making a lot of money. We weren't middle-class or anything like that, but we knew that we had a roof over our head and that we had food on our table." "In Livingston [California], mother organized student interns from Stanford, and opened up temporary medical services." He proudly described her efforts to create a clinic and the founding of Federación de Clinicas Rurales, which benefited the town of Alviso. He explained that "she went to Washington, D.C., and they brought in millions of dollars into California rural areas to build clinics...up and down the state." His mother also invested in educational endeavors. "My mother was part of the Deganawidah-Quetzacoaltl University, or D-Q University, land takeover,"[2] and "she was part of those two groups: a North American Indian group, and Chicana/o activists."

Alvarez's family would give him the foundation he needed to become active. His upbringing, the historical

FIGURE 48 Felix Alvarez with "No Dogs, Negros, Mexicans" sign. Courtesy of Felix Alvarez.

knowledge he learned from his ancestors, and the ethical principles he adopted from growing up in his family and the community gave him the direction necessary to work for social change. In his efforts to engage social justice and social change, Alvarez followed a trajectory that had been carved out by changes agents who had taken ownership of their community needs so as to make a difference for Raza.

EDUCATION AND COMMUNITY MENTAL HEALTH ACTIVIST: JORGE GONZALEZ

Born in Mexico, to a Mexican mother and a father who was a political refugee from Guatemala, Jorge Gonzalez described growing up as a two-stage process. The first took place in Mexico City, where he grew up surrounded by "an extended family that took two and sometimes three apartments. So that my aunts and my uncles and my grandparents were with us as a whole." His aunts and uncles influenced him. For example, he had "an aunt who was into things that were Spanish and she was a Flamenco dancer, and an uncle who was a bullfighter and more into things that were Mexican." On the other hand, "my mom was interested in things that were American such as U.S. music." In Mexico, his family was lower middle class. "In this country, we would be considered poor the way that we lived because basically it was paycheck to paycheck, but we were not poor in the kind of poverty that exists in Mexico."

His maternal grandfather was the patriarch, and an avid reader who told stories about the *Revolución*, "about the importance of fighting injustices." His maternal grandmother was the matriarch of the family, "a very kind person that worried about the poor and gave food away to people. She was religious and even claimed some visions." However, "we were not extremely religious. I mean we wouldn't even go to church on Sunday. I would say we were more spiritual than religious, and my grandfather was anti-church, but he prayed to the Virgin." Because of all the people who convened at his grandparents' home—those who came from the provinces with their musical instruments, peers from the labor movement, and Spanish refugees from the civil war—Gonzalez was exposed to "a very rich experience growing up in Mexico."

His second growing-up phase was in the United States, "because my mom married an American. So, we immigrated, and then the extended family was no longer there, it was now a nuclear situation." When he arrived in the United States, given the lack of resources in Mexico, Gonzalez was impressed with what he found in school. He remembered they had "lockers, microscopes, and they give you this, they give you that, and you don't have to take a chair with [you] to the classroom. So, I became more interested in school. In Mexico, I liked learning but it was hard for me." In the United States, he entered the seventh grade. Literate in Spanish and knowledgeable about the culture of Mexico, he had a "history, I had my identity, all those kinds of very important things." For that reason, his transition was "not as hard for me as it is for Chicanos or people coming from other kinds of background, so I took advantage of education, and I got good grades all through school and high school." What he did not expect was the racism he would experience or the limited expectations some teachers would have for him. "I got discouraged from going to college, even though politically in school with offices in student government . . . my counselor told me 'college is going to be hard, you should go in the army.'"

Gonzalez experienced inequalities in school. He recalled, "My grandfather had warned me about things like that because he had been in the United States and I sort of understood it, but it was still painful." He recognized the ways in which Chicanos acted as a result of the treatment they received from those who discriminated against them. Yet in general his socialization was positive, and his parents were very supportive. "They basically let me do my things, stood by me, didn't interfere, and my parents gave me independence—it fit for me. So, it wasn't bad."

A blended family, with his mother and stepfather at the helm, there were five siblings, two sisters and three brothers, of whom he was the oldest. Only one brother graduated from college, at Berkeley, with an undergraduate degree in English; "the rest are high school graduates, you know, some college classes." The communities in which he interacted, particularly schools, were populated by groups that stayed with their own. "[There were] two areas where Raza, working-class whites, and blacks [lived]—the Avenues—and then at the other end was a town called Saticoy, basically a lemon-growing region and that's where Mexicans lived—a couple of Asian families,

Chinese." Many people from the community went to Oxnard, "because I think among the working-class people there was more mixing." Ventura was a more segregated community. "I was in a dilemma where I lived," he said, since the area "historically had been agricultural, very segregated," recalling that "in my junior high, we were bussed, . . . passing a white middle-class school, and they would take us to Cabrillo," near an area called the Avenues, "which was the working-class minority school—Mexicans, some blacks, Oakies."

Things would change in high school. Gonzalez attended a school that served a middle-class community, and within that environment, everyday relations sometimes involved "fights because of racial remarks, but there was more of a connection among the people of the working class, regardless. We would go to the movies and hang out together." He spoke about a painful experience he endured: "They assigned an Anglo girl to take me around. Daily, she would wait—the first week, or the first couple of weeks—and she would take me around, introduce me to the teachers, the kids. It turned out she started liking me. Then, one day she didn't wait. She wouldn't talk to me . . . her mother didn't want her hanging with Mexicans." Racism would surface in other environments. Gonzalez recalled, "I was up for football in high school, and I remember we were going to play Oxnard High School." In a pep talk given by the coach—in this mostly white school—he "compared our team with Oxnard's, making racist remarks, such as 'Steve [our quarterback] was more intelligent.'" Gonzalez "stopped the guy, and said, 'Why are you saying that? You mean just because the guy is Mexican you don't think he's intelligent?'" Despite their sense of superiority, "Oxnard beat the shit out of us . . . they—all the Mexicans and blacks—ran us all over the place."

Although it took him some time to pick up on the racist behavior, Gonzalez internalized much anger. "At high school I was picking it up. It was a frustration because I ran around with a lot of white people, running around with people with whom I had something in common." He associated with academically driven peers and recalled Raza saw him as "a *traidor* or *vendido* to his people, but it wasn't at all where my mentality was, no way." Gonzalez recalled being told by those in student government, "We don't think of you as a Mexican," to which he retorted, "What do you mean by that? I am a Mexican." It would not be "until the Chicano movement that you realized the depth of things." When he ran for student government, it was the voting block of "Mexicans and working-class whites—the kids who hung around outside of campus smoking—that voted and gave me the edge." Because of other Raza student and his ability to create coalitions with working-class whites, Gonzalez would create a path toward social justice in high school.

Gonzalez attended Ventura Junior College for two years. It was there that he became opposed to the Vietnam War, and "caught a lot of flak from Chicanos because they said 'it was a white thing.'" His Mexican upbringing allowed him to understand war with a "kind of anti-imperialist, anti-interventionist mentality, to me that was really clear; I don't think that as an individual I ever saw this threat of communism in all of that stuff." He explained that he was not antimilitary, "but anti-intervention, and then knowing what the U.S. had done to Mexico." Gonzalez explored his options and "found out there was a draft counseling center, and I got myself a volunteer attorney, this Jewish lady—extremely knowledgeable, and very nice—and she found legal ways to get me off." He explained, "I think I got drafted, actually got my induction papers a couple of times, and she found loopholes for me," with college as a deferment strategy.

He did not see this as the turning point in becoming active. For him, his activism began when "my parents turned me on to the farm workers movement." As a transfer to San Diego State, among forty-five Spanish-surnamed students in a campus that enrolled 19,000 students, Gonzalez became involved with a group of students to form a Raza organization. "There were maybe five of us, among them was [Chicano poet and activist] Alurista. . . . I became one of the leaders; one of the people promoting the development of a Raza organization." Their efforts yielded the first Chicano history class, "even before UCLA," he added. But Gonzalez said, "Where I really learned was outside the classroom, in the Chicano studies classes, and in the political process of putting the college administration up against the wall to delivery Chicano studies . . . that's where I learned more psychology."

When he completed his BA in psychology, he took jobs that pointed him in the direction of social work: "For example, in job training, being a counselor to the trainees. I was a labor organizer for the restaurant workers union . . . and gained counseling, organizing, and political skills." Then, Gonzalez relocated to San José to join his wife, whom he married in 1978. He was recruited by the League for Revolutionary Struggle to translate for a political newspaper and later became involved with youth and immigration issues, co-founding Youth Getting Together and Raza Sí!.[3] Raza Sí! focused on and serving immigrant families and children, regardless of legal status.

Gonzalez returned to school to complete a higher education degree. In graduate school, having amassed much work experience in the field of social work, Gonzalez found himself repeating the same patterns of his undergraduate experience. "I kept being an activist, and I kept just doing the minimum to get the degree. So I can't really say I've been in an academic situation where I have totally focused on that." It would be the community, rather than his studies, that drove his agenda. After completing his master's in social work, Gonzalez focused on education and immigrant rights. He remained active with the League for Revolutionary Struggle, one of the leftwing political groups that inspired his vision for social change.

As a professional social worker in the field of mental health, Gonzalez was approached to run for the San José Unified School Board. He continued his work with Raza Sí! When Youth Getting Together folded, Gonzalez became a lecturer for San José State

University's Social Work Program. He would be one of the many residents of Southern California who would relocate to work for social justice in San José.

COMMUNITY ORGANIZER AND UNION PRESIDENT: MIKE GARCIA

Born in Los Angeles, California, Mike Garcia described his household as "very macho; the males dominated the *familia* . . . all my uncles were working-class, hardworking men, and very traditional." His mother was a stay-at-home mom, because his father would not let her work. His father was born in an area of East Los Angeles called Maravilla, otherwise known as El Hoyo. Garcia's mother came from another part of the city, from a traditional Mexicano family from Aguascalientes. On his paternal side of the family, my "father's dad was never around." According to family lore, his grandfather was an "Español who fled during the revolution, and married my maternal grandmother, supposedly because she was a maid, and that's what he was used to back in Mexico." Garcia's paternal grandmother "was stoned Indian [Indigenous looking], she spoke Nahuatl," and his "grandfather visited and would come make babies and leave." It was not clear to Garcia why he did that, and he often wondered if it "was because my grandfather was dreaming about what he lost in Mexico?" In his view, "Dad was attracted to her family because it was more traditionally Mexicano."

Garcia grew up in a small nuclear family, with an older brother and a younger sister. His older brother was "a lifer in the National Guard, he's in charge of a lot of people now, but he doesn't project himself as a leader." His younger sister was "very fun person," but she was not a leader, and neither parent is a leader or activist. Garcia explained, "My dad wasn't all that political; he believed in just working hard and surviving. He came from a really harsh upbringing and just programmed himself to think that working hard was the way." Garcia added that his father "grew up in Depression-era East LA with a father that wasn't around, it was really rough. All of them had a rough life, but he worked hard to get his way out of the barrio." Apolitical, his father was never involved and instructed Garcia to "work hard and not question authority."

To Garcia, "Mom was the sweetest person—good mother and everything"; he had no conflicts with her. "The conflicts I had were with my dad because I questioned everything. Also, he didn't like anything I did." Garcia attributed these conflicts to "anger that he never resolved. He wanted me to get what he wanted for himself, but what he wanted didn't match with me." Garcia rejected any aspirations that his father would have had for him. Garcia came of age during the 1960s, thus the times were not the same for his father and him. "My experience was different than his, in a lot of different ways, the eras themselves. When I started getting intensely active, we ended up in a lot of conflict, and I ended up leaving home. His focus was work, survive, and take care of your family. And do better than where you came from." When he was six years old, the Garcia family moved to the San Fernando suburbs, "a white area of the Valley." The influx began with "two families, then three families, and now where my dad lives is predominantly Mexican." His family was among the first few who relocated there. In his new community, Garcia "did not understand the social arrangements, having grown up in an all-Mexican barrio." He explained: "I didn't understand it. I didn't know it. I think it affected my self-image because you get subjected to all the names and stuff, and then by the time I went to high school—it was 50 percent Mexican—and you see some change in that area of Los Angeles. Now, you go out there and there are no white people." As an example of that segregation, Garcia spoke about a time he was driving with his friends on "Ventura Boulevard in the area with open restaurants and stuff, that's exclusively white, they just pulled us over, and my friend resisted." The cops threw his friend "to the ground, trying to search him or something and beat him up. They were saying, 'What are you doing in this side of town? Why don't you just go back to San Fernando?'"

The neighborhood that he moved into "was mostly working-class—everybody's father was either a construction worker, plumber, or PG&E worker." At the time of our interview, the neighborhood had become "mostly a Mexicano neighborhood. The white people have left, and everybody else is coming." With urbanization, Los Angeles slowly absorbed the valley, and with development came the building of freeways. "My dad's house is right across from the freeway, you know, it feels very urban now, from when I was there." With urbanization, the problems they had fled returned. "So now it's a very violent place—urban problems have besieged it, gangs, shootings, killings. It's become pretty bad."

At school or work in the valley, Garcia witnessed white supremacy. "Whites were favored over browns. However, I didn't realize that until after I left." When he was in school, he thought of becoming a firefighter, but there was no example to guide him. "In those days there were no Chicano teachers, all the schools had white teachers, and the coaches preferred whites." Even as a member of the football team he experienced discrimination: "I started one game and he pulled me right out, after one mistake, even though I played a great game, it made me think, 'I must be a bad player.'" Garcia would not understand that this was a form of racism until later, when he "realized that had its effects, especially in sports, you want to excel, you want to be the best person."

Despite the difficulties, self-sufficiency was fostered through hard work. This was not necessarily talked about; it was modeled by "just the fact that all the men in our family were very hard workers—different trades, or warehousemen, or whatever, sign or house painters." The children had to work too. "We had to work around the house, and do our chores, and we went to work at an early age; our father just really pushed work. He never gave us any money; he just made us work for it."

As a young adult, Garcia was involved in community efforts to create access to recreational activities for youth, and he would later become one of the most influential leaders in the Service Employment International Union. His upbringing prepared him to fight against oppression, especially as it pertained to working-class people, and in particular to immigrants, who were the most exploited and marginalized. The union became his life, and his life was union work. "I got carried away, building the union. It's in my blood."

Leading a union "is a big responsibility, moving in one direction, so I get obsessed by it." The only regret he had is that it takes him "away from the family more than I want to." Garcia said, "I've been trying to hold it together; it's a balancing act. It takes communication, give and take, and compromise. I try to be there, to keep the family as a first priority. Sometimes I don't do it so well, and sometimes I do it better—it's a question of focus." His responsibilities as a union activist leader have imposed a great burden on the family, although he said his wife, Gloria, is "proud of my accomplishments, sees the importance of union work, and is proud to be associated with me, and glad that we have a decent living—that my job provides for us." A recent marital separation gave him an opportunity to regroup on the meaning of family. "The separation showed me how much of my father is in me. Taking care of my responsibilities, I couldn't walk away from it—that's what he instilled in me."

A Chicano and a unionist—those two forces grate against each other, but he sees himself in both. He said, "I see myself as a crusader in the labor movement, because I think that its power needs to be expanded into the Chicano community, and there's a lot there that needs to happen." His views begin with the premise that Chicanos are "working-class people above anything else," and this allows him to see that he is "serving a very important role, still making it difficult to get involved with anything in the community while building my union, building our movement. But I also recognize that the unions and the community shouldn't be divided." He elaborated, "I see myself as a working-class person that got educated versus an educated person. I'm proud to have a long history of working with my hands. I'm not afraid of work, and I have a work ethic that got me where I am. I see myself as a person that believes in a strong sense of the family, and I struggle to maintain that role because with it my life's efforts are more important." As a unionist who is an activist leader, "I'm president of the local and a professional leader involved in administration, personnel, management, leading staff meetings and the organization—being the center point, holding people accountable, setting goals and objectives—we go to retreat every year—in a very structured and accountable method of keeping track of our records and driving the organization forward." His work is time-consuming: he oversees twenty-four staff people. "We keep on growing, we're buying a new building, and three offices, and six thousand members; leading contract campaigns; speaking at general membership meetings; driving organizing campaigns," and being active "day in and day out, twenty hours a day." Along with work duties, Garcia is involved in other activities in the SEIU. He has organized "Chicano/Latino caucuses, and I've been at the core . . . now for a year and a half, and it's moving along."

Because the union is comprised mostly of white members, Garcia has had to force the international on issues that impact Latino workers. For example, "we got them to set quotas for hiring. We've been institutionalized by SEIU as part of their oral conference." Still, wanting to ensure that the people he represents are included, he said that "we're putting an agenda together and a list of issues we want the international to move on, and we have gotten them to be more responsive to the Latino membership, and a lot of people are being attracted to it, from all the different SEIU unions in the state." Garcia has witnessed firsthand that Latino caucuses advance the labor movement, and "as long as you play the game right, and you don't threaten them too much, and we are tactful," the union can make changes. He has been instrumental reactivating Latin American Council of Labor Associations (LACLA) to democratize the union, and he has become active with them as the organization of Latino unionists that supports the AFL-CIO. He is very proud of his efforts all over the state because LACLA links unions with the community. Still, Garcia acknowledged that his "focus is on the labor movement because I can't be everywhere, but that's another area where I've concentrated my efforts."

Garcia conceded that "we stumbled on how to organize undocumented workers." He noted that "problems are so deeply rooted that whenever you attack a problem from the surface, you get temporary progress, but the roots are still there." He says you have to try to engage workers in the context of their reality.

Garcia spoke with immense pride about "the locals I left behind—Denver and San Diego—strong active unions—and was glad that I've been able to grow, hang through it all, and I've been able to hold my family together." When the labor movement was dying, the SIEU was "growing by leaps and bounds; I'm really proud of what we have built with the union."

Throughout his endeavors, Garcia created a multiethnic approach to organizing "with blacks, Samoanos, Filipinos, and whites. It was fun pulling everybody together; whatever we did, we couldn't do anything wrong because it was so bad." He also had the opportunity to work with Eliseo Medina, "the master organizer, or the one individual that really taught me how to organize," and it was a great experience. He said he learned much from the Chicano movement, from "Rudy Acuña, the intellectual organizing of José Carrasco in the classroom setting, [but] as far as hands-on, structured, disciplined organizing, and the very keen sense of strategy—it was Eliseo Medina." From him, Garcia recognized that the local was not very disciplined. "Medina comes out of the farm worker movement, if we didn't arrive on time at an eight o'clock staff meeting, Medina had the doors locked." He also learned from Marshall Ganz, whom

Medina "brought for a whole week of planning and strategy sessions." For example, "the circular organizing planning strategy where you put the plan into effect; you organize the situation; decide and put into effect; analyze the plan, come back, meet, strategize; put another plan into effect; and go around until you come across something that's moving. We had great training under Eliseo." Garcia never imagined himself as president of a union. His work has been his education; not having had "training, I have a commonsense approach to managing people."

Though he was invested in community organizing, the union was always priority for Garcia. Yet, as far as SEIU is concerned, "community people have varying perspectives of the union, and a lot of it is based on their hands-on experience." He added that "most people don't have union experience or working experience; they've never worked with their hands for a living—they may have floated around from community agency, to community agency, but they don't understand the labor movement." For Garcia, "the work of the union is complex and has currents going in different directions—progressive forces and regressive forces, and power players, and do-nothings: there's Hispanics and Chicanos who have sold out to a certain way." So, for example, "some community people didn't even understand why labor was involved—they didn't even recognize César Chávez as a labor leader, which he was first and foremost." Garcia attributed their ignorance to a lack of experience organizing in the workforce, as most have not had to fight exploitation as workers. "Hispanics see the movement like 'a political force'—how to get their votes; the labor council has a good political machine, and they're key in getting people elected."

In regard to community relationships with labor, Garcia thinks "it's tied to a lot of different things. Our perspective of working with the community is just one of the many things the labor movement doesn't understand." For him, "they are trade unionists involved with elections and rooted in its demise, in their failures, actually." In this context, Garcia learned from José Carrasco that unions know how to sustain an organization, but they lack the "know-how to build them. They inherited their unions and organizations; it was handed to them, and that creative aggressive style of unionism is built into the union movement, but it's not part of their experience—that threatens them." So, "in terms of community, I'm looking for signs of hope that we'll pull people together." But it frustrates Garcia when members of the community seek his support. He feels powerless because he is "absorbed with union work because I can't do more. I'm doing my piece in building a very powerful thing, pero, I'm hurting for the community."

One of the community partnerships Garcia was able to participate in was the Coors boycott. "That was the first time we took on the Hispanic establishment, over the Coors issue, basically putting labor on the right side of things with the Chicano community, versus the Hispanics—Gloria was the chair." The issues merged his union and community interests. Still, while he tried to keep involved, some people expressed frustration at his limited involvement. "People need to understand that building our union is a full-time job, and I have to spend most of my time on that." Still, Garcia was thankful that he has two community organizers that "represent the local in those issues" even though "they're getting turned off because they're getting sucked into the war, and they don't want to be out there."

Despite the struggles, Garcia was interested in building partnerships. "Community labor coalitions and anything that relates to my area of work I will get involved, like immigration reform, labor—organizing the labor movement to become more active in the community—to show that it's not just a bunch of white guys. We're developing progressive Latino leaders." Of upmost importance for Garcia is the belief that labor needs "to support the Latino community, and the Latino community needs to understand labor issues, because we are a working people; we make up the majority of workers in this city and in this town." In dealing with racism and economic struggle, "we need collectivism as working people, as well as community organizing to make change, because labor has so much to offer us in terms of structure, it is a power that goes untapped." "I want to pull all of it together. That's why we have a community organizer on staff and are expanding it to other unions that want to feed off of our success; they're coming in and they're sending organizers and money, and we can potentially have a big organizing project right here in the East Side."

In his career, Garcia dealt with race and class inequalities; in doing so, he has tried to build coalitions around common interests. Still, it was not an easy journey; there had been countless obstacles and challenges to overcome. For example, "racism was the struggle that I had early on with the union but learned that being an effective labor leader in a white world of obstacles [allows] opportunity for change. I think the fact that I'm Chicano is why I am so effective, and I look at it that way, and anybody that can't handle it, well, that's their problem." "Sometimes it's hard to reflect on things that I wanted to see happen for years, like organizing some of these nonunions that I got so angry with [in] my wars early on, because I didn't have the skills, experience, and support to beat them." Yet, his tenacity paid off. "Companies like Lohman, Sir Thomas, and Service by Medallion—an ongoing enemy—we're really kicking their ass. They're feeling it. The power that we have right now, moving things so fast, and getting much recognition and attention." The mistreatment and bullying Garcia experienced from these nonunion firms has helped turn the tide around, creating a climate of support for the union and publicity in their favor. The treatment he received from their goons was well documented by the local media, and it might have been what broke "Medallion, because I think Oracle's already talking about getting rid of them; they want to resolve the issue." As a workers' organization, Garcia said, "We got our share of good press over the years."

As Garcia reflected on his career, he said there have been many instances of support that have brought him success. "In my career everything kind of turned around. I know

FIGURE 49   Mike Garcia's memorial of life collage. Photo taken at memorial by Josie Méndez-Negrete.

the Apple victory was a big, a big turning point, and I know the hunger strike was the thing that broke their back." While he could not predict the outcome of their struggle, Garcia recognized that "things are moving really fast," and the union is growing by leaps and bounds.

POLITICAL POLICY AND CULTURAL ACTIVIST: PETE CARRILLO

Pete Carrillo was born in Phoenix, Arizona, into a traditional household: "The women would cook and the men would drink." His father would go play cards at the neighbors', and "they'd be there and all the women would be sitting in one part of the yard and would not participate in the game, they would bring out all the food." It was a family that was "very fast-paced, and there was always something happening in the house—a large family of seven brothers and sisters, and my mother and father." Pete was youngest child, with "four brothers and two sisters, who are leaders in different ways." For example, "I have one brother—he's a blue-collar worker—and he works in a factory." Because he's "someone who is very steady and someone that they can come and ask questions of and get answers to, so people look up to him as somebody who is very stable."

The family bought and moved into the house in in which he grew up when Carrillo was less than a year old. He grew up in "a working-class blue-collar neighborhood that had primarily whites and Mexican Americans. There was a lot of families with a lot of kids." Economically, the neighborhood in which he was raised was "one of the poorest sections, known as South Phoenix because it was south of the river."

He recalled that his family and neighborhood generated an exciting environment. Also, being the youngest in the family, "I had a tremendous amount of attention paid to me, and that actually was good, it was good while I was growing up, and then it also created problems as I became an adult." Carrillo perceived his family life as stable and good, although "I remember different aspects of it that were punctuated with good and bad things." Initially, his neighborhood was composed of whites and Mexican Americans, but it gradually became more blacks and Mexican Americans. He recalled that "we all coexisted in a relatively civil manner. There were times in which tensions would flare up but these were minimal." There were a series of confrontations that he experienced at the hands of white kids who lived in the neighborhood and their friends. "These guys would come in their flatbed truck driving through the fields in front of our house, and we'd be sitting there playing baseball or doing something." They made obscene gestures and slung racial slurs at them, calling them "tacos," "taco benders," and "chili chokers." They would goad Carrillo and his friends, who were "pretty good throwers, and I was on the baseball team, and could pitch real good to chuck these mud clods at them, . . . we used to hit them all the time. And they would jump off the flatbed and start running and in all kind of different directions calling us names and everything. But they would repeat it, every week. And, I thought it was hilarious, but that was the only racial incident that I can recall."

Carrillo spoke about one conflict that he got into at school. "In elementary school I used to like to play foursquare. I also played sports such as football and baseball, and sometimes basketball." Foursquare had a particular appeal to Carrillo, not so much as to play it, but to be around "this girl that I liked." He and another male friend would go play foursquare with the girls, but the coach did not like it. To teach them the social protocol for gendered games, the coach paddled them. Carrillo felt that was the only rule they were violating was the "sexist, traditional role that this person thought we ought to be assuming, and the paddle didn't seem to dissuade us from doing that."

Because they continued to participate in "girl games," one day the coach called them into the office and informed them that "the next thing I can do is embarrass you." Later they were summoned to the principal's office, where the coach called them out for continuing to violate the rules. He declared that "the paddling isn't helping, so go to the nurse's office." There, they were instructed to choose a dress to wear and told "once you make that decision, then you have to have it on all day. If all you want is to hang out with the girls, then put on dresses." Carrillo recalled that he picked "a yellow dress with red polka dots, I thought it was hilarious."

Carrillo would experience other conflicts about race and class. There were weekly fights at elementary school. "We knew when a fight was going to occur—alley A was where the boys fought, and B where the girls fought—at least once a week we were treated to pretty good fights, in both alleys."

Despite the conflicts, Carrillo perceived his education as "multifaceted and multidimensional in that it [was] intertwined with both formal and informal education that has been equally valuable." In his view, "my high school education was very valuable for many reasons, including my own awareness of issues and also the value of getting a degree." Although he was active in sports, "I wasn't viewed as a jock . . . I was more of a bookworm, intellectual, but a defiant intellectual." Even though he graduated from school, college education was not emphasized in his family, since "it wasn't an interest, our parents didn't know how to emphasize that to us. I know deep down in their heart they wanted us to go to school, but it wasn't something that they really pushed."

FIGURE 50 Pete Carrillo in high school. Courtesy of Michal Mendoza.

Despite the lack of encouragement, Carrillo matriculated at Phoenix College, and then he went for a semester to Pima College in Tucson, where his brother lived, but a college education was not for him until much later in life.

He would experience informal and alternative education opportunities through work and community involvement. In this way Carrillo gained knowledge that, he said, "I don't think you can get that in a formal institutional setting. . . . I had a rare opportunity to gain experience in terms of public policy, issues in the community, awareness issues, and direct experience in terms of living on the edge." This drove him to the point of almost "being put away for a while, so that in itself, living on the edge in South Phoenix, was a tremendous education." Given his life experiences, Carrillo "does not mind putting on a double-breasted suit and a nice tie and talk to politicians or anybody in a high position," as he does not fear "talking to somebody who is involved in a gang because I've had that experience."

Thinking about his parents, he said, "My father wasn't active but my mother was active in her own family because she was the one that graduated from high school." As a result of her bilingual literacy, "she was the one that did all the paperwork for the parents—she could read, write, and speak both languages, and actually it was through her that I got my political bent." His mother was active in the community, getting her start in formal organizing with "the March of Dimes and the one that was related to muscular dystrophy—MDA." She would collect money for the Jerry Lewis telethon "every time they had their fund-raisers. And so she used to take me with her and so I used to go listen to her talk about the MDA." Her social skills were highly developed. "She knew everybody in the neighborhood. I mean literally knew everybody in the neighborhood." As a result, she often canvassed for political candidates: "She got around the neighborhood distributing literature, leaflets for Senator Barry Goldwater."

Carrillo would have an opportunity to be mentored by his mother and to learn her political ideology. He recalled helping in a campaign "in 1972 when a young man by the name of Alfredo Gutierrez challenged a black fourteen-year incumbent for the state senate . . . Clovis Campbell." His mother allowed him to work with her when she became one of "the precinct coordinators to get out the vote, which I thought was absolutely fabulous, and I learned a lot." He said that his mother was well respected and that gave Carrillo much pride. There would be times when he did not want to help, but his mother urged him to participate: "Hey, the campaign is almost coming to a close, they really need your help and they're depending on you, so you should probably go over there." That campaign was truly a grassroots effort because of his mother. Carrillo picked up people to go vote and remembered that on the eve of the campaign, "a group of us went into the black neighborhoods, which were adjacent to our neighborhoods and we leafleted it with Alfredo Gutierrez's literature." Gutierrez was elected and "became one of the most influential legislators in Arizona's history, and perhaps the greatest orator in the senate, and his second year he became the majority whip."

Carrillo's mother had a tremendous influence on him. "She had something to offer if there was a need," and she acted to meet those needs. She was not an organizer motivated by self-interest: "My mother really thought about it intellectually," and what drove her was her desire to empower other people. On the other hand, his father was invested in his work. "He was a steady blue-collar worker." Although he had opinions about politics, "he didn't get involved and worked in the same place for thirty-seven years—the only job he had was at Borden's Creamery."

FIGURE 51 Pete Carrillo and his mother, Longenia Abeytia Carrillo. Courtesy of Michal Mendoza.

For Carrillo, it was not an easy decision to move from Phoenix to San José. The opportunity came thanks to "an invitation from my uncle, Ernie Abeytia, who ran a store at San Antonio and King Road by K-Mart. He suggested I would have a good time." When the call came, Carrillo was working for North Phoenix High School as a community worker. "I had just completed my second year there and we were on these ten-month contracts," so during the school break he went to "spend a couple of weeks and check it out." During the visit he was expected to help in the store, and he had to contend with the demanding personality of his uncle. Carrillo explained, "I used to take care of the store at night, which I didn't mind, and I used to have to make 100 pounds of menudo starting on Friday, which I didn't mind at all because I know how to make good menudo now, but he had his way of wanting me to do things, which I usually complied with, but he always thought that when I did something the way he wanted it, that he wanted it done differently after that." One Sunday, when his uncle came to the store to inspect his work, he criticized Carrillo for not having carried out his orders as expected. "I didn't say anything to him, out of respect," but the following day he informed his uncle, "I'm going to go look for a job, any job. It didn't matter to me what kind of job because I'm only going to be here for a few weeks and then I'm going back to Phoenix." He applied for work at the Opportunities Industrialization Center (OIC). "I remember it so clearly, I filled out my application," and having done community work was in his favor, "there was a position open for a follow-up counselor. So, I applied for that, and I didn't hear anything." However, "right after the Fourth of July," Carrillo received a call that he had been hired.

He would still have to deal with the challenges of moving. For him, coming from Phoenix, "it was a very traumatic experience. I've always felt a strong need for community involvement, civic involvement, doing things for the community, and at the same time I like to hang around with my friends." Consequently, in a new community and with a new job, Carrillo recognized "that sometime soon something was going to break. I had this feeling that what was going to break was me going to prison because that's where a lot of my friends were headed." With the option to turn his life around, Carrillo decided "to get away from that environment—actually, a good part of the reason for my staying here." Still, the move would be a very difficult one. He added, "the most important reason for me was leaving my family. I was the only one in my family that had left. I've got one brother that lives in Tucson but every other brother and sister lives in Phoenix. So, and here I was the youngest leaving the nest."

In San José, Pedro Carrillo put his formal and informal knowledge into use turning the lives around of those who found themselves in situations he was still trying to overcome. He would create community from scratch, while keeping the support of his uncle, as he engaged social change one person at a time.

GRASSROOTS ACTIVIST, LAWYER, AND POLITICIAN: TONY ESTREMERA

Tony Estremera's parents were born in Puerto Rico and "knew each other in the neighborhood—they met at family gatherings." His parents attended some elementary school. Estremera's father was a farmworker who migrated to the United States to look for work: "he took a boat to Florida and worked in agriculture up and down until he made enough money—from Florida up to upstate New York—picking all the way back and forth, until he made enough money, and then he got an apartment in New York, got a job, and sent for us." Moving to New York was like another world for him and the family. They had no idea it would be as difficult as it was. Linguistically, culturally, and climatically, differences created a traumatic experience for the family. "Being in places where you don't speak the language, or even if you do, you know how different it is, how far away you are, and there we're educated with a few bucks in our pocket. But here, they have nothing. They don't have any property, they don't have any money, and they don't have anything—it was traumatic—didn't speak the language."

Estremera grew up in a big family, with eight children, his parents, and his aunts. His early upbringing was in the "hustle and bustle of New York, arriving October of 1955 at the age of five." He grew up, "with a big family, it was loud, crowded, and had a real exciting kind of early childhood"—much noisier than in Puerto Rico. What was uppermost in his mind was "the transition, because, you know, it's a real significant part of your life, so I remember the trauma of change." He recalled that "when we landed in New York City we had little tee shirts on, because we never knew what cold was, and I remember the cold. It was significant to me. And, I remember the first time I saw snow and things like that, so it was really a significant change, and as you can imagine English was really heavy." For them, English was a foreign tongue. Estremera—the middle child, with three older brothers and three younger brothers plus a sister—was the first one to graduate from high school. His siblings have some high school, but only "one of my little brothers finally finished. Then my oldest brother quit; he had a semester to go."

When it came to enrolling in school, they had no choice. His parents wanted a better life for them. "They never understood, but they knew that [school] made a difference. And, they were very insistent about it, although I had dropped out of high school at an early age also, but I went back. However, they were very insistent about work and the work ethic; I mean, I worked since I was in second grade." His father was a taskmaster and kept them on a short leash. However, "we didn't have male-female trips—everybody got up, everybody got an assignment, you know, we washed the walls, I mean, I remember we did everything." In addition to helping in the house, "the bigger guys took care of the younger guys. There were certain unwritten rules; it is the way things went."

Among the teachers who instructed him were some "pretty good ones." However, because he lived in the ghetto, "the institution itself didn't look out for us." He loved math and science and considered attending a school with that emphasis, but "I took an entrance exam which I didn't pass, which really devastated me, mostly because I thought that I did pretty good." It would not be too long before Estremera recognized that the blame belonged to the institution, realizing that "it's not really my fault, and that's when I became a rebel." Estremera knew, "I was not stupid, we had moved around; we went to nine different elementary schools," and that constant relocation and the tracking system relegated him to the bottom. When they moved to Brooklyn, "I ended up in the middle of the sixth grade, then when I went to the seventh grade, they tested all the kids." There "my scores were so high, they put me in 701—the class where you become the most cultured." Estremera became part of the elite, but then he "took the Regents exam and failed. So, I became a rebel and started not going to school, not taking anything from anybody, not taking any shit."

Ethnically, Estremera learned to see himself as a "Chicorican. The reason I say that is because you know how it is." He explained, "In Puerto Rico, there's three different groups: there are people who want independence, people who want it to stay the same, and people who want statehood. So, really there are three different groups. In New York, there are Puerto Rican Chicanos. They don't belong to these three other groups. They don't have an affinity with the island. They don't really understand it." Estremera himself is twice removed from the island: "born in Puerto Rico, I grew up in New York City, and I'm kind of like a California guy—I came as a teenager—so, culturally I'm more Mexican than anything else." He perceives himself as "Chicano 1,000 percent, because the politics in Puerto Rico and New York are just different, really different from here." Even though Estremera was born in Puerto Rico, "I'm not an islander in that sense." He said, "I visit my relatives. They don't even speak English, which is very unusual. They refuse to learn. Puerto Rico is a very Latin American country and considers itself pretty Latin American."

Estremera came of age during the Chicano movement. However, while he spoke, read, and wrote Spanish, his affinity with Latino culture was not that strong. It was working in this movement that he cut his activist teeth, with guidance from such activists as Sofia Mendoza and Fred Hirsch. He continued his trajectory with the student movement and later took on political and policy interests, holding positions as a community college board member and other public posts. All of this was possible after he joined Job Corps, which moved his family to San José and then to "Pleasanton, and . . . to East San Jo because I met a few guys, and one day a mailman approached him about his education. 'Hey, how're you doing? How come you're not in school?'" That was how Phil Marquez "talked me into going back to high school." Marquez also invited him to attend a community gathering. Later he would meet Dick Johnson, director of admissions for Santa Clara University. But before that, he would become involved with United People Arriba (UPA), attending its second meeting with his parents and siblings (who had been at the first meeting) at the urging of Fred Hirsch. He recalled: "I was the second youngest there; they thought I was feisty, and they kind of pushed me along—they were working on getting a light at King and Story Road. So, they got me to speak in front of the council about that. And from then on, it was one issue after the other." He lived in the Sal Si Puedes barrio, where students were bused to Piedmont Hills High School. "We were poor kids; we all worked, and I'd get home at 11:00 or midnight . . . Then, at 5:00 a.m. I'd get up to catch the bus and sat around in school for an hour or two." His assigned school was Overfelt, a new school built for residents of the community, but it was not solely a matter of overcrowding; they bused the students as part of a desegregation plan. "So Al Morales and I, and the Mosely brothers . . . we got our folks involved; we missed the bus because we walked and slept in the hallway, made a big deal about it." He had learned how to organize and to bring people together. This helped him to get peers and adults to protest the district taking them out of their neighborhood.

Estremera became a union member as a high school student. He worked with his father as a member of Local 19 of the Hotel, Motel, and Restaurant Workers, and he often found himself "picketing—all the restaurants, everything in Santa Cruz." When he enrolled at Santa Clara "there were less than twenty people of color out of about 3,500 students." It would not be too long before the people of color got together and organized. "All twenty of us started the Mexican American Student Confederation, and the same twenty started the Black Student Union. So, we had both groups, and we were all members of both; it was tough." It was not long before the school newspaper labeled them "functionally illiterate" using words like "unable to abstract, like animals, functionally illiterate, those kinds of things." It was not only the males who experienced mistreatment at Santa Clara University. "I remember two Chicanas that we had on campus complaining that white guys threw pennies at them. It was very painful."

Once again, they rallied activists in their community, and thanks to United People Arriba, UFW supporters, and massive community support, the university established an ethnic studies program. He recalled, "In 1967, Santa Clara University had been dubbed the most racist university west of the Mississippi by the Office of Equal Opportunity—the quarter before, they had enrolled one Latino, Rudy Madrid, [who was] later joined by Al Morales and Esau Herrera and a few others that were in school together. It was pretty bad there for a while." Students activism and community involvement would also push the creation of Project 50, a summer program that would recruit Raza and other students of color to matriculate at Santa Clara University. With a BA in history and specializing in Latin America, Estremera applied to and was accepted to Bolt Law School, where he obtained his law degree.

Soon after law school, Estremera married Yolanda, and "because she got paid four to five times more," she supported the household. He continued to be very involved, usually making $400 to $500 dollars a month, as a partner with Mandy Haws and Jaime Gallardo. In their private practice, the attorneys provided legal services to the most marginalized in the community. Still, Yolanda, coming from an apolitical family, did not share Tony's interest in politics or his commitment to the community. However, they would become active in marriage encounters, group meetings for married couples, and that "really helped us and gave us the tools—she has the facility with intimate conversation and easy expression of emotion, so we always had good talks, but initially this was also foreign to her." Their different upbringings, in an urban versus

For San Jose
City Council
District 3

**TONY
ESTREMERA**

Ballot #138

The Neighborhood
Candidate

FIGURE 52 Tony Estremera running for San José City Council, District 3. Courtesy of Michal Mendoza.

a rural setting, also led to class differences, but what allowed them to overcome them was their willingness to "listen and negotiate." Tony Estremera had no hesitation in saying that his "wife is in charge; she is the boss simply because she has such a greater dedication to the home." She is the closest person to him and "is very sensitive to my concerns and my worries, and she counsels me in a real personal way."

Estremera was inspired by people who were "influential because of how they lived, what they taught others." In his view, activist leaders are those that work for the greater good and "create something beneficial for everybody; it's not someone just going through the motions of being a leader because you inherit a title or something . . . it's going through a concerted effort of making things different, or changing things, of doing something for everybody's good." Based on this philosophy, Estremera preferred to join forces with others. He never wanted to forget his origins, and at every opportunity he relied on that background to advance the causes for which he has struggled. "My father was a farmworker. I'm the only guy who graduated from high school. I can't forget that. I will never forget that. I learned from my community involvement that the only reason that we bridge our gap was because there are a lot people who really did sacrifice for us. And that is the thing that always stays with me. I will never forget."

As he recounted his history of involvement, Estremera recalled that since he ran for secretary of his class in the sixth grade, he was involved in many efforts to improve or change the communities with which he identified. From the age of sixteen, he became active with United People Arriva, Community Alert Patrol, Mexican American

Student Confederation (MASC, which later became MEChA), La Raza Lawyers Association, Service Employees International Union (SEIU), and the Cannery Workers Committee. Through his labor work, Estremera became active with the Campaign for Economic Democracy (CED), an independent, progressive California-based political movement led by Tom Hayden, and in redistricting for San José, to change the electoral process from at-large to district elections. In San José, CED worked with the trade union movement and community activists with the goal of building a progressive coalition to fight big business and bureaucracies. Estremera's work with CED brought him inside the politics of power to work with individuals such as Zoe Lofgren, Susie Wilson, and Tom McEnery.

In all his endeavors, Estremera continued to pursue public office. Inspired by those who mentored him, he wished "people to remember me as a guy who wouldn't give up just because it's hard, as one who really tried to live with his principles and didn't forget where he came from." With that philosophy in mind, Estremera sought to work with people on a personal level, with an understanding that "you have to work with coalition politics," and acted with the sensitivity of not being "overly ethnocentric."

After a stint in private practice, he was hired by the Legal Aid Society of Santa Clara County in its San José office. By this time, his activism had taken him in the direction of public service, and he ran for public office. He challenged Blanca Alvarado, a city

FIGURE 53 Tony Estremera, second from right, in an election flyer for city council. Courtesy of Michal Mendoza.

council incumbent, and he ran for the Downtown council chair, losing to Susan Hammer. With two campaigns under his belt for city council, and he ran against Manny Diaz for the Downtown district, which he lost. He would later run for the San José Evergreen Community College Board and served as its chair.

Estremera expressed his concern over the state of leadership in the community and called upon those activist leaders who had worked for the betterment of the community to continue investing in it, since "we've got students now who are very involved but . . . they are invested only for their self-promotion and self-interest." To create change, Estremera believed in coalitions that facilitate speaking across differences. He felt that as long as they start from a place of honesty and integrity, activist leaders could still come together for the common good.

CONCLUSION

Male participants from the Baby Boomer Generation in San José grew up invested in the greater good of their community, while focusing on creating social change. For some of them, their parents were involved in social and political activities. From his family, Felix Alvarez gained the foundation to become active in any area he chose. His upbringing, the historical knowledge he received from his ancestors, and the ethical principles he learned and practiced growing up in his family and the communities in which he lived gave him the direction necessary to work for social change. Jorge Gonzalez, after completing his MSW, continued to focus on education and immigrant

FIGURE 54 Mike Garcia during the Justice for Janitors campaign. Photo of photo by Josie Méndez-Negrete, taken at his memorial.

rights, while remaining active with the League for Revolutionary Struggle and Raza Sí! As Mike Garcia reflected on his career, he mentioned many instances of support that had brought him to his current place in life.

Pete Carrillo would have an opportunity to use his formal and informal knowledge in turning around the lives of those who found themselves in situations he himself was still trying to overcome. He created community from scratch, engaging in social change one person at a time. Tony Estremera, among his other endeavors, continued to pursue public office, inspired by those who mentored him, to whom he had promised never forget his origins. He called upon those activist leaders who have worked for the betterment of the community to continue investing in it.

10

• • •

CHICANAS OF THE BABY BOOMER GENERATION

Women of the Baby Boomer Generation contended with expectations not placed on their male siblings. For example, Delia Alvarez challenged the notion that it would be her brother alone who was to obtain a higher education, although her goal was an afterthought, rather than a plan. But when she said, "Wait a minute, I want to go too!" her parents honored her request and supported it. Josie Romero, Cecilia Arroyo, and Elisa Marina Alvarado would provide services to the community while tending to the cultural, health, and policy needs of their community. A mental health activist at the national and regional level, Romero would establish an institute for the study of Chicano families, while Arroyo would work with county planning and other health providers to make health and mental health services accessible. Alvarado, as the director of Teatro Vision, transmitted educational and cultural knowledge to her community, while working as a gerontology social worker for a local nonprofit. With all her professional life invested in education, Rose Amador ventured into vocational education and employment, displaying the commitment of a person who understands that there are a multiplicity of ways for making change. Employment, advocacy, the preparation of the un- or underemployed, were some of the many ways in which Amador worked to create a community that would improve the lives of those who are socially marginalized, such as Chicanos and Native Americans. As a co-founder of La Raza Roundtable and Native Voices, Amador continued to make visible the lives of those who would otherwise remain in the shadows of Silicon Valley.

ANTIWAR MOVEMENT TO HEALTH ADMINISTRATION: DELIA ALVAREZ

Alvarez was born and raised in Salinas, California, and her mother came from "Colton, California, with roots in Huanímaro, a village near the town of Penjamo, Guanajuato."

Among her maternal relatives, she knew her "grandmother—Mamá Mona—who died in 1967," but never met her maternal grandfather, who died in the 1920s. Her father's origins are in Jerome, Arizona, and he identified with the "Español side—the other side." His family originally came from Teocaltiche, a village "northeast of Guadalajara." Even though he descended from a line of "mestizos," her grandfather claimed "the Spanish side. He was very light, and my mom dark." The paternal side ended up in Arizona when "Mexicanos would travel back and forth to work in the mines," and her grandmother was born in one of the northern states of Mexico.

Inspired by Mamá Mona, who "bought a plot of land in Salinas on the poor side of town; a little house, it was cute," Alvarez grew up valuing the acquisition of real estate property. She has pictures of her grandmother "holding me as a baby, and I remember the roses, a lot of flowers, the corn." Before moving to Salinas, Mamá Mona had a little house in Colton. Without making a connection to the repatriation of Mexicans, Alvarez said that "in the 1920s, the family had to sell their property because they went back to Mexico, although they didn't last there long and they came back to the States." Because of their belief in acquiring land, Alvarez's upbringing was different from most Mexicans who lived in labor camps in Salinas.

In Salinas, the Alvarezes did not reside in a middle-class community but lived in the barrio "with the Oakies in the old part of town, the Eastside of Salinas." She recalled, "I didn't know the difference . . . there was a lot of richness, even though we were poor." Most importantly, she was "able to play and there were kids and a good life." Still, "life was rough, and my dad was a blue-collar worker, so we lived from paycheck to paycheck." With financial uncertainty, her "dad was changing jobs a lot . . . he started drinking . . . and my teen years were difficult; it was not like the earlier years with a lot of family and excursions to the beach in Santa Cruz," of which she had fond memories. Her younger sister was born later and missed the hardships, and Alvarez was thankful for the stability of having had "a mother who stayed home to raise us."

Alvarez remembered that throughout her early years "there were many Braceros in Salinas," and she was often aware "which ones had just come in, they were very poor peasants." Their presence intensified the racism she was beginning to notice, which exposed her to negative remarks such as "Well, look at those Mexicans," with a caveat of "Oh, Delia, we don't mean you." These tensions were traumatic, especially in regard to an identity she had "always been on the border about," since she was taught "to never deny our people, you know, we are Mexicanos." She also had to contend with the embarrassment of "Market Street, where my dad used to go to the bars; it was a painful time." Her dating options would be limited too, "because the guys weren't interested in me; it had had to do with being Mexican." For Alvarez, those days were filled with "confusion and conflict." Because she grew up in a neighborhood with a sizable number of Oakies, she participated in their social life. "I was in two or three weddings—I mean when we got out of high school—and here I am the little darkie with the Oakies." The way Alvarez saw it, she was included "because we went back years, they accepted me, and I wasn't quite sure where they were with my people," clarifying that "the ones that I was closest to didn't make the derogatory remarks. It was the others."

Even as a child, Alvarez knew her own mind. She remembered that when "I was about twelve or thirteen, I decided I didn't want to make tortillas. I could not make tortillas." One day she refused: "'That's it.' I rolled up the tortilla dough and threw it in the sink." There were no consequences, and because of this and other acts of resistance against gender expectations, Alvarez believed that, from early on, her parents "recognized I was different, but I was a good kid." Whether she wanted to or not, "I had to take care of my sister, while my mother had to work to send my brother to college." Often, she got the notion that her "mother felt guilty that I was robbed of being able to play with my friends" or of having "a more normal upbringing." However, because she was an excellent student, "my father was very flexible in breaking tradition—he made better tortillas than I did." Her family saw her as "a tomboy," and she recalled her "dad saying, 'You should have been a boy.'" Among her siblings, she "would be the one out there willing to work on the car or in the yard," and rather than wash dishes, she "went out and watered the lawn."

When Delia Alvarez was a junior in high school, her parents became active with Community Service Organization (CSO). "A gang fight in Gonzalez, and the ways Mexicans were depicted in the paper," pushed them to become involved. She remembered that her dad was part of a CSO committee, and "there was a meeting with the paper. So, they went to San José for CSO's big conventions. As a kid, I saw my parents, and my father a little bit involved with that." Now "my parents are divorced. And my dad remarried. So he's living in San José. Then my mother's living in Santa Clara. And my brother is in Rockville, Maryland, with his second wife and two boys." Alvarez herself was not married, nor did she expect to be. Marriage was not on the agenda. Rather, she aimed to achieve and do things not expected of a young woman of her time, "like college and travel."

In her perspective, Alvarez grew up in a family in denial whereby no one noted what was right in front of them. She clarified, "There was a lot of denial about my dad's drinking . . . about my lifestyle. My parents don't want to know. My brother doesn't want to know. My sister didn't want to know. I think in my thirties, because I was professionally accomplished, it was okay for my parents that I was not married." The time would come where her parents could rationalize her lifestyle because they saw her as "married to a profession." Then "I became caught up in my brother's imprisonment for eight and a half years," and she missed "the opportunity to get married." Yet, no one pushed her in that direction. "Both parents were very happy that I wanted to travel . . . they were excited for me to do that." After returning from a twenty-month trip, she rekindled the one relationship that might have led to marriage. She elaborated, "When I came back home I thought I was madly in love with a divorced man with five children. That never would have worked. He was very traditional, but I wanted to have a child, that would be the only time in my life, I was about thirty."

At the time of our interview, Delia Alvarez said she "would like to have a partner. If a partner is young enough and I know this sounds crazy, but had a baby or child, I would be open to that." She was invested in other relationships: "I mean it's all of the relationships because you have to work at all of them." She added that "now, I'm thinking of getting old with somebody and sharing," this is "the first time in my life I'm thinking of a relationship that's going to last a long time." She felt free to pursue whatever relationship she determined was best for herself.

Alvarez's path to leadership began early: "I think I've been prepared to do that all my life, I mean, I never really stopped to think about it." She took pride in "being a tradition breaker, of growing up in Salinas where I have a lot of fond memories, family support and care and attention, and the care and love that was very instrumental in providing stability." Even "as a little kid who questioned traditions, and who wanted to be better, I had the motivation to be different and be okay with it." Alvarez was nurtured by a "kind of inquisitiveness and a consciousness [of] breaking tradition." She expressed pride "in the fact that I completed high school, the fact that I went on to college, being the first in the family, and one of very few Latinas." She said that "as the pioneer, it was challenging and scary because I had nobody to look to for a role model, and so I just did what I saw and wanted to do, but better."

A leadership path first opened when she was elected to office in junior high school. Alvarez said, "I was student body treasurer, then I ran for student court—different organizations," and because of "good grades I ended up being in all this stuff." Her activism in school continued until she graduated in the top tier of her high school class. After that, with a handful of Chicanas, she went to San José State College, where she did not become a student activist until "the '60s, when I was a social worker." Under the supervision of Lino Lopez, "since I was one of very few Chicanas who had a college degree, I got involved in as a volunteer—I wouldn't say organizer—but as a supporter in the MAYO [Mexican American Youth Organization] organization. Then I went to work at MACSA in '69, where I followed up organizing, and pushing that effort with students." For Alvarez, the work she did in her community was exciting, and she was inspired by the group "when I was a social worker, with a group that started a union." Even though she perceived herself as "always in the middle of it," for her, union organizing "was a whole different scene."

Her brother Everett Alvarez was captured in Vietnam in 1964. Initially, her family and the community did not mobilize: "We didn't buck government, that was unthought of, but it was like '69 when we started a family petition drive" for his release. In her view, that organizing effort was "just an innocent thing, but then we did quite a bit. I learned a lot, how to mobilize people, families, and I was always the natural coordinator, director, even with the kids." Soon after, "we organized a family drive that was just earmarked to bring public attention that there were still prisoners of war. I mean, my brother had by then been a prisoner for five years, and the American public has low memory retention." By this time, "people were jaded by the war," but their drive to get the prisoners of war released garnered much publicity. She recalled that "it was just families, you know, huge extended families, different people that got involved." Alvarez "became the core organizer" and as a strategy for organizing, she "started the Family Picnic in late '69." Her reach soon went national, and in the '70s she focused on "families that had prisoners of war or were missing in action," and thus their efforts were publicized throughout the nation.

Initial organizing "entailed having to identify others who felt the same way that we did. We were with the other families, following that network." She did extensive traveling in her organizing and sought ways to pull in those who shared her family's experience with words of encouragement such as: "Hey, let's get together. We feel the same way. We want the war to end, we are opposed to war and we need to develop a voice." The struggle for her brother's release began from nothing, so it required "a lot of direct contact and identifying those who would be part of the core leadership that believed in the concept." In that quest, she went "to Detroit, Virginia Beach, Santa Fe, and I would go to antiwar rallies afterward." Interestingly, "we never organized as families, and so I was just providing that initial leadership. It took a lot of leadership" on her part. Still, her endeavors to free her brother and other prisoners of war during the Vietnam conflict brought much "backlash." Alvarez was tagged "a communist from all kinds of people." Most painful to her was the reality that Mexican men in San José tried to devalue her with their machismo, "when my brother came home and he didn't come out in support of the antiwar stuff," these men took his response as devaluation of her work. Her brother understood that he was limited in what he could do because he was a soldier. Yet, "Chicanos were like, 'oh yeah, now he's going to put her in her place,' because they had a hard time with the national exposure that my mother and I got."

Her leadership abilities and activism placed Delia Alvarez at the center of power in Santa Clara County government, when she took the first of many of the positions she held. Still, her involvement and activism did not make for an easy life, especially when she could not fully be herself. Because of her lifestyle, Alvarez's "life has been rough . . . but, I came out. I've gone through all the changes myself, and I'm much more comfortable." When she was outed as a lesbian, Alvarez regretted the lack of support she received from those whom she had previously worked with or supported, especially from politicians, who, she says, tend to speak out of both sides of their mouths. Those individuals who would go to big gay political events such as "BAYCOP [Bay Area

Construction Opportunity Program], because I've seen it, you know, 'I'm for all.'" But when it comes to your own, "they're not there to support you."

Pushed out from her job as director of Santa Clara County Health Department, Delia Alvarez gave second thoughts to confronting those who would tarnish her reputation. She was "not humiliated during the whole process, and that shocked people." The way she saw it, her time had come to remove herself from the public eye, and during those very public attacks she opted "to not do anything." Clearly, she had no regrets about the contributions she had made to public service and the county of Santa Clara.

Although perceived as "controversial because I've been involved in a lot of things," Alvarez said she felt "respected as a role model, a tradition path breaker, even when, from men there's a distant respect." She articulated that "some might not agree, but I basically have succeeded." Through her experience working in corporate government, a "very rough system," what happened to her in 1992 was "very painful." As Alvarez looked back, she realized that she was raised to see herself as an agent of change who fought for her rights as well as those of others. In addition to affirming her ability to take charge, her parents raised her to be "proud that we're Mexicans and never deny it." At the same time, her parents imparted the belief that "you've got to be white to succeed," and "so it was okay to be with the Oakies, because they were white, even though they were Oakies. So, they were my girlfriends, from grammar school to junior high, and then into junior high when I started going to slumber parties and such." It was these social interactions which framed her upbringing in the context of race and class, even when her parents socialized her to believe that the way to succeed would only be by embracing white notions. For this reason, this centered her in the ambivalence of race, having to negotiate racialization through ethnic affiliation and the ways in which whites, her primary socializing peer group, perceived Mexicans.

Even when the rights of males were perceived as having more value, her ideas and dreams were given merit by her parents, so she did not feel less valued for being female. Throughout her upbringing, her parents taught her to act on the side of justice. However, it would take interacting with Braceros, Chinese, and other people of color for her to gain clarity on issues of racism in her community. "In my teen years, there were two thing that were going on that were very painful. I started really understanding racism, and I had to deal with the fact that I grew up Mexican, thinking that 'you've got to be white.'"

It was not be until she retired that Delia Alvarez understood the price she paid by standing up for principles of justice, equality, and fairness. Most painful to her was that the community in which she'd invested so much did not support her in time of struggle. "So, the price I paid is that the community didn't support me when I was being outed" in a very public arena, nor were politicians there to give their support. She recalled that being outed made her "uncomfortable," since she had lived with the conscious decision to separate her sexual politics from her work or political involvements. She had made a clear decision that "I wasn't going to be visible because I'm not going to do that to my parents. . . . I was just going to deal with it when it came up, and I was just not going to talk about it." However, people who knew her and had worked as activists alongside her, who really cared about her, "were scared to death about me being outed—more than I was." However, those who should have supported Alvarez left her out in the cold.

Alvarez's lived experience and socialization among whites and her educational experiences taught her to navigate the cultural power of her community, preparing her to professionally advance in the county government bureaucracy, which encompassed community, education, and public services. With integrity and commitment, Alvarez achieved many successes, leaving a legacy of someone who contributed to the administrative bodies of country government, and who was recognized among women activists as a point of access and influence for the betterment of her community.

STUDENT ACTIVIST TO VOCATIONAL TRAINER
AND CULTURAL ACTIVIST: ROSE AMADOR

Rose Amador was born in San José, California, when her parents were on a visit from the East Coast. "My father was born in Mexico and raised in Chicago and my mother was from Pennsylvania. So, after I was born they went back to Chicago, and I grew up in Pennsylvania." Amador grew up among whites, as "there were no Chicanos around, almost no other nationalities, not even Asians." She added, "I really didn't experience a lot of discrimination; it was a very small, little town." She was enrolled in "an old small school where there was one in each grade, the teacher had everyone in your family, type of thing; it was a real close-knit community." That type of environment meant that she knew "the same kids from kindergarten all the way through sixth grade—it was comfortable, secure, and a good experience." In "Pennsylvania we were accepted," she said, clarifying that "racial division was between blacks and whites, and we were associated with whites because it was very segregated, although I didn't really reflect on how bad it really was until much later." She passed "'The Hill' where blacks lived" and walked to school by themselves, and we "played with whites, but no one associated with blacks." "We were accepted as whites, but my dad would often remind me to be proud of being Mexican, telling us all about the stories of the Revolution, everything about Mexico—there was never any doubt that we were Mexican."

When they moved to Santa Clara because of her father's job, "there were different feelings. There were only a few Mexicans, the real rough ones with high hair and makeup." She "got along" except for those times when white people would tell her,

"Well, you're not like the others." For her, "that was really awkward and made me feel uncomfortable." Her father was involved in the community, and "I think that it is where I get it from." In her recollection, "there were very few Hispanics or Mexicans" where they lived, and still her father "managed to even start a Latino group—the AMVet," and other organizations in Chicago such as "the American Legion and things like that, and he belonged to the Masons; he was always involved."

The family returned to California when Amador was about twelve years old, and "even here he was very active in the community." For example, "he was involved with the GI Forum and always involved with something." Her mother was mostly "involved in school things, PTA and stuff like that, and in the GI Forum, with the women's groups. However, she was not involved on her own, she was just involved with my dad."

Based on what she experienced with her parents, Amador said her own involvement started in "kids club in elementary, Job's Daughters, and organizations in high school." She perceived herself as orderly and recalled "always trying to organize everything." It was her father who told her she was a leader, when she helped "with my father's organizations, the fund-raisers, decorating and things—those days kids used to do a lot of that stuff with the GI Forum."

In her work, as in her activism, Amador perceived herself as "open and receptive to people and information," adding, "I stand up for what I believe. I'm motivated. I follow through and normally accomplish what I set out to do." To illustrate her point, she said, "I put on a great menudo cook-off. That was fun. I was proud of that because it was the first time I had ever done something like that, put on a major festival; it was a co-sponsored by Kiwanis and the Hispanic Chamber." Coordinating with such a traditional organization required a collaborative effort. And even though Amador delegated and directed volunteers efficiently, she still "ended up doing it all, because volunteers weren't doing it, and we're associated with it, and if it flops it reflects on us, too." She took much pride in telling me that more than "10,000 people filled Cunningham Park, and it was the first year ever." For her, the event "was a lot of work and a lot of fun and quite an accomplishment."

In her career as an activist leader, Amador contended with experiences that were exceptionally painful and traumatic; experiences that she would turn around for the greater good of the community. While she openly discussed those tensions, I extrapolated some lessons she learned from her time at Service Employment Redevelopment (SER). During her tenure there, she moved up the ranks quickly. "Hired on as a counselor, about six months later, I became a coordinator of the program." Soon after, Amador was promoted to run "the East Court operation, from which I moved to Planning and, this was all in four years, then to deputy director." Amador was "assistant director right before we closed down" because of an FBI investigation into fiscal improprieties and other alleged charges. Through that experience, Amador learned many lessons,

including that people, and women in particular, should not compromise their principles. "I've always done that . . . figured out ways to do it or have someone help me do
it—without fear of reprisals or devaluation—people assume . . . I'm doing what I set as
my goal, but it wasn't." By way of example, she offered that she remained in her position
out of commitment to her community.

She had gone to SER when looking for an alternate employment experience while
she was at San José State because "I was bored, I didn't like what I was doing; I had
worked there two years, and I didn't like being away from community work. I hated
it. It was just so dry." It was her father who pointed her in the direction of SER when
she asked him if he knew anyone in the community that had openings. He referred
her to the director of SER at the time, since there were "positions there and they had
some new grants." Even though some of the positions didn't appeared suitable for her
because of the skill sets required—she had never done counseling before—Amador
took a risk and applied. Often, she has relied on this experience "when I'm mentoring";
she encourages mentees to "take risks but learn as much as you can, learn the requirements; the more you know, the better it is for you," with the advice that "you could
always use it another way."

Her experience at SER brought with it difficult lessons, and it was something she
would not wish on another person. She explained: "It was horrible, but I wouldn't have
done it a different way. I did what I had to do—I felt that it was the right thing to do. I
had to do it. Still, there was guilt that I made Chicanos look bad, because it was a big
public thing—it was all over the papers and everything." Because she "did the right
thing," Amador was able to transition from the closure of the program and continue her
work providing vocational education and employment training when she became the
director of Center for Training and Careers (CTC). She reflected, "I had the capacity
to take on many roles to promote access to employment and to advocate for under-
served workers." As a result of her work and because of her commitment to improving
employment access and policies, Amador was twice elected as chair the now defunct
Chicano Employment Committee (CEC). "I chaired CEC for a couple years and I
think during that time we had a lot of victories, accomplishments, and the organization
had a lot of visibility and it got recognized by a lot of public bodies. Actually, I was seen
as a threat to a lot of people at the time." Thus, in her capacity as director of CTC and
because of her expertise with the community, Amador was their representative in the
Program Officers Association of the Private Industry Council. Also active in the GI
Forum, Amador was selected as an outstanding member and worked with the Chicana
Scholarship Foundation. In addition to community organizations, she sat on different
boards, such as "the Economic Development Board for the City of San José with such
special interests as Kimball-Smalls, the developers, and all the people who can afford
to attend the mayor's fund-raisers, and mostly the CEOs of banks."

Amador managed to balance her work and activism and at the time of our interview was "active with the National Council of La Raza because the organization I direct is an affiliate of theirs." Almost as if in disbelief of her accomplishments, Amador said: "I've gotten to be in some arenas that just overwhelm me." She attributed this to father's promotion of self-sufficiency: "He was always pushing. 'You have to go to school, you have to do this, you have to do that, and provide for yourself.'" It was unclear to Amador whether he pushed because she was one of the oldest in the family, the second daughter to be born, because "he never really pushed my brothers that much to get involved in community things, but he did with us." From her father she learned that "a leader is someone to whom one looks for advice and helps at direction or sets the course of things." Also, that the meaning of leadership is not just "taking a stance on something or having opinions on something, it is actually doing something about issues."

Toward that end, Amador surrounded herself "with good and positive people." What motivates her to act is that she is someone who "likes to work with people, who likes to help people, and is sensitive to the Chicano community." She was proud "when something I do is accomplished, and I feel that I have a role in making that change take place or making whatever happened happen." For example, Amador became involved with the GI Forum pageant and "took it over, made them change a lot of their rules so, it wasn't a beauty pageant any longer but made it a big production. . . . Not everybody was content with its direction, and while I've heard complaints, a lot of these things are just fun for me." She also chaired a GI Forum convention a few years back, adding "that it was something I had never done before and would never do again, but I did it." During that process, she often wondered if "I would ever survive—it was so much work and I did most of it myself" because her co-chair dropped out. "We had [the convention] in San José and we had Senator Feinstein as our speaker." All the events were sold out, but it was a lot of work for her. A person who has the tendency to "really tend to a lot of details and scripting everything that's going to happen, all the way through the lunches, all the way through everything, you know, everything went very smoothly." She was more than satisfied with her effort.

Amador was concerned with current climate for activist leaders, witnessing "the mistake leaders are making, and it's kind of related to that camp thing, is that by not forming alliances you burn out the potential for relationships." Her philosophy is that "you ought to create alliances, just agree on that issue and go on, because you might need that person for another issue." In her perspective, "this kind of thing is happening a lot and creates those gaps, so down the road this issue comes up, and that means if that camp is against it then we're going to be for it." Instead of action in unity and strength, "the issue gets dissolved somewhere, lost in the whole process, whereas the whole community could be so much stronger through alliances." The way Amador saw it, there is "alienation going on where, 'okay we just don't agree here, so therefore I'm going to hate you the rest of your life,' kind of thing." For example, "I see a big division between the Latino Issues Forum, other organizations, and the students at San José State." The *Mercury News* divides the issue, sees it, and underscores sides, "you're on this side and I'm on that side." However, it is "not about being opposite sides, it's mis-understanding." Such as the case of the Mexican Heritage or the Cultural Gardens or the notion that its foundation is displacing residents of the community. "'Okay, you're displacing people,' but what they fail to say it's a couple of businesses that are white-run." Amador said, "It boggles me that Chicano activists are so concerned about these two white businesses trashing on this corner, and then these other people who are renting here aren't complaining because they're going to get moving money to move into a different place. So, it doesn't make sense. I think it is more personality-wise."

In her view of the issues, their objectives are misplaced. As was the case with the Fallon statute, "Oh, don't waste the money on the statue. What about the homeless?" Clearly, "they don't understand that redevelopment money isn't going to go to the homeless, it'll go to another building downtown. Let it go to our community, for a cultural center." Another issue had to do with the chief of police: "It is the first time we get a chief of police, and they have to go out and say, 'We want a citizen review board,' to undermine his authority. My question is, 'Okay, fine, but why didn't I hear this when McNamara was there? Why weren't you out there in the streets when McNamara was there?'" For Amador, "this is bothersome because we struggled so hard to get Chicanos in this position, and then the students come to make their job more difficult." What remains in the balance is their knowledge of history and how informed they are about the struggles that others have built to bring us up to now.

Amador's father went to the seventh grade, and her mother graduated from high school. Although Amador finished a BA in management in the early 1990s, her edu-cational trajectory did not follow a traditional path. While she herself did not make a direct connection, this may have been in part a result of their move to Santa Clara and of her difficult transition into a new school. In the seventh grade, she was place in the C track at school with the other Mexican kids, despite having all As. It was not until her mother complained that she was put in the higher track. Gender too became an issue at school. "When we were in high school there was more emphasis on boys," Amador stated, while "a stigma was assigned to females in tracks such as home economics, typing, and so on."

When she graduated from Wilcox High School in 1967, she "had A-B average—pretty good grades in high school." She went directly to De Anza College, where she received a Chicano Studies degree with honors, although she became distracted by her activism with "MEChA, and on campus. . . . I just got too involved and too side-tracked, so I went a little bit to San José State," then she dropped out because education became less of a priority. Amador took a different path when she "started working for Economic and Social Opportunities (ESO) and running one of their programs, and the big drawback was marriage." Those changes in her life—work and marriage—set her back in her education. It was not a shock for her family that she would return and complete her degree; nor were they surprised that "I was the first one to be involved in the Chicano movement."

Rose Amador's moved into vocational education and employment, displaying her understanding that there is a multiplicity of ways for making change. As one of the founders of La Raza Roundtable and Native Voices, Amador worked to make visible the lives of those who would otherwise remain in the shadows of Silicon Valley.

WOMEN'S RIGHTS, PLANNING, AND POLICY: CECILIA ARROYO

Cecilia Arroyo was born in Cupertino, California. Her mother came from Phoenix, Arizona, and her dad from "a place called Lluvias de Oro, Chihuahua, a place that no longer exists because the village is underwater." Her father came to the United States when he was five or six. Among her extended family, her parents were the most successful. As the oldest of three children, two girls and a boy, and the oldest grandchild, Arroyo's life took a "whole different other dimension," since she had to set the pace for other people—that was her job. Noticing the contradictions displayed or the double messages sent by adults around her, she saw herself as having "a different way of looking at the world." She recalled, "I was told that you had to do certain things, although you could see that people around you in your extended family didn't honor those obligations, but nevertheless they were your obligations." In that context, Arroyo learned to make up her "own mind, to be a certain way, and that was all there was to it." She "grew up in a very typical Chicano household," even when the "women in my family are very strong—mother, and my maternal grandmother are strong role models."

As she looked back at her childhood, Arroyo spoke about their first move. "We grew up around Cupertino close to De Anza College. It was all Chicano except for a few Oakies." The neighborhood was a village where her "paternal grandmother was on one side, next door, and my maternal grandmother was around the corner." Other extended kin included "a Nina or godmother who was down the block, and so it was a family neighborhood." However, the birth of her younger brother pushed the family to move out of Monte Vista. One of her earliest memories is when "my mother put her foot down and told my dad that she had to work." Her mother going to work would be the only way that the family could move. Arroyo said, "My dad was just totally appalled and said, 'No, no, you can't work.' She said, 'I have to.'" Despite his doubts that they could afford to move to another home, her mother took on "the night shift at the cannery, at

FIGURE 55 Cecilia Arroyo, far left. Courtesy of Michal Mendoza.

Libby's, and that became her work every summer." Thus, the family was able to move to Santa Clara, and Arroyo witnessed the strengthen of the women in her family, which would guide her future path.

In her twenties, she met her husband, Ron Arroyo, "when he was working at the University of California, Santa Cruz. . . . He is Puerto Rican from Hawaii, who in 1945, when the Second World War hit, relocated with his family to San Francisco because of the war." Before meeting him, she considered herself "very old, a *vieja*," and she was sure she would remain a spinster. "I had just convinced my grandmother at the age of twenty-six that I was not going to get married." She had also informed her mom and dad, "I don't think it is in the cards." Soon after that, she met her future husband, and after a ten months' courtship, they became engaged and were married by the time Cecilia turned twenty-eight.

Her activism was not truncated by her marriage. She explained, "It actually became much stronger because Ron gave me the support: 'If you want to do it, do it.'" She was employed by the Santa Clara County Planning Department, which she soon left for four years to work at the Association of Bay Area Government (ABAG). Then she returned to Santa Clara County in 1987, after the Chicana Coalition had begun. It was at this organization that Arroyo recognized that she was "doing the leadership thing, because I was doing things that nobody else was doing. And basically, my contribution to the Chicana Coalition was a political link because that is my strength."

Giving birth to two sons did not hinder her involvement. She had the support of her husband and her mom and dad. She said, "My mom still helps me take care of my children and that is the only reason that I am able to have jobs that require evening work or weekend work. I've always got a backup, so it is not a problem." Her "husband is a cook," and he tends to the evening meals when she arrives late from work or her meetings, "but they do appreciate it when I cook." She added, "This is the fine line with which I've been able to make a difference in my mind to find it acceptable." Her marital relationship was unlike the relationships she had witnessed growing up: "My father was the kind of typical Chicano male that said, 'I need a glass of water.' He could be sitting in the kitchen right next to the sink but it was your job to bring him the water." Unlike her father, her husband "knows that he can get water for himself and will do it. If I want to give him water I can. But it is not necessary." Her marriage became a source of support for her in her investment in social change endeavors.

Arroyo had to establish boundaries with her sons, Ronaldo and Luis. She explained, "I will set boundaries more than my husband because he is much more, he's used to a much more flexible environment." As a Chicana, she grew up with more restrictions, and she relied on that experience to guide her sons. This has often created conflict between them, as her husband told her, "You can't do that. You can't continually tell them no." She retorted, "Why not? That is the way I grew up." But Ron provided Cecilia an alternative perspective: "Hey, when I was his age, I was out. I was hanging on streetcars." But she could not imagine

FIGURE 56 Cecilia and Ron Arroyo. Courtesy of Diego Salazar, thanks to Corinne Gutierrez.

that much freedom for her sons: "The last year and a half has been really hard for me to understand why my sons need to go to a party and there has to be a party every week. I don't think so." However, because of Ron's advocacy she learned to "agree that it is okay."

San José State was the place where Arroyo first confronted sexism. She explained, "I never got along with those obnoxious pigs at San José State. There were male students with their wives in the same class who treated their wives badly. Never in the world would I marry such a pig." She found it offensive, and she had to deal with the contradictions and expectations that were "pounded in my head that I had to marry a Latino." She began to contemplate her options and think about what she wanted in a relationship. "So, in my mind, when my sister and I went to Mexico for a summer, I thought I would check things out and see how they are in Mexico. Well, what I found out in Mexico is that everybody played, they dillydallied, and I didn't want a *callejero* or man of the streets, I was not going to tolerate that." In Mexico, she and her sister were recognized as "Norte Americanas, not as Mexicanas, my sister and I were in cultural shock," not having seen themselves as gringas.

As a university student, Arroyo was trying to find her place in the new world she had entered. Arroyo pointed out that she "wasn't active at San José State." Instead, she became active in the community, where was more receptivity for her involvement. "When WOMA [the Women's Alliance] got off the ground, I got involved with Oaxinas de Paz. Then there was a third, what did we call it—it was like the women of color—so it was broader than just Chicanas or Latinas, and then the Chicana Coalition was really the keystone to all of that because that was when we were really were doing things right and being involved and making an impact. We have done that well." She would also become involved with the Chicana Foundation and the GI Forum, with women's issues. Arroyo "held officer positions, if not the chair the then vice-chair or the secretary, but it was always in those leadership positions." However, her leadership skills did not always translate to work, since there she was "most comfortable behind the scene, because I don't want to be the elected official that goes out there and does this and that, but I like to do all the good staff work."

Arroyo attributed her initial involvement to her friends in college, explaining her activism focused on "my friends, primarily women, it was a real natural thing for me to go into Chicana women's issues." For her, it was "women-centered organizing," rather than "feminist, white women's issues," which compelled them to do things differently. Chicanas were not interested in creating an exclusive venue for leadership. "Although the men had their problems with our involvement, it didn't mean that we were necessarily out there by ourselves. So we would do things to bring them along," elaborating that "in this valley, the people who have the most credibility and can get things done well are the women, not the men."

Arroyo became involved in politics after graduating from college, and "that's been the consistent factor." In the struggle to bring about change, she has worked "to support women candidates, Latina candidates, not just Latinos." She added, "I think I've made my major contribution, and I've made a difference. The Chicana Coalition was critical in that regard, and the Latino Issues Forum" as well. However, her involvement was not all about electoral politics. "I guess when you think about the '70s, that's what most of us did. We advocated for people's rights, not only their employment rights but to make sure that we had certain positions covered in the public sector."

Because Arroyo came into the movement with the greater good of the community in mind, she proudly stated, "None of those things ever benefited me, nor did I ever do them to benefit myself. That's one of the things I feel good about." With the demise of the Chicana Coalition and the ebbing of the Latino Issues Forum, and "since the fall of '92 with this new job, I haven't been involved in much of anything." At the time of our interview, because of her compromised health, her activism was not as intense. "Still, I have been on the board of the Children's Discovery Museum, I am on the State Central Committee representing my assembly district. I'm on the Community Foundation Board of Directors, I'm on an advisory committee for San José State in the Urban Planning Department, I am ex officio for San Jose Development Corporation, and I'm on the advisory board for my son's Catholic School." Invested in creating coalitions, Arroyo also noted that she "worked with the Asian community and have helped them through the Asian Americans for Community Involvement," adding, "I've been there when they've needed me." Arroyo spoke about her ability to become involved with various ethnic communities as she "crossed different community lines," adding "if you look at gay issues, I have worked on AIDS issues within the county." Also, "if you look at some black issues, I have my work with some black graduate students I've mentored." She has done so "since prior to graduate school, when T. J. Owens plugged me into the NAACP—I've got good relationships there." Arroyo also has worked with "Indian Health Center, on the Indian on Native American issues I think I'm pretty good." She said her activism had "covered the bases."

She has learned to value her relationships, especially her link "to Latina women, recognizing that my leadership has evolved through the process of friendship and doing joint projects with other women from my grade school days, my little clubs, to doing things in college." Whether it was "fund-raising and working with the GI Forum, or the whole issue of working with women and how we as Latinas pursue an issue, or how we form a unified front—we're not jealous of one another." Arroyo took much pride in having participated in making change without regard as to who benefited.

Arroyo's parents promoted self-sufficiency and self-reliance. "It was always emphasized that no matter what happens we should be able to support ourselves and not depend on anyone including the husband." Unlike other members of her community, "my parents were not very religious, so we didn't have the religious community to relate to and they didn't do a lot of civic things." Still, as a result of their values, Arroyo worked for "empowerment in terms of self-determination, showing that I respect diversity and I think everyone has a right to pursue what they think is important to their own community." Education would be an entry point into activism.

For Arroyo growing up, there was always the assumption that she would go to college, and not to just any local college. "In fact, one of my counselors tried to get me to go to school out of state, which was never to be considered by my parents, that was just not an option." But it was not a problem for her to go to the local state college, so she "went to San José State all the way through," living at home through her graduate education. But living at home in the late 1960s meant she did "not really [understand] the whole world around us, still insulated in the small world because I was still at home."

At college, she would create a social family and relate only "to Chicanas, not Chicanos." And that was the beginning of her activism. "To just get involved, to understand what some of the issues were, but not to go off the deep end, because as I told you I also worked. I didn't have a lot of time. My friends who got over involved didn't do well in school, and the bottom line for me was always that I had to do well in school in order to graduate and get out. So that I was clear on my end goal so I didn't get all crazy." To finance her education, and owing to her business training, Arroyo worked as a secretary. "I got a job at City College and I worked a year in the counseling department," where she soon decided it was not an environment that supported her goals. Thinking "these guys are locos, I split." She looked for other employment and found "a job at the old Economic Opportunities Center as secretary to the executive director."

With an MA in regional planning and urban development, Arroyo was able to work inside the bureaucracy and to guide those who were interested in accessing or creating services in health, housing, and transportation. When Cecilia Arroyo died of cancer in 2009, she was organizing her papers to document the work that she carried out with the Alviso Health Center, the American Indian Center, and Gardner Health Center, organizations in which she created resources for those who would otherwise not have had medical or other services.

COMMUNITY AND MENTAL HEALTH ACTIVISM: JOSIE ROMERO

Born in Eagle Pass, Texas, Josie Romero remembered her family as "very healthy, very supportive, but having very little, and being very poor," although she "felt you belonged, you always felt that somebody was there for you." She grew up in "family where grandpa and grandma were always watching to make sure that mom and dad did the right thing," and their extended family was there to make them feel secure.

FIGURE 57 Josie's Romero's parents. Courtesy of Diana Martinez, whose image appears between her grandparents.

Her ethnic heritage is mixed: Her paternal side of the family was German and "were distanced" even though they were all raised in Mexico. Her maternal side of the family, on the other hand, "were Indian and Mexicanos, and they were much more united, and involved."

Romero's father was born in in El Moral, Coahuila, on the border with Texas, and "he was second-generation German who was born and raised" in Mexico having arrived in the northern part "after the First World War when Germans went underground." The family legend was that "her paternal grandfather was a mayor in Germany and apparently had attempted to overthrow whatever government was in place and went into exile *a España*," and from there "*pa'* Mexico."

Her mother was born in Eagle Pass on the Texas side of the Rio Grande. Her maternal grandparents had land on both sides of the border, and her mother was second-generation Tejana. Both parents were living on the Texas side before it became part of the United States, making "half of the family Americanos and half Mexicanos." Romero said her mother was an activist but not in the traditional sense, emphasizing that she was always very involved in el barrio, "helping little old ladies that were alone, she would always make sure that they ate, she would wash their clothes and she would send us with anything special we would make like tamales, or caldo." Her concern for

FIGURE 58 Josie Romero (far left) and her sister, visiting their aunt in El Moral, Coahuila. Courtesy of Diana (Romero) Martinez.

those in need was always in her mind. "She would remember a lady that was sick in the neighborhood, or one that was alone—we sort of adopted them, and then when she doing things for herself, she would move on to others."

Her father also did what he could for their community. He knew what it was to be poor. "We never applied for welfare, or anything like that, and I'm sure that we would have qualified because we had so many of us." Still, self-sufficiency and self-help were foundational values for the family. Many times "my father told us he had brought us to this country, and he alone was going to support us," as he did not want them to be a charge on the government. For him, this was an issue of pride, because it was *una vergüenza pedir ayuda*, shameful to ask for help. So, "we worked in whatever was available" to do the best they could without asking for a handout.

Romero credited her family's values and beliefs for finding a balance in her work and activism, and for raising kids that did not give her much trouble or prevent her from being active. The support of her family and her community reassured her that "I'm not alone, as there were always people who were excellent role models." For her, family sayings or "*dichos* and words of wisdom to live by" best reflected her actions. Phrases like "*No hay mal que por bien no venga*, or Get up and get going, it's kick-butt time" kept her inspired. As difficult as life might have been, because of her responsibilities and poor health, Romero said she would not trade her life for any amount of money, because "I've accomplished a lot, and my purpose as a mother has been reached. I've done a lot and I will continue . . . to defend and protect my people to the end, working for my community." Clearly, Romero was successful at negotiating her personal and professional lives, and she took pride that "I've never allowed a job to control me. I've always shaped the job to fit me, rather than shape me to fit the job."

Romero married when she was twenty-one, and her marriage lasted for twenty-two years before ending in an amicable divorce. She met her husband, Arturo Romero, "at school—we're from Eagle Pass, Texas, and he was my neighbor across the street." After they married, the couple moved to California, "because half of his family lived there, and it was where his sister was employed, and where he found a job." Settled in Gilroy, Josie Romero found "a small community with the migrant feel" with which she was familiar. She welcomed it. "When I was homesick for migrants—I was always working with them anyway, if I wasn't assigned to the group—I volunteered." It was in the camps that she found a feeling of kinship, and she recalled "getting in trouble because I wasn't supposed to be in the labor camp, but . . . I would go anyways." She experienced Gilroy "as small enough where you knew who was involved where, and it was sort of like all you had to do was make two or three phone calls and everybody came together—*eramos los mismos gatos*—it was the same people responding to community needs." Soon she found herself volunteering for a "gang task force or facilitating something or other." In addition to working in labor camps, she "became very active in the community, as a result of my job as school liaison," enraged by "injustices and too many situations where our kids were not being treated equitably, and little by little, I joined advocacy groups and I never stopped."

For Romero, it was not easy to negotiate marriage and activism. She explained, "As a wife and mother I worked very consciously on balancing things, to not add stress but to reduce it." She attributed this lesson to a grandfather that "taught me to think things through." Reflecting on her experiences as an activist leader, she detailed how she was able to become involved. "I was super organized. There were certain days to do the wash . . . for the kids . . . for him, and certain days for the community. . . . I never robbed the time that legitimately was theirs, unless there were emergencies." Even though she embraced domestic responsibilities with intense commitment, there were times when Romero felt resentful that all of these responsibilities fell on her. Often, she felt angry about all she did to keep others happy and to balance resentments. For that reason, she set out to show her husband in particular that "I wasn't involved just because I wanted to be away from home. There were legitimate needs, and slowly I decided to fight his ignorance with education." She achieved this by "involving him in discussions such as the need for lawsuits or why workers were treated unfairly in the migrant fields." When she was working with César Chávez or the United Farm Workers union, she would "involve him in situations, so he could see the reasoning behind why people needed to contribute their time to defend and promote equality." Thus, rather than become defensive about her involvement, Romero would show her husband why "I'm not going to sit back and see these injustices happen."

Romero raised two children, her daughter, Diana Isabel, and her son, Arturo. Her daughter is a nurse, and Romero says she's "sensitive and kind, unlike me—a very public shameless activist leader—my daughter leads quietly and behind the scenes, often coming to me with issues." For example, one day she told her mother about a Mexican lady whom she saw being mistreated because she did not speak English. "You should have seen the way he treated her, and I got so angry." So Romero asked, "What did you do?" and her daughter replied that she went right up to him and said, "When you treated that lady like that, you insulted me, because she's from my culture, and my race, and I didn't like it. It felt humiliating, and I'm sure that if my feelings were hurt so were hers." Proud that her daughter stood up to protect someone's rights, she queried her daughter about the action she took: "'Where did you learn that?' She said, 'You.' And I said, 'What did I do?'" Her daughter described other things she had observed and brought up other conflicts she'd experienced with her supervisor, and she would often consult with Romero about the best way to deal with them. "Mom, I have this problem. This is what I want to do. How else should I do it?" Her daughter was happy to consult with her, knowing that her mother's advice would yield positive results.

With her son it was different, although he too is beginning to become involved. Romero said that "he's doing an internship in Washington, D.C., with the Coalition of Spanish-Speaking Mental Health Organizations." Like Romero, her son displayed an "extreme interest in working with young people, and also was very much focused on righting inequalities." Romero expressed pride that her children were displaying interest in leadership, showing her that "her own activism translated into something good."

Romero first became involved early in her school days; she was a member of "the safety patrol, volunteered to interpret when they lacked someone who spoke English, or cleaning up, or taking a group from one place to the other." She provided one-to-one support to peers and adults alike. In addition, "I was the captain of the baseball team, or the basketball team." As her mother told her, "*Que todo el tiempo le gustaba dar ordenes*, I would always be giving orders." Unlike Romero, her siblings did not take the opportunity to become active or to lead, but she pointed out that they did not have the same opportunities. "When the three oldest came to this country, they were already at an age that they didn't want to go to school. They were embarrassed because they didn't speak English." Her sister went to school for a year, but "she quit because they made her undress in PE, she was very prudish, very conservative." Romero said, "It was different for me because I shed my clothing—*no me importó, me encueré*—I took my clothes off when I was told." In the final analysis, "they dropped out because it was more acceptable to go work"; all her siblings would drop out of school in the ninth grade.

She grew up to never think less of herself and to always believe in her own power. In her family, Romero experienced males "getting away with doing what they wished." Because of that, she decided she would teach "my son and daughter to be more equal and responsible" for getting things done in the house. She declared that "I always felt gypped because the girls did double work by also working in the fields." In addition to gender inequality, as part of a migrant family she would confront other inequalities. Poverty was another structural inequality she had to contended with, although Romero clarified that "it wasn't painful because we didn't wish for anything, *no deseábamos cosas que no podíamos tener*—I don't remember wishing for anything or asking for something that we couldn't have." Upon reflection, she recalled one exception: "I wanted a real coat, because I always had hand-me-downs, but it was comfortable for us. It was maybe that my mother was very, very good, and thrifty. You know, she would manage the money where we worked six months and we could live a whole year on it; she would always buy at the garage sales and she would always buy at the secondhand stores, and she would always take good care of our clothes." All of her mother's efforts made it so that "most of the time we looked decent." At least as far as she remembers: "We don't have a whole lot of pictures to show" from that time.

A spirit of resistance marked the "beginning of my education; it was sort of like there's something wrong with you, but we'll tolerate you . . . as migrant farm workers we went like to twenty schools a year." This made it more difficult for Romero to obtain an education. "It was difficult to catch up with the work: we started getting algebra, a lot of history, and a lot of English, and not every school covered the concepts under study." Thus, her school experience produced feelings of "extreme frustration and anger that made me feel cheated." Very few teachers showed an interest in them, "except for those in Texas." There was one teacher who really believed in her and "encouraged me even though I might've gotten there this week, next week I took a test and I got a hundred—I had a very good memory, and the teacher was really supportive, he helped me thrive." In the classroom, "I loved to compete with boys. I loved to prove I was smarter, especially if they were friends—we competed with each other." When they moved to another community, "they wouldn't accept the courses I had taken, and when I went to ninth grade I was told that I would have to stay in Texas to graduate, which totally discouraged me." I said, "Well, these people know that my parents weren't going to leave me in Texas alone."

So, at age fourteen "I went to work at Newberry's and other such stores, moving on to Levi's jeans until the age nineteen, but I was always working." While she was happy to contribute to her family, when she got married she impressed upon her husband her desire to continue her education. He agreed that he would support her, but his promise came to naught, and "it I took ten years to go back to school, get my GED, my AA, my BA, and my master's." For her, it was difficult to do it alone, without support, and undergoing three back surgeries in the process. However, "I did it!"

She described her educational journey in more detail: "I started with my GED, when I was working as a school liaison, then I went to Gavilan College on a part-time basis, working and raising kids, and also raising hell in Gilroy." She could not go full-time, so "I went back on a part-time basis," receiving a GED six weeks later, moving on to community college to finish an associate of arts degree. In Romero's experience, "a couple of professors were very supportive, and a couple of Latino professors were quite supportive, and my job endorsed my efforts because they expected it, so it was easy for me to justify being in school." It was "because it was an expectation for work and I could do it during work time—the county gave us ten weeks to go to school; it was very legitimate." For any classes that weren't offered during the allotted time, she took evening courses, and that "was always acceptable, because to maintain the job I needed to stay in school." She then went to San José State, where she "followed the same pattern, although it was disappointing to continue the BA level on a part-time basis." Having had major surgery for a congenital back problem, it was "more difficult when I entered the master's in social work program."

For her MSW, Romero chose administration as her concentration "because I loved to manage money, and the specialization came with more control." During this part of her education, the county did not support her efforts which was a challenge. Nonetheless, she continued working, performing her work responsibilities and continuing her efforts to democratize services for those who relied on Santa Clara County for their mental health needs.

Her earliest leadership intervention came when she was only "nineteen and working at Levi's doing the hems." One day they did not meet a production quota. "The bell rang for us to stop, and they told us we would be staying late because we had not finished." In response to their orders, "I put the scissors down and I went right up to the boss and said, 'Try to stop me,' reminding him that 'the contract says we're done at five.'" With that, she initiated a work stoppage. It was not clear to Romero "what gave me the courage. I could have been fired on the spot, but I caught him off guard." When she returned to work the next day, Romero realized "I was still angry, yet I went to the supervisor and asked to talk to him about the rules: 'I don't know if they're going to be different than the contract says. I want them in writing, and I want to talk to the boss to make sure we understand each other.'" When the women saw her, "they rallied behind me. This might have been something they wanted to say, but they were afraid. I wasn't afraid—next month I was leaving," so she had nothing to lose. For that reason, "I took that risk, but mostly because I felt insulted and humiliated—the way he treated us."

Specializing in disaster social work, Romero was often called to serve in national disasters. Also, she continued to work on issues of equity and mental health services and worked to create equity in public service. At the time of our interview, she had not been as active because she was focusing on her institute, the Hispanic Institute of Family Development. Still, "I've made a conscious decision to continue serving in the Criminal Justice Board, the Board of Developmental Disabilities, the Social Services

Board, the Gardner Health Center Board, and the Council on Aging." She was invited to serve on the board at MACSA and said she would probably join. However, "every two years I rotate, because as I learn and understand how systems work, I aim to translate it for people in the lay community, with the hope to influence them to include us and make them better."

PROGRESSIVE ORGANIZING TO CULTURAL AND MENTAL HEALTH: ELISA MARINO ALVARADO

Elisa Marina Coleman, now Alvarado, was born in San Francisco in 1953; she is the oldest of six siblings, including one brother and four sisters. "I grew up dealing with a big family and a lot of activity in the house, and everybody having a sense of a dad working really hard for a certain quality of life and security." Her mother stayed at home: "It was a pretty traditional family." She said, "My friends were in awe because we were into arts and music, culture, history, and my father always had lots and lots of books; he was a Spanish teacher." A transnational family, they traveled to Mexico every year, "and we would visit my grandmother in San Diego." She grew up "middle-class, and with a kind of an intellectual orientation where I related to being Mexican, until I got into the Chicano movement." Proud to identify as a Chicana, Alvarado is of Cuban, Irish, Mexican Indian, Purépecha, and *un poquito de* English and Irish ancestry. She has long concluded that "in this country, for a lot of different reasons and my biological racial mixture and Indigenous experience, we are the result of colonialism and imperialism." So for her, choosing to call herself Chicana is not necessarily an identity, it's more of a historical consequence.

Her father was born in Guadalajara, Mexico, and is of mixed heritage—Purépecha from Michoacán and Irish. Her paternal "great-grandfather was—*cómo allá dicen mayordomo*, or an Indigenous representative of the Pueblo; he was one of the first people who learned Spanish." She has been told that "there was a book in which somebody interviewed him around the *mitos* [myth] stuff written in Spanish and Purépecha." Her paternal grandmother "married an Irishman who worked in the oil fields; he was a pipe fitter and supposedly laid the pipes for the Tijuana Bullring, and he is buried in Oaxaca." Alvarado's mother was born in Hollywood, California, and had an Irish and English ancestry, tracing her lineage to the Smithsons of the Smithsonian Institute. Her maternal grandfather was Cuban and "came to Hollywood pursuing the entertainment business. So we always imagined him as being kind of a Desi Arnaz."

Her father taught Spanish at Foothill College and De Anza College and she remembered him as "definitely very active." She saw him as "a fighter for the just respect of Chicano students, curriculum, and Latino teachers, yet he was always just struggling, and he had a good relationship with MEChA." During the Cambodian bombings, "he was one of the organizers of the walkout" at school. She saw him as "being frustrated." Her mother, on the other hand, was not active outside the home, although Alvarado recalled that "she had a pretty liberal perspective: she was against the Vietnam War." Alvarado said her grandmother had much influence on her in her growing-up years, "because she was a reader of humanistic books and really into studying with an incredible interest in her own intellectual development." Her grandmother's dream as a girl was to become a writer, and according to Alvarado, "she managed to get a couple of articles into the *New Yorker* magazine under a male pseudonym." In different ways, the elder women in her family inspired Alvarado to become tenacious.

Thinking back to her upbringing in San José, where Alvarado has lived since she was in fifth grade, she recalled it as a Chicano Mexicano town, with farmworkers and laborers. She said that as citizens of San José "we're marginal, even though we've got this barrio or this huge, this demographic shift, but we're not part of the power relationships, you know, the mainstream, we're not represented." For her, "San José has a front of being a progressive city, but still has the feeling of an agricultural town." It is both a large and small environment where those who are not central to the narrative of San José become irrelevant to the city.

In 1978, "on the day of a huge demonstration in San Francisco," Elisa Coleman married her first husband, Jorge Gonzalez. The couple timed the ceremony in a way that allowed people to go the demonstration and the wedding afterward. After the marriage, they remained in San José. She said they talked about it a lot: "he was in Los Angeles but it turns out that he was needed to work for a political newspaper [for] which he was the translator. So we stayed." She saw her marriage as enhancing her political work, "but at times it was very hard and I think that having a marriage, being with somebody, and not lose myself in it, you have to have different things in your life, not just the movement."

Alvarado said her husband supported her cultural activism and commitment and her dedication to Teatro Visión, a woman's theater group of which she is a co-founder and director. "Teatro has become the most central activity of mine outside of the home, away from my job. We love the movement, but we're not willing to give up everything; some people give it day and night." She added that her husband is "a person that has a good political consciousness and understands that what I'm doing is important." Still, "most tensions surfaced because of time with the Teatro, and for me the household has been on ongoing struggle" because she felt it should not be her sole responsibility but something they both shared.

Elisa and Jorge have a son—Emilio Gonzalez—an intelligent young man who is into electronics and but is not interested in being involved in the community. Alvarado explained that their activism had been "very hard on Emilio, and basically, I gave up touring but still doing the work, having children—it just made sense" to stop. Thus, rather than traveling to perform, the troupe created a home-based company with a seasonal schedule and a membership base.

As a Chicana, Alvarado "has a sense of belonging . . . commitment, and desire to do something for the collective Chicano people." Her ethnic identity "really strikes at what I do." Also, "in my mental health endeavors, I approach work as an artist. . . . not defining reality per se, but shaking and moving through and seeing what else can we see; another dimension of this reality . . . as an artist, *curandera*, healer—I try to merge mental health with the Teatro." Alvarado traced her activism to the antiwar movement, although she "can't remember any specifics," except for organizing "a teach-in."

Her entrance into activism was through cultural work; political involvement came later. She began as a tutor with Educational Opportunity Programs and Services (EOPS). Also, she was "very involved in the creation of a Third World Coalition, and an Asian American Student Organization." At the College of San Mateo, "we were very active with BASTA, with the *Los Siete* defendants, so I was definitely pretty involved—that was around '73 or '74." In addition, "I was involved with political prisoner defense and MEChA, where I continued on with that."

At the height of her activism, Alvarado received a "scholarship to Cornell in anthropology." However, because "it wasn't really close to my family and it was mostly white people there, I did not accept their offer. I freaked out at the idea of being so far away and not knowing any Chicanos." Later, she was accepted by the University of California, Santa Cruz, "but I was told I couldn't get [financial aid] because my father made too much money." She sought her mother's support, and while she could vouch for Alvarado's having lived on her own for three years, it was not sufficient for her to qualify for financial aid. So "I got myself into San José State, and I took classes in that powerful political economy program where Gail Southworth and Jim O'Connor taught." For her, "it was a very interesting time to be there, and I got involved." Soon enough, though, "instead of studying, I was doing cultural work, so I joined the Teatro—Teatro de la Gente—and didn't go back to school until I returned to social work ten years later."

Meanwhile, she worked as a case manager and community worker, which "I really enjoyed," but the position did not last long and she found herself back in school because of "cutbacks and the need to have a license and a degree to work in a mental health setting." She decided to apply to graduate school, and she soon realized that the School of Social Work was the place for her. "I was excited as I began to look at it more closely—here was a school with a certain mission to work with Latinos, train social workers to work with Latinos. I realized the social work profession is about social change, and also how it moves into people's individual values, and lives, and their families, which I think, as I was aging, you know, kind of looking at that too, being married, and so on." She enjoyed working on her master's, even though the program "lacked depth in terms of a real understanding and application of the power of racism, the dynamic of racism with mental health, and class, and certainly gender." In her perception, "the teachers were really out of touch. There were a couple of women who were powerful, but that was it." Nonetheless, she remained in the program until she completed her MSW.

Elisa Marina Alvarado's involvement has focused on "family, the Chicano community, the arts community, and the left—in terms of the labor movement and Central American nonintervention and progressive politics." She sees herself as invested in social justice, the central philosophy of her activism and community involvement. As such, her work is reciprocal, whereby relationships begin with "responsibility and mutual support, and as an educational process, where activism comes with responsibility of passing along knowledge, with the purpose of creating social change." Alvarado believes "a leader is essentially a teacher, a person who develops critical consciousness, self-awareness, and has the ability to look at options, moving from awareness to action whether it's with an individual or a group. It is a process where people look at a problem, or a situation, or a need or a desire, and then don't just stay in a space of complaining, or wanting, or dreaming, or whatever, but move into manifestation of change." Being an activist leader is not about doing everything yourself. In Alvarado's view, those invested in social change "keep an eye on the overall process, on the goals and notice if and when we're straying, and call for commitment to that, or changes it, if it needs to be changed."

Alvarado is the product of "public schools from kindergarten on up. English was my first language and I didn't master Spanish until later," even when "as a seven-year-old we lived in Peru, and one year in Mexico with my family. Those experiences were very powerful, because education was advanced, challenging, and demanding." These experiences instilled in her "a certain approach for education and study skills that I really didn't get here, at least not in elementary school." In the Bay Area, Alvarado went "to school in the pinnacle of '60s activism. Even in sixth grade I started being aware of the antiwar movement, and rock and roll, and other things." However, "in junior high and high school, I started to get an attitude about school, and provoked things" that resulted in her dropping out. Wanting to be rebellious, "I participated in organizing a walkout, and sold the Black Panther paper on campus," and because of difficulties in school, "I had home teaching, and I ended up finishing up the requirements in junior college." Most members of her immediate family have a formal education, "beginning with my father. He has an MA in language arts and teaches Spanish, taught linguistics, and reviewed texts for teaching Spanish." However, her mother "never finished her BA in French." Most recently, Alvarado's "brother received an MA in drama, my sister got a BA in graphic arts, another sister has a BA in biology, with another sister in the process of going back to school." Education is highly valued in her family.

In the 1960s she was inspired by social activism in the Bay Area. Role models such as "the Black Panthers, who made a big impact on me, and the Young Lords Party" helped Alvarado convey the message "you can't look down on us." Despite all her work in the movement, Alvarado did not perceive herself as an organizer, even when she put together a walkout, which turned into a teach-in, during the Vietnam War. Her activism and leadership began in junior college, when she was not yet eighteen. "I got involved in a support Los Site thing—the campaign that was going on; on campus, we were organizing a Third World Coalition." There were other issues surfacing, such as lack of programs and resources for minorities. Also, in the early 1970s she became involved with the Barrios Unidos movement, police brutality, and political prisoners. From there, she became involved with "Venceremos, you know, different heavy-duty groups; they were starting to look at China and Cuba."

Back in San José, Elisa Marina Alvarado participated in community organizations that focused on issues of police violence, such as the Community Alert Patrol. She recalled, "There was a series of police shootings—there was a black man that had been shot, then they killed Treviño." Alvarado also worked with "rent relief, the farm workers movement, and Teatro—I was the North American coordinator of the Trabajadores de la Cultura—Frente de Trabajadores de la Cultura—that had branches in Mexico and Latin America." In addition, "I worked with the Paulo Freire Project, and did community education that formed the basis for my performances, held ESL meetings, and organized a tenants' union." Alvarado became involved with the Angela Davis Defense Committee and the American Indian Movement, for whom she helped "collect food to send to Wounded Knee out of La Confederación," and worked on efforts to "free American political prisoners." At San José State, she became involved "in the walkout because of cutbacks in the Economics Department." She added, "I've done a lot of controversial stuff. And, you know, immigrant rights, and then certainly all along Teatro and educational rights," developing a performance to educate the community on the Bakke decision, and youth work.

As a founding co-chair, Alvarado worked with the immigration rights organization Raza Si! "Police brutality became an issue for the youth, because for them it was something that was just, you know, they have this tough exterior but they were frightened and angry." So, in the beginning it was "in terms of seeing the universality of their experience . . . barrios or *clicas* or gangs . . . going through the learning of how much impact you have if you try to change a city council. So, I was like allowing them to have those choices and learn from them, and just kind of building where they were at, and supporting them in their efforts to organize things." That context became the beginning of Youth Getting Together, showing barrio young people that they could make an impact on city policy, "in terms of what was going on like forcibly taking pictures of youth," and from there "they began to make statements like opposing the *migra* when they began to do the raids in the streets." Then the youth started connecting with MEChA and "collected food, which allowed them to look at their experience. 'Where are you from? Your parents are farmworkers.'"

Alvarado recalled that working with Teatro became really difficult for her, "whether it was self-esteem or shyness or something else," but with the women "in Teatro de la Gente there was a lot of unhappiness." She attributed this to "manipulation and exclusion from decision making and feeling exploited, as they worked their butts off from sunup to sundown." Alvarado pointed out that men made the decisions, but soon the women called for discussions about how tasks got decided and the division of labor. Child care became a key issue, and because the director would not listen to their demands, "the members went to the board, and the board turned around and told the director that we were going to them behind his back." It was such a controlling environment that members would be sanctioned and forbidden to speak to other members unless it pertained to logistical or other business matters when rehearsing or on tour. The contradictions Alvarado confronted were not because of race and class; it was gender that became a site of struggle when working with Teatro.

She spoke about her experiences with males, or with Chicanos, in terms of activism and leadership. She talked about situations in which her work with males traumatized her as a *teatrista*. "I'm working closely with a prior director of Teatro . . . to put a collaborative agenda together, as Teatros, to create a community organization and build a cultural center, but underneath there is a sort of mistrust." Alvarado added, "We're able sit down and work through it, and I'm really open to seeing if this time we can follow the agenda and move forwards with our plans."

At the time of our interview, Alvarado planned to retire from Teatro Vision in 1993. In addition to past involvement with many nonprofit and public organizations, she served on the Campaign for Human Development Board for about four years. And, while she had been invited to sit on other boards, she had not accepted "because of wanting to do some performing." She was not interested in advancing her presence or profile in the community. Instead, as an activist or professional, Alvarado wanted to expand her creative outlets. For her, teatro has become the venue by which she would continue to make a mark on her community.

POLICY AND POLITICAL WORK TO COMMUNITY ACTIVISM: KATHY CHAVEZ NAPOLI

Kathy Chavez Napoli is the oldest daughter of eight siblings, "three older and two younger brothers, and two younger sisters." She grew up in a large extended family, where "there were always people around, and my parents, my mother comes from a very large family, so there was always a lot of people: aunts, uncles, cousins, friends."

FIGURE 59 Kathy Chavez Napoli and her family. Courtesy of Kathy Chavez Napoli.

Her mother was born in Somis, California, and later moved to a small farming community near Fresno, and her father traced his origins to Susanville, California, and is of Maidu Indian ancestry.

Although her parents were not active in the community, her oldest brother, who is a baseball coach, was a leader. Still, "my mother was always being asked to translate where I grew up on Summer Street." The people in the neighborhood "were limited English speaking, so she was always being asked by friends and neighbors to do translations and to kind of help ease the way in different situations." Chavez Napoli said that "you had to be self-sufficient in a family of eight children, otherwise you'd get lost in the shuffle." Even though the "boys were catered to, girls had to do extra things, and more pressures were put on them, with certain higher standards; the boys got away with things, but the girls couldn't." As the oldest girl, she emphasized that additional responsibility came with one's place in the family.

Life was not easy in Sal Si Puedes, as "my mother didn't drive. I remember going to the José Theater, seeing all the horror movies, also a couple of times getting picked on by older boys at the movies, but mostly it was pretty positive." She went to catechism with Sister Bravo. She could still remember the taste of "stale doughnuts. Father

McDonnell. First communion at Guadalupe Church, walking to Mayfair and Lee Mathson, and walking by the church, seeing dead people—weird lip color, no blood on them—that's mostly what I remember growing up."

Chavez Napoli also recalled close family interactions. Because her father was not social, they had very few friends. "My uncle and family would visit mostly," and she and her family visited the Five Cities area, where her maternal grandparents resided. In addition to growing up inside a close family circle, Chavez Napoli has memories of a "father that was very, very strict, and we couldn't go over other people's houses, we never stayed overnight." She added, "If Dad found us in the street when he came home, we would all get hit." The family kept to themselves. "My father had a truck and a station wagon, and we would drive around, never going to traditional places like the museum or the circus, only to Alum Rock Park and driving around the city. He was the boss, he was the one who spoke to everybody, the wife just stayed at home—this is almost with everybody I knew—and there wasn't a lot of social interaction with others that I saw because we didn't go to a lot of things." In retrospect, Chavez Napoli "didn't have the kind of upbringing that a lot of the Mexican people have. So I didn't have the appreciation of the culture or the songs; my parents didn't listen to Mexican music." In her household, the sounds of home were primarily "cowboy and English music because that's what Dad was comfortable with, that's what he was raised with—I didn't have the traditional kind of upbringing." She recalled stratification by gender, such as "wives serving the husband's food, the wives not saying anything. The husbands there talking and doing whatever they want as long as they wanted, and the wives having to wait until they were ready to go." She did not remember "equal conversations where the woman's opinion was asked for and appreciated."

Chavez Napoli experienced discrimination at school, although "I really didn't look at them as race because it was something that wasn't talked about. In those days, race was white and the farmworkers." In her socialization, "Mexican people were like nonexistent and so were Native Americans." These social interactions conveyed the message that neither group was valued, it was "Oh, you're Indian! You're lower than low, lower than black, lower than anyone." Because her ancestral lineage is "Native American Indian, the system deliberately misleads us, we would lose all that we have." That knowledge was a source of loss for her: "I don't speak my native language or know where my native home is, and the government deliberately tore apart Indian families."

A woman of Native American Indian and Mexican descent, Chavez Napoli spoke about the destruction of the "Mexican and Latino communities," pointing out that the community's losses happened "because we didn't know the rules." But she rejoiced in knowing that "we are getting educated, and fighting to get that knowledge, and then going to city council and seeing them change the rules right before our eyes—these things made me get involved." With a greater understanding of the circumstances, she felt as if "I didn't have a choice . . . I was compelled to speak. I have to speak . . . I couldn't just stay silent." It was an ethical responsibility to make a difference in the lives of those who were the most marginalized.

Kathy Chavez and her husband, Bill Napoli, "were high school sweethearts," and they married five years after they met. "We're kind of unusual in that we met when I was a senior and he was a junior, and I went on to college," thus delaying marriage to make sure that she graduated, "because I didn't want to get sidetracked, and my mother was very, very supportive." Her mother advised her to finished college, even when her father was "completely against her going to school." She attributed his resistance to her becoming educated to his status and experiences as a Native American Indian and Mexican. He'd say, "You don't have anything to learn from that white men's school." When she opted to attend college, Chavez Napoli and her father "had a very big falling out," but her mother urged her on. "She worried that if I went, and then got married, I would drop out because I had kids, or that other things would interfere." Chavez Napoli did end up marrying while still in college, but she waited five years. With only two classes left for her to graduate, they took their vows.

Chavez Napoli and her husband had two boys and also raised her niece and nephew. They assumed responsibility for raising them after her brother was incarcerated, and "his wife married someone else, and didn't want the kids. She abandoned them." Chavez Napoli and her husband got legal custody. She described how it happened: "One day on Thanksgiving weekend she dropped them off at my mother's house and never came back. So, on a Sunday my mother was worried about my sister-in-law; she thought something had happened to her, she didn't know what was going on because she hadn't heard from her. We talked to her parents, her mother, and we couldn't find her, and then finally we came to realize that she had just abandoned them." When they went to court, the judge asked the children's mother: "Do you know what they're doing, that they're going to get legal custody?" She nodded and "walked out with her new husband. It was really hard for the kids," and it took a long time before they "felt secure enough to talk about her, and before they felt safe with us. It was hard."

Chavez Napoli said that her husband is supportive, not only in relation to family but also in ensuring that she is safe and secure. For example, "during the Giant stadium controversy, my family was getting threats, and I was getting threatened a lot, instead of just saying, 'Get out of it, and don't get involved anymore,' he asked her 'to buy another little phone, so I can know where you are all the time, and just call me, and tell me where you're going to be so that I'll know.'" All he asked was for her to phone regularly and make sure she locked all the doors, since "we had bomb threats, we had somebody thrown in jail, and what's really sad about is that Mexican people have also made threats against me."

Kathy Chavez Napoli's path to activism began in high school, "in shorthand class . . . the teacher was being very condescending, and the teacher and I just weren't getting along, so I asked to be taken out of the class, and they said that wasn't possible." Without thinking it over, Chavez Napoli responded, "I'm sorry, but I'm not going to stay here." It was at that time that "I decided I'm going to do what's best for me, not what I'm told is best for me." For her, issues of "equality and fairness, and accountability—fiscal accountability—have always been central." "It was my early experiences in the family, where we didn't have a lot of people who would advocate for justice, for equal treatment, for applying the rules equally to everyone without changing the rules as you go along just because you're the wrong color for their standards." Poverty and race were barriers that gave her insight to understanding the difficulties her community faced, although she was not cognizant of her class position until much later.

The activist seed surfaced "when my parents were forced to move out of our neighborhood when the Highway 280 came through." While she was not able to become involved with her family's displacement, their removal was foundational in her struggle for the betterment of her community. As best as she could recall, "there were no community groups advocating for fair compensation for losing your home because it was a poor minority community." Chavez Napoli never stopped questioning whether her family received a fair settlement, or whether the state cared that "you had to go into debt all over again, and you had a smaller house because you couldn't afford one, they could care less, and there were no community agencies really fighting for you in that way." The only institution that played any type of role was the Catholic church, but it "was a very small kind of moral support role, but nothing significant." Because of this, she would become involved in issues she found to be unfair and unjust, especially unfairness premised on the notion that as a people "you don't belong here and we don't have to pay you what's right. We have much power and money. You're just the wrong color and you speak the wrong language, and so you don't count." By this time, she knew she was Native American, so she felt she had more of a right to be here—her Indigeneity was the safeguard that gave her absolute confidence.

As an activist leader, the biggest issue Chavez Napoli took on was in 1986–87, when an outside enterprise targeted San José to set up an autowrecking business. "They went and lobbied and artificially created a glut of abandoned cars, with the message, 'Hey, we're your savior. Support us and we'll clean up your mess.'" In her view, "the city basically ignored the local business people, and we went in there and said, 'Hey, deal with us.'" However, "at every turn we lost—at the Planning Commission and city council." It took four and a half years to win, and this was because "we took it to court and we got neighborhoods to support us, and this large out-of-town corporation lost the court battle." She is not one to take lightly issues that impact her community and her family. "So, that was the first one and I was just real proud of that, but it was hard going all the time." However, "I'm one of those kinds of people who doesn't give up—I'm stubborn—like my father." The fact is that when "somebody tells me I can't do something, it's like saying that I can because I'll prove you wrong."

Still, she has had to contend with being "a minority woman who dares to speak up, and how dare I?" In the case of "the stadium issue, they were questioning where I lived," without looking into the residence of "the six or seven white males who are very influential, very wealthy white males who don't live in San José, but all of those white males want San Joseans to tax themselves." That information never came out in the media. Yet, they questioned Chavez Napoli, "a native San Josean, who went to school here, owns property in San José, and maintains two residences—one is in the city, and one is in Coyote Valley, but it's in the county." The detractors would often question her civil activism, asking, "Where do you live?" to which she would retort, "Hey, go ask those white males. Don't come bugging me. It's a nonissue. Let's talk about the issues here." Because the stadium was a pet project of moneyed interests, "I was always getting attacked, and the media has always labeled me as a rabble-rouser." To describe her demeanor as an activist leader, they use terms such as "shouting, and complaining, and whining when we bring things up, or 'There she goes complaining again.' They don't do that with white people." She believes that the establishment views her as a threat, but "I'm not compromised. I haven't sold out. I don't want or need a job. I'm not getting a kickback one way or another, and the Latino community respects me, but I speak for anybody who has to work hard, and has to earn it, so they don't want to pay more taxes and they don't want to have to do without services. They want to be safe, they want their kids to be educated, it's the same kind of issue." Because of her position and integrity, and because "I do my homework, I do the research, I read the report, and I know how to do a budget because I run my own business and know what profit means, they really view me as a threat." And "since I wasn't raised in a traditional way, they can't predict what I'm going to do."

As she reflected on her involvement, Chavez Napoli spoke with pride about her work on the issues she had taken on. From the Studio Theater victory (see above, pp. 124–25), to stopping a company from coming in and competing against the wrecking yards, to defeating the Fallon statue in the Plaza of San José, to the stadium tax: "those were all things that I was involved with and of which I'm very proud," but she also took pride "in the things that we quite didn't succeed at, because we tried to save the Mi Tierra Community, even though they moved them." In her view, without community involvement, "people wouldn't have recognized that they had a right to speak up for themselves, and the city would not have relocated them in such a nice facility." After all, the powers that be "were basically trying to intimidate them and tell them that they didn't have any rights at all." In the final analysis, Chavez Napoli has become involved for the best interest of the community. Her notions of activism focus on "integrity and commitment to the average person," with emphasis on "bettering the situation of hardworking honest people, and with the objective of creating safety" for future generations. In Chavez Napoli's view, race and ethnicity are irrelevant in activism and leadership. "It doesn't really matter what color you are, the only thing you have to do is recognize that you have to overcome certain obstacles. It doesn't matter what color you are because you can be purple and if it's an economic obstacle you're still going to have to overcome it—whatever color you are." She added, activist leaders "recognize that obstacles take on different forms: some are economic, some could be color, some could be education, some could be experience, and some could be emotional." Thus, to overcome these obstacles, "leaders must get people to hear ideas and share each other's vision." For Chavez Napoli,

> A leader is a comprehensive kind of a person who cannot always have the right answers but who can point you in the right direction to find answers, who cannot be everything for you but who can point you in the right direction. It is somebody who is a big enough person that doesn't need to take the credit, as long as that person facilitates what your goal is, helps you focus on what you need to do, and sometimes that person can just be there to support you.

Moreover, "a leader represents different things to many people, such as with the Studio Theater, which was an issue of too much power in the hands of Mayor McEnery" when he decided to give the Studio Theater to a private business—the San José Repertory Theater. With this issue, her approach was to work within the system. "So I immediately called the mayor's office and asked what was going on, and they didn't respond. Then I went to the theater operator to make sure that I wasn't misunderstanding what was going on, because I was reading newspapers. That's when I got involved [in] something that was viewed as a losing battle, they told me I can't do it, and I showed [I] could." Chavez Napoli went into the fight with all she had, acknowledging that "we may not win on this, but we're sure going to fight." Eventually, "we had so much support that the mayor had to back down on that," and in less than four months the community had won. From there other issues came up, and she was approached about the Fallon statute. Once again, "the budget limits were not followed—more than tripling the approved budget—a pet project of Tom McEnery. So we went after him on procedure and policies, and again he had to back down. So we won." The more she learned about the system and its players, the easier it became for her to take on the more powerful in Silicon Valley.

Talking about education, she explained, "My mother finished eighth and my father went to third grade." As for herself, "I've done graduate school. I've been in graduate school—I just didn't finish." She proudly stated that she was "the first in my immediate family to graduate from high school and go through the ceremony." To be the first on "both sides of my family among at least two hundred cousins, some who are twenty and thirty years older, is quite an accomplishment." She started school at Mayfair, now called César Chávez Elementary. She recalled that it was a caring and dedicated environment, because of a kindergarten teacher—Mrs. Amore—who set the tone. Chavez Napoli said that she was proof that if children have "a positive experience those first years, then they will always love school, even if they have bad teacher afterwards." Contrarily, "if they have a bad teacher, it can usually carry over." She pointed out that it was not just the teaching that paved the way and expressed appreciation for her parents' "voracious love of reading," which contributed to her schooling success. She felt thankful for "that strong base."

With the opening of "Mildred Goss [Elementary School], which was very much a white school in a nice neighborhood," things would change for Chavez Napoli. Those who went to that school lived in brand-new tract homes, and "we were kind the outsiders. I can remember one real negative time when this girl kept picking on me and called me 'a beaner.'" She had not heard this word as an insult and could not recall her response at the time, but they were both "sent to the principal's office. I got in trouble. And she didn't." That happened in fourth or fifth grade, but "it was so negative it sticks out in my mind." In Lee Mathson Middle School, "I got along well, then I went to San José High School," and it was there that she noticed class distinctions. "I saw the difference between poor and middle class, and that's where I really learned that I was real poor."

As best as she could recall, at San José State there were "probably only 250 Latinos/Chicanos in the whole school." She matriculated in 1970, and while she attended rallies and other such things, she never organized them because she lacked the time, since she had "to pay most of my own way to go to school." Then as now, education was key, and Chavez Napoli looked forward first to becoming educated and to learning the rules of the game. "So that's what I did. I wasn't really visible in the community," although she was a mentor "for SHARE, a program that linked students up with young elementary school kids." Her community work was all one-to-one, and she

FIGURE 60 Kathy Chavez Napoli's high school picture. Courtesy of Kathy Chavez Napoli.

feared speaking in public. If she had been asked, she would have said, "No way, I would have said no way." At that time, she thought her "contribution was to get educated and become a teacher and help teach other kids. That was my goal."

The reason Chavez Napoli became involved in local issues was "to show my children that they need to look out for themselves, that they need to speak up for themselves and their community, because if we don't, nobody will." She added, "The reason I got so visible was because I know what it's like to be displaced," and she retold the Highway 280 and Summer Street stories that inspired her to make things right. To those who saw the building of the freeway as progress, it did not matter that "my father had completely remodeled our four-bedroom house." "Everyone received the same money, and those houses there were thirty to fifty years old, they were small, and he went to court to try and fight that, and there was no winning." Her parents went from owing their own home outright to "going into debt all over again for thirty years, and getting only a two-bedroom house, because that's all he could afford, and so that really devastated my father."

The loss of that home pushed her father to consume more alcohol; it became a problem, and "he never fully recovered." Those memories inspired Chavez Napoli to take on the Studio Theater issue because "it was very close to where my parents now live." Moreover, they had already destroyed the Guadalupe Auzerais area with the convention center, and there was talk "about extending eminent domain to where my parents lived, and they wouldn't have survived another kind of relocation, another kind of displacement." She asked her parents, "Do you go to that theater?" When they both said yes, she decided she would do anything she could to keep that amenity available for her parents. Given her own good life, she decided to do something for those who, like her parents, would be left without entertainment in their neighborhood. "I felt that I needed to say something because no one was saying anything. I asked everybody that I knew to say something and nobody did. I looked around and nobody said anything, so I did. And, I felt very strongly that it was in a way fighting for my parents, from the twenty-some years before, when there was no one there. I really got involved and became visible."

Even though in high school she was a member of a business club and of Future Business Leaders of America, she said, "I never really thought I was going to be a business leader, I just joined it because it was fun." She took business courses because she thought she could find employment, since "I never had the hope of going to school because I knew we didn't have the money, my parents didn't have the money." In her senior year, "probably sometime in March, people from EOP at San José State came and said, 'Hey, if you wanna go to school, you can go. It doesn't really matter about your finances. We can help you.'" She had taken the necessary tests, and her grades had always been good, and "with that they said, 'We can help you.' So, that's how I got in."

It took a long time for Chavez Napoli to find her voice and power. She explained, "Our culture does not teach you to blow your own horn, it does not teach you to recognize your own accomplishments and give yourself credit." For her, "it was during the Studio Theater issue," after having been president of the Auto Recyclers Association four or five times, that she was recognized as a Latina leader in a male-dominated world. It was not an easy path, and people would often scream at her to "just shut up." So, at those meetings "I had to insist on better treatment." But "after the Studio Theater some of the same people I represented as a president told me, 'You know, Kathy? You really did a hell of a job.'" And "my landlord of twenty years came and said, 'I'm really, really proud of you.'" It was his compliment that made her look at herself and think: "We did that. It was pretty good." However, she still did not fully value her activism and leadership. "It wasn't until I was already thirty-five or thirty-six that I recognized it."

CONCLUSION

For Chicanas of the Baby Boomer Generation, the lessons learned were many. Although at the time of our interviews some may not have been as fully involved as they were

at the apogee of their involvement, they were continuing to serve the city they loved. For example, Chavez Napoli was still serving on the boards of various organizations, including the Four Cs, the Lupus Foundation Board, and the Alviso Community Organization board.

Although they have since died, in their oral histories Arroyo and Romero spoke about lessons learned. For example, Cecilia Arroyo, in her activist work, learned to value relationships, especially her link to women, to Latinas, recognizing that leadership evolves through the process of friendship and doing joint projects with other women. Whether it was fund-raising or working with the GI Forum, Arroyo affirmed that there was no jealousy among the Latina women working together to pursue an issue or

FIGURE 61 Elisa Marina Alvarado, director of Teatro Visión. Photo by Jesús Manuel Mena Garza.

form a united front. For Josie Romero, migration made it more complex for her to obtain an education, which led her to drop out of school. Later she went back to school, and although it took her ten years, she eventually obtained her GED, AA, BA, and MA degrees. It was difficult for her to do it alone—without support and having endured three back surgeries—but she did it.

Elisa Marina Alvarado frequently reflected on her often-traumatizing experiences with men, Chicanos, in terms of activism and leadership. In addition to involvement with many nonprofit and public organizations, Alvarado served on the Campaign for Human Development Board. Although she had been invited to sit on other boards, she opted out because her heart was in teatro. In Alvarado's activism and leadership, she aimed to create change in the most creative outlet she has, and teatro was the venue in which she made her mark in her community.

Finally, for Chavez Napoli, her family's displacement from their neighborhood was foundational to her later engagement in activism for the betterment of her community. Her Indigenous, Native American background gave her absolute confidence in her right to belong here.

The next chapter examines the ways in which women of both generations engaged the structural inequalities of social change as they became involved in improving the lives of those who must content with race, class, and gender in the pursuit of social justice and social change.

11

• • •

CHICANA AWARENESS, CONSCIOUSNESS, AND RESISTANCE

Systemic and Structural Interactions

M ost scholars of leadership begin by expounding upon the ascribed or assigned attributes and characteristics of individuals.[1] Founded on functional and conflict-oriented assumptions, most of these leadership theories depart from pluralist and managerial theories,[2] and leadership is perceived in terms of the individual.[3] Within an individualistic framework of leadership, Chicanas, while perceived as individuals with ethnic affiliations, are not assumed to be capable of accessing and amassing a power base unless they willingly seize the opportunity, which is theoretically available to any-one. At the same time, the common assumption exists that they lack the necessary attributes for leadership, and thus miss out on such opportunities.

As with conventional studies of leadership, various theoretical perspectives from a variety of disciplines have been used to examine Chicano leaders and leadership. Many Chicano scholars have replicated a male argument in leadership research, marginaliz-ing women or minimizing their activism by placing their analysis in the context of a male perspective.[4] Evidence shows that women made significant contributions to the Chicano movement, yet accounts of the exploits of Rodolfo "Corky" González, Reies Lopez Tijerina, José Angel Gutiérrez, and César E. Chávez, commonly known as the four horsemen of the Chicano movement, abound today, while Chicana leadership remains overshadowed. In the present, as in the past, culture and domestic everyday activities remain the expected realm of women, and leadership exercised within this sphere tends to be neither recognized nor valued. Even Mario García, in his account of Mexican American leadership in El Paso, Texas, places women in a male equation of gender, failing to address their leadership for its own value.[5] In contrast, feminist theorists provide analyses that expand our current understanding of leadership.[6] They advance the public world of politics as exclusive gendered domains.[7] For example, many Chicana scholars critique analyses of women's involvement in the *movimiento*,[8] arguing that their exclusions are due to women's subordination by way of labor division and invalidation based on gender.

In this final chapter, I rely on oral histories collected from 1992 to 1994 to examine the ways in which eleven Chicanas engage race, class, and gender interactions to carry out their involvement as activist leaders. I explore the ways in which they internalized and understood interactions, and how their experiences serve to illustrate a reflective awareness of their social positions inside relational strategies for the creation of social justice and social change.[9] To begin with, Chicanas start with the assumption that their gender influences how they are treated or perceived in their respective social locations. Moreover, they advance a womanist consciousness, while others rely on a feminist frame of reference, without naming themselves feminists.[10] Also, most rejected traditional notions of femininity, as their activism was premised on believing in justice, equality, and fairness as enacted in a multiplicity of social locations. These activist leaders use knowledge of themselves, their respective social positions, and their social environments to confront issues embedded in their interactions, marking their experiences within structures of inequality to analyze Chicana involvement. Chicanas in this study have worked as program directors, elected officials, grassroots organizers, business owners, administrators of educational institutions, and educators, intent on creating institutions of change.

Chicana/Latino leaders, with some exceptions, have not been recognized and have largely remained invisible within the dominant society. Yet, in matters of everyday life, these activist leaders have served as sources of empowerment and change for their respective communities. Identified as one of the four main organizers of the Chicano movement, and recognized as grassroot organizer in San José, César E. Chávez raised the consciousness of the United States about the plight of farmworkers. In coalition with liberal idealistic leaders—Jews, middle-class Euro-Americans, Catholic nuns and priests, and students, who were a prominent force in this alliance—Chávez and the United Farm Workers waged a struggle for human dignity and recognition of workers. Because Chávez fit traditional attributes of leadership, he received recognition as a charismatic leader. To this day, he is considered a key and primary figure in the union's formation and evolution.

On the other hand, Dolores Huerta, vice president of the UFW, a leader in the union since its inception and instrumental in contract negotiations, policy formulations, and boycott actions, was not afforded the recognition given to male union leaders.[11] While a number of Latinos and Chicanos have been acknowledged as leaders by dominant and Raza communities, contributions made by Chicana activist leaders have been overlooked, with a few important exceptions.[12] For the most part, the androcentric historical account of Chicano leadership and activism obscures Chicanas.[13] While Emma Tenayuca and Luisa Moreno are noted for their progressive and union activism, and Josefina Fierro de Bright is recognized for her political involvement, inside analyses of leadership are generally grounded on assumptions of a universal and male understanding of power and authority.[14] The inclusion of such women leaders has served to complement or illustrate the exploits of masculinist models. Strength, rationality, and decisiveness are attributes assigned to those who exercise leadership or power.[15]

WHAT MAKES AN ACTIVIST LEADER?

Chicanas and Latinos/Chicanos in this study concluded that leadership is more than believing or speaking a certain way; it is acting out a philosophy that creates change to benefit the collectivity over the individual. For them, it is not enough to talk about change; they work to create it. Taking a stance and acting upon issues that have had a negative impact on others is part of their active involvement. Moreover, key to their activism is their ability to listen, to observe, and to keep an eye on the overall process, along with the flexibility to modify their approaches, albeit less readily so for Latinos, who tend to keep their eyes on the prize.

According to Chicanas, social change is best undertaken when those who enact leadership are grounded and have a sound understanding of the community needs, while firmly evaluating their own and others' expectations about change from a common perspective. For Ernestina García, an educational activist and community organizer, working for social change means to "do what one can *para cambiar las cosas* [to change things] . . . *pa' mejorar* [to improve] people . . . *y ya que otros mejoran* [and when others improve] maybe I'll get a share *pero* [but] not for our benefit . . . *es para que mejoremos todos* [it's so all of us improve]." For her, and the other Chicanas interviewed, the process of creating social change is not about personal gain, although it can be an end result of exposure and recognition. Without exception, the participants in this study expressed that their involvement placed priority on what would benefit the greatest number of people.

In Santa Clara County, a leader is expected to express self and community understanding, addressing issues faced in their everyday interactions. Sofía Mendoza, a community organizer, political activist, and recognized leader, offered that a leader must "be where the people are at: dress like the people, speak like the people, be one of the people." Also, that it is not enough to exercise leadership among others; leadership starts at home. For Mendoza, "leadership begins with the exercise of justice, fairness, and equality within the leader's private world." Thus the domestic sphere, as well as the greater society, is a site of change.

Chicanas experience, practice, and perform their activism differently from their male counterparts. For these participants, a preferred strategy is not to stand or act alone, but to work collaboratively. Blanca Alvarado, a community and political activist, vice mayor, and past chair of Santa Clara County Board of Supervisors, summarized it as a process that occurs among others: "It is being able to be out there, not as a stand-alone person, but as a person who can work to meet common objectives with groups of people." In her view, a preferred mode of interaction is working with a group and in the direction of the group, instead of working individually. For her, leadership originates within a shared vision for the common good of all involved.

In the engagement of relational processes of interaction, each individual is accepted as an integral part of the process and is not released from their responsibility for "taking charge or being willing to lead in certain events, situations, or incidents." According to Josie Romero, a community and mental health activist and the founder of an institute for the study of the family, when you enact your activist leader potential, it calls for knowing when to lead "without being asked to guide, mentor, support, and direct." Furthermore, "enabling others to act should be emphasized, rather than doing for, which is a disabling approach to creating social change; one must take equal responsibility" in the process. In activist leader interactions there is ownership for contributions and respect for those who work for social change. Change does not happen through the charm or special attributes of an individual; it evolves in interaction with others. Esther Medina, a feminist activist and administrator, saw leadership as "joining people who are already involved in what they already want to do, and somehow empowering them to do it." Among Chicanas, collective strategies drive their actions. Although not always in the frontlines, Chicanas in this study directly wove their notions of change into the continuum of their everyday lives. They saw struggle as an integral aspect of improving the quality of life for their group and community, understanding that improvement of the group and the community results in a better environment for themselves and their families. Self-sacrifice is not a word in these women's vocabularies or interactions, because their driving concepts are resistance, struggle, and change.

For Chicana activist leaders in San José, power relations are a constant part of their interactions, as they struggle with and negotiate involvement, confronting external forces (outside the Chicano community's sphere of influence) and internal structures that impinge upon their leadership. Gender status places Chicanas in conflict with misperceptions held about them by dominant groups as being exotic, foreign, and willing to collude with patriarchal power. They also have to contend with cultural expectations centered on their gender, as they struggle with stereotypes of *marianismo*— submissiveness, abnegation, and passivity.[16]

In addition to being activist leaders, Chicanas manage domestic responsibilities and public life and negotiate gender relations, incorporating domestic responsibilities into their involvement. Chicanas in this study indicated that while the private and public worlds of action meld in their daily interactions, the so-called private realm did limit and shape their activism insofar as it is embedded in the everyday gendered interactions of their lives—for them, there is no separate sphere.

GENDER RELATIONS: NOTIONS OF DIFFERENCE

The Chicanas in this study stated that gendered relations have been part of their consciousness as women. Growing up, they were expected to be molded within patriarchal notions of femininity, domesticity, and *marianismo*. Bombarded with traditional messages of how to be a *niña* (girl) or a *mujer* (woman), they spoke of experiencing gendered structures of subordination, regardless of their generation. Cecilia Arroyo, a planner and political and community activist, recalled gendered interactions and expectations within her family: "My brother was treated very differently, although he was ten years younger. It was a whole different scenario for my brother. He knocked heads a lot with my dad. I became the go-between that protected my brother. Still, my brother could do things that we [my sister and me] would never have imagined because he was a man." Notions of difference guided Arroyo's understanding of her brother's position as a boy in the family. She spoke about having to negotiate feelings of nurturance and protection for a brother for whom she was expected to assume responsibility. The conflict of having to protect her brother from the problems caused by his own behavior was intensified by the parental attitude that "boys will be boys."

Kathy Chavez Napoli, who grew up with a Mexican-descent mother and an American Indian father, said that "boys were much more valued than girls." She gave a cultural explanation for that behavior: "Even in my father's culture—the Native American [he is Maidu, one of the four tribes in the Susanville Indian Rancheria]—boys were always free to do what they wanted, to be what they wanted: they got more attention, they got more things, their opinion mattered. That was the way it was." In both Chavez Napoli and Arroyo's interactions, boys were more valued and occupied a central place in the everyday lives of the family. As she thought about gendered interactions, Chavez Napoli thought that her socialization as a girl still influenced her perception of herself as an adult woman and recognized leader. This is particularly clear in her position as the president of an otherwise mostly male business. She finds herself constantly having to examine and reflect on the gendered interactions that surface among the membership and mediating any differences that might be caused by these interactions.

As the eldest of three siblings, Delia Alvarez, an activist and retired administrator, recalled experiencing divergent gender socialization. She explained: "I remember my dad saying, 'You should have been a boy.' I would be the one willing to work on the car, or I was out working in the yard—I didn't want to wash dishes. If I went out and watered the lawn, I didn't have to wash dishes. I quickly learned that I would rather be out there mowing the lawn. I remember my dad always saying, 'You are a tomboy. You should have been a boy.'"

Having decided that female roles were constraining, Alvarez purposely engaged in behavior traditionally considered male. For example, she found a way to get out of doing domestic chores by mowing the lawn, washing the car, and learning to do small motor repairs, thus endearing herself to her father so that he would teach her and invite her to participate in nontraditional work. In this way, Alvarez developed a strategy for doing the things she enjoyed without feeling constrained by gender. She carried out nontraditional tasks without experiencing repercussions. Because of a "tomboy" persona, Alvarez was allowed to stretch her parents' expectations. Thus, rejecting gendered roles gave her the freedom to engage in activities ascribed to both sexes, as she chose.

Elisa Marina Alvarado similarly recalled the value that her father placed on his son's education but not on hers. She said her father "never really encouraged us [girls] to value education . . . he never really sat down and advised, 'Okay, m'ija [my daughter], how are you going to attend Cornell?' 'How can we help you to go to college?' No. All my education, filling out the application, the plans, it was all up to me, totally. I don't think that he really thought that we would go through with it." Although Alvarado was from a more recent generation—from the 1970s rather than the 1950s—she internalized the traditional expectations of marriage and a family. These notions emerged from the belief that girls were not the focus of the family's investment, since they would soon become someone else's responsibility. In the 1970s, boys were still expected to achieve and pursue a public life, while girls, like their mothers before them, were expected to remain within the bounds of feminine or domestic spaces, unless their role was to support male achievement.

In their analyses of gender relations, Chicanas expressed a complex view of relations between men and women. When speaking of men and women's relations within the confines of an organization, Ernestina García recalled some interactions she'd had with male activists. The first one sheds light on men's misapprehensions about women's organizational abilities:

¿Sabes que me dijeron a mi? [You know what they said to me?] Y me lo dijo loud and clear—I'll never forget. Jack Brito told me, "Sabes porqué [Do you know why] you are running the organization? Te voy a decir en un sentido porqué [Once and for all I'll tell you why]. Because when us men figure this tool doesn't work anymore, we throw it out the door, we let the women pick it up. We figure they can't do anything because it's not working anymore anyway. So we figure they can't do nothing with it, and that's why."

Fully aware that this was a misogynist statement, García used this recollection to challenge the myth of gender powerlessness. To keep Chicanas out of the social justice and social change arena, Latino males with class and gender privilege imposed internal limitations and barriers in the organizations they ran.

For these activists, gender discrimination was a familiar social experience. García spoke about a time that a Raza organization she worked with hired a secretary. Since men held the leadership positions, they expected to hire a candidate that would support and protect their interests. However, because women made up the majority of the membership, they got the organization to hire their own candidate who would give inside information to female members. For example, the secretary reported an organization leader who "gets the men jobs. Any job that comes in goes to him—he's pulling *movidas* [moves]." The women decided to do something about the situation. García said:

> We go upstairs into the bathroom *estaba allá arriba de* [that was above] Kragens *un cuar-tito así, y luego la oficina, y acá la secretaria* [it was a little room like that] (marking the parameters in the air), and then the office, and the secretary here (pointing to where she sat). We took turns *con un vaso* [with a glass], put it against the wall. We could hear real loud *lo que estaban hablando allí los hombres* [what the men were saying], and marked down *esto, y esto, y esto* [this, that, and thus]. We came out *para que no se dieran cuenta* [so they would not notice], taking turns is how we caught them. *Fíjate!* [Can you imagine!]

A surreptitious game of espionage ensued, wherein the women developed a rotation system to go to the bathroom upstairs to hear how resources were being distributed for the job bank. This took ingenuity and organization, and to this day the women who participated in the action get a laugh out of the strategy they devised "to keep the men honest." These types of activities were not limited to their public and activist involvement. In their daily struggles, Chicana activist leaders devised many creative ways to challenge unfair treatment of Raza, without failing to claim their rights as women.

RACIALIZED INTERACTIONS: BOUNDARIES, OPPORTUNITIES, AND LIMITATIONS

In addition to negotiating relationships among family members and the nuances of gender, participants in this study negotiated racial structures of inequality in their daily interactions. Each woman spoke of her awareness of racial differences and marginalization in the dynamics of her community. For example, Delia Alvarez realized how she was perceived because of race relations in her hometown, where the railroad tracks marked the boundary of the segregated part of town. Both class and racial differences were used against her and her people. Despite the pain she experienced, Alvarez acknowledged and accepted her ethnic/racial origins, discussing racial relations in her town: "Only the whites lived in the good part of town. We used to go there at Christmastime. When my sister was small, my brother and I would drive. We would look at the nice homes because those are the ones that had the lights. Literally, there was that side of the tracks and this side. I was very aware of that." Alvarez and the other Chicanas in this study realized that race and ethnicity were implicated in how they were perceived and in what they were allowed to achieve. Without exception, Chicanas had negative experiences as individuals of color, yet they turned their experience to their advantage. Specifically, they did not reject who they were within their own culture, nor did they come to "accept" the "white way" or assimilate into the dominant group. They learned to negotiate the subtleties of racism as competent and capable individuals, understanding their experiences through their personal and cultural values. Moreover, these negative experiences inspired them to make a difference in their respective communities. For example, rejection of Spanish by the dominant culture became a site of resistance for many of the subjects. García and Mendoza, who were punished for speaking Spanish when they were in school, both had a history of activism and long-term support for bilingual and bicultural education.

Racism, while a great source of pain for the women in this study, fueled their commitment to creating an equal society. For example, Elisa Marina Alvarado remembered racial conflict as a subtle, painful, and indirect experience when she saw how her "Mexican-looking, darker sister" was treated. "People didn't say things, but then if things kind of broke up—like the little girls taking sides, *disgustos* [quarrels or disagreements]—racism came up, especially with my sister. She came home crying because somebody called her nigger. I had a kid tell me to 'smile because we can see the white of your teeth, otherwise you're too dark.' It was very stupid stuff, coming from kids, my level, and the overt kind of stuff." The subtler affronts were experienced at the hands of mainstream educational institutions that marked the participants because of their Mexican heritage. There were additional complications for some. Elisa Marina Alvarado was confused about her ethnic heritage. She felt herself an outsider, because she did not have access to her racial and cultural background as the child of a Mexican father and an Irish mother. She struggled with the meaning of race in multiple contexts—both the Mexican and Anglo worlds.

Race was a complex issue for the Chicanas in this study. Chavez Napoli, who was born and raised in San José, is thankful that Mexican Americans, Chicanos, and Latinos are now perceived as visible groups of people who have political power and have the numbers to make a difference. The previous invisibility these groups, along with the tolerance for attacks on immigrants and minority bashing, is no longer something Chicanas or Latinos accept without question.

CLASS RELATIONS: WE WERE ALWAYS DIRTY, NO MATTER HOW CLEAN

In addition to gender and racial discrimination, Chicanas in San José also had to nego-tiate class dynamics. However, having a poor or working-class background was not something that initially generated trauma for Chicanas in this study. Most spoke of not realizing that they were poor until they were able to compare their situation to those who were better situated economically, which did not not occur until they ventured into the world of public education.

Alvarez, speaking about her social and economic position, observed that those who were better off lived in "better homes, everything was better." She remembered that she "used to fantasize a lot about what I wanted, and I was going to have it." On the other hand, some recalled comparing their situations ethnically rather than economically as children. Romero, for example, remembered that her economic situation was not particularly painful. It was as an adult and as an activist leader that she became aware of her socioeconomic position because of the unequal, unjust, and unfair treatment given their economic class.

> ¿Cómo te diría? [How could I tell you?] No queríamos cosas o no deseábamos cosas que
> no podíamos tener—porque no sabías [We did not desire things nor did we wish to have
> something we could not have—because we did not know]. I don't remember wishing for
> anything or desiring something we couldn't have—Mother was thrifty. She managed the
> money we earned working for six months; we lived on it a whole year. She would always
> buy at the garage sales. She would always buy at the secondhand stores. She took care
> of our clothes. I assume that most of the time we looked decent. I don't know. We don't
> have a whole lot of pictures to show.

Most of the participants' families of origin were good at managing their resources. As Romero observed, poor families managed their income carefully because they had to make ends meet to live under the fiscal constraints of seasonal or low-paying jobs. Romero's experience resonates with that of Blanca Alvarado, who does not recall pov-erty being unique to her childhood experience, suggesting that children all over the Southwest experienced it as well. Alvarado said, "There were clearly the 'haves' and the 'have-nots.' At Christmastime—the only time that we ever got a piece of candy or a piece of fruit—we went to the superintendent's house or the priest's house or to the teacher's house to get 'May Chreesmas, May Chreesmas,' and we would get a piece of candy." The physical separation imposed by poverty was not something that Alvarado questioned at first. She only grew keenly aware of poverty and disparity over time. She noticed that some of the "haves" did not shop at the company store, as her family did: families with means went downtown to shop. Unlike Alvarado's family, wealthy families had their own physician and had no need of the company doctor for their medical care. Alvarado did not recall seeing them in the doctor's office, "so it was clear they had their place and we had ours."

Alvarado and other activist leaders in this study understood that noticing difference did not mean acceptance of the inequality that came with having fewer economic resources; they noted the separation of those who had means and those who lacked them. The Chicanas in this study, like Alvarado, were keenly aware of the disparity, especially as it related to older people, who were the poorest of the poor in their neighborhood. As a child she realized that her side of town was not like everyone else's. She recalled always wanting something better for her people and herself and often wondering what that better life would be like for her.

FEMINIST CHICANAS OR *LAS ADELITAS*: IF THAT'S WHAT IT MEANS, I'M NOT A FEMINIST

Along with internalizing negative and derisive messages of race, class, and gender, which were informed by cultural markers, Chicanas learned to examine and reflect on their experiences inside nuances of power from the position of Other within a feminist ideology. Their identity as women, cast within a nationalist Chicano and traditionalist Mexican culture, provided them with an arena in which to negotiate the intersections of race, class, and gender without having to claim their actions as feminists. Because they became adults during the women's movement, some situated themselves within feminist ideologies and claimed feminist values as the foundation for their activism and leadership, without actually calling themselves feminists. Still, four of the eleven Chicanas in the study claimed a feminist identity, but even when accepted it, they diverged in how they positioned themselves: one located herself in the radical camp, which she defined as completely anti-male, women-centered, and revolutionary; three others associated more closely with cultural feminism, that is, with a feminism that promotes the culture of women without excluding men as partners and leaves patriarchy intact.

Bea Vasquez Robinson, a longtime political and anti-domestic violence activist, identified as a radical feminist, clearly basing these notions on her belief in women, emphasizing that women are no different from men. "I believe in women," she explained. "I believe we have the same rights as men. We have the same strength and the same abilities and deserve everything equally as men with no exceptions—I am a feminist because I care for women." While she referred to herself as a radical feminist, she assigned a liberal feminist ideology to herself when discussing women's rights. Despite her identification with feminism, Vasquez Robinson experienced contradictions with feminist politics because of her race and class consciousness. In the early years of the second wave of feminism, she clearly assessed the feminist movement as race and class biased. She illustrated her position with an address she gave to a conference on family violence where she chastised domestic violence activists for what she perceived as a lack of support for bilingual services. She recalled her position: "I'm never ever going to quit believing the way I do. It's okay with me if you don't want to have bilingual services.... Every time there's a grant available on the national level, I'm going for that grant. ... From the get-go, I'll offer more services. You don't see the importance of bilingual services, and that's fine with me—you just keep going on your white middle-class ways." Vasquez Robinson's agenda deviated from that of women of the dominant culture who were middle-class. She targeted race, class, and language insensitivity as the crux of her difference with them. From her experience working in the domestic violence field, Vasquez Robinson concluded that feminists can only overlook language if they are unconcerned about reaching the women who are most affected by structural inequalities—immigrants, the poor, and monolingual Spanish speakers.

Vasquez Robinson's notions of feminism were more radical than those upheld by Alvarado and Medina, who identified with the culture of women as a site of strength. Alvarado spoke to this issue in discussing her notion of feminism: "I am a feminist because I'm very, very happy with my femininity; I love being a woman. Feminism, which is kind of the word that has been coined to advocate and crusade for women's issues, is all about justice and equality. It is not inconsistent to be a feminist if one

FIGURE 62   Bea Vasquez Robinson (at the far right) at the International Women's Conference. Courtesy of Bea Vazquez Robinson.

has been a crusader for justice, for minorities; it just goes hand in glove; there is no separation." Alvarado did not make gendered distinctions regarding justice and equality. For her, social justice includes Chicanas and Chicanos because of their common experiences as minorities. In contrast, Esther Medina placed herself within an understanding of cultural feminism, claiming to have been "born a feminist now that I look back." Like Vasquez Robinson, she acknowledged confronting race and class issues in her leadership interactions with middle-class white feminists. Medina explained, "They did not want to hear that there was [race and class] oppression and sexism; the reason women are poor is because of that, and they [feminists] couldn't understand that." She criticized what she perceived as their emphasis on the reorganization of language over focusing on "changing the hiring process, so women can get in." Medina underscored the need for structural change: "If you get women hired, it would be very hard for people to keep saying 'firemen.'" If society makes spaces for women to have equal access regardless of race and class, the struggle for gender-neutral language becomes a moot issue. Her struggle for Chicana feminist rights was different because it was grounded in structure rather than on individual rights. Medina's identification with cultural feminism had been in conflict with the race and class consciousness that informs her activism, yet it has been useful to her as she sorted out the conflicts she experienced with Chicanos based on gender and cultural tradition.

Differences are also present among Chicanas who do not identify with feminism as an ideological reference point. Although these women disclaim ties with feminism or a feminist ideology, a woman-centered or female consciousness emerges in their struggle for social justice and equality by way of contesting the power of patriarchy. For example, as García shared her meaning of feminism, she provided insight into this female consciousness:

> *Yo creía que una feminista era alguien que está contra los hombres.* [I thought a feminist was someone who was against men.] *Yo no estoy ni en contra ni a mitad, no puedo estar en contra porque estuviera a contra de mi padre, mi esposo, y mis hijos.* [I am not against nor halfway on this—I can't be against because if I were, I'd be against my father, my husband, and my sons.] *Ves, yo no soy feminista, pero a la vez, las ideas que traigo yo y lo que quiero cambiar—si los hombres se oponen porque yo soy mujer* [See, I am not a feminist. But, at the same time, the ideas I hold and changes I want to carry out—if men opposed them because I am a woman]—I wouldn't put up with that.

García acknowledged the power differentials found in a sexist society, clearly recognizing the limitations imposed on her, as a Chicana, by race and class. She acknowledged the barriers set up by male privilege, yet she emphasized that she would not accept unequal treatment from males because she is a woman: "I wouldn't put up with that."

For Alvarez, differences between men and women were irrelevant. In her women-centered understanding of struggle, she incorporated family, ethnicity, and Chicano rights while rejecting feminism, which she perceived as individualistic in its motives. She explained: "I think a Chicana will give [a different] definition because we are very family oriented. I don't come first, it's my family. . . . Also, we have a cause, where white women don't have a cause; they're searching for a cause and we have our cause. We're fighting for our own people; they are fighting for their individual rights." Mendoza situated inequality on multiple fronts, emphasizing that it is an issue of justice for both sexes. She saw sexist treatment as a structure of oppression that inflicts equal damage on men and women, but she nevertheless argued against feminist liberation. She added, "How can I talk about liberation when my husband isn't liberated? He isn't . . . I'm against male chauvinism." She pointed to patriarchy as the source of their oppression. For Mendoza, social justice issues emerge within a race and class analysis; sexism, in particular, is a condition that hurts those perpetrating it and those who are targets of it. Thus, Mendoza concluded, gender subordination cannot be reduced to simplistic oppositions. Agreeing with Mendoza, Rose Amador, an educational activist and the executive director of a training program, maintained that women in the dominant culture, when arguing for feminist causes, have pitted their rights against those of minorities. According to her, white feminists focus only on their own issues, minimizing problems that pertain to women of color, poor women, or minority men. Amador explained: "When I think of feminist, I think of statistics. They say, 'Well, we have minorities, starting with white women.' It's always seen as more competition for Chicanos in general. To me it's rather negative. I would say I was a Chicana, but not a feminist, unless it's a feminist Chicana." While emphasizing that she believes in people's rights, Amador explained that the arenas of struggle in which she contends embrace more than gender issues, and competition for resources is at the core of these inequalities.

Romero provided a bicultural reflection on feminism. Romero called herself a feminist, yet she emphatically rejected any affiliation with mainstream notions of feminism. She elaborated:

> A feminist, in my Mexican culture, is *ser una mujer, una mujer que se comporta con dignidad, una mujer que respeta, y una mujer que sabe su lugar . . . que sabe darse su lugar en público y donde quiera* [being a woman—a woman who carries herself with dignity, a woman who respects, a woman who understands her position . . . who knows how to situate and comport herself in public or wherever]. If you define feminist just the way *gabachos* [Anglos] do, no!

Chicanas in San José, whether claiming a feminist ideology or not, espoused a female consciousness to gauge an analysis of power from multiple perspectives. They have had to "make sense" of their gender identity and how it informs their involvement, while accounting for class and race. All the while, they have had to carve out and develop an understanding of activism and leadership—with their families and other institutions—that yields an activist approach founded on relational interactions rather than traditional ideologies. For these Chicanas, multiple understandings have served, and continue to serve, as analytical tools in their involvement.

Chicanas have engaged the subtleties and complexities of race, class, gender, and culturally nuanced interactions in their struggle for social justice and equality. These women have learned to engage and manage a myriad of power interactions, negotiating a multiplicity of identities in their activist leader endeavors because they are conscious of their raced, classed, and gendered social locations. Moreover, these relationships have allowed Chicana activist leaders to gain and sharpen understanding of the subtleties of power. With their Chicana consciousness, they have learned to engage their involvement grounded in relationships with those who, like them, are interested in pursuing social change regardless of leadership perspective.

Whether identifying with a feminist ideology or not, Chicanas based their work for change on the centrality of their relationships, as they refuted notions of *marianismo* and claimed activist leader voices. And without privileging a Western feminist analysis or invoking it as the catalyst for their involvement in social change, Chicanas in this study identified women-centered worldviews as their point of departure. This female consciousness thus informs activist leader interactions for Chicanas in San José.

In general, Chicanas in this study have shown that the politics of identity are complex. From them we have learned that identity shapes and guides their actions within the politics of daily life. Through them we learn that race and racialized ethnicity, gender, class, and cultural experiences qualify and shape their involvement. On the other hand, Latino/Chicanos have learned to negotiate race and class inequalities, creating and building coalitions and alliances on those issues that are most likely to improve conditions for Raza without rejecting their socioeconomic background or the ethnic identity they have learned to embrace as part of the family legacy, and even when having navigated privilege of class, they have struggled to improve the lives of Raza.

CONCLUSION

What Chicana and Latino/Chicano Activist Leaders Teach Us

Those who participated in this study believe that social change begins with a reflective mindfulness of self, being one with the community, in the context of family values that are often altruistic; even when those efforts fail to yield desired results, they generate positive lessons. These participants were able to cull much knowledge and insight from negative experiences of race, class, gender, and sexuality in their homes and communities. For these reasons, their activism begins in an imaginary that conceptualizes lived experiences in past recollections of their involvement. For them, it is the interconnectedness of mind, body, and spirit that allows them to negotiate race, ethnicity, sexuality, and socioeconomic class as a people who have known poverty and have overcome its limitations. Emotional intelligence and the ability to engage power in all its nuanced qualities frame the ways in which they have gauged unjust and unequal treatment, as guided by emotional traumas with which they have had to contend inside sociocultural violence experienced and witnessed in their homes and communities. Therefore, through cultural and emotional intuition—the ability to understand the cultural fabric of multiple communities as well as to take ownership and understanding of emotions inflicted or shaped by trauma—these activist leaders struggled to make things better, weighing the ways in which they and their people were socially positioned as Mexicans. Premised on agency and the desire to bring about social change, their actions were informed by notions of equality, fairness, and justice in the context of the traumas and inequalities they experienced and witnessed, without assigning blame to their social position as working-class people.

Unlike Chicanos/Latinos from the Depression Generation, Baby Boomer Chicanas dealt with oppression and the internal dynamics of class and gender in the intersections of family interactions, as evidenced, for example, by a lack of investment in their education because they were expected to become future homemakers or, at best, find indoor employment away from agricultural or manual work. Early in childhood, Chicanas of this generation became aware of the ways in which socioeconomic and gendered structures of inequality excluded and marginalized them because of their gender, race and racialized ethnicity, class, and sexual identities. Although they lacked access to education, through relational interconnections Chicanas learned oppositional and alternative ways of dealing with difference in their everyday surroundings at home, in their community, and sometimes in educational institutions. As gendered individuals, in contrast to Latinos/Chicanos, whom they perceived as entitled and privileged, Chicanas negotiated a multiplicity of power relations in their everyday interactions. Yet, both Chicanas and Latinos/Chicanos fought for Raza as they took up labor struggles, educational rights, and access to employment.

Regardless of generation, the political imaginary of these activist leaders was informed by parents who expressed a political ideology that privileged democratic ideals. All shared a strong work ethic and a belief in self-sufficiency as core values, anchored in the working-class experience. Beyond mutual aid societies to which they contributed, alternatives such as welfare or public assistance were never considered. Mothers and fathers promoted self-reliance through work and self-sufficiency, advancing employment as the route to success and social change, although some considered education for their sons.

Latinos/Chicanos from the Depression Generation became eligible for education and housing through their military benefits. For its part, the Baby Boomer Generation gained access to education and employment through the Higher Education Act of 1965, which provided options not readily available to previous generations. It was through that social intervention that higher education became more readily accessible to all, even though San José's institutions of higher education focused on the recruitment of male students. In the Baby Boomer Generation, one Latino/Chicano completed a law degree, three obtained MAs, one a BA, one with some college. However, it would not be until after the birth of the Chicano movement, when Chicanas became involved in a wider breadth of activities, that a greater quality of life would become available for generations to come. In pursuit of equality, fairness, and justice, both Chicanas and Latinos/Chicanos of the Baby Boomer Generation actively challenged the status quo and created options where none had existed before. Guided by an ideology of service and a consciousness of responsibility, based on what they had experienced in their families and communities, Chicanas and Latinos/Chicanos advanced social justice, inspired by ancestral legacies of activism and based on their community needs, taking on issues such as bilingual education, Mexican American content in the K–12 curriculum, health, affirmative action, anti-police and anti-domestic violence issues, and affordable housing.

Both Depression and Baby Boomer Generations struggled for their people's rights mediated inside the injustices they survived. In their own body and experiences, Chicanas of the Depression Generation in San José internalized the ways in which poverty and class, gender, and race informed their involvement, gaining lessons from their interactions with systems of power to improve the lives of those who were as bad off or worse than they had been. In that context, and in the struggle against the social boundaries that limited their aspirations, these activist leaders of both generations created access to resources not previously available to people in their community. Thus, Chicanas of the Baby Boomer Generation (born 1942–49) fought for social justice and continued to advance the struggle for social rights in their respective areas of influence as access to education became more readily available. For some in the Baby Boomer Generation, federal policies became the equalizer. Still, like earlier generations, they were guided by an ideology of service and a consciousness that promoted social justice. Based on what they had experienced in their families and communities, these activist leaders built on their ancestral legacies to improve the lives of their people and their communities.

With the vision of creating change and advancing Raza rights, the Depression Generation's point of departure was cultural affirmation, services, and education for immigrant and working-class communities. Latinos/Chicanos, more readily than Chicanas of this generation, moved up professionally, with three PhDs, three graduate degrees (MA and MSW), and one with a tenth grade education and some college. Among Chicanas of the Depression Generation, one completed the eighth grade, one attended some college, and three graduated from high school. Still, all were equally invested in improving conditions for poor people, women, and workers in their community, and especially in opening options for educational access for future generations. The Baby Boomer Generation accessed education and employment in ways not previously available. Moreover, with the birth of the Chicano movement, Chicanas became involved in a wider breadth of activities that would garner a greater quality of life for generations to come.

Throughout their upbringing, activist leaders of both generations were influenced by parents who were active in their respective communities. From community investment to membership in cultural, civic, and social organizations, parents imparted a consciousness of service and an ideology of care that promoted the well-being of the community, particularly of those who were most marginalized. Because of their experiences with racism, classism, and sexism as differential treatments in the spaces they occupied, Chicanas and Latinos/Chicanos contested and resisted the ways in which inequality and oppression maintained disparities in their respective communities. While the historical record has still to be fully unearthed and examined, this project had documented the ways in which activist leaders of the Depression and Baby Boomer Generations have built on their ancestral activist paths to create change, in their quest to improve the sociocultural conditions of Raza. Still more has to be done to understand the ways in which oppression and marginalization have colluded in entrenching the invisibility of a people who have made and continue to make contributions to their people and the communities in which they were raised. The lived experiences of these activist leaders and their ancestors evidence a people invested in their communities who strove to create a fair, just, and equal environment for all.

DEBUNKING THE MYTH OF DISINVESTMENT IN SAN JOSÉ

From those who participated in this study, I have learned that Chicanas and Latinos/Chicanos internalize an active and reflective mindfulness of being one with their environment, in an imaginary that conceptualizes an active social justice ideology that engages past recollections of their experiences as insight and consciousness in their involvement regardless of race, class, gender, or sexuality. Thus, these actors engage a sentient self whereby through mind, body, spirit, and soul they have learned to negotiate race and racialized ethnicity, socioeconomic class, gender, and sexuality as people who intimately know poverty and were driven by their experiences to make things better for others. As such, the interactions they enact display agency and relational notions of change informed by a philosophy of equality, fairness, and justice, as witnessed and engaged inside their families and communities.

While others have written about leadership, the narrative in this book is enacted in the voices of those who lived the events. While each oral history is a book in itself, I focus on the ways in which Chicanas and Latinos/Chicanos have struggled to create an environment of inclusion in a nation that has declared them second-class citizens. With their stories, they share their upbringing and relationships with their families as they recall their cultural, social, and political lives in San José. Moreover, because their families have been repositories of activism and leadership by modeling for and instructing their children, they created an ethic of community service and support for the greater good of their people.

Among the contributions of these activist leaders, some worked in unions and in politics, while others tended to their neighbors or participated in religious activities of their communities. Their involvement began not for self-promotion or personal gain but with the aim of improving the community in which they resided and the lives of their people. Ernesto Galarza and César Chávez were these activist leaders' fellow travelers and were emulated by those who took part in the struggle for social justice and social change. Mothers, fathers, and significant others within and outside their private and public communities, along with gendered, raced, and classed experiences, provide a foundation for understanding the ways in which the participants understood their activist leadership interactions. Knowledge of self, knowledge of family history and their respective communities, and awareness of social, cultural, and political environments, along with historical, contextual, and situational influences, moved these Chicanas and Latinos/Chicanos to work for change.

Raced, classed, and gendered experiences, which were primarily negative (with some alternatives presented by their families of origin) allowed activist leaders to advance from awareness to consciousness about injustices, whether they were raised in Mexico or in segregated Chicano barrios throughout the Southwest. Even now, when most activist leaders claim lower middle- to middle-class status and many are college educated, they have not forgotten their class origins and continue to fight for the needs of working-class Chicanos/Mexicanos, grounded in the knowledge that they have struggled with poverty and racism. Yet, Chicanas, while socialized within traditional notions of femininity, mustered the encouragement to become involved without being hindered by their gender. The history of activism in their families, and both negative or positive relationships with significant others, have influenced their formation, stoking their ability to negotiate and engage in leadership interactions from an insider perspective—classed, raced, and gendered notions of leadership—that demonstrate commitment to social justice.

From their oral histories, genealogies of empowerment emerge to show how families, communities, and leaders have influenced these activist leaders to improve social, political, cultural, and economic conditions for Raza in San José and in Santa Clara County in general. In carrying out their activism, these Chicanas and Latinos/Chicanos have had their values tested. These were relational spaces where they were socialized, mentored, and instructed to value and demonstrate concern in support of working-class Raza, regardless of value differences. Also, despite gender, race, and class, these activist leaders were influenced by perspectives they gained in their interaction with their families and communities, which informed their involvement in the struggle for Raza rights. Still, hidden in the shadows of their narratives are stories of inequality inside the home, whether because of gender or color, as well the ways in which power has privileged men over woman, in the context of relational interactions that maintain power inequalities among genders and sexualities that deviate from the patriarchal imperative of heteronormative expectations. While some of these narratives emerged in the stories that were shared with me, more work needs to be done to make visible the collaborative ways in which men and women of color go about enacting their everyday life.

NOTES

PREFACE

1. I use Chicana and Latino as identity categories based on the respondent's primary choice. Most leaders used multiple identifiers to describe themselves and those with whom they interacted. Other categories used by the activist leaders included Mexican American, Mexicano and Mexicana, and Hispanic. Referents like Tejano, Chicorican, and Indian also were used as self-designations. In my master's thesis, "What Are you? What Can I Call You?: A Study of Chicano and Chicana Identity," I argue that Chicano(a) ethnicity is historically located and that it changes with social, political, cultural, and economic conditions in time. Ethnic identity is not a prescriptive, rather it is a fluid and malleable process that reflects changes in the social and political climate. As such, individuals use multiple categories to negotiate their identities in a variety of situations. Also, situations inform not only how a category will be used but also how it will be constructed and reconstructed in interaction. Female cohorts chose Chicana as their primary ethnic identity, while male cohorts opted to rely on Latino, although Chicano is a term they use in their activist leader endeavors, depending on the context and situation.
2. See Acuña (1988), chap. 11, for a discussion of the Mexican American Generation.
3. See Pérez (1999) for a discussion of a decolonial methodology that unearths and makes visible the forgotten stories of Chicanas. She relies on a metahistorical approach, whereby archaeology and genealogy become ways to record and reclaim their histories as part of a nation that has relegated them to the margins of history.
4. Méndez-Negrete (1995). This study was initially written using pseudonyms, for the city as well as the participants, because one participant withdrew permission to use her oral history. That participant has reconsidered and given permission, so I am using the real

names of the participants in this book. The study takes place in the county seat of Santa Clara County, San José, California, with over about two million residents. The population of Chicanos/Latinos is about 36 percent of the general population, with a larger percent of Chicanos/Latinos residing in the county seat municipality.

5.   Anselmo "Chemo" Candelaria was an activist leader during the Chicano movement in the 1960s and '70s. He passed away on April 7, 2012, in Peoria, Arizona, where he had relocated from California because of the high cost of living. Born in San Francisco in 1943, he was raised in Sal Si Puedes. He attended James Lick High School and was enrolled there when he started the Brown Berets, a precursor of the Black Panthers and the Brown Berets of Los Angeles. Joe Rodriguez wrote in his obituary: "Tensions between the police, Black Berets and other Chicano activists exploded in the summer of 1969 during the once-popular Fiesta de las Rosas parade in downtown San Jose. Dozens were injured, including three police officers, and 23 people were arrested. Among them was Candelaria, who was dragged away yelling instructions to his Black Berets in Spanish and English. But instead of booking him into jail, the officers took him to Agnews, a high-security hospital for the severely handicapped and mentally disabled. Candelaria was held for 72 hours until a local priest recognized him and demanded his release" (*Bay Area News Group*, April 13, 2012; updated August 15, 2016).

6.   I found this information on a website, "The Post War-1970s, Women Cannery Supervisors," which has now been taken down.

CHAPTER 1

1.   Spanish American has been the designation taken by residents of this Colorado area. For a discussion on ethnic identity and preference of terms, see García (1985), Muñoz (1989), and others who have engaged the concept of ethnic identity and self-naming.

2.   During the Great Depression, Mexicans were seen as an excessive charge on the relief roles. Under the Hoover administration, and Secretary of Labor William N. Doak, Mexican workers were targeted for removal. Many Mexican Americans and their U.S. citizen children were also deported to Mexico. Although none of the participants of this generation were targeted for removal, some of their ancestors might have been.

3.   See Epstein (1981) for a discussion of this theory.

4.   Seven out of twelve Latinos traced their work ties to the agricultural industry. More females than males settled in California via their respective migrant stream. Nine females were born in Santa Clara County. All the males came from other parts of California or the United States, with one from Mexico.

5.   It is hard to imagine being in Carrasco's place. However, it is not difficult to conceive of the torment he experienced when surrounded by the peers who mocked his poverty. I share a hometown in common with Carrasco. My memory is not of garbage cans, but of language

isolation. A similar insensitivity and disregard surfaced when my peers and teacher refused to speak to me in a language other than English. The first six months of school, I lived in a world of silence, and dominated by a language that I had yet to make mine.

6. Family rank, size, and composition were recorded for each of the participants, to assess family influence. Males were evenly distributed in sibling family ranking order. Females, on the other hand, were concentrated in other than the eldest category. That is, most were not the oldest child, but the second or fifth, and later.

7. Josie Torralba Romero was born on September 24, 1944. She passed away on November 4, 2004, at the age of sixty.

8. Ernestina García had been struggling with language oppression since she could remember. Born in Arizona to a migrant family, she experienced firsthand the pain of racism through language oppression. She remembered forcing herself to memorize English words so as not to be kept after school because she could not respond to the teacher. While now fluent in both languages, García expressed herself in Spanish because it is a language of empowerment, while English, for her, is a language of inferiority and oppression. In support of her struggle, I have decided to use the language she expressed in our *pláticas*.

9. The Alianza Hispano Americana was founded in Tucson, Arizona, in 1894, as a mutual aid society for Mexicans in the Arizona territory. The Arizona Archives Online collection shares documents "as legal evidence of financial transactions among members and within lodges. The materials include membership files containing legal and insurance records, lodge correspondence, administrative files like meeting minutes and financial papers, and printed materials." The materials are mostly written in Spanish. The Alianza was known to advocate for Mexican American education and civil rights. Available at http://www.azarchivesonline.org/xtf/view?docId=ead/asu/alianza.xml; Spanish-language version at http://www.azarchivesonline.org/xtf/view?docId=ead/asu/alianza_spa.xml.

10. Portions of this section were published in Méndez-Negrete (1994).

11. What Mendoza and Medina recall reflects the coalitions of resistance that were formed to protest lowered wages and bad living conditions, and their fathers' involvement in organizing farmworkers to fight for their rights.

12. Born in 1929 in Arizona, Ernestina García passed away on July 9, 2005, after a lifetime of activism and caregiving.

13. Chávez was posthumously awarded the highest recognition given to American citizens, the Medal of Freedom. Helen Chávez, his widow, accepted the award from President Clinton.

14. An integral part of his organizing strategy was door-to-door campaigns. Acuña (1981) says that "he built his union going door-to-door in the barrios where the farmworkers lived" (269).

CHAPTER 2

1. Jorge Ubico Castañeda ruled Guatemala from February 14, 1931, to July 4, 1944. A general in the army, he was the only candidate on the slate for president when he ran in 1931. He was removed from office by a pro-democracy uprising in 1944, leading to the ten-year Guatemalan Revolution. See Grieb (1979).

CHAPTER 3

1. Sofia Magdaleno, who married Gilbert Mendoza, was born on December 22, 1934, in Fillmore, California. She died in San José on March 14, 2015.

CHAPTER 4

1. The racialization project of segregating Mexicans at school occurred throughout the Southwest. Montejano (1987) documents that farmers were not interested in educating Mexicans: "In some districts, local policy restricted Mexican children to an elementary education" (192). One grower representative said that "educating the Mexican is educating them away from the job, away from the dirt. He learns English and want to be a boss. He doesn't want grub" (193). "By 1930, Mexicans were the second largest demographic group in Arizona—60% White and 26.2% Mexican" (U.S. Bureau of the Census, 1932, in Powers 2008). During this period, school districts in Arizona and across the Southwest began to segregate Mexican American students in Mexican schools or classrooms. Moreover, it was concluded that "because students were geographically assigned to neighborhood schools (which were mostly filled with Latinos in the urban areas and Whites in the suburban areas) it was found that segregation was 'not unconstitutionally segregated,'" by Judge Robert Peckham in 1976 and again in 1981, and in Los Angeles in 1985, as reported by David Savage in the *Los Angeles Times*, December 1, 1985.

CHAPTER 5

1. A collection of the magazine archives can be found at the Martin Luther King Jr. Library, San José, in the California Room, on the third floor. Also, see "El Excentrico Magazine Project" on Facebook for additional information.

2. According to the *Los Angeles Times,* "George Anthony Sanchez, 26 . . . is behind bars and charged with 106 felony counts in 26 sexual assaults and linked to at least seven other rapes." Retrieved June 11, 2017, http://articles.latimes.com/1987-12-26/news/mn-7460 _1_ski-mask-case.

3. Mendoza participated in many research projects, including Rosaldo's cultural citizenship study from 1990 to 1994, which took place as I was conducting my study. She among others contributed to an understanding of cultural citizenship in their quest for knowledge, sharing the concept as a process of engaging "the norms of the dominant national community, without compromising one's rights to belong, in the sense of participating

in the nation-state's democratic process . . . cultural citizenship offers the possibility of legitimizing demands made in the struggle to enfranchise themselves. These demands can range from legal, political, and economic issues to matters of human dignity, well-being, and respect" (Méndez-Negrete 1994, 57).

CHAPTER 6

1. La Confederación de La Raza Unida identified and launched many struggles, including in support of at-large elections and against police brutality through the Committee on Public Safety (COPS), which José Villa co-chaired. In an article in the *East San Jose Sun,* April 7, 1976 (7), Dara Perlman argued that conditions for Chicanos were such that it went beyond the Treviño case, and that redistricting was but one solution that would bring Chicanos to the seat of power, where they could access economic, political, and social resources; redistricting in and of itself was not the solution to income and education gaps faced by Chicanos.

2. *La Palabra* was a journal/magazine launched in San José in 1969.

3. David E. Hayes-Bautista (2012) conducted a historical analysis of the celebration of the first Cinco de Mayo as a California initiation and an outcome of the *"juntas patrióticas mexicanas* . . . who went to deliberate lengths to create and maintain the public memory of the Cinco de Mayo" (88). Women were an auxiliary group among those participating. According to Hayes-Bautista, in Northern California, on May 5, 1862, with the takeover of the city of Puebla, "the junta [*juntas patrióticas mexicanas*] in the mercury-mining town of New Almaden, just south of San José, organized nearly twenty-four hours of commemorative activities," which started on "May 4, when a marching band paraded through the streets of 'Spanishtown,' past houses decorated with laurel arches and illuminations," carrying "an inscribed banner or placard in the Mexican national colors of red, green, and white, as well as portraits of President Benito Juárez and Zaragoza" (90). While Los Angeles "officially sponsored commemoration of the battle on May 25 and 26, 1863" (148), since then Latinos continued shaping the Cinco de Mayo tradition (153). With the resurgence of immigrants from Mexico, the "first-generation immigrant community organized their celebration" (156), and the importation of Braceros and other immigrants promoted the celebration of Cinco de Mayo, even when the Spanish media would argue that the "Cinco de Mayo holiday was *not* a Mexican holiday, but they were at a loss to explain" its meaning or origins (160)—it was celebrated and the "first commemoration of the battle of Puebla . . . originated in California" (160).

4. In May 1968, Roosevelt Junior High School walked out to protest racist treatment and the lack of teachers and course materials on Mexican American studies.

5. *Diaz v. San Jose Unified School District* (which later would be referred to as *Vasquez v. San Jose Unified School District*) was a class action law suit filed in 1971 on behalf of Spanish-surnamed students and their parents, seeking "injunctive relief to effect of desegregation." In August

1974 the court found that the district "acted without segregative intent and consistently adhered to a neighborhood school policy" (n.p.). A second hearing, with an additional five amicus briefs, decreed that San José Unified School District was guilty of de jure segregation of its schools in violation of the Fourteenth Amendment. For a discussion of the remediation structure that called for reassignment of faculty, hiring of monitors, and various enrollment strategies, including dropout prevention, extracurricular activities, and bilingual education, see https://law.justia.com/cases/federal/district-courts/FSupp/633/808/1678053/.

6. The South Bay Second Wave Feminist Oral History Project, MSS-2006–0630, San José State University Special Collections & Archives, which identified the year in which Janet Gray Hayes was elected as the first female mayor in the United States of a city of 500,000 people. It is reported that "from 1975 to 1979 the number of women in public office increased from 4.7% to 10.9%, with the largest increase at the local and state levels" (n.p.). For additional information, consult the SJSU Special Collections & Archives.

7. See Chacón (1995) for an account and analysis of the conflict over the installation of this public art piece.

8. OIC-CET was brought to San José with the support of Father Anthony R. Soto, Hermelinda Sapien, who participated in this study but requested to not be included in the book, and other community activists; Russell Tershy was its first executive director. OIC, founded in Philadelphia by Reverend Leon Sullivan, was "dedicated to the elimination of poverty, unemployment, and illiteracy . . . so as to ensure a meaningful quality of life for families and individuals . . . by offering education and vocational skills training." Accessed June 30, 2017, https://www.idealist.org/en/nonprofit/967807022ba4432d9fb2a2504 d4209ca-opportunities-industrialization-center-inc-philadelphia.

9. The second-longest-held American POW, U.S. Navy pilot Everett Alvarez's plane was downed on August 5, 1964, in the aftermath of the Gulf of Tonkin incident. He was held for eight years and seven months by the North Vietnamese in the prison dubbed the Hanoi Hilton. He was released on February 12, 1973, during Operation Homecoming, after spending 3,133 days in captivity. He is the coauthor of two books written about his prison war experiences: *Chained Eagle* and *Code of Conduct*. Accessed July 2, 2017, https:// en.wikipedia.org/wiki/Everett_Alvarez,_Jr.

10. Ralph Guzman, a political scientist at the University of California, Santa Cruz, was the first researcher to study war casualty reports from Vietnam. He released his findings in 1969, concluding that Chicanos were only 11 percent of the population of the southwestern United States but represented 19.4 percent of dead. Accessed July 2, 2017, http://www.dailybulletin .com/veterans/20150321/vietnam-war-50-years-later-giving-a-voice-to-latino-veterans.

11. See Oropeza (2005) for a discussion on Alvarez's politicization and work with MACSA and La Confederación de la Raza Unida, where she fought for better health care and housing for Mexican Americans, among other issues.

CHAPTER 7

1.   Anti-Mexican and Indigenous exclusionary practices, laws, and policies were the result of the "white hegemony that emerged in Arizona . . . to exclude certain ethnic groups . . . from social, political, economic, and cultural power from before statehood" (Santa Ana and González de Bustamante 2013, 19–20). Arizona only became a state on February 14, 1912, when enough white settlers had migrated into the region.

2.   Origins of El Presidio de Tucson began with a small fortress built in 1775 by Captain Hugo O'Connor, who selected the site "on the east side of the Santa Cruz River." For additional information, see https://www.tucsonaz.gov/info/search-el-presidio-de-tucson.

CHAPTER 9

1.   During the massive repatriation of Mexicans from 1929 to 1936, it is estimated that a half a million to over a million were deported, among them citizens and their children. In *Decades of Betrayal,* Balderrama and Rodríguez (2006) noted that children who were sent back never gave up on their desire to return to the United States. Like Alvarez's father, many came back and worked hard to get their lives in order. Balderrama and Rodríguez argued that because of the shame associated with deportation, few, if any, told anyone about their experiences, as was the case with Alvarez's father.

2.   Established as a collaborative by Chicanos and Indigenous activists in California, Deganawidah-Quetzalcoatl (D-Q) University was set up to provide an educational experience "that honors and utilizes traditional knowledge and contemporary technology to empower individuals to build stronger tribal nations." Accessed March 16, 2016, http://www.d-q-u.org/.

3.   See Yolanda Reynolds, "Raza Si! Celebrates 10 Years of Community Involvement," December 7, 1990, in *La Oferta Review* 12, no. 60, San José, California.

CHAPTER 11

1.   A prior version of this chapter was published in *Frontiers* 20:1 (1999): 25–44. It was reprinted in Niemann et al. (2002).

2.   Hollander and Offermann (1990); Weber (1978), 3–62.

3.   Kats and Kahn (1978); and Yukl (1981).

4.   See, for example, Acuña (1988); Camarillo (1984); Mario T. García (1989); Gómez Quiñonez (1990); McWilliams (1990); and Carlos Muñoz Jr. (1989).

5.   M. T. García (1989); see also Gómez Quiñonez (1990), 55–74, 115–43.

6.   Examples include Bunch (1980); and Denmark (1979).

7.   Kanter (1977); and Bunch and Schwartz (1976).

8.   Cotera (1979); Mora and del Castillo (1980), 7–16; Alma García (1980); Nieto Gómez (1974); Pesquera and de la Torre (1993); and Pardo (1991).

9. Relational leadership strategies are those processes or activities that anchor relationships with others. That is, regardless of ideology, leadership style, position, or issue, these women accomplished change through or because of their relationships with others, using common ground as the foundation for change.

10. Kanter (1977); and Pardo (1991).

11. Acuña (1988), and Gómez Quiñonez (1990).

12. Rose (1990).

13. Acuña (1988); A. García (1989); M. T. García (1989), 153–55, 146–50, and 155–57; and Gómez Quiñonez (1990), 50–51.

14. M. T. García (1989); and Weber (1978), 212–99.

15. Gardner (1984); Hollander and Offerman (1990); and Rost (1991).

16. Reyes (1998), 1979–92.

REFERENCES

Acuña, Rodolfo. 1988. *Occupied America: A History of Chicanos.* New York: Harper & Row.

Alvarez, Rodolfo. 1973. "The Psycho-Historical and Socio-Economic Development of the Chicano Community in the United States." *Social Science Quarterly* 52 (March): 920–42.

Anzaldúa, Gloria. 1987. *Borderlands: The New Mestiza = La Frontera: The New Mestiza.* San Francisco: Aunt Lute.

Anzaldúa, Gloria E., and AnaLouise Keating, eds. 2002. *This Bridge We Call Home: Radical Visions for Transformation.* New York: Routledge.

Alarcón, Norma, Ana Castillo, and Cherríe Moraga, eds. 1989. *The Sexuality of Latinas.* Special issue of *Third Woman* 4.

Baca Zinn, Maxine. 1982/83. "Familism Among Chicanos: A Theoretical Review." *Humboldt Journal of Social Relations* 10 (1): 224–38.

Bacon, Dave. 2015. "Social Justice Unions Claim Deep Roots in Silicon Valley." *Reimagine.* https://www.reimaginerpe.org/20-2/bacon-Valley-union-history.

Balderrama, Francisco E., and Rodríguez Raymond. 2006. *Decades of Betrayal: Mexican Repatriation in the 1930s.* Albuquerque: University of New Mexico Press.

Barrera, Mario. 1979. *Race and Class in the Southwest: A Theory of Racial Inequality.* Notre Dame: University of Notre Dame Press.

———. 1990. *Beyond Aztlan: Ethnic Autonomy in Comparative Perspective.* Notre Dame: University of Notre Dame Press.

Blackwell, Maylei. 2011. *¡Chicana Power!: Contested Histories of Feminism in the Chicano Movement.* Austin: University of Texas Press.

Bunch, Charlotte. 1980. "Womanpower: The Courage to Lead, the Strength to Follow, and the Sense to Know the Difference." *MS,* July, 44–48, 95–97.

Bunch, Charlotte, and Susan Schwartz. 1976. "What Future Leadership?" *Quest* 2 (Spring): 2–13.

Camarillo, Alberto. 1984. *Chicanos in California: A History of Mexican Americans in California*. San Francisco: Boyd & Fraser.

Chacon, Ramon. 1995. "Quetzalcoatl in San Jose: Conflict over a Commemoration." *California History* 74 (3): 329–39.

Cotera, Martha P. 1976. *Diosa y hembra: The History and Heritage of Chicanas in the U.S.* Austin, Tex.: Information Systems Development.

Del Castillo, Adelaida R. 1980. "Mexican Women in the United States: Struggles Past and Present." In *Mexican Women in the United States: Struggles Past and Present*, ed. Magdalena Mora and Del Castillo, 7–16. Occasional paper, no. 2. Los Angeles: Chicano Studies Research Center, UCLA.

Denmark, Florence. 1979. "Styles of Leadership." *Personnel Journal* 2 (2): 99–113.

Epstein, Barbara. 1981. *The Politics of Domesticity: Women, Evangelism, and Temperance in Nineteenth Century America*. Middletown, Conn.: Wesleyan University Press.

Flores, William V., and Rina Benmayor. 1997. *Latino Cultural Citizenship: Claiming Identity, Space, and Rights*. Boston: Beacon Press.

García, Alma M. 1989. "The Development of Chicana Feminist Discourse, 1970–1980." *Gender and Society* 3 (2): 217–37.

García, David G. 2018. *Strategies of Segregation: Race, Residence, and the Struggle for Educational Equality*. Berkeley: University of California Press.

García, Mario T. 1984. "Americans All: The Mexican American Generation and the Politics of Wartime Los Angeles, 1941–45." *Social Science Quarterly* 65 (2): 278–89.

———. 1989. *Mexican Americans: Leadership, Ideology and Identity, 1930–1960*. New Haven: Yale University Press.

Gardner, John W. 1984. *Excellent: Can We Be Equal and Excellent Too?* New York: W. W. Norton.

Gill, Vandna. 2010. "'Race' and Immigration: The Self-Destructive Cycle." H525: Immigration, Education, and Identities in the United States, Harvard Graduate School of Education.

Gómez-Quiñonez, Juan. 1990. *Chicano Politics: Reality and Promise, 1940–1990*. Albuquerque: University of New Mexico Press.

Grebler, Leo, Joanne W. Moore, and Ralph C. Guzman. 1970. *The Mexican-American People: The Nation's Second Largest Minority*. New York: Free Press.

Grieb, Kenneth J. 1979. *Guatemalan Caudillo, the Regime of Jorge Ubico: Guatemala, 1931–1944*. Athens: Ohio University Press.

Griswold del Castillo, R. 1975. "La Familia Chicana: Social Changes in the Chicano Family of Los Angeles 1850–1880." *Journal of Ethnic Studies* 3 (1): 41–58.

Hardy-Fanta, Carol. 1993. *Latina Politics, Latino Politics: Gender, Culture, and Participation in Boston*. Philadelphia: Temple University Press.

Hayes-Bautista, David E. 2012. *El Cinco de Mayo: An American Tradition*. Berkeley: University of California Press.

Hernández, Kelly Lytle. 2009. "'Persecuted like Criminals': The Politics of Labor Emigration and Mexican Migration Controls in the 1920s and 1930s." *Aztlan* 34 (1): 219–39.

Hollander, Edwin P., and Lynn R. Offermann. 1990. "Power and Leadership in Organizations: Relationships in Transition." *American Psychologist* 45 (2): 179–89.

Jiménez, Francisco G., Alma M. García, and Richard A. Garcia. 2007. *Ethnic Community Builders: Mexican Americans in Search of Justice and Power: The Struggle for Citizenship in San José, California*. New York: Altamira Press.

Kanter, Rosabeth Moss. 1977. *Men and Women of the Corporation*. New York: Basic Books.

Kats, Daniel, and Robert L. Kahn. 1978. *The Social Psychology of Organizations*. New York: Wiley.

Levy, Jacques E. 1975. *Cesar Chavez: Autobiography of La Causa*. New York: W. W. Norton.

Lewis, Oscar. 1979. *The Children of Sanchez: Autobiography of a Mexican Family*. New York: Vintage Books.

Madsen, William. 1973. *Mexican-Americans of South Texas*. Case Studies in Cultural Anthropology. San Diego: Harcourt School Publishers.

Márquez, Benjamin. 1993. *LULAC: The Evolution of a Mexican American Political Organization*. Austin: University of Texas Press.

McWilliams, Carey. 1990. *North from Mexico: The Spanish-Speaking People of the United States*. New York: Praeger.

Menchaca, Martha. 1995. *Mexican Outsiders: A Community History of Marginalization and Discrimination in California*. Austin: University of Texas Press.

Méndez-Negrete, Josephine. 1994. "We Remember César Chávez: A Catalyst for Change." *San José Studies Special Issue* 20: 2, 71–83.

———. 1995. "'. . . Es lo que haces!': A Sociohistorical Analysis of Relational Leadership in a Chicana/Latino Community." PhD diss., University of California, Santa Cruz. Ann Arbor, MI: UMI 9605562.

———. 2002. "Awareness, Consciousness, and Resistance: Raced, Classed, and Gendered Leadership Interactions in Milagro County, California." In *The Frontiers Reader: Chicana Leadership*, edited by Y. F. Nieman et al., 239–58. Lincoln: University of Nebraska Press.

Molina-Pick, Grace. 1983. "The Emergence of Chicano Leadership: 1930–1950." *Caminos* (August): 9.

Montejano, David. 1987. *Anglos and Mexicans in the Making of Texas, 1938–1986*. Austin: University of Texas Press.

Mora, Magdalena, and Adelaida del Castillo, eds. 1980. *Mexican Women in the United States: Struggles Past and Present*. Los Angeles: UCLA Chicano Studies Research Center.

Moraga, Cherríe. 2000. *Loving in the War Years: Lo Que Nunca Pasó Por Sus Labios*. Boston: South End Press.

Moraga, Cherríe, and Gloria Anzaldúa. 1983. *This Bridge Called My Back: Writings by Radical Women of Color*. 2nd ed. New York: Kitchen Table/Women of Color Press.

Muñoz, Carlos, Jr. 1989. *Youth, Identity, Power: The Chicano Movement*. London: Verso.

Muñoz, Carlos, Jr., and Mario Barrera. 1982. "La Raza Unida Party and the Chicano Student Movement in California." *Social Science Journal* 19 (2).

Ngai, Mm. 1999. "The Architecture of Race in American Immigration Law: A Reexamination of the Immigration Act of 1924." *Journal of American History* 86 (1): 67–92.

Nieto-Gómez, Anna. 1974. "La Feminista." *Encuentro Femenil* 1 (2): 34–47.

Oropeza, Lorena. 2005. *¡Raza Sí! ¡Guerra No!: Chicano Protest and Patriotism during the Viet Nam War Era*. Berkeley: University of California Press.

Pardo, Mary. 1991. "Creating Community: Mexican-American Women in Eastside Los Angeles." *Aztlán: A Journal of Chicano Studies* 20 (1/2): 39–71.

Pérez, Emma. 1993. "Speaking from the Margin: Uninvited Discourse on Sexuality and Power." In *Building with Our Hands: New Directions in Chicana Studies*, edited by Beatriz M. Pesquera and Adela de la Torre. Berkeley: University of California Press.

Pérez, Emma. 1999. *The Decolonial Imaginary: Writing Chicanas into History*. Bloomington: Indiana University Press.

Pesquera, Beatriz M., and Adela de la Torre, eds. 1993. *Building with Our Hands: New Directions in Chicana Studies*. Berkeley: University of California Press.

Pitti, Stephen. 2003. *The Devil in Silicon Valley: Northern California, Race, and Mexican Americans*. Princeton: Princeton University Press.

Powers, Jeanne M. 2008. "Forgotten History: Mexican American School Segregation in Arizona from 1900-1951." *Equity and Excellence in Education* 41 (4): 467–81.

Ramos, Henry A. J. 1998. *The American GI Forum: In Pursuit of the Dream, 1948–1983*. Houston: Arte Público Press.

Regua, Nannette. 2012. "Women in the Chicano Movement: Grassroots Activism in San José." *Chicana/Latina Studies* 12 (1): 114–52.

Regua, Nannette, and Arturo Villarreal. 2009. *Mexicans in San José*. Charleston: Arcadia Publishing.

Reyes, Migdalia. 1998. "Latina Lesbians and Alcohol and Other Drugs: Social Work Implications." In *Alcohol Use/Abuse Among Latinos: Issues and Examples of Culturally Competent Services*, edited by Melvin Delgado. New York: Haworth Press.

Rosaldo, Renato. 1994. "Cultural Citizenship in San Jose, California." *Political and Legal Anthropology Review* 17 (2): 57–63.

Rosales, Rodolfo. 2000. *The Illusion of Inclusion: The Untold Political Story of San Antonio*. Austin: University of Texas Press.

Rose, Margaret. 1990. "Traditional and Nontraditional Patterns of Female Activism in the United Farm Workers of America, 1962 to 1980." *Frontiers: A Journal of Women Studies* 11 (1): 26–32.

Ross, Fred. 1953. *Get Out If You Can: The Saga of Sal si Puedes*. Berkeley: University of California Press.

Rost, Joseph C. 1991. *Leadership for the Twenty-first Century*. New York: Prager.

Ruiz, Vicki L. 1998. *From Out of the Shadows: Mexican Women in Twentieth-Century America*. New York: Oxford University Press.

Santa Ana, Otto, and Celeste González de Bustamante, eds. 2013. *Arizona Firestorm: Global Immigration Realities, National Media, and Provincial Politics*. Lanham, Md.: Rowan and Littlefield.

Segade, Gustavo V. 1978. "Identity and Power: An Essay on the Politics of Culture and the Culture of Politics in Chicano Thought." *Aztlán* 9 (double issue): 85–99.

Segura, Denise A., and Beatriz M. Pesquera. 1988–90. "Beyond Indifference and Antipathy: The Chicana Movement and Chicana Feminist Discourse." *Aztlán* 19 (Fall): 69–92.

Segura, Denise A., and Jennifer L. Pierce. 1993. "Chicana/o Family Structure and Gender Personality: Chodorow, Familism, and Psychoanalytic Sociology Revisited." *Signs* 19 (Autumn): 62–91.

Tirado, Miguel David. 1970. "Mexican American Community Political Organization: The Key to Chicano Political Power." *Aztlán* 1 (Spring): 53–78.

Villareal, Arturo. 1991. "Black Berets for Justice." Master's thesis, San José State University.

Weber, Max. 1978. *Max Weber: Economy and Society: An Outline of Interpretive Sociology*, edited by Guenther Roth and Claus Wittich. 2 vols. Berkeley: University of California Press.

Yukl, Gary A. 1981. *Leadership in Organizations*. Englewood Cliffs, N.J.: Prentice-Hall.

Zavella, Patricia. 1984. "The Impact of 'Sun Belt Industrialization' on Chicanas." *Frontiers: A Journal of Women's Studies* 8 (1): 21–27.

Zavella, Patricia. 1987. *Women's Work and Chicano Families: Cannery Workers of the Santa Clara Valley*. Ithaca: Cornell University Press.

Zavella, Patricia. 1988. "The Problematic Relationship of Feminism and Chicana Studies." *Women's Studies* 17:123–34.

Zavella, Patricia. 1991. "Reflections on Diversity Among Chicanas." *Frontiers: A Journal of Women Studies* 12 (2): 73–85.

INDEX

Individual index sections per time period discussed follow the general index.

Abeytia, Ernie, 54, 223

Acuña, Rudy, x, 216

activism: grassroots activism, xii, 10, 22, 66, 126; active in unions, xxiv, 33, 88, 288; cyclical processes of activism, 81; writing as activism, 24, 115, 150, 196

AFL, xxiv, 216

AFL-CIO, xxiv, 216

Agricultural Labor Relations Board, xiv, 116

Alvarado, José J., 39, 74, 155, 168–69, 171

Alvarez, Everett, 134, 235

Anzaldúa, Gloria E., xv, xix

Armas, Phyllis, 147–48

Arroyo, Ron, 244, 245–46

August Twenty-Ninth Movement (ATM), 37–38

Baca Zinn, Maxine, xix, 19

Bacon, David, xxiv, xxv

Barrera, Judge, 116

Barrera, Mario, xiv

Beall, Jim, 116

Belluomini, Rudy, 75

Bernabe, Lucio, xxv

Bird, Rose, Justice, 116

Black Berets, xxii, 37, 118

Black Student Union, 98, 177, 227

Blackwell, Mailei, xi, xx

Brown, Jerry Governor, 116, 200

Brownstein, P. and Christensen, T., 113

Camarillo, Albert, xiii, xiv, xviii

Campos, Dan, 120

Candelaria, Sal "Chemo" xxii, 102, 292

Catholic Church, 40, 94, 125, 150, 153, 171, 175, 177, 196, 264; Catholic schooling, 176–77; Catholic Social Services, 74, 168; Catholics, 97; El Grupo de Santa María; El Santo Nombre Society, or La Sociedad del Santo Nombre, and La Soledad, 40, 153

Casey, Father, 148

Centro de Acción Autónoma (CASA), 37

Chávez, César E., xxi, 21, 24–29, 40–41, 79, 106–7, 116, 122, 129, 153, 168–69, 171, 188, 217, 251, 267, 271–72, 288

Chicana Coalition, 66, 118, 134, 201–2, 245–47
Chicano Employment Committee (CEC), 88, 117–18, 120, 139, 142, 240
Chicano Student Union, 98, 101, 177
Chicano studies, 52, 85, 115, 150, 138, 212, 242
Comisión Honorífica Mexicana, 38–39, 155–60, 170, 183
Community Service Organization (CSO), xiii, xxi, 11, 39–40, 168, 206, 234
Confederación de la Raza Unida, v, 84, 95, 101–2, 107–8, 110, 117
Cordova, Liz, 97
Cotera, Martha, xvi
Council of Churches, 97, 107
Crist, Mrs., 74, 168
Cursillo Movement, 147, 149

Deganawidah-Quetzacoaltl University (D-Q), 209
Diaz, Manny, 230
Diaz, Richard, 75
Duarte, Anita 117

Escalante, Fran, 135
Excentrico, 75
Equal Opportunity Education Act of 1965, 93, 203, 221, 257

familia, xv, xix, 4, 7, 16, 78, 159, 231; family environment, xix, 5, 8, 11–13, 31, 33, 51, 53, 63, 137–38, 158, 163, 174, 196, 220, 174, 238, 248, 256, 267, 274; families of origin, xxvi, 31–32; family hardships, 6–7, 26, 30, 44, 50, 167, 233; family histories; family solidarity, xix, 172; family values, 4, 11, 13, 21, 26, 56, 79, 105, 146, 151, 164, 182, 187, 248, 250, 257, 280, 285–86, 289; family wages, xxiii, xxv, 41, 44, 174–75, 182, 293; followed the crops, 9, 48–49, 61; German extended family, 51; parents' support, 8, 41–42, 133

Fannin, Paul, Senator, 14
Feinstein, Dianne, Senator, 143, 241
Fierro, Lenny, 108
Fierro de Bright, Josefina, xviii, 35, 273
Fiesta de las Rosas Parade, 96, 109, 101–2, 292
Fifth of May or Cinco de Mayo, 40, 96, 106, 267
Fletcher, Claude, 116
Flores, Reynaldo, 147–48

GI Bill, 46, 64, 165, 196
GI Forum, xiii, xvii, 12, 36, 42, 64, 86, 88, 92, 106, 117, 139, 142, 206, 238–41, 246–47, 269
Galarza, Ernesto, xxv, 21–24, 35, 111, 113, 118, 184, 288
Gallardo, Jaime, 227
Gallegos, Herman, 136, 168
Gamio, Manuel, xxiii
Ganz, Marshall, 216
García, Doreen, 97–100, 103, 176
Garcia, Gloria, 215
Garcia, Richard, 147
García, Tony, 63, 97–99, 105, 175–76
Garza, Al, 120, 172
Garza, Henry P., x
Garza, Humberto, 21, 86, 109, 120, 163
gender, xi, xviii, xix, xxiv-v, xxvi, 3–4, 9, 13, 15–17, 19, 21, 29, 30–31, 32, 49, 52, 56, 61–62, 72, 82, 93–94, 116–17, 118, 130, 132, 144, 172, 197, 199, 201, 203, 234, 242, 253, 258, 260, 262, 271–72, 274–75, 276–77, 279–80, 282–83, 284–85, 287–89; gendered structures of inequality, 30, 93, 144, 272, 286; gender and sexism, xviii, xv, xix, 16, 30, 82, 117–18, 199, 201, 282–83, 287; gender politics, xvi, xxiv, 13, 27, 30, 61, 94, 116, 172, 258, 272, 284, 288
Goldwater, Senator Barry, 12, 14, 222
Gomez, Manny, 169, 171
Gómez Quiñonez, Juan, xi, xiii, xv–vi, 33, 37
Gonzales, Linda, 150
González, Rodolfo "Corky," 271

Gray Hayes, Janet, 172, 199, 296
Guadalupanas, 160
Guadalupe Church, 102, 108, 148, 168, 262
Guerrero, Lalo, 74, 168
Gutiérrez, José Angel, 271

Hammer, Susan, 125
Hardy-Fanta, Carol, x
Haws, Mandy, 227
Hernandez, Ike, 33, 88, 143
Herrera, Esau, 227
Hirsch, Fred, 226
Hispanic Health Leadership Program, 136
Holocaust, 18, 62
Huerta, Dolores, 188, 272

Ibarra, Jack, 101, 109, 120
Infante, Pedro, 74, 168

Jackson Kings, xxii

KLOK, 90, 74, 168, 171
Knight, Charles, Superintendent, 23, 109, 111
KOFY Radio, 171

Latino Issues Forum (LIF), 114, 117
League for Revolutionary Struggle, 212, 231
Locatelli, President, 180
Lofgren, Congresswoman Zoe, 139, 141, 229
Lopez, Esther, 139
Lopez, Lino, 101, 127, 133, 235
Lopez Tijerina, Reies, 271
LULAC, x, xiii, xvi–vii, 139, 142, 206

Madrid, Rudy, 101, 227
Madrid, Sonny, 136
Márquez, Benjamin, x, xii
Marquez, Phil, 55, 226
Martinez, José, 139
Mayfair, 19, 169, 262, 267
McCorquodale, Dan, 139
McDonnell, Father, xxi, 168, 262
McEnery, Mayor Tom, 123–25, 229, 266

McEntee, Jim, 148
McNamara, Chief Joseph, 87–88, 91, 112,
    143, 242
McWilliams, Carey, xviii
Medina, Goyo, 39, 45, 186
Mendoza, Gilbert, 186–87, 294
Mexican-American Movement (MAM), 35
Mexican American Political Association
    (MAPA), 64, 101–2, 116, 118, 172
Mexican American Youth Organization
    (MAYO), 134, 235
Mexican Consul, 170, 252, 296
Mexican Revolution, xiv–v, xx, 33, 35, 44–
    45, 49, 56–57, 74, 156, 160, 168, 185, 194,
    213, 238, 280, 294
Mineta, Norm, Mayor, 109, 204
Model Cites, 187
Molina-Pick, G., 35
Molina, Gloria, 172
Moraga, Cherrié, xix
Moreno, Luisa, xviii, 35, 273
Mosely Brothers, 227
Movimiento, xiv–vi, xix, 27, 41, 55, 78, 83,
    106, 118, 135
Movimiento Estudiantil Chicano de Aztlán
    (MEChA), xv, 55, 83, 138–39, 176, 189,
    229, 242, 256–57, 259
Mujeres de Aztlán, 118
Muñoz, Carlos, xii, xiv, 35, 297
Murphy, Chief Charles, 112

Nieto-Gómez, Anna, xvi, xviii

Obledo, Mario, 90, 109
Ortea, Señora, 45, 183
Owens, T. J., 247

Partido de la Raza Unida, xv
Pérez, Emma, xix
Pesquera B. and Segura D., xviii
Plan de Aztlán, xiv
Plan de Santa Barbara, xiv
Plan Espiritual de Aztlán, xiv

Rainbow Ballroom, 182

Raza Unida Party, 36–37, 138, 302

Reed, Sally, 137

Rintala, Marvin, xii

Rios, Richard, 138

Rodriguez, Lupe and Gil, 139

Rosales, Rodolfo, xix

Ross, Fred, xx–xxi

Roybal, Edward, 171

Salazar, Javier, 125

Sal Si Puedes, xxi–xxii, 12, 19, 52, 55, 102, 122, 125, 171, 226, 261

Sanchez, Armand/o, 135–36, 150

Sanchez, George Anthony, 88, 294

San José Unified School Board, 109, 111–12, 212, 247, 296

Santa Clara County Planning Department, 66, 126, 245

Santa Clara County Welfare Department, 66

Santa Clara University, 81, 180, 185, 226, 244

School of Social Work, 111–12, 136, 150, 212, 257

Shirakawa, George, 114

Silva, Raquel, 101

Sixteenth of September, 40, 92, 96

Soto, Ramón, 10, 39, 145–46

Southworth, Gail, 257

Spider, 83

Sullivan, Leon, 148, 296

Tenayuca, Emma, xviii, 35, 273

Tirado, David, xxii

Treaty of Guadalupe Hidalgo, 33

Treviño, Danny, 84, 90, 112–13, 135, 259, 295

Treviño, Shirley, 135

UCAPAWA, xxiv

United Farm Worker, (UFW) xxii, xxv, 11, 24, 27, 41, 53, 81, 97, 139, 162, 167, 206, 227, 251, 272, 162

University of Bridgeport, 196

University of California, Santa Cruz, 244, 196

Vasquez, Francisca, 12, 40, 192

Vasquez, José, 98, 109, 196

Villa, Pancho, 185

Villarreal, José, 86, 154–55

Wilson, Susie, 229

World War II, ix–x, xxv, 39, 157, 182, 206, 244

Yzaguirre, Raul, x

Zavella, Patricia, xxiv–vi

Zazueta, Fernando, 117

Depression Generation

CHICANAS

Alvarado, Blanca, xxvii, 4–5, 11, 13, 20, 25, 28, 39, 43–44, 58–59, 73–74, 94, 114–16, 121, 143, 166–69, 170–72, 229, 274, 279

   Bicentennial Commission, 116

   Center for Employment Training (CET), 116, 118, 171

   Club Tapatio, 74, 168, 172

   Comisión Honorífica Mexicana, 170

   Hispanic Charity Ball, 117

   KLOK, 74

   Latino Issues Forum, 114, 117, 143

   League of California Cities, 116

   Mexican American Political Association (MAPA), 116, 118, 172

   Most Holy Trinity Church, 271; Los Amigos, 94, 171, 172

   Opportunities Industrialization Center (OIC), 115, 171

   San José City Council (first Chicana Elected), District 5, 4, 114, 173

García, Ernestina, xxvii, 7, 12, 25–56, 40, 43–44, 58, 60, 88, 95, 97–99, 101–1, 103–5, 135, 173, 175–76, 179, 181, 273, 276

   Black Student Union, 98, 177, 227

   Chicano Student Union, 98, 101, 177

   Comité Pro-Estudiantil, 101–3, 106

   Fiesta de las Rosas, 101–2

   Frito Bandito, 102

MAPA, 101–2

Las Mujeres de Aztlán, 118

Medina, Esther, xxvii, 4, 17, 20, 23, 39, 43, 45, 58, 62–63, 75, 77, 138, 181, 184, 186, 274, 282

   Comisión Honorífica Mexicana, 183

   Economic and Social Opportunities (ESO), 138, 243

   Latin American Club, 75, 184

   Mexican American Community Services Agency (MACSA), 78, 185

   Santa Clara County Human Relations, 185

   Women's Programs (ESO), 243

Mendoza, Sofia, xxvii, 11, 20, 22–25, 28, 30, 38, 43–45, 58, 63, 89, 95–97, 101, 107–13, 126, 135, 185–89, 190–92, 223, 226, 228–29, 244, 273, 278, 283, 293–94

   Community Alert Patrol (CAP), 109–11

   Community Improvement Center, 95, 108

   East Valley Medical Clinic, 109

   Family Services Association, 126

   Lemon Grove strike, 24

   Roosevelt Junior High School, 96, 187, 189

   Spanish Club, 63, 191

   United People Arriba, 95–96

Vasquez Robinson, Bea, xxvii, 9, 12, 17, 20, 27, 40, 43, 45, 58–59, 61, 98, 192–95, 197–99, 200, 202, 280–81, 203, 280

   bilingual services, 194, 199, 281

   Bay Area Construction Opportunity Program (BACOP), 197–98, 202

   National Coalition Against Domestic Violence, 197

   National Organization for Women (NOW), 201

   National Women's Centers Association, 199

   National Women's Political Caucus, 201

   Women's Alliance (WOMA), 194, 202–4, 246

LATINOS/CHICANOS

Brito, Jack, xxvii, 21, 23–24, 40, 43, 46–47, 65, 85, 89, 90–92, 96–97, 101, 112, 107–9, 120, 153–54, 165, 276

   California Youth Authority, 108

   Community Progress League, 97

   Corrections and advocacy work, xxvii, 89–91

   Criminal Justice Board, 254

   Highway Commissioner, 90, 153

   Treviño, Danny, 90

Carraso, José, xxiii, xxvii, xxviii, 5–6, 21–24, 39, 43, 46–47, 64–65, 86, 93, 96–97, 107–9, 111, 154–56, 216–17, 292

   bilingual education, 22

   Chicano Federation, 115

   Comisión Honorífica Mexicana, 39, 155

   Community Resource Teacher, 108;

     English Teacher, 107

   Council of Churches, 97, 107

   Roosevelt Junior High School, 64, 96, 107

Castro, George, xxvii, 11, 13, 16, 24, 38, 43, 47–48, 63–64, 151–52

   GI Forum, 64

   International Business Machines (IBM), 47, 63, 151

   International Ladies Garment Workers Union (ILGWU), 11, 38, 152

   Mexican American Political Association (MAPA), 64

   Society for the Advancement of Chicanos and Native Americans in Science (SACNAS), 64

Covarrubias, Lou, xxvii, 33, 43, 48, 64, 88, 91, 126–29, 158–59, 160–62

   Comisión Honorífica Mexicana, 160

   Family Services Association, 126

   Latino Peace Officers Association, 126–28

   Mexican American Command Officers Association (MACOA), 127

   Next Door, 127

Garza, Victor, x, xxvii, 8, 21, 23, 28, 41, 43,
  48–49, 64–65, 85–88, 92, 109, 120, 139–
  41, 162–64
  Berryessa School Board, 86
  ENLACE Program, 88
  GI Forum, 64, 86
  Latino Issues Forum, 88
  Proposition 187, 86, 88
  Raza Round Table, 87
  Service Employment Redevelopment
    (SER) Jobs for Progress, 87
Soto, Antonio, xxvii, 10, 13, 15–16, 23, 30, 32–
  33, 39, 43, 49–50, 63–65, 98, 145–51, 164
  Alianza Hispano Americana, 13, 35
  Braceros, 10, 33
  Chicano Deacon Program, 148
  Chicano Priests, 147–48
  Cursillo Movement, 147, 149
  Emeritus from San José State and CET,
    10, 151
  Federation of Christian Ministries,
    149–50
  Job Corps Center, 149
  Comunidad, 146–50; Comunidades de
    base, 149–50; Liberation theology, 149
  Mexican American studies, 150
  Second Vatican Council, 147–48
Villa, José, xxvii, 12–15, 22–23, 40, 43, 49,
  109, 64, 111–13, 155–58, 185, 295
  bilingual education, xxvii, 112–13
  Braceros, 113
  Mexican American Graduate Studies
    (MAGS), 64, 111, 136
  Mexican American Community Ser-
    vices Agency (MACSA), 111
  New Mexico's Normal Teachers' Col-
    lege, 158
  Treviño, Danny, 112

Baby Boomer Generation
CHICANAS
Alvarado, Elisa Marina, xxviii, 7, 20, 29, 41,
  43, 51, 67–69, 78, 82, 84, 114, 232, 258–59,
  269–70, 276, 278

American Indian Movement, 84, 259
Angela Davis Defense Committee, 84,
  259
Bakke Decision Coalition, 259
Barrios Unidos, 114, 259
BASTA, 83, 257
Black Panthers, 259
Campaign for Human Development
  Board, 260, 270
Frente de Trabajadores de la Cultura,
  xxvi, 84, 145, 259
Los Siete, 84, 257
Movimiento Estudiantil Chicano de
  Aztlán (MEChA), 83, 257
Raza Sí!, 114, 259
Story Road Apartments Tenant Strike,
  84
Teatro de la Gente, 83–85, 257, 260
Teatro Visión, 84–85, 232, 259–60, 269
Venceremos, 259
Wounded Knee, 84, 259
Young Lords Party, 259
Youth Getting Together, 212, 259
Alvarez, Delia, xxviii, 8, 11, 20, 39, 43, 66,
  132, 134–35, 137, 232–37, 275, 277
  Oaxinas de Paz, 66, 134
  Mexican American Services Agency
    (MACSA), 135–36, 235
  Mexican American Youth Organization
    (MAYO), 134, 235
  Paris Peace Conference, 136
  Public Health, 137–36, 237
  Santa Clara County Health Depart-
    ment, 66, 136–37, 237, 255
  Vietnam War, 134–35, 236
Amador, Rose, xxviii, 11, 14, 20, 32, 42–43,
  51, 66, 69, 87, 137–39, 141, 232, 238, 243,
  283
  American Legion, 42, 239
  Center for Training and Careers
    (CTC), 87, 66, 138, 142, 240
  Chicano Employment Committee
    (CEC), 139, 142, 240
  ConXión, 66, 138

GI Forum, 12, 42, 86, 139, 142, 239, 240, 241–42
Hispanic Chamber of Commerce, 142
image, 12
Job's Daughters, 239
Masons, 42, 239
National Council of La Raza, 142, 241
Native Voices, 232, 243
Raza Roundtable, 143, 232, 243
Raza Unida Party, 138
San José Job Corp Advisory Board, 142
Private Industry Council, 139, 142, 240
Service Employment Redevelopment Center SER Jobs for Progress, 66, 138–39
SER National Board, 88, 138–41
Arroyo, Cecilia, xxv, xxvii, 9, 20, 43, 50, 66, 132, 232, 243–48, 269, 275
Alviso Health Center, 248
Asian Americans for Community Involvement, 247
Association of Bay Area Government, 66, 245
Chicana Coalition, 245–47
Children's Discovery Museum, 247
Indian Health Center, 247–48, 255
NAACP, 247
Oaxinas de Paz, 246
Women's Alliance (WOMA), 246
Chavez Napoli, Kathy, xxviii, 12, 14, 19–20, 28, 32, 43, 52, 67–69, 121–26, 260–70, 275, 278
Alviso Community Organization, 125, 269
Auto Recyclers Association, 67, 129–30, 198, 421
Fallon Statue, 121, 124–25, 143, 242, 265
Four C's or Santa Clara County Coordinated Child Care Council, 125
Giant Stadium, 124–25, 263
Lupus Foundation, 125, 269
San José Repertory Theater, 266

Santa Clara County General Plan Review Committee, 126
Studio Theater, 122–25, 265–66, 268–69
Romero, Josie, xxvii, 6–8, 12–4, 18–20, 23, 27, 30, 33, 43, 51, 67–9, 81, 129–132, 232, 249–54, 269, 274, 279, 283, 293
Board of Developmental Disabilities, 254
Chicano Mental Health Association, 66–7, 132
COSSMHO, 131
Council on Aging, 255
Emergency Social Work Network, 132
Family Institute for Santa Clara County, 67, 132, 254
Raza Clinical Case Conference, 132

CHICANOS/LATINOS

Alvarez, Felix, xxiii, xxviii, 5, 14–15, 24–27, 29, 43, 52–53, 70–71, 78–81, 82, 121, 207–9, 230
Alum Rock School District (Board), 70, 81, 121
Center for Community and Cultural Activism (CCCA), 70, 80
Federación de Clinicas Rurales, 209
Misa Chicana, 78
Sacred Heart Church, 78, 148
Teatro Campesino, 70, 81
Teatro de los Pobres, 70, 78–79
Carrillo, Pete, xxviii, 12, 14, 21, 43, 53–54, 70–71, 118–20, 121, 140, 217–24, 231
California for Fair Representation, 120
Center for Employment Training (CET), 54, 118–19, 140, 142
Chicano Employment Committee (CEC), 117, 119, 131, 192–93
March of Dimes, 222
Mariachi Festival, 117
Mexican Heritage Corporation, 70, 88, 117, 119
Muscular Dystrophy Association (MDA), 222

Carrillo, Pete (*continued*)
  Opportunities Industrialization Center
    (OIC), 115, 118, 148–49, 171, 224
  San José Best Program, 120
  West Valley Community College
    District, 119
Estremera, Tony, xxviii, 41, 43, 54–55, 70–
  71, 136, 224–29, 230–31
  Campaign for Economic Democracy
    (CED), 229
  Cannery Workers Committee (CEC),
    xxv, 229
  Community Alert Patrol (CAP), 55,
    110–11, 115, 228
  Job Corps, 55, 149, 226
  Legal Aid Society of Santa Clara
    County, 202, 229
  Mexican American Student Confedera-
    tion (MASC), 55, 227
  Project 50, 227
  Raza Lawyers Association, 88
  San José Evergreen Community Col-
    lege Board, 70, 230

  United People Arriba (UPA), 55, 95–
    96, 226
Garcia, Mike, xxiii, xxvii, 4, 7, 43, 55, 70–71,
  213, 219, 230–31
  Coors Boycott, 217
  Justice for Janitors, 70, 115, 230
  LACLA, 216
  Local 1877, 4
  Service Employees International Union
    (SEIU), 70, 115, 229
  Service by Medallion, 218
  Sir Thomas, 218
Gonzalez, Jorge, 10–11, 28, 33, 41, 43, 55,
  70, 114, 209, 230, 256
  Chicano Park, 115
  Cleaning Up Silicon Valley Coalition,
    115
  Draft Counseling Center, 212
  Network for Immigrant Rights and
    Services, 115
  Raza Sí!, 10, 41, 70, 114–15, 212, 231,
    259
  Youth Getting Together, 212, 259

ABOUT THE AUTHOR

Josie Méndez-Negrete is a professor emerita of Mexican American studies in the Department of Bilingual-Bicultural Studies, the Mexican American Studies Program, and the College of Education and Human Development at the University of Texas at San Antonio. She is the author of two previous books: *A Life on Hold: Living with Schizophrenia* takes us inside the heartbreak of mental illness. *Las Hijas de Juan: Daughters Betrayed* narrates a story of domestic and sexual violence in her family.